The Sonarman'

To Graham
Happy Birthday
2010!

Love, Sue

The Sonarman's War

*A Memoir of Submarine Chasing
and Mine Sweeping
in World War II*

H.G. JONES

McFarland & Company, Inc., Publishers
Jefferson, North Carolina, and London

Royalties from the sale of *The Sonarman's War* are donated to
the Belk Library of Appalachian State University in Boone, North Carolina.

LIBRARY OF CONGRESS CATALOGUING-IN-PUBLICATION DATA

Jones, H.G. (Houston Gwynne), 1924–
The sonarman's war : a memoir of submarine chasing
and mine sweeping in World War II / H.G. Jones.

p.   cm.
Includes bibliographical references and index.

ISBN 978-0-7864-5884-4
softcover : 50# alkaline paper ∞

1. Jones, H. G. (Houston Gwynne), 1924–
2. Jones, H. G. (Houston Gwynne), 1924– — Diaries.
3. World War, 1939–1945 — Naval opertions, American.
4. World War 1939–1945 — Naval operations — Submarine.
5. Anti-submarine warfare — United States — History — 20th century.
6. Sonar — History — 20th century.
7. Minesweepers — United States — History — 20th century.
8. World War, 1939–1945 — Personal narratives, American.
9. United States. Navy — Biography.
I. Title.
D773.J66   2010   940.54'519092 — dc22   2010025079

British Library cataloguing data are available

Front cover images: SC-525 underway off Beni Saf, Algeria, September 1943;
SC-525 with the captain, executive officer, and the chief boatswain's mate
on the ship's flying bridge (both from Author's collection)

Manufactured in the United States of America

*McFarland & Company, Inc., Publishers
Box 611, Jefferson, North Carolina 28640
www.mcfarlandpub.com*

Table of Contents

Preface   1

1. The Agony of Waiting *December 1941–September 1942*   5

2. "You're in the Navy Now" *September–December 1942*   10

3. Farm Boy in the Big Apple *December 24, 1942–March 4, 1943*   17

4. Introduction to Africa: French Morocco *March–August 1943*   22

5. Closer to the Front: Algeria and Tunisia *August–December 1943*   42

6. Agony at Anzio *January 1944*   58

7. "No-Hands Ward Ambassador" *January–March 1944*   75

8. *Cinq-Deux-Cinq* While I Was Away *January 26–March 10, 1944*   86

9. Back Aboard, Back to Anzio *March–July 1944*   95

10. Attacking the "Soft Underbelly" of Europe *July–September 1944*   109

11. Another Side of War: Ashore in Sicily, Italy, Corsica
    and France *January–September 1944*   127

12. Back to the "Good Ole U.S. of A." *September–November 1944*   150

13. Stateside Interlude: Norfolk and Panama *December 1944–March 1945*   161

14. Hiatus: California and Hawaii. *March–June 1945*   168

15. Bloody Okinawa *June–August 1945*   178

16. Finishing Off the Japanese *August–October 1945*   193

17. Formosa, China, and Japan Again *November 1945–January 1946*   203

18. The Long Way Home *January–March 1946*   212

Chapter Notes   225
Bibliography   239
Index   245

On the s ... t Anzio, I returned to the beachhead wl ... our awful months in 1944, and I learnec ... lello Sbarco di Anzio, I — like other ret ... s greeted as a special guest and awardec ... my participation on that bloody mor ... n. If our erstwhile enemies remember, !

In the ... iuthor Rick Atkinson asked, "What hap ... ger tell their stories?" To an octogenaria ... ed through and documented his particip ... vernor of North Carolina as trying to c ... lat question constitutes a call to action.

This ... iry than upon documentation ranging f ... notes made and photographs taken dui ... letters to and from family and friends w ... ly of the federal government, includin ... ports of military commanders under w ... ned my understanding through account ... icular military operations. Most of the p ... x earned through magazine sub-scriptio ... abominable processing in a for-eign country, the resulting pictures ... ure the excitement, danger, and drabness of the lives of common seamen and petty officers aboard antisubmarine and mine warfare vessels during historic events such as invasions at Anzio and Southern France and the landing of occupation troops in Japan.

I do not pretend to present a full story of antisubmarine or minesweeping warfare. This is simply a rambling and chatty story told through the first-person pronoun, for mine was the experience of but one of millions of young men who, voluntarily or through conscription, answered their country's call and served in the ranks.

Of the thousands of books and articles about the role of American armed servicemen, the vast majority were written by commissioned officers who viewed wartime experiences from a privileged position of authority. Conversely, few book-length narratives have come from the pen or typewriter of lowly soldiers or seamen who carried out their officers' orders. As one who rose in rank no higher than petty officer second class (but who in postwar professional life could boast of being the only petty officer with an admiral as his assistant), I am acutely sensitive to the short shrift given to millions of dogfaces and seadogs who performed remarkably during the war but never set foot inside an officers' club. More of their voices deserve to be heard through the written word. I feel compelled to give my version in intimate detail with the hope that other fellow octogenarians — or even nonagenarians — may be emboldened to do the same. As a historian, I join Rick Atkinson in wondering what will happen to the history of the war when those of us who "lived it" can no longer share our first-hand accounts.

Of the published material on the Navy's role in World War II, a disproportionate amount of it relates to capital ships; precious little recognizes the service of vessels below the size of destroyers and submarines. For example, except for Theodore R. Treadwell's *Splinter Fleet* and Edward P. Stafford's *Subchaser*, there is little in book form on the lowly "One-Tens," the 110-foot wooden submarine chasers such as *SC-525*. And except for Arnold S. Lott's *Most Dangerous Sea* and Barbara Brooks Tomblin's *With Utmost Spirit*, almost no public attention has been given to the "Two-Twenties," the 221-foot minesweepers, such as *Speed* and *Strive*, that could truthfully say, "Where the fleet goes, we've already been."

My book seeks to document just a few contributions to the Allied victory made by those unheralded small ships and their enlisted crews. If the reader tires of references to vessels known only by letters and numbers, let him or her be reminded that each little wooden Sugar Charlie carried about two dozen enlisted men under the command of three low-ranked officers, the latter usually just a few months out of college and with very little naval training. Even the larger metal-structured minesweepers carried crews of only about a hundred enlisted men and a dozen officers, none above the rank of commander. Three intermediary classes of sister ships — 173-foot Peter Charlie subchasers (the largest commissioned vessels without names), "One-Eighties" (184-foot metal minesweepers with names), and 136-foot wooden yard minesweepers (designated YMS plus a number) — play less a role in my story only because I did not serve on them and have little first-hand knowledge of their experiences. Yet they too fall into the category so eloquently saluted by Rear Admiral Samuel Eliot Morison this way:

> Let us also remember the "small boys" — the gunboats, minecraft, destroyer escorts, PTs, beaching and other lettered craft, even the lowly "yard-birds" and small cutters. These, largely officered by reservists, were forced to perform functions and make long voyages for which they had not been designed. The production of thousands of these in wartime, the training of them at special schools set up for that purpose, the operation of them under the most hazardous conditions, are beyond praise.[1]

Those classes of small seagoing craft are deserving of the nation's highest recognition, and to every man who served on the "small boys," I dedicate this book. I wish that each of them could tell his own story, as I am now privileged to tell mine, warts and all.

As will be painfully and sometimes embarrassingly observed, I have not tried to hide juvenile and misguided thoughts and behavior that, while demeaning in hindsight, cannot be separated from virtuous thoughts and actions of a teenager entering manhood contemporaneous with his war experiences. History is what was, not what we wish it had been, and a sanitized autobiography would have accomplished little except to hide a guilty conscience. If for no other reason, revelations of stupidity, misjudgment, and depravity remind both the author and the reader that few of us live up to highest ideals, and that imperfections, whether admitted or concealed, are inherently human. Because I have not glossed over my share of indiscretions, perhaps my mistakes may be a reminder to the reader of his or her own. For, as the Persian poet Omar Khayyam reminded us all,

> The Moving Finger writes; and, having writ,
> Moves on: nor all your Piety nor Wit
> Shall lure it back to cancel half a Line,
> Nor all your Tears wash out a Word of it.[2]

1

The Agony of Waiting

December 1941–September 1942

My diary entry for September 12, 1942, was simple and to the point: "Ship Ahoy! Enlisted in U.S. Naval Reserve."

The future might be uncertain, but at least — and *at last* — I had mustered up the courage to assuage my cancerous sense of guilt. For me this was a day of celebration, of liberation, so when in front of the Navy recruiting office in Greensboro, North Carolina, I ran into my former college schoolmate, Jimmy Hauser, I must have exhibited the youthful exuberance that he remembered from our first meeting more than a year before. Certainly my fellow mail clerk at Jefferson Standard Life Insurance Company, Ed Taylor, was puzzled by my spontaneous generosity when I persuaded him to join me, at my expense, for a movie at the Carolina Theater later that afternoon.

* * *

The exhilaration of September 12 was in sharp contrast to nine months of agony that began at Lees-McRae College the previous December 7. I was the first member of my family to finish high school, and through an unlikely combination of good fortune — a scholarship, a loan, the sale of a small patch of tobacco, and self-help campus work — I had fulfilled my intense ambition to enter college. Although I was raised on a tenant farm, I soon adjusted to campus conveniences such as indoor toilets and steam heat, and I sought valiantly to adapt to the use of collegiate English. To say that I was completely comfortable in my new milieu would be an exaggeration, but I was on my way toward full-fledged college studentship when at 2:31 on a Sunday afternoon the radio music in Room 212 of Virginia Hall was interrupted by a flash from the Associated Press reporting the bombing of Pearl Harbor. Like my classmates, I was stunned, confused, and demoralized by this catastrophe. However, having shown a sixteen-year-old's interest in the presidential election of 1940 by wearing a Wendell Willkie button, I instinctively knew whom to blame: the president of the United States. "Call us 'Isolationists' if you will, but we should have looked after our own business rather than England's and Frances's [*sic*]," I angrily scrawled in my diary. This was only one of many journal entries that I would live to regret having made.

The next two weeks were so consumed by exams, college activities, and attention to the broken leg of my buddy Roy Hall — I even put my temperamental radio in his hospital room — that I entered little more than routine reports. Besides, we were all excited about going home for the holidays. By the time I was back on the farm in Caswell County, however, I was feeling conflicting loyalties. I had worked so hard to get to college, but now my country was at war. How could an able-bodied American boy remain in college when my two cousins, John Fowlkes and Billy Jones, in the uniforms of the 34th Engineers Battalion, may have been killed by Japanese bombs on Schofield Barracks almost within sight of Pearl Harbor? My juvenile mind vacillated between my interest in my career and my obligations to my country. As early as December 18 I was debating whether to return to college after the holidays, and on the 29th I wrote, "Don't know whether or not to go back to LMC." The ambivalence increased as radio reports brought more bad news from the Pacific.

My mother's illness was neither serious nor inconsequential, but it gave me an excuse for my decision, and three days before my eighteenth birthday, I wrote, "Really heartbroken. Won't go back to L.M.C.... Nerves completely shattered. Never felt this way before." On January 4, I revealed my decision in letters to Leo K. Pritchett, the dean and registrar who had so generously opened the door for my college entry; Alison B. Stirling, whose patient instruction and mentoring had heightened my interest in college librarianship; and John Foster, my former roommate. All three responded with wishes for my mother's recovery — sympathy that pricked my conscience because I had not been entirely forthright in explaining my decision to quit school.

During several weeks at home, I hid my anguish behind farm duties — milking Kate the cow, slopping the hogs, building a new pig pen, cleaning the brooder house, and chopping wood. My family wondered what had come over me, for I had never before exerted myself at these tasks. But I also found some diversion by visiting relatives, hanging out on alternate evenings between Jimmy Hodges's and Robert Smith's country stores, and watching my Cobb Memorial High School basketball teams play Murphey at the rickety old Park Springs arena. I rode Queen, my favorite mule, through the snow to play Rummy with a cousin, Nellie Jones Hodges; and one night I attended a square dance at Edna Chance's new log bungalow. (I always enjoyed seeing Miss Edna, for she bragged that "Number 7" — the 1938 Chevrolet school bus that I drove the previous year — arrived so punctually each morning that she adjusted her clock.) It was also during these few weeks that a neighbor, Paul Poteat, was indicted for murder in Virginia; my former schoolmate, Sgt. Fred Cooke, was killed along with actress Carole Lombard in a plane crash near Las Vegas; and war came closer home when a Nazi submarine sank a ship off the North Carolina coast.

I had been interested in the Navy for more than a year, and now that on January 7 I became subject to conscription, I reasoned that I should volunteer before the Army could draft me. However, I was not required to register immediately, so I assumed that I could take temporary employment in a defense industry, earn enough to repay Uncle Kester Fowlkes the $50 that he had lent me, and choose my date for enlistment. The decision was made a bit easier when I was assured that John and Billy had survived the bombings in Hawaii. I inquired of shipyard work in Norfolk, but when I talked with the federal employment officers, they suggested that I take an office job to replace young men who were being drafted. That, they assured me, would also be patriotic. Consequently, I was given a clerical test in which I placed in the middle third — not a distinguished record, but enough for me to be interviewed by C. E. Bennett, the assistant secretary of Jefferson Standard Life Insurance Company in Greensboro. Bennett put me at ease, showed me around the impressive seventeen-floor building, and offered me a job as file clerk in the Planning Department on the sixteenth floor — from where I later would boast of holding one of the "highest positions in the company." My salary was $65 per month.

Two days later I found a comfortable second-floor bedroom with meals at 338 Church Street, in easy walking distance from the office. My landlords were Worth and Marjorie Feree, he an insurance agent, she a fine cook and housekeeper. In addition to another resident couple, Guy and Kathryn Routh, there were several boarders for animated conversation. A favorite pastime in the evening was bridge, a game new to me and one that I never mastered. My room was pleasant and food was good, but the monthly cost of $40 left me only $25 per month spending money. Obviously, paying back Uncle Kester would take a while.

After a two-day trip to Lees-McRae for my belongings, a quick date with my old flame Barbara Simpson, and an emotional farewell to my schoolmates, I started working at Jefferson Standard on January 26. My task, under crusty J. C. Barefoot, was to retrieve and re-file policy folders. Among the Main File's clerks — all male — were Douglas Brooks, Clark Foster, Ned Fowler, Tom Huffines, Bill Sharpe, Mokie Stancil, and Ed Taylor. I quickly learned that except for jobs held by women, file clerks were at the bottom of the career ladder, and each of my fellow workers aspired to the next-step promotion, the Mail Room. (By August 17, however, I recorded in my diary, "Girls have taken over Main File," evidence of the manpower drain during the coming months.) As the new kid in the department, I figured I would be in the Navy before an opportunity for promotion arrived. So I set out to be the best file clerk on Barefoot's staff.

The work was more boring than burdensome. Long before computers were even envisioned, each policy holder's file — totaling more than 700,000 in 1942 — contained a variety of documents providing evidence of issue, beneficiary, loans, and payments. A dummy card was substituted when a file was pulled for insertion of new documents. The most tedious tasks involved filing cancelled checks and repairing papers that had become tattered through repeated handling. Neatness and accurate filing were marks of a good clerk. I must have been a satisfactory employee, for when Bill Sharpe was promoted to the Mail Room, the departmental supervisor, Jack Causey, gave me the consolation of a compliment on my work. Then after two months I too was given a raise of $10 per month and a new assignment in the Mail Room. With my mail satchel, I bravely learned the route through the labyrinth of offices and was privileged to say "good morning" to officers all the way up to the president, saintly Julian Price. Returning to the building one day, I stepped on the elevator at street level and was shocked to see the president standing there in his stocking feet. He sensed my surprise and explained that a panhandler had approached him on the street, asking for money with which to buy shoes. "I asked him what size he wore," Mr. Price said, "and when he told me that he wore my size, I gave him mine." When he reached his office, the president simply phoned down to Younts-DeBoe and ordered a new pair for himself.

I also adjusted quite well to my new surroundings. In addition to evening card games and conversations, I frequently attended twenty-five-cent movies with Ed Taylor, Ned Fowler, and David Neal (the latter a friend from Caswell County studying at King's Business College). A distant cousin, Doris Fowlkes, then at Greensboro College, introduced me to fellow students; and Margaret Graham, the red-headed daughter of the manufacturer of Bug Death insecticide and a relative of my Fowlkes cousins, broadened my social contacts in Greensboro. Soon I was dating females whose names would fade with time, all the while corresponding with Barbara Simpson and other girlfriends. Radio provided an ear to the outside world, and February 25 was a special night, for the most famous orchestra leader in the country, Glenn Miller, broadcast a national "Salute to Lees-McRae." It was the first time millions of people had ever heard of the little college at Banner Elk, North Carolina.

Much of my spare time was devoted to reading — including John Steinbeck's *The Moon*

Is Down and Pearl Buck's *The Good Earth*— and to writing. Having edited my high school newspaper and honed my talents by contributing community news to the *Caswell Messenger*, I had also broken into the dailies with a few stories. I was emboldened to visit Jack Horner and Smith Barrier in the sports department of the *Greensboro Daily News*, who instantly recognized me as a "freebie" and authorized me to report on high school basketball games in Caswell County. I interpreted this as a commission, so I returned home for as many games as possible and took pride in seeing my stories in print. I was even more thrilled when a story on Cobb Memorial High School was given a two-column headline and my personal byline. Locally, the Greensboro Red Sox, and particularly pitcher Joe Ostroski, who won his twenty-first baseball game in September, captured my interest and occupied many evenings. Roy Hall moved in with me a couple of weeks but left before his rent check for Mrs. Feree bounced. My letter remonstrating him was intercepted by his mother, who embarrassingly sent a replacement check with profuse apologies.

Frequent visits home by bus kept me from being homesick, and, as always, services at Locust Hill Methodist Church and the Third Sunday in May — the annual all-day preaching and dinner-on-the-grounds at Pleasant Grove Primitive Baptist Church — enabled me to maintain childhood contacts. My father's bay horse and buggy — the only luxuries in his drab life — reminded me of my younger years before he was able to buy his earliest second-hand Ford T-Model. Not all visits were happy; Felix Chambers and two other young neighbors died in an automobile wreck. And on the death of Lees-McRae President Edgar H. Tufts, whose daughter Anna Lois I had dated for climbs up Beech Mountain, I sent my first telegram, not realizing that the copy would have to be mailed from the nearest Western Union office in a larger town.

I was so proud of my North and South Carolina championship in the Future Farmers of America's public speaking contest the previous year — my topic was "The Place of the Farmer in National Defense"— that I wanted to encourage other students back at Cobb Memorial to participate in the competition. I had received nothing but a little publicity, so, to stimulate interest, I purchased a silver cup, had it engraved by Schiffman's Jewelers, and sent it to Fred B. Harton, principal, and E.W. James, the agriculture teacher who succeeded my former mentor, A.I. Park. This first cup (I continued the practice for several years while in the Navy) was won by my childhood playmate and distant cousin, George Robert (Bobby) Smith, Jr., who would become a prominent physician and author of a book on diet and obesity.

*   *   *

That seemingly idyllic three-quarters of a year concealed a morbid anxiety. They were, in fact, the worst nine months of my life. At the core of the conflict was my ambivalence between enjoying the present and my sense of obligation to my country — the same conflict that led me to abandon college. I registered for the selective service system on June 30, but I still wanted to go into the Navy. I simply couldn't muster the courage. The fact that I was not working in a defense industry (my intention back in January) compounded my sense of worthlessness in face of my country's danger. Japan's seemingly unstoppable advances in the Pacific and the Nazi's rapid domination of Europe produced a gnawing fear of defeat among many Americans. Rumors often outran fact in the press and on the radio, and many Americans, despite President Roosevelt's reassurances, were pessimistic. Wartime rationing was adopted, and on May 7 I registered for sugar stamps, which I signed over to Mrs. Feree so she could purchase the limit for our table. Back home my father registered for gasoline and a variety of scarce products needed for war purposes. American Tobacco Company, which employed several neighbors, announced that "Lucky Strike Green" (the printer's ink on cigarette packs) had gone to war. War bond campaigns and metal scrap drives were hastily arranged. As soon as Guilford County announced the installation of a Civil Defense Control Center in the county courthouse, I rushed to sign up as Volunteer #7088 and regularly performed air warden duty on the roof—my introduction to binoculars. The air raid siren went off when an unidentified airplane came within sight, and a power failure could produce suspicions of sabotage. Air raid shelters were rapidly designated. Such jerry-rigged precautions were not far-fetched in 1942, when the war was going badly for the Allies.

My sense of guilt was aggravated by a condition that I was not able to analyze at the time. My life was a series of highs and lows, and the swings between extremes were regularly recorded in my diary. My mental condition worsened in May when a strange illness led the company nurse, Mrs. McAdoo, to turn me over to Dr. William Norment, who diagnosed my trouble as thyroid gland disorder. I was put on a regimen requiring several weeks of "hypos," pills, and quarts of liquid medicine. Although my physical ailment was ameliorated, there was little effect on my morbid psychological malady. Scenarios of suicide were recorded in my diary: June 19 — "Most terribly [*sic*] day in long time. I'm simply all to pieces — tired of everything.... Tonight may be the moment."; July 13 — "Feel terribly again tonight. Had it out with myself, but no good." For many nights, a glass filled with cigarette tobacco soaking in water sat on the mantel, for I had read that a heavy dose of nicotine was the most painless way to die. In July I precipitously took out life insurance in the amount of $2,500, with my parents and siblings as beneficiaries, without reading in the fine print that suicide would nullify its double-indemnity provisions.

My life was probably saved — unknowingly — by my fellow Jefferson Standard employee, William J. Sharpe, a black-haired, dark-skinned, quick-witted mountaineer from Smoot, West Virginia. Bill was already in the Main File when I arrived in January, but I was drawn more immediately to Ed Taylor and Ned Fowler, who frequently joined me at movies. Greensboro's several theaters, all within walking distance, offered cheap admission, comfortable seating, and frequent feature changes. Bill was first mentioned in my diary on March 18, when I recorded our bowling party, along with the added judgment, "Bill is really a swell guy." Having been my guest for a meal, he began having his lunch with us at Mrs. Feree's. We soon found that we shared several interests, and we frequently double-dated, for he had the luxury of an ancient Plymouth automobile. He was especially solicitous during my illness, listened to the troubles that I poured out, and provided a calm and mature response to my problems. When I was at my lowest, he knew how to distract me by "goosing" me near my armpits, a weakness that I tried to conceal from everyone else. On June 30, Bill and I registered together for the draft, and on September 10 he accompanied me to the Navy Recruiting Station. Try as I might, I was unable to persuade him to sign the enlistment papers. He had a good reason: He had met Anna Rose of Newton Grove, a lovely auburn-haired woman who became his bride with the help of my loan of $20 when I left for the Navy. Bill later served in the Army and became a successful businessman as proprietor of Bill Sharpe Office Equipment Company. After the war, he and Anna, with their daughters Carolyn and Sandy, provided me with something akin to a second home while I was teaching at nearby Oak Ridge Military Institute.

The time had come for a life-changing decision.

2

"You're in the Navy Now"

September–December 1942

Even in wartime, an eighteen-year-old was a minor, so my enlistment in the Navy required my father's notarized consent. That legality was taken care of in the presence of Attorney R.T. Wilson in Yanceyville on September 18, 1942. While my parents were not thrilled at seeing me go off to war, they had learned to view me as a good but very strange boy, not at all like my brothers and neighboring males, whose future was tied to the land. My mind was never really on the struggle to eke out a living from the soil; I was always trying to figure out how to get away from the poverty and drudgery of the tenant farm. Having taken typing at a time when only "sissy" boys chose that subject, I preferred pecking on a type-writer to following the south end of a mule plowing northward. That's why I spent my pennies on postal cards with which I "ordered off" for an incalculable assortment of free literature revealing innumerable ways to escape — in fantasy if not reality — my drab surroundings. For example, my bedroom, the attic of the log "front room" of our humble four-room house, sagged under the weight of nearly two hundred catalogs of colleges, many of whose school colors I still remember. From them I had learned about Lees-McRae College's self-help program that provided my initial escape.

So my folks were not surprised by my decision to abandon the farm, and they were no doubt amused during my last days at home when I worked off my excitement by chopping wood for the tin heater and iron cookstove. A Navy enlistment was unusual in the Kill Quick-Locust Hill area, and it sparked curiosity among my neighbors, few of whom, I among them, had ever seen — much less been aboard — a ship. That was fortunate; otherwise my own ignorance of what lay ahead might have been exposed by my loquaciousness. I visited and was visited by inquisitive relatives and neighbors; and several evenings were passed at Crossroads, Robert Smith's store that became the unofficial community center at the junction of U.S. 158 and the Park Springs Road.

Although I was anxious to enter my new world, I still entered the words "Sad about leaving" in the little leather-covered five-year diary in which I had scrawled my innermost thoughts from age fourteen. (My first diary entries, 1937, were made in a small green paperback, spiral-bound notebook.) I returned to Greensboro and stayed with my friend Bill Sharpe until September 22, when he saw me off at the railroad station for my first train ride. The next morning at the Naval Recruiting Station in Raleigh, after passing the first thorough physical examination in my life, I was accepted as an apprentice seaman in Class V-6, United States

Naval Reserve. The physical revealed a lot about myself. At 68 inches tall and 132 pounds, I presented a "normal" appearance — ruddy complexion, light brown hair, "Blue VIII" eyes, 20/20 vision, 15/15 hearing, 34-inch chest at inspiration, pulse of 90 before exercise, and blood pressure of 120/80. Everything else was normal except that one tooth overlapped another. An inked print of my right index finger forever associated my physical body with the paper record.

My enlistment became official with the assignment of serial number 656 97 02 imprinted, along with my blood type A, on an oval stainless steel tag attached to a string that hung around my neck. Then, along with other recruits classified as AS (we joked that one more "s" and our rank would perfectly describe us), I was put aboard another train for Norfolk, Virginia. Bussed to the Naval Operating Base, I was assigned to Platoon 526, Unit X, United States Naval Training Station. My platoon commander, Chief Specialist M.S. Orr, quickly won the respect of the strange assortment of about eighty juveniles whom he sought, in four weeks, to whip into sailors.

My boot camp trauma began with another inspection, standing naked before an officer who seemed a little too personal in his questioning and touching. I was especially uncomfortable with the short-arm inspection, and only later did I understand why he so thoroughly examined my rear end. My first lie as a sailor was to respond affirmatively to the officer's question about my sexual experience with females. After all, I was now a *sailor*! My lying boast, I assumed, was duplicated by most of my platoon mates who, like me, wouldn't dare admit to being a virgin, thus exposing ourselves as the butt of jokes around the barrack. Later in the day, as I saw bushels of hair crudely shorn from the heads of my colleagues, I felt like a fool for having paid a quarter for a haircut the previous Friday. A Lees-McRae classmate, C.S. Deweese, previously admired for his rich black hair, rushed up to me exclaiming, "Look what they did to me!" We were in the Navy now.

During the issuance of clothing and gear, each recruit called out his various sizes, but the storekeeper was not reluctant to substitute his own judgment. He grumpily stacked on the counter clothing that would turn a farm boy into a sailor: a bewildering array of strange items in *blue* — traditional wool dress jumper, fourteen-button trousers, flat hat, undress outfit, denim shirt and trousers; in *white* — cotton jumper, vertical-buttoned trousers, Dixie-cup hats, T-shirts, nainsook drawers, handkerchiefs, towels, mattress and pillow covers; in *black* — heavy pea coat, silk neckerchief, watch cap, sweater, bathing trunks, sox, shoes, overshoes; and then, web belt, canvas leggings, and rubber pancho. All of that was just the beginning: Still to come was the sailor's bed — a narrow thin mattress, pillow, and canvas hammock complete with ropes secured at both ends with metal grommets. Finally, there were the traditional *seabag* — a canvas sack about 32 inches tall by 13 inches in diameter when filled — and a small *dittybag* for toiletries. And, as if an afterthought, the storekeeper slapped down a whisk broom and the tenth edition of the 800-page *Bluejacket's Manual*. It occurred to me that the loquacious naval recruiter back in Greensboro had not warned me that all of my belongings must be carried in a single seabag, nor that, when I transferred from station to station, I would carry my bedding with me, rolled into the hammock, wrapped around the bag, and loaded onto my shoulders. Each recruit spent hours practicing the proper way of rolling his clothing and packing his belongings in a predetermined order in the seabag to conserve space and minimize wrinkling. He also spent much time laying out his hammock; neatly coiling the lines and placing mattress, pillow, and blankets in the exact order; then rolling the hammock and lashing the complete bedding around his pre-filled seabag; and, finally, hoisting his worldly possessions to his shoulders. We were never given statistics on how many men suffered a hernia or sprained back, but it was not until near the end of the war that enlisted sailors were relieved of the burden.[1]

Although in the gymnasium at Lees-McRae I had slept in a large room with a half-dozen other students, that was a far cry from NOB's acre-size military barrack equipped with little more than double-decker bunks and a large toilet (called a head) and shower. There were no lockers, for all of my worldly possessions were held by that seabag into which clothing was rolled and packed in an exact order. Carried separately was a stainless steel meal tray, to which were attached a spoon, fork, knife, and scallop-shaped drinking cup. A properly equipped sailor seemed to be prepared for almost any eventuality.

Our drillmaster, a handsome fellow named Tumlin, and his assistants were products of military schools, and they, under Chief Orr's close supervision, whipped us into a fairly cohesive platoon. Even so, only after seemingly interminable hours on the drill field did our leaden feet, in brand-new shoes, respond to military cadence. Our ears rang with barked orders — 'Ten-shun! Hup-two-three! A-bout face! Wherever we went, we formed a column, often in alphabetical order of surname, and a first rule of the military forbade line-breaking. Classes — to which we marched in step — occupied most of the time that was not spent on calisthenics, drills, rifle firing, and swimming practice. We learned that a rope was a line and that Navy lines accommodated an assortment of knots — square, slip, overhand, cat's-paw, granny, and a dozen others — and we were expected to be able to tie each one. Smokers were taught the meaning of "The smoking lamp is lit [or out]" and warned that the butt of a cigarette was to be finely "stripped" so that the trash would easily meld into the ground. A flipped or stomped butt was cause for demerits. And, of course, we learned "Anchors Aweigh" and several other naval songs, especially the moving Navy hymn:

> Eternal Father, strong to save,
> Whose arm hath bound the restless wave,
> Who bid'st the mighty ocean deep
> Its own appointed limits keep;
> O, hear us when we cry to Thee,
> For those in peril on the sea.[2]

In retrospect, meals were good, but of course at the time we grumbled that nothing was fit to eat. Mechanical potato-peelers apparently had not yet been introduced to the military, and galley duty rotated from one man to another. There was no shore liberty, so recreation was largely limited to athletic contests, card playing, movie watching, radio listening, letter writing, telling yarns and listening to scuttlebutt, studying, and, for those who brought along a little cash, carbonated drinks and caloric snacks at the canteen. There was time for vaccinations, however, and during boot camp I endured three shots for typhoid fever, two for tetanus, and one for cowpox. Beginning on October 10, I spent three days in sick bay with acute catarrhal fever, which was treated with "Acetylsalicylic acid gr. X Soda Bicarb. Gr.X. Q.4.H," whatever that was. The officer specifically noted that the malady was "not due to misconduct."

Few close friendships were formed in the four weeks of boot camp, and after we posed for our group photograph on October 19, we scattered in many directions. However, I felt some kinship with R.H. Jernigan, Bill Wood, B.F. Turner, O.D. Harris, W.M. Thompson, and H.A. Kendall — almost all of them called by surname. My buddy Earl Marlow of Sarasota, Florida, went on to become a torpedoman, but I lost touch with him. I especially developed a friendship with Wade A. Harris of Albemarle, North Carolina, who was assigned to gunnery school in Quonset, Rhode Island. We corresponded until I received a letter from

In the October 19, 1942, boot camp picture of Platoon 526, Naval Training Station, Norfolk, I am standing at far right in the second row from the top. Chief Specialist M.S. Orr was platoon commander.

another sailor informing me that Wade had gone down at sea with his TBF airplane on July 15, 1943. I was shocked, and I shared my sense of loss to his mother, Martha Harris. On October 4, I received a letter from Mrs. Harris that touched me deeply: "Wade wrote me the sadiest [*sic*] letter when you left Norfolk. He said he was so lonesome and blue because his best buddy had left him and it sure was bad to get to like someone so good and then have to part with him." Even in grief, one can draw satisfaction for having had a positive influence on a friend. How many of the other seventy-nine platoon mates died for their country, I shall never know. I was fortunate to be among those who survived to enjoy the liberties for which we were at war.

Each "boot" underwent a battery of tests — physical, written, oral, and auditory — to determine who among us might have talents leading to ratings other than that of common seaman. I assumed, on the basis of assurances from recruiting officers, that my typing skills would lead me toward the rating of yeoman, the Navy's classification of a typist/secretary. I was a little incredulous, then, when an officer reported that my auditory test revealed a "musical ear," for, not knowing the difference between a G-clef and a G-string, and with a voice more practiced in calling the pigs ("sooooie, sooooie"), I had been an embarrassment to the glee club at Cobb Memorial School. I was horrified at the specter of being sent to a music school. It was then that I first heard the word "sonar."

The following entry was made in my service record on October 20: "Completed 4 weeks Recruit Training covering all assignments in Navy training course. Qualified swimmer. Received instruction at indoor rifle range. Received gas mask instruction." That introduction to the Navy having been completed, I went home on my first leave, riding the bus both ways. I recorded in my diary, "Back home after a month's grand time at Navy at Norfolk. It's swell. In [Anti-] Submarine Sound School. 8 day leave. Glad I joined. May go to Key West, Fla." In my dress blues, bearing a single white stripe on my sleeve and around my shoulder, I was the most popular boy in the neighborhood. Naturally I visited my old friends at the high school and at Jefferson Standard Life Insurance Company, posed for pictures with both sexes of all ages, and Bill Sharpe and I visited my sister and her family in Reidsville. Toward the end of the month, I returned to NOB, Norfolk, was assigned to another barrack, saw a few of my platoon mates who also were awaiting new assignments, and was bored with little to do except participate in work parties, including the indignity of galley duty. Mostly we talked and fantasized about our next station. Fortunately, however, evening liberty was allowed from time to time and was usually spent at movies in Norfolk or Portsmouth. I was never notified of my promotion on November 7 to seaman second class.[3]

On completion of my leave, I followed orders to proceed to the Fleet Sound School in Key West, Florida. For the first time I stuffed my clothing and gear into that canvas seabag, careful to roll each cloth item and pack it in the exact order specified in the *Bluejacket's Manual*. Even more difficult was the rolling of the mattress and pillow into the hammock and lashing the canvas roll around the bag. But the real test came when I, weighing only 132 pounds, hoisted the heavy assembly onto my shoulders. Even the physical training in boot camp had not prepared me for such a burden, and I was not alone in struggling to carry the ensemble to the waiting bus, then transferring it to the train at the rail terminal in Norfolk. The train to Miami November 14 was unmemorable, but the bus trip over the Florida keys was spectacular. Having never been to Florida, I was happy that the scenery lived up to that state's tourist advertising, and I arrived in Key West during its best weather. There, however, a heavy presence of the military dulled the views so invitingly depicted in magazines. Regardless, I saw little of the town because we were seldom allowed off the naval base.

Those of us selected for sonar training were assigned to a barrack at the Fleet Sound School, located near Fort Taylor in an area later designated as the Truman Annex because President Harry Truman spent vacations nearby. (The buildings later housed the Joint Inter Agency Task Force East.) Within view were submarines and surface vessels, the identities of which we had not yet learned. Furthermore, before arrival we had been given neither orientation nor literature about the mysterious word "sonar," so we were as green as grass about both our mission and our surroundings. Soon, however, we read that the word was an acronym for "*so*und, *na*vigation, and *r*anging," a system developed to detect an

Home from boot camp with a single white shoulder stripe signifying my initial rating of apprentice seaman, I was photographed with my Greensboro friend William J. Sharpe.

underwater object by listening for an echo from a sound wave sent out from a dome beneath a ship's hull. Within the suspended dome were hundreds of small nickel tubes, each encircled with copper wire and mounted on a diaphragm. Electric current caused the nickel tubes to expand, thus moving the diaphragm and sending out an impulse, a "ping." Although the hydrophone and a primitive form of echo-location had been invented during World War I, it was not until the 1930s that the technology was first installed in a limited number of American destroyers. The system's importance grew in the face of the expansion of the German submarine fleet, and in 1939 the Navy established its West Coast Sound School at San Diego and Atlantic Fleet Sound School in New London, Connecticut. As the threat of war increased, the Navy recognized the role of craft smaller than destroyers in detecting submerged vessels, and by 1941 the construction of specialized craft, ranging from 221-foot metal-hulled fleet minesweepers down to 110-foot wooden submarine chasers, was accelerated.[4]

The training of officers and enlisted men for antisubmarine warfare was also accelerated; officers were trained in Miami's Subchaser Training Center, and the New London school was moved to Key West for the instruction of enlisted personnel in operating underwater sound equipment. I was to be among the little fraternity of a new rating, *sonarman*, a designation so new that it was initially called *soundman*. From North Carolina, off whose coast German submarines were sinking American ships, I began to feel that I might play a genuine role in the war, and the mental conflict that vexed me the previous summer was soon dissipated. Maybe I knew nothing about music, but I had ears sensitive enough to distinguish tones. That was an essential talent, because the pitch of an echo, together with its distance as judged by a rangefinder, produces a doppler effect and can reveal the movement of the detected object. I had found my niche. Preparing for the niche, however, was not easy. My mind did not easily grasp technological theory or scientific terminology, so the theories behind sonar were less clear to me than its practical value in the war against the Axis powers. Only my ears would make me a good sonarman.

The first weeks at Key West were spent largely on an Attack Teacher, a British invention that had been installed the year before to train sailors in antisubmarine tactics. The shore-based contraption mimicked shipboard echo-sounding and offered experience in operating the equipment and in honing the operator's interpretation of echoes. Lessons on the Attack Teacher resembled a twenty-first century computer game in which an elusive target (a make-believe submarine) seeks to outwit the sonar operator on an imaginary surface vessel. If a ping elicits a contact (an echo), the operator determines the nature of the contact by the clarity of its sound (sharp for a metal object, squishy for a whale) and, if it is determined to be a submarine, measures its distance (by electronically timing the emission of the ping and its returning echo) and its movement by observing the compass variation and the pitch of the echo — up-doppler (advancing) or down-doppler (receding). With confirmation of the object as a submarine, the "surface ship" hurriedly attacks it by firing mousetraps (hedgehogs) from a distance and by sailing over the site and dropping depth charges. Upon completion of the simulated exercise, a team evaluates the operator's antisubmarine skills.[5]

After practice on the Attack Teacher, one could become so "ping-happy" that he might imagine hearing the outgoing signals for an hour afterward. Seagoing training was another matter for one who had never been in a canoe, much less an oceangoing ship. My first trip at sea was not only historic; it was aboard a historic ship, one for which a fellow Tar Heel, Josephus Daniels, had been partially responsible. As Secretary of the Navy during the First World War, Daniels called upon Henry Ford for the construction of small steel-plated patrol ships capable of hunting down and depth-bombing German submarines. Although sixty vessels were built by Ford's company and sailed through the Great Lakes and St. Lawrence River to the Atlantic, the war ended before a single one of them could face the enemy. Nearly a quarter-century later in another world war, a survivor, too antiquated for modern antisubmarine warfare, was pressed into service as a training ship at the Fleet Sound School. Steel-hulled USS *Eagle PE-56* had a displacement of 615 tons with a draft of nearly nine feet, length of 200 feet, beam of 33 feet, and speed of up to 18 knots.

Another relic from World War II, USS *Dahlgren* (DD-187), alternated with *PE-56* as a training vessel. Larger at 1,190 tons and length of 315 feet, this old destroyer could reach a speed of 35 knots. Four months before I sailed on her, the *Dahlgren* had rescued survivors of the torpedoed tanker SS *Pennsylvania Sun*. Of course, we future sonarmen were ignorant of the history of these vessels and viewed them as little more than old hulks.

Each daybreak, trainees in Key West boarded one of these lumbering old vessels, which left port and rendezvoused in the vicinity of a World War I American R-class submarine, with which she played a game of hide-and-seek. It was aboard them that scores of echo-sounding sailors learned to detect an underwater obstruction, analyze its nature (sandbar, whale, school of fish, submarine, wake of another ship, etc.), and chart its length, depth, and movement. The routine was simple: a trainee sat before the sonar equipment and turned a little wheel five degrees, sent out a "ping," waited a few seconds for an echo, then turned another five degrees, and, hearing no echo, repeated the sequence over and over. Because the ship's own wake would distort the impulse when pointed toward the stern, the search was usually directed forward of 100 and 260 degrees. The captain, upon confirming a suspicious contact, generally turned the ship in the direction of the target to get a clearer contact, to minimize exposure, and to be prepared to launch hedgehogs (rocket-fired depth charges that exploded on contact with a firm object) or speed over the target and roll off (or fire from the K-guns) depth-charges that exploded at a specified depth. Even though he was but an enlisted man, the sonarman's judgment was crucial to the ship's safety, because it was his "call" to analyze the contact, determine its nature and characteristics, and pass his judgment to the officer on the bridge. Ultimately, of course, reaction to that analysis was the responsibility of a commissioned officer. To earn the confidence of his superiors, therefore, was the highest aspiration of a sonarman.

On December 19, having survived both the rigorous training and several cases of seasickness as *PE-56* or *Dahlgren* bobbled on rough seas, I completed my course of study and was promoted to sonarman third class (with the acronym SoM3c). Neither a rating badge nor the title sonarman had yet been approved officially, so we were authorized to attach to our left sleeve the insignia of a quartermaster third class, the eagle facing the wrong direction, giving rise to comments like "left-armed quartermaster" or, more derisively, "queer quartermaster." I sewed mine on proudly, but my ego was not enhanced by my final grade: 84 out of 100, no better than 21st in a class of 58. Figuring that to be a C, I realized that I had more work to do before gaining the confidence of a future commanding officer.

When a transfer list was posted on the bulletin board, we excitedly jostled each other to learn our future assignment. There were exclamations as well as groans. When I ran my finger down to my name in the J's, I found a cryptic line: "R/S NY (fft USS SC-525)." Translated, that meant Naval Receiving Station, New York, for further transfer to a submarine chaser numbered 525. I soon learned that the receiving station occupied Pier 92 in New York City, but I had no idea of the location of *SC-525*, a 110-foot wooden submarine chaser. On December 22, 1942, my fellow sonarmen and I left behind the warmth of Key West and headed northward.

3

Farm Boy in the Big Apple

December 24, 1942–March 4, 1943

Just after daybreak on Christmas Eve, 1942, a train disgorged seventeen newly rated naval sonarmen in New York City's Pennsylvania Station following a two-night ride from Florida. It had been a rather boring trip except for a little show put on by several black women while the cars paused in the middle of the street that divides Nash and Edgecombe counties in Rocky Mount, North Carolina. Taunted by sailors leaning out of the train windows, the amused ladies responded with an impromptu strip-tease, their contribution to the morale of the servicemen. For farm boys from a fundamentalist background, this was just one of many shocking scenes that would open our eyes and ears to a less-inhibited lifestyle in a rapidly urbanizing world.

One of my Key West classmates, a native New Yorker named Frank J. Zanino, was sufficiently concerned about my provincialism to take upon himself my introduction to the Big Apple. Before we reclaimed our seabags, he led me through the milling crowd to the street level, pointed upward through the morning haze, and gave me my first sight of the towering Empire State Building. That exact view remained vivid in my mind long after the built environment in the area was radically altered years later, and my pal Frank took justified pride in giving me my very first glimpse of the canyons separating skyscrapers that I had seen only in pictures. The scene was so alluring that years later I returned to the city for graduate work at New York University.

We were bussed between the tall buildings to Pier 92, which jutted from the foot of West 52nd Street into the Hudson River.[1] The street end of the enormous structure housed offices and facilities, but the main portion consisted of a cavernous 70,000-square-foot barrack filled with multi-decker iron beds capable of sleeping several thousand sailors. Our contingent from Key West was soon dispersed by indiscriminate assignment to bunks, and the comradeship developed during sonar training was vitiated as we melded with the other men. The fact that this was only a way-station between assignments meant that here, too, few close friendships would be formed. For the purpose of muster, I was assigned to Section One.

I slept soundly through Christmas eve. Captain W. H. Pashley, commander of the Receiving Station, ordered that a special dinner be served Christmas day, and the commissary stewards laid out a spread uncharacteristic of the drab but fulfilling meals to which we enlisted men had become accustomed. The menu, printed in 4,000 colorful double folders, included the usual turkey and ham, along with oyster cocktail, fruitcake, pumpkin pie, and other delicacies, topped off with cigarettes. We new arrivals gorged ourselves and envied those lucky enough to be allowed liberty during the remainder of the day. My exploration of the city — so near but so far — would have to wait.

None of us knew how long we would have to wait for transfer to our new station, and while I had learned that *SC-525* was in Africa, no one could give me an idea of when I might be provided trans–Atlantic passage. "Hurry up and wait" was characteristic of the military, and the first several days were passed in the pier by mustering, exercising, eating, sleeping, playing cards, and gabbing. Soon, however, my name appeared on a list for a work detail, and a memorable one it was. A young officer was put in charge of a small group that was taken by bus to Bayonne, New Jersey, where we labored the entire day in sub-freezing weather loading an ammunition ship. As the afternoon wore on without lunch, it became obvious that there had been a snafu, for the officer could find no one with authority to order a meal for us. This "ninety-day-wonder," as we called recent college graduates who were commissioned after minimal training, was deeply embarrassed over our mutual predicament when it became clear that we would be returned to New York too late even for supper. He won our respect when he found enough cash in his pocket to buy each of us a candy bar at a nearby canteen. That officer deserved a commendation for sacrifice and humanitarian aid in the face of bureaucratic bungling.

The next detail appeared a bit ridiculous. With another sailor, I was issued a rifle and instructed to walk the outside deck of a pier south of the Receiving Station. For what purpose? To guard a sunken ship. This was not, however, just "another" ship. It was the former SS *Normandie*, put in service by France in 1935 as the largest, fastest, and greatest ocean liner built to that time — the ultimate in seagoing luxury. She had made her 139th Atlantic crossing when Germany occupied France, so the lavish ship was seized by the United States while tied up at Pier 88. After we entered the war, *Normandie* was refitted as a troop ship and renamed USS *Lafayette*, a recognition of France's role in the American Revolution. Finishing touches were being made on February 9, 1942, when sparks from a welder's torch ignited a pile of life jackets. The fire spread rapidly because no one could figure out how to turn on the ship's state-of-the-art fire-extinguishing system, and harbor fireboats poured so much water into the ship that she capsized beside the pier. From that time until the next year when the vessel was refloated and moved to Brooklyn, armed Navy men like me from Pier 92 protected the half-sunken, side-lying hull from souvenir hunters. Plans to convert the liner to an aircraft carrier were abandoned, and the once luxurious floating palace was ignominiously scrapped at Newark in 1947.

Interesting, to say the least, were my assignments aboard a dangerous floating brig tied up to Pier 90. Built in Germany in 1900 as the cargo ship *Keil*, the 4,500-ton vessel was seized and rechristened USS *Camden* (AS-6) when the United States declared war in 1917. Before that war's end, the aging freighter carried coal to Britain and France. Afterward she was converted to a submarine tender that operated in both the Atlantic and the Pacific until decommissioned in 1931. As World War II approached, *Camden* was again pressed into service as a floating barrack with the designation *IX-42*. By early 1943, she was outfitted as a brig with iron-barred cells to which enlisted men convicted of serious offenses were committed. Again, my assignment, complete with a sidearm, appeared to be overkill, because I was more amused than frightened by fellow sailors on the other side of the bars. Later it occurred to me that perhaps not all of those who spun their yarns to me were as tender and innocent as they pretended. Nevertheless, I developed empathy for several of the prisoners whose future, I feared, would forever be circumscribed by youthful indiscretions. That compassion did not extend to one tough old bastard whose monkeyshine antics lost their humor when he hoisted himself to an overhead pipe, hung himself upside-down by his ankles, and masturbated to the applause of the other prisoners.

My talent as a brass-polisher was honed aboard USS *Prairie State*, which looked more like a huge wooden floating hotel than the battleship USS *Illinois* (BB-7) that she had been in an earlier life. Launched in 1898, the 11,500-ton, 375-foot long *Illinois* was out of date by World War I, so her superstructure was removed and the metal hull was surmounted by a strange-looking three-story wooden building that served as an accommodation ship in New York harbor. In 1941, to free the Illinois state name for a projected new Iowa Class battleship (that was never built), she was redesignated *IX-15* and given the state's nickname. By 1943 *Prairie State* was tied up in the Hudson River near Columbia University, serving as a Naval Reserve Midshipmen Training School. From the river the old hulk looked like a carpenter's nightmare, but her interior revealed earlier elegance as a flagship that sailed around the world with the Great White Fleet of 1907 to 1909. I became attracted to the historic vessel and several of the midshipmen, so whenever the opportunity appeared, I gladly volunteered to polish brass on the venerable curiosity. Circumnavigating Manhattan with the Circle Line in 1952, I found *Prairie State* docked at Pier 23 in East River, still providing quarters for sailors. She survived until 1956, when in Baltimore she was finally cut into scrap by the Bethlehem Steel Company.

Some of my comrades considered these and other manual tasks beneath the dignity of a newly rated petty officer third class, but I reveled in the opportunity to live and work in New York for more than ten weeks. Afternoon and evening liberties were fairly frequent, and I took every opportunity to go ashore (a misleading term inasmuch as the "shore" was just outside the front door). For a country boy, New York was a candy store of surprises, and I tried to take advantage of every one of them.

Strangely, though, my first experience on the streets of the Big Apple was not on liberty but on official assignment. Only a few days after arriving at Pier 92, I was stunned to be ordered to shore patrol duty. With a wooden billy club in my hand, an "SP" insignia wrapped around my arm, and leggings covering my ankles, I — a youngster from North Carolina — suddenly possessed authority to apprehend servicemen (regardless of branch or rank) who violated either civil or military law. Never a violent one and so timid as to run from a prospective altercation, I was scared witless when I failed to get an exemption from the order. With several other men selected for SP duty that night, I was driven to a military discipline center for our beat assignment, and it was only after I was paired with a veteran Army sergeant that my anxiety was somewhat relieved. I quickly learned that the soldier was an old hand at MP duty, and he just as quickly put me at ease with his patient explanation of what we might encounter during the night. Not having expected the opportunities of the evening, I had eaten a hearty noon meal; the experienced sergeant had not made the same mistake. So, with him always in the lead, we walked into bars, restaurants, and other business establishments, looked around, and, not infrequently, accepted invitations from owners to visit kitchens for whatever delicacies we desired. That evening for the first time I tasted pastrami, and it has remained one of my favorite foods. I was relieved that we ran into no disciplinary trouble, and the evening turned out to be quite satisfying. A few days later on my 19th birthday, I facetiously scribbled, "... there was no Fifth Avenue Parade."

I carried to New York a stereotypical assumption that was dispelled by the warmth with which the city treated military personnel. During the ten weeks, Frank Zanino, whose family ran Sam's Cigar Store in Astoria, served as a congenial guide to the city so familiar to him.

Furthermore, a uniform was a ticket to a wide assortment of entertainment, and I felt welcome wherever I went. The cost of my liberties was lightened by servicemen's free or reduced admission fees to museums, cultural activities, sports events, and theaters. An inveterate recordkeeper, I listed two pages of events that I attended (and kept ticket stubs for many of them). On my fifth night in the city, I went to Madison Square Garden to see Southern California defeat Long Island University and University of Kansas defeat Fordham on the basketball court; ten days later I was at the Garden again to see Long Island beat University of North Carolina Pre-Flight School and New York University trounce Manhattan. Among other memorable games for which I had complimentary tickets was one featuring the then tallest team in the world, West Texas State College; and on February 18 I watched my first ice hockey game as the Detroit Red Wings defeated the New York Rangers. On a more sophisticated level, I saw and heard Arturo Toscanini conducting the NBC Symphony Orchestra in *Brahms Cycle IV*, and I attended the auditions of Thelma Altman and Gustave Longtin at the Metropolitan Opera, conducted by Wilfred Pelletier. I listed more than fifty motion pictures, their stars, and the theaters in which they were seen, ranging from *Casablanca* to *The Man Who Came to Dinner* and *Yankee Doodle Dandy*. But more memorable were stage performers whose names would mean more to me as the years passed. During the war, the larger theaters booked live entertainment to supplement the film on the screen, and I saw and heard the orchestras of Ray Block at CBS Studios, Jimmy Dorsey at the Roxy, Benny Goodman and Johnny Long at the Paramount, Sammy Kaye and Guy Lombardo at the Strand, and Fred Waring at Vanderbilt Studios. Equally exciting was the opportunity to attend stage plays featuring Jack Benny and Rochester in *The Meanest Man in the World*; Dorothy Lamour and William Holden in *The Fleet's In*; George Raft in *Scarface*; Red Skelton in *Whistling Dixie*; Ray Milland and Paulette Goddard in *The Crystal Ball*; and Robert Young in *January for Margaret*. There were also stage appearances by Fred Allen, Carol Bruce, George Jessell, Al Jolson, Danny Kaye, Roddy McDowell, Rose Marie, Claude Rains, and some talented youngsters that I could not have known would become famous in the postwar years.

Another popular liberty destination was the Stage Door Canteen on West 44th Street, which, with a twin that opened in Los Angeles, inspired the film by that name and Irving Berlin's haunting lyrics from, "I Left My Heart at the Stage Door Canteen." I also took the opportunity of attending religious services conducted by famous theologians such as Norman Vincent Peale at cathedrals and churches about which I had heard but never imagined I would be able to attend.

Liberty was granted on an alternating schedule, so I was not always able to go into the city with my buddies from sound school. Before one liberty, the father of Lenox B. Wharton, Jr., of Crisfield, Maryland, notified his son that he was wiring him money in care of the American Red Cross at Times Square. Unfortunately, the son was not on the liberty list for several consecutive days, so he asked me to pick up the money for him. Knowing that I would be required to show identification, he gave me his entire wallet. The Red Cross worker was hospitable, looked at "my" driver's license (this was before photos appeared on such documents), and asked me several questions designed to confirm my identity. Just as she was about to count out the money, she asked for my father's full name. My mind went blank and my face reddened. The disguise was betrayed, and she sighed and commented, "And they wonder why we ask these questions!" In my embarrassment, I explained the situation, and, remarkably, the lady kindly accepted my story without suspecting me of having found or stolen the wallet. Of course, I did not get the money, and my chagrin was magnified when, upon explaining the situation to L.B. back at Pier 92, he pointed out that his driver's license clearly showed him to be a "Jr."

Throughout my ten weeks at Pier 92, most of my sound school mates were transferred to their ships. For example, classmates Frank Zanino and Nuzio J. Caravaglia were sent west to join USS *Schroeder* (DD-501), which earned ten battle stars against the Japanese. Bob Ferrell of Danville, Virginia, not far from my birthplace, went aboard USS *John Rodgers* (DD-574), then in the Atlantic but soon to transit the Panama Canal, head for the Pacific, and win a dozen battle stars in the war against the Japanese. I learned little about my future ship, USS *SC-525*, except that she was a 110-foot wooden hulled submarine chaser equipped with sonar gear. Between work assignments and liberty in the Big Apple, I tried to envision what it would be like on a vessel little more than half the length of *Eagle*, on which I experienced my first *mal de mer* off Key West. Regardless of the apprehension, I looked forward to getting aboard. I had already been given additional vaccinations for typhoid and typhus, so I figured that I was ready for wherever the little ship would take me.

On March 3, 1943, while I was confined to sick bay with influenza, Wharton — having finally obtained his money and forgiven me for my stupidity — rushed in with news that we were scheduled to be transferred the next day. The thought of being left behind by my Key West buddies was unbearable, so without official discharge, I snuck out of sick bay, packed, and boarded a bus the next morning for the embarkation dock. For months I worried about being recorded as AWOL, and I wondered what entry was made in my official record. When sixty-some years later I obtained a copy of my medical record, there was no mention of my having been checked in *or* out of the sick bay. For once, I was the beneficiary of sloppy book-keeping.

4

Introduction to Africa: French Morocco
March–August 1943

Weakened by influenza, I strained to shoulder my packed seabag and bedding on the morning of March 4, 1943, as I joined hundreds of other sailors forming a line to busses that carried us from Pier 92 to Staten Island. Upon arrival at the embarkation dock, there was mass confusion as each of us attempted to retrieve his individual bag, identifiable only by name and serial number stenciled on the side of the canvas cylinder.

I carried orders simply reading "NOB Casablanca fft USS *SC-525* for duty." Casablanca, French Morocco, had been much in the news because of President Roosevelt's meeting with British Prime Minister Churchill there in January. The name of the North African city was also familiar to me because only a few weeks earlier at the Hollywood Theater near Times Square I had seen the motion picture *Casablanca*, starring Humphrey Bogart, Ingrid Bergman, Paul Henreid, and Sidney Greenstreet. But 3,600 miles of the Atlantic Ocean separated New York from my destination, and the first sight of my means of transportation — the troopship *John Ericsson* — was quite daunting as she sat beside the dock at Staten Island.

I was to learn later that *John Ericsson* was in prewar life *Kungsholm* of the Swedish-American line. Built in Hamburg in 1928 with a gross tonnage of more than 21,000, a sparkling art déco interior, and a capacity of more than 1,500 passengers, *Kungsholm* in the '30s provided luxurious accommodations during cruises on several oceans. Her popular entertainment director in 1941 was J.D. Salinger, future author of *Catcher in the Rye*. After war was declared on Germany, the United States government took over *Kungsholm*, stripped her of fancy furnishings, and outfitted her as a troop transport named for John Ericsson, the Swedish engineer who designed USS *Monitor* of American Civil War fame. For Army and Navy men who scampered aboard that Thursday morning, there was little evidence of the former glitter, for many bulkheads that once surrounded private suites had been ripped out to open large barrack-like rooms filled with multi-decked bunks. Formerly sumptuously decorated with crystal chandeliers and fancy table settings, the dining room was now filled with long rows of drab tables reminiscent of other military mess halls.[1]

Separated from familiar faces and disoriented on board an unfamiliar craft, each man, with his bag, sought his way through the confusion to a designated bunk, where he grabbed as many inches of storage space as remained unclaimed. Once settled, many returned to the open deck to wave goodbye, only to be disappointed because just a few dock workers and vehicles remained in sight. Ours was only one of hundreds of monthly troopship departures from American ports, and secrecy guarded news of sailings, which soon became so routine that relatives and friends seldom knew about embarkations. Still, the open deck was crowded when the lines were cast off and the New York skyline receded. Some pointed to the tiny silhouette of the Statue of Liberty; others picked out the Empire State Building and landmarks on Manhattan Island. Almost to a man (and a few uniformed females), we wondered if and when we would see our native land again. We were also sobered by the realization that we would be a target on the surface of the submarine-infested ocean before reaching the dark continent of Africa, where the war against Rommel's Afrika Korps in Tunisia was at a critical stage.

The *John Ericsson* took an inner position as the huge convoy formed off the New Jersey coast. Troopships, freighters, and tankers were surrounded by destroyers and patrol craft that provided air, surface, and sonar surveillance. The fear of aerial attacks was virtually dismissed, but a torpedo fired from a submarine was capable of penetrating a protective shield. The frightening effectiveness of German U-boat warfare demanded constant vigilance, so defensive actions, including blackouts at nights, were strictly observed throughout the voyage. We would have been even more troubled if we had known that in that very month alone — March 1943 — 108 American ships would be sunk by the more than a hundred German U-boats operating in the North Atlantic.[2]

We were blessed by not knowing what lay ahead: two weeks at sea in crowded quarters, boredom, personality conflicts, oppressive odors, seasickness, and, for me, a severe case of influenza that I dared not report to the medical officer for fear of being courtmartialed for abandoning sick bay without proper release.

The dispersal of various units around the ship and the absence of flat drilling surfaces minimized military formations and activities, so time passed slowly. The lethargic tended to lie around, getting little more exercise than was required to walk to meals; most just paced the decks; a few kept in shape climbing the manifold ladders; a few practiced calisthenics. Tables between meals were commandeered for playing cards and checkers; even a few chess boards were seen, but I had not yet been introduced to that game. Movies filled many hours; gabbing occupied many more. Abandon-ship drills were impromptu. Most disagreeable to me was the absence of anything productive; few books were available; I was not a card shark; and, although I had become more sociable after leaving the farm, I was still something of a shrinking violet. Furthermore, I had not yet become comfortable when my Southern accent was ridiculed by a Brooklynite or a "Joioseyite" for saying "y'all" instead of "youse guys." Understandably, then, the fourteen days on *John Ericsson* were not among my happier weeks in the Navy.

The Allied occupation of coastal areas of North Africa was just four months old as our convoy approached Casablanca, which from the sea looked like any other city except for a greater profusion of roof colors. After the Vichy government of France came under German domination, Operation Torch — history's first ship-to-shore operation across an ocean — was launched in November 1942 with the hope that French troops in Africa would welcome liberation by American and British forces. The miscalculation resulted in a costly invasion both along the Atlantic coast of French Morocco and on the Mediterranean coast of Algeria. When the French forces resisted the landings, the large portion of their fleet at Mers el-Kébir (MEK) near Oran was effectively destroyed, and the harbors at Algiers and Casablanca were left strewn with sunken vessels.

As *John Ericsson* was piloted through the minefield toward the sprawling Casablanca harbor on March 18, an astounding number of vessels darted about within the breakwater extending far out into the Atlantic. Miles of docks, radiating from a tall maritime building that served as a landmark, were occupied by Allied ships in varying stages of loading and unloading. Tall cranes moved along tracks, filling waiting trucks and rail cars. Smaller vessels formed nests, one along-side another.

My first sight of devastation came at the mouth of Casablanca's harbor. There sat the dead battleship, *Jean Bart*, previously the pride of the French Navy. In November she had engaged USS *Massachusetts* in a battle in which she sustained eight direct hits. Subsequently, she suffered cannibalization by the removal of her fifteen-inch guns and navigational gear, leaving the derelict as little more than a monumental landmark to greet the hundreds of Allied ships entering the busy harbor.

A more gruesome scene came into view a hundred yards or so farther inside the harbor. It was the forward three-fourths of a British ship that had just been towed in, its stern sheered off in the aft sleeping quarters. The picture is still burned into my memory: severed bodies dangling from mangled metal bunks, the remainder of each body having been sheered off by a torpedo and lost to the sea. Now I knew what war was, and I wondered if some sonarman third class might have failed to detect the enemy submarine that fired the deadly torpedo.

Except for these two indelible scenes, there were few signs of damage from the American invasion four months earlier. The huge battleship, partially sunk at Mole du Commerce by dive bombers from the carrier *Ranger*, had been moved to the side, and most of the other French victims had been cleared out — a tribute to the hustle and efficiency of the Navy's advance base unit. The broad expanse of the harbor and my inability to identify various ship silhouettes provided little hope for me to spot a tiny vessel on which, I presumed, would be painted the letters and numerals "*SC-525*." Later I learned that my little subchaser stood out-side the minefield — neither recognizing its first and only sonarman nor being recognized by me — as *John Ericsson* carried me through the swept channel.[3]

My orders were to report to the commander of the Naval Operating Base from where, presumably, I would be immediately directed to my ship, wherever it was located among the hundreds of vessels operating in the Moroccan Sea Frontier. But I had forgotten the old adage, "Hurry up and wait," so instead of a ship, a shore barrack was my home for the next eight days. Except for a few menial assignments, my sound school mates and I simply loafed, ate, smoked, and gabbed — for no liberty was granted — pending transfer to our ships. From the base buildings, however, we could walk the miles of moles and docks, so long as we remained within the fenced preserve. These meanderings gave me an increasing familiarity with the superstructure of different seagoing vessels, recognition that would be useful to me as a look-out aboard my own ship in coming months. I was issued a ration card allowing me to pur-chase from the base canteen a limited number of scarce items, such as candy bars and toiletries. Despite having been grown up around tobacco, I had never regularly smoked cigarettes, but a combination of boredom and long walks around the base introduced me to a baser habit, cigars.

My most memorable experience at NOB was also the most painful: a three-day battery of vaccinations, several duplicating those already taken in boot camp. I was more fortunate, however, than one poor fellow whose record was misplaced by the pharmacist's mate, sub-jecting him to an entirely new battery of treatments. The impending separation from a group of my sound school mates, who had sailed across the Atlantic with me, was also painful, for we had no idea of whether our ships would operate together. Norman Ellis went to *PC-475*, Rick Rickenback to *PC-472*, David Sechler to *PC-826*, Almon Teel to *PC-482*, and Lenox Wharton to *PC-480*. I already knew that the PCs (called "Peter Charlies," the largest commissioned warship without a name) were metal ships sixty-three feet longer than my wooden *SC-525* and Jim Proctor's *SC-619* (called "Sugar Charlies" or "One-Tens"), so Jim and I were a little envious.

Still, both the PC (patrol craft) and the SC (submarine chaser) were popularly called subchasers, and the confusion was compounded by the Navy's decision to assign hull numbers without regard to class of vessel. For example, number 496 was applied to *PC-496*, but the next number was assigned to *SC-497*.

On the warm afternoon of March 26, I received orders to proceed to my assigned ship at a specified pier. With all of my earthly possessions — including my bedding — balanced on my shoulder, I staggered to the dock only to receive a rude shock: *SC-525* was still on sea patrol and would not return until the following morning. Suddenly, I was homeless in Africa. Apparently, however, such a misconnection was not unusual, for a sailor on watch invited me to spread my hammock on the forecastle (always pronounced "fo'-c'sle") of his ship, a sister subchaser. He also invited me to chow, after which I spent the evening listening to horror stories spun by old salts who took advantage of my ignorance of the *real* Navy. On the open deck, under the same stars that shined on my native Caswell County, I spread my mattress atop my canvas hammock and slept little because the harbor hummed with activity throughout the night. It was comforting, however, to know that Casablanca was finally beyond the range of German aircraft.

When, on the morning of March 27, USS *SC-525* slipped in and tied up on the port side of my overnight host ship, I must have seemed quite rumpled after sleeping in my white uniform. As I walked the gangplank and dropped my bag to salute the flag, I was met by a chubby character dressed in dungarees more rumpled than my whites. He extended his hand and gave his name as George. When I responded, "Houston," he said, "Oh, a Texan" and, without giving me time to correct him, instructed me to leave my bag and come with him into the tiny bridge, not much larger than a playhouse. There, finishing an entry into a log, a khaki-clad officer looked up, extended a hand, and said, "Ah, you're here." He appeared no more than 20 years old, and so informal was his greeting that I did not catch his name — nor did I think to salute. Observing an ensign's bar on his shirt collar, which also appeared in need of ironing, I assumed that he was a second or third officer. He welcomed me aboard and instructed George to get me settled. As I strained to get my seabag past the 3"/23-caliber gun toward the bow, George explained that I had just met the ship's captain, Ensign Harry William (Bill) Reece, a Jayhawk from Scandia, Kansas. It was something of a surprise to be aboard a seagoing combat vessel commanded by no more than an ensign, the lowest-ranked commissioned officer in the Navy. But, then, I was aboard the Navy's smallest commissioned combat ship.

A logistical problem arose when we reached the forward hatch — hooded to divert bow spray — down which ran the vertical ladder to the forward sleeping quarters. Having solved the problem when he came aboard a few weeks earlier, George instructed me to untie my bedding from the seabag, then go down the ladder and catch each as he dropped it through the hatch. Suddenly I, a 132-pound stranger, was standing in the crew's quarters catching two loads of canvas while several pairs of eyes gazed upon me. In a flash, though, George slid down the ladder and yelled out something like, "Well, guys, here's the fellow who gets the interesting mail." Before I could wonder what he meant, everyone seemed to be talking at once in what I interpreted as a friendly but inquisitive welcome. Several approached and shook my hand; others just waved or simply ignored the intrusion.

As the crew member with least longevity, I expected what the old hands considered the least desirable berth, but when I was pointed toward a canvas-covered pipe bunk triced against the bulkhead, I was not disappointed. It was the top rack (in a tier of three) on the port side forward. A bench locker beneath the bottom bunk, plus a tiny upright locker behind the ladder, provided minimal storage for the contents of my seabag; the bag itself I folded under the head of my mattress. Only later did I learn the negative aspects of my sleeping space, which was adjacent to the single most heavily used facility on the ship — the head, containing the compartment's only commode and tiny washbasin. Furthermore, only caulked slabs of wood separated my body from the deck overhead and the sea water lapping the other side of the hull. I had much to learn, for I was now among twenty-six other men whom I did not know and aboard a seagoing vehicle completely unfamiliar to me.

Only one name registered in my mind during that first contact with the other fifteen men with whom I was to share the forward crew's quarters the next year and a half — that of George, the plump, fair-skinned, dark-haired sailor who had met me at the gangplank. He was George Franklin Klumpp of New Orleans, a radioman third class. His bunk was below mine, and he was to become my closest friend as the months passed. During the day, however, I met or at least saw the enlisted men who bunked in the aft crew quarters, which, when the bunks were folded against the wall, doubled as the mess hall. The galley was little more than a cubbyhole, and abaft the compartment was a tiny lazarette. Eventually I met the two other ensigns, John C. Waldron of Merion, Pennsylvania, and Hugh P. McCormick of Baltimore, Maryland, both of whom shared with the captain the cramped ward room just forward of the engine room and beneath the bridge. About their only convenience not shared by the enlisted men was a tiny shower stall.

I was later to learn of the early history of *SC-525* (one of 438 wooden subchasers built during World War II) through a study of its deck log and from oral reports for the months before my arrival. Following commissioning at Philadelphia Navy Yard in May 1942 and successful passing of sea trials, the ship was assigned to the Submarine Chaser Training Center in Miami, Florida, for the introduction of new Navy personnel to antisubmarine warfare. When not taking officers and enlisted men on sonar maneuvers, she patrolled the Florida coast as a defense against German U-boats. Lieutenant W.M. Martin had been relieved as commanding officer on October 4 by Ensign Reece, with Ensign Waldron as the executive officer. In late October the ship sailed for Naval Operating Base, Norfolk, Virginia, and there Ensign J.G. King reported aboard as commissary officer and E.L. Miller as Boatswain's Mate First Class.[4]

At Norfolk, *SC-525* was outfitted for war. Then on November 6, with the crew unaware that American forces were within two days of invading French Morocco and Algeria in North Africa, she sailed east as a part of Task Force 39, commanded by Captain R. M. Zimmerli in the tanker *Maumee* (AO-2). Launched during World War I, *Maumee* was the first surface ship in the Navy to be powered by diesel engines. Her executive officer back then was a young lieutenant named Chester W. Nimitz.

Known as the "Spitkit Convoy," the force was screened by minesweepers, PCs, SCs, and much larger vessels. Without capacity to distill water and with small diesel tanks, the little subchasers regularly bucked the roiling seas to pull alongside *Maumee* for life-sustaining fuel and water, supplied through hoses as the vessels rolled with the waves. After a short stop in Bermuda, the convoy encountered a nightmare of engine problems and several submarine scares before arriving safely outside the American-laid minefield protecting the harbor at Casablanca, French Morocco. On November 25, Ensign Reece docked *SC-525* at Phosphate Mole, stationed a three-man gangway watch, reported to NOB, and ordered that no reveille be sounded the following morning. Three days later four sister ships — *SC-515*, *-516*, *-517*, and *-529* — sailed northward, leaving *SC-507*, *-519*, *-524*, and *-525* to provide antisubmarine defense along the coast of French Morocco.[5] For the next several months, these vessels repeatedly relieved each other in patrolling outside the minefields, the monotony broken to escort ships sailing for other ports along the coast — Fedhala, Port Lyautey, Safi, and Agadir. Occasional submarine contacts resulted in no recorded sinkings, and *SC-525* could thus far claim only one possible hit on the enemy: In the early hours of December 31, several Junker 88s and Folke-Wolf 200s attacked the fleet at Casablanca. The guns of *SC-525* fired at an FW-200, but instead of claiming a victim, Ensign Reece modestly recorded in the log, "She was smoking & losing altitude on the way out of town."

More tedious entries reported the usual wartime problems — broken-down engines, blown head gaskets, bent propellers, contaminated diesel oil, conflicting orders, and slow delivery of mail from home. On the brighter side, one example of naval comradeship occurred at sea when on December 9 the oiler USS *Mattole* (AO-17)) responded affirmatively to the plea of *SC-525* for fresh water and diesel oil. Perhaps the tanker's officer on duty had once served in the "splinter fleet," for Ensign Reece gratefully wrote in his deck log, "*Mattole* invited *SC-525* crew to come aboard for canteen stores, showers, small stores, and movies." For the men on the little subchaser, whose small tank of fresh water could be used only for cooking, face-washing, and brushing teeth, Christmas had come early with warm showers on the rolling Atlantic off the African coast.

I was soon to learn and respect the "plankholders" — crew members assigned before the commissioning of USS *SC-525* at Philadelphia on May 1, 1942. Still aboard ten months afterward were Michael J. Balog, gunner's mate; James E. Bennett, Jr., machinist's mate; John B. Bringman, quartermaster; Edward Cain, machinist's mate; Boleslaus L. Cieslak, signalman; Albert Le Riche, ship's cook; Walter L. Marzean, electrician's mate; John F. McLaughlin, radioman; John F. Minster, motor machinist's mate; Albert Price, machinist's mate; Otto H. Promp, Jr., motor machinist's mate; Edmund E. Runof, fireman; John S. Schira, motor machinist's mate; and J.R. Vestal, gunner's mate. Together they comprised half of the crew. Although not a plank holder, Chief Boatswain's Mate Edward Lewis Miller, the highest ranking noncommissioned officer, immediately took a special interest in me, a fellow North Carolinian, and I, in turn, later sought and received good advice from him on a myriad of matters.[6]

Getting to know the crew was easier than learning every foot of *SC-525*, a wood-hulled submarine chaser measuring 110' 10" long and 17' 11½" wide, propelled by two GM straight eight diesel engines with a maximum speed of sixteen knots. Built by the Mathis Yacht Building Company in Camden, New Jersey, the little vessel's shallow draft — no more than seven feet — enabled her to get close to shore, a benefit when leading landing craft into invasion beaches.[7]

Space was always at a premium on a subchaser with a complement of three officers and twenty-four enlisted men. Living quarters were crowded, but additionally the deck was so cluttered that walking from stem to stern was hazardous even when in port. Forward of the pilot house were the 3"/23-caliber cannon (which, shortly after my boarding, was replaced by a 40-millimeter BoFors Mk3 gun), two Mk20 rocket-propelled launchers (called "mouse-traps" or "hedgehogs" capable of firing off eight antisubmarine projectiles), ready and ammunition lockers, booby hatch, anchors, winch, davit, vents, and jackstaff. On the quarter deck just aft the pilot house were two 20-millimeter Oerlikon antiaircraft guns, flag bag, and deck lockers. Farther aft were two K-guns for hurling depth charges to port and starboard, fourteen roll-off lethal depth charges ("ashcans"), a 50-caliber machine gun, two fifteen-men life-

World War II
Class SC497 Subchaser

Ship Particulars:

Length Overall	110' 10"
Extreme Beam	17' 11.5"
Maximum Draft	6' 6"
Displacement (Tons)	98
Engines	Two GM straight 8 Diesel Engines (8-268A), 500 bhp
Speed	15.6 knots
Fuel	Diesel Oil
Armament	1 Single Bofors 40 mm (forward)
	3 Single Oerlikon 20 mm (midships)
	1 Twin 50 cal. machine gun (aft)
Depth Charges	6 Single release chocks
	2 K-guns
	2 Mark 20 mousetraps each mounted with 4 7.2" ASW projectiles
Complement	3 officers, 24 enlisted
Endurance	1,500 nautical miles @ 12 knots

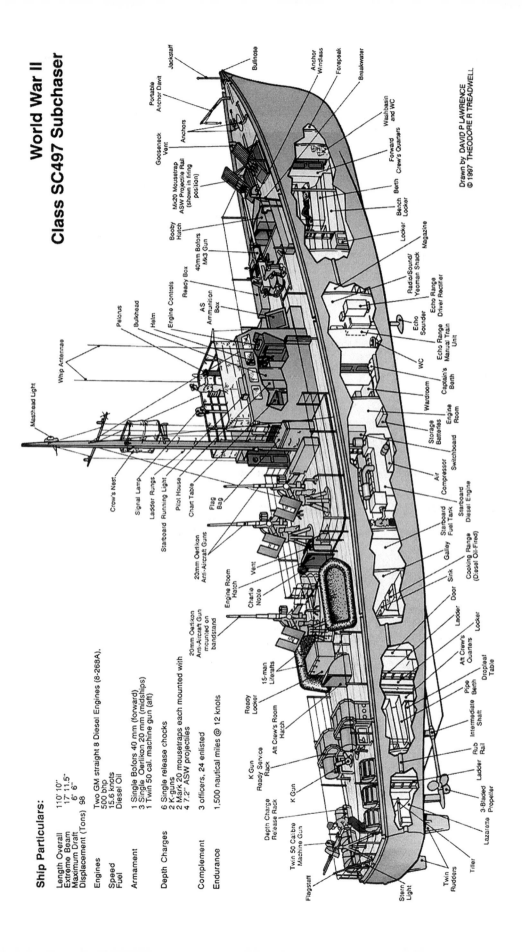

Drawn by DAVID P LAWRENCE
© 1997 THEODORE R TREADWELL

rafts, an oared wherry (alternately called dinghy, pram, or whaleboat), hatches to the engine room and aft crew's quarters, more ready lockers, several vents, and the flagstaff. Various small arms were strategically located around the vessel. Obviously, jogging was not a practical activity, and there was no exercise room.

The *Cinq-Deux-Cinq*, as I grandly named my new home (no doubt to display my high school French), was not equipped with radar in March 1943, but that enormously useful navigational aid was installed shortly thereafter, its presence revealed by a distinctive dome mounted on the masthead. The sonar console and radar screen were located in a tiny chartroom of the pilothouse. The echo sounder was retractable under the hull. Because of blackout requirements, canvas flaps shielded the small amount of light required by the navigator and radar and sound operator. The closed space often became overheated, stuffy, and permeated by diesel fumes — a perfect prescription for seasickness during rough seas.

I was too green to worry that just abaft my sleeping quarters was the magazine, which held all of the ammunition except small amounts stored in ready boxes on the deck. Beyond the magazine came, in order, the radio and yeoman's shack, the officers' wardroom, engine room, fuel tank, galley, aft crews' quarters (which served also as the mess hall), and a tiny lazarette. Ironically, the officers suffered most from the loud noise of the diesel engines, but they shared the luxury of their own head while sixteen enlisted men shared the forward oneholer, located behind a thin partition about four feet from my bunk. Besides, located farther aft, they escaped the worst of the pitching as we plowed through heavy waves. The 40-millimeter gun and the mousetrap projectile rails were located above my bunk, but they posed no problem, because I was always on deck when they were fired.

The subchaser was controlled from the bridge — a squarish box, slightly sloping upward, with rectangular portholes — located just forward of the mast and directly above the ward room. The main section housed the gyrocompass, helm (a large, wood, spindled steering wheel), engine telegraph and controls, voice tubes, public address microphone, and captain's (or officer of the watch's) chair. Behind a bulkhead were located the sonar recorder, radar monitor, chart table with navigation instruments, maps, and deck log into which entries were made at least every four hours. A normal watch in the pilot house included the officer on duty, helmsman, and sonar operator, but during general quarters, the small space was crowded also with the captain, navigator, radarman, engine room operator, and usually two or three other men on call. Topside was the flying bridge, its three-foot metal railings usually covered with painted canvas to deflect the wind. In this open-air area were located the ship's signal lamps, pelorus, telescope, voice pipe, and any other convenience permitted by the captain. At GQ, crew members without a specific battle station crowded onto the flying bridge, which was, with the exception of the crow's nest, the best location for observation.

Subchasers were notoriously unstable in heavy seas. Every small ship sailor can tell stories of hanging onto the railings during violent seas in blizzard conditions, and every helmsman can recall valiant efforts to hold the correct compass heading as huge waves tossed the little "Donald Duck" as if it were a cork. A combination of narrow beam and shallow draft was a prescription for bronco-riding experiences. Two threats were always present in heavy

Opposite: SC-525 was one of the SC-497 class of submarine chasers. Although each ship was unique, the configuration of SC-525 closely resembled this schematic. For a year and a half I slept in the forward berth just above the one on which a sailor is shown lying in the drawing. My sonar console was in the pilot house; the echo sounder was under the hull (courtesy Theodore R. Treadwell).

Taken from the flying bridge, this photograph shows the bow of *SC-525*, including the covered 40-millimeter gun, hatch to the forward crew's compartment, hedgehogs, and ship's anchor. My berth was 36 inches below the hedgehog rack at center left.

seas: first, the vessel could be caught in a trough between huge parallel waves that swamped the deck before the entire craft was tossed back up as a cork; or second, when the ship was headed directly into the breakers, one enormous wave could lift the bow upward to the angle of a water ski, then — after momentarily shuddering atop the wave — throw it into a forty-five-degree dive against the next onrushing wave, leaving the bow awash and the screws completely out of the water, whirring like airplane propellers. Conversely, while sitting momentarily atop a wave, the little vessel could corkscrew and radically yaw off course. One who has served on a subchaser in rough seas never forgets the shuddering of the little wooden ship the moment that it reaches the top of a giant wave; he holds his breath, and his stomach sinks as his entire world plunges into the trough with a jarring and deafening thud, accompanied by sound of, at best, creaking timbers, and at worst, flying objects. Each such experience endangered any object that was not tied down and any sailor who had no convenient hand-hold, particularly if climbing a ladder or attempting to walk the deck. The most frequent victims were utensils and tableware thrown athwartships in the galley, but the violent movement of the ship was often powerful enough to break loose even the most carefully secured objects. Once our long mess table in the aft crew's quarters broke loose and crashed against adjacent berths which, by opportune timing, were unoccupied. We were forever begging cups and plates from supply ships after losing so many during rough seas. Such violent motions made sleep almost impossible, and more than once, while in bed, I was thrown against the port bulkhead and into the underside of the deck directly over my top bunk. Fortunately, the canvas on which I lay, lashed to the aluminum pipes by cord, sagged enough to prevent my being thrown out into the compartment, but with so little space between bunks, George often bumped me from below. During rough weather, the term *terra firma* meant for us "the more firma, the less terra." We believed the old adage, "The only cure for seasickness is to sit on the shady side of a country church."

Mike Balog, our quartermaster, swore that *525* once took a fifty-eight-degree roll during heavy seas. While I cannot attest to the accuracy of his measurement, I can say that on many occasions it *felt* like we were on the verge of capsizing. On the other hand, soft waves on a shimmering seascape could rock our boat gently like a cradle. The little 110-foot vessel was almost never still, for even in port the wakes from other ships caused our hemp fenders to rub against, up, and down the dock pilings, producing a mournful sound.

The tenor of life aboard a subchaser was determined to a large extent by the personality and demeanor of the commanding officer, almost without exception a "ninety-day wonder"—a young man right out of college with only a few months of naval training before being commissioned in the Naval Reserve. On the *525*, we were fortunate, because naval etiquette was relaxed. Except for his khakis, Ensign Reece looked and sounded much like a member of the crew. We addressed him respectfully as "Mr. Reece," but there were few occasions when we saluted him. Ensign Waldron, in size and bearing, was a little more formal, but Ensign McCormick, like the captain, moved easily when in company with enlisted men. This relative informality gave the crew a sense of comradeship rather than of enforced discipline. Not all subchaser crews were so blessed.

A one-bell landing was the ultimate accomplishment of any officer. To accomplish that, he carefully approached a dock at just the right declination of angle and speed so that a single order ("one-third back") allowed a propeller to gingerly push the ship against the dock with no more than the sound of hemp fenders rubbing against wood. That was not a particularly difficult task when maneuvering between calm waters and a stationary pier, but a real challenge arose upon approaching another moving ship in heavy seas for the purpose of taking on fuel, water, or provisions. Even though the latter operation usually did not involve actual contact, it did require the captain's skill in approaching the mother ship. The SC, whose masthead often reached no higher than the deck level of the mother ship, made its approach from an aft quarter, avoiding the wake; then, by adjusting its speed, the small ship maneuvered parallel to and within a few feet of the larger one to accept the monkey fist of a line thrown down from above. Thus loosely secured, but at a distance of perhaps fifty feet to avoid collision, the two vessels maintained parallel headings and speeds as the water or fuel line was extended for the replenishment. Provisions, even men, could be transferred by breeches buoy on a hawser running between the two ships.[8] On long-distance convoys, this tricky maneuver had to be repeated every few days in order to keep the subchaser supplied with fuel and fresh water.

For a country boy brought up on biscuits, eggs, and pork, I adjusted only reluctantly to shipboard navy-style breakfasts. We had eggs — oh, did we have eggs — but they were eggs without shells. The product came in powdered form that, when mixed with water and cooked in a huge pot, yielded the faint taste and smell of the rotten eggs that my mother always threw to the hogs. Hotcakes, with syrup poured through a hole made by a knife-gash through the top of a gallon can, were a novelty for me, and I liked them when in port but dreaded them on a rough sea. Shredded beef on toast ("SOS") was good until its novelty wore off. Spam seemed a delicacy until it too became boring. But I thought someone was pulling a joke when we were served beans for breakfast. My New England buddies learned what a hick I was because I had never been introduced to the tradition of Boston baked beans in the morning. Other meals were more traditional, but nearly everything came from cans or cartons. The word "dehydrated" became a part of my vocabulary, and even today the word evokes the memory of dehydrated potatoes that, no matter how the stuff was boiled, still had no potato taste. I sometimes felt that we survived the war only because catsup ("ketchup") came in gallon cans, sufficient to provide at least a familiar taste to otherwise unpalatable foods. Still, with all of our complaining, we were thankful that we had sufficient food and that we were spared from C-rations, K-rations, and other packaged issuances furnished to the troops.

For the first eight months in 1943, the Sugar Charlies and Peter Charlies repeatedly relieved each other in providing antisubmarine protection outside the minefield shielding the port of Casablanca. Each ship was assigned a sector to patrol — sometimes a straight line for miles, back and forth; sometimes a dog-leg course, back and forth — each with a name such as Love or Yoke. Entries in the log were divided into four-hour segments, often beginning with "Steaming as before" or "On normal patrol," and recoding changes of course and speed, names of ships detected, and actions or observations deemed of importance. Here are selected entries from the log of the *SC-525* for August 21, 1943:

> 0540, Sounded Reveille. 0545, Started main engines. 0602, Underway for Able patrol. Proceeding at various courses out of harbor. 0612, Held GQ drill, started sound gear, and set depth charges for patrol.... 0837, Secured starboard engine and started patrolling area around Buoy Able. Various courses were used. 1025, Received message from *PC-474* saying they would return at daybreak tomorrow with three merchant ships.... 1205, Steered clear of incoming *YMS-26, -27, -77* and also outgoing carrier and escorts.... 1530, Carried out gunnery drill on HOMN ... 1908, Five-ship convoy passed patrol station. 1907, Started port engine. 1908, British destroyer *I-75* passed through station heading in. 1921, Spanish vessel, *Ebro*, passed [patrol station] and dipped colors. 1940, Battle stations drill. 1958, Secured port engine. Section II on watch. 2110, Held 40 mm. gun drill.

The following day, immediately after a general quarters drill at 1653, the captain entered, "Allowed swimming over the side of 20 minutes, after stopping engines and securing depth charges." Even while some of the crew enjoyed a little horseplay in the salt water, we sonar and radar operators maintained surveillance against enemy submarines.

With customary watches of four hours on duty and eight off, each man had specific assignments, but to vary the monotony, enlisted crewmen frequently "swopped off" between flying bridge lookout, helmsman at the mahogany steering wheel, and radar and sonar operation. I of course was on call 24/7 in case of a sonar contact. Engine room personnel had fewer opportunities to vary their activity. No crewman was beneath "falling in" to perform menial jobs ranging from throwing lines during docking to holy-stoning the deck during rain. The three officers followed a similar schedule, the captain sharing eight-on/four-off assignments. And, of course, they were on call even when off duty. For example, when I detected a solid object on my sonar, the officer of the watch was summoned immediately.

Patrol assignments varied in length from a single sortie to several days at sea, after which the ship returned to port for routine maintenance, including from time to time, a trip into drydock for scraping the wood hull. Not only were barnacles damaging to the wood; when heavily infested, the ship's speed was affected.

During daylight hours off Casablanca, our constant "companion" was El Hank, the 213-foot white masonry, minaret-topped, lighthouse located about two miles southwest of the breakwater. Amazingly, "Old Hank" had withstood the November invasion, during which the 194- and 138-millimeter guns around its base carried on a fierce duel with American ships, including direct hits on the battleship *Massachusetts* and cruiser *Wichita* and near-misses on several other warships. Navy veterans of Operation Torch remembered the landmark with respect.

Ensign Reece's curiosity about his sonarman was evident when on my second day aboard he took me to NOB and put me through the test of an Attack Teacher to ascertain my auditory acuity. After spending a couple of hours sending out electrical impulses — and, if an echo was returned, interpreting its nature, movement, and distance — I truly felt the part of a "ping jockey." The captain showed no disappointment, however, so I returned aboard reassured. On my first voyage to sea on my new home, I adjusted easily with the shipboard sonar gear. Fortunately on my early tests, I detected echoes that I was able to define variously as schools of fish, shallow banks, anchored buoys, and wakes of entering or departing vessels. My confidence was somewhat shaken, however, by an experience ten days later.

Breaking the monotony of routine patrols were assignments as antisubmarine escort to protect another ship or a convoy of vessels. Each such detail was welcomed because it enabled us to visit other ports where, inevitably, we found English-speakers with whom we could exchange scuttlebutt. On April 6, only ten days after I reported aboard, *SC-525* was assigned to escort a ship to Gibraltar. This was my first major test as a sonarman, for by then French Morocco had been successfully occupied and most of the troopships and supply vessels from the States sailed directly through the strait to Oran and the other Mediterranean ports. On both the Atlantic and Mediterranean sides of the Strait of Gibraltar, however, German U-boats lay in wait and exacted a heavy toll on Allied ships. My anxiety increased as we approached the strait, and it was a great relief to sail with our ward into the harbor at Gibraltar without having heard a single suspicious sonar contact.

Instead of the liberty to which I had looked forward at "The Rock," my first day was spent — this time with all three officers — at a British Sonar Lab equipped with more sophisticated gear than I had previously encountered. Even the pings sounded as if they had a British accent. I preserved the answer sheet for one "Doppler Test and Drill"; on it I erred on 13 out of 72 ping tests, a score of just over 80 percent. A memory flashed through my mind: the sight of the bodies dangling from the torpedoed tanker's stern in Casablanca. Had that torpedo come from a submarine that escaped detection by an "80-percenter" sonarman? The captain did not appear to be disappointed with my performance, but I could sense that I had not fully impressed the executive officer. My self-confidence and esteem would have been enormously elevated had I known that Ensign Reece shortly afterward wrote on the back of my photograph: "Houston G. Jones. Sound Man 3/c. Pelham, N.C. One of the best sound operators in the business — best I ever worked with. Young, clean, Southern, handsome, well-liked, not exceptionally industrious, but dependable and bright. He had one year of college, interrupted by war. Came aboard fresh from sound school in March. Recommended for O.T.S. (V-12)."[9]

My mediocre performance on the doppler test was followed by a memorable liberty that included a hair-raising ascent of "The Rock" from where, with its famous monkeys, one could visualize the strategic importance of Gibraltar, a thumb pointing southward from Spain. On a clear day, the view was spectacular: below, the bustling harbor, haunted by enemy submarines lurking outside; to the north, Spain, no friend of the Allies; to the west, the Atlantic; to the south, Tangier in Spanish Morocco; and to the east, the Mediterranean, teeming with Allied surface vessels and Axis submarines. One could almost believe the story of Hercules standing there pushing the European and African continents apart, and imagine the battles between the Moors and Christians over control of the Iberian peninsula long before Gibraltar began flying the British flag in 1704. The stoic British at Gibraltar carried on in spite of the war, and we felt at home. Embassy Hall featured on stage Soro and His Symphonic Girls and the Three Sisters Mendoza. Five movie theaters advertised in the *Gibraltar Chronicle*, and with several shipmates I saw *That Night in Rio* (featuring Alice Faye, Don Ameche, and Carmen Miranda) and *The Shadow of the Thin Man* (featuring William Powell and Myrna Loy). The newspaper reported the linking of American and British forces as they battled Rommel's troops at Akarit, Tunisia; it also carried a German report that their submarines had recently sunk fourteen Allied ships in the Atlantic and Mediterranean. I regretted that my trials on the Attack Teacher caused me to miss a visit to a bar straddling the border between Spain and British territory where, according to Stash Hallas, the wine was good and scantily dressed girls danced on tabletops. My prized souvenir — a large, colorfully glazed British lion emblematic of the strength of Gibraltar — went unacknowledged until the following year when my mother finally admitted, "Son, it arrived in so many pieces we didn't know what it was, but we didn't want you to know that."

SC-525 was a lone wolf on our return to Casablanca, and it gave me time to marvel that my first foreign liberty had not been in Africa but rather in Europe. In fact, I had not yet been into the city of Casablanca, so I was anxious to explore outside the Naval Operating Base and see something of this city, the name of which had become familiar around the world due to the recent "unconditional surrender" conference between President Roosevelt and Prime Minister Churchill, and the release of the popular motion picture by that name. The "Dark Continent" had hardly been mentioned in my high school studies, so my intellectual introduction to Africa came through the study of *A Pocket Guide to North Africa*, a forty-four-page pocket-size booklet.[10] The remarkably well-written booklet gave a sensitive review of the history of the Moslems, who centuries ago conquered much of the Mediterranean region but in recent decades had been under the political (but not religious and cultural) domination of the French, Spanish, and Italians. I was particularly struck by the reminder that

> Your chief concern is with the nine-tenths [of the North African population] whose ancestors have lived along this coast for centuries, and whose life is still regulated by ancient traditions and beliefs.... They can tell us what the Germans and Italians are doing if they like us or they can tell the Germans and Italians what we are doing if they dislike us. Winning their friendship is therefore an important step in the winning of the war.

After warning us of customs — the peculiar role of Moslem women ("Never stare at one. Never speak to her in public.") and the Moorish abhorrence of pork — the booklet introduced the monetary system (the hassani, a coin outdated but still in circulation, and the French franc, which in 1942 was pegged at 2.28 American cents), and the common practice of haggling over prices ("Never pay the asking price"). Tea, sugar, or cigarettes were recommended as gifts ("Be generous with your cigarettes"). Of course, we were cautioned against offering a Moslem alcohol, and we were instructed to shake hands very gently, to remove shoes if we entered a native's home, and to tear bread and eat with our fingers. This was my first exposure to the metric system and to the language, originally Berber, but almost universally Arabic in the twentieth century. However, we soon learned that from Morocco to Tunisia, French was the second tongue of most urban Moslems, and virtually all signage was in French, so few Americans bothered to adopt Arabic terms except greetings like "shah 'l kheir" (good morning), "WA-ha" (yes), and, of course, the street trading terms "sha-HAL" (how much does it cost?), "bi-ZEF bi-ZEF" (too much), and "IM-shee! Seer fee HAL-ek!" (scram).

Because I had not yet become chummy with any particular shipmate, I deliberately slipped ashore alone for my first liberty in Casablanca. I simply wanted to see the historic sites, and my first purchase was a large folding map of the city "avec plan de la ville et nomenclature des rues." Boulevard du 4e Zouaves, lined with palm trees, led directly from Bassin Delande, where we docked, to Place de France, whose tower provided a landmark. Just outside the gates to the naval base, the broad, palm-lined boulevard separated two worlds. To the left (northwest) rose tall, modern buildings; to the right (southeast), an agglomeration of low structures was partially hidden behind an irregular masonry wall. Later I would learn something of these two contrasting worlds, but first I wanted to get my bearings and see more of the city beyond Place de France. It was not to be that day, for when passing the Opera Bar — one of the French bars approved for American servicemen — I was accosted by several crew members whose names and faces I had only begun to associate. Wanting to "fit in" to the extent of at least being sociable, I joined them with the intention of nursing one drink until I could escape to continue my sightseeing. The area was patrolled by MPs and SPs, but their interest was in preventing physical violence rather than dictating drinking habits, so the bar was quite noisy as conviviality reigned among the crowd in military dress. Each time I took a sip of my cognac, a companion tried to refill the glass. So I slowed my sips as my shipmates continued to drink. As curfew approached, all of them were drunk, but I only felt a buzz. It was I, a backwoods boy unaccustomed even to moonshine, who helped the staggering sailors back to the ship. That experience confirmed to my companions that the new fellow was one of them. By this time I had learned what George was referring to when he introduced me in the forward compartment as "the fellow who gets interesting mail." While I was in New York, Frank Zanino had taken me to a risqué stage show where we signed up for some girlie literature. The package, addressed to me at Pier 92, was forwarded to my ship and, because of the eight days I spent at NOB, had reached the ship before I arrived. Now, in the eyes of some of my shipmates, I had demonstrated the two characteristics of a proverbial sailor: sexaholic and alcoholic.

Having wasted my first liberty in Africa, my next one was better planned, for I had studied the map and decided to find Parc Lyautey, around which were grouped several buildings including Casablanca's hôtel de ville with its clock tower. I made excuse for not joining the "Opera Bar Gang," as I began to think of the drinking quartet, and sought to slip through Place de France without being observed. The group, nevertheless, spotted me walking the southwest side of the boulevard, beckoned me over, and forced a drink on me. Already tanked up, they surprised me by insisting that they accompany me to the park. The senior was a large man, well liked, and a natural group leader, so the other three readily agreed. However, as we walked along Avenue du General d'Amade, the guys became less interested in seeing the park than in finding women. Several times they indicated their interests to locals, one of whom signaled to the driver of an approaching horse-drawn carriage, its curtains closed. With words, French or Arabic, and gestures, a universal language, the two men communicated; we were told that the lady passenger invited all five of us aboard. Someone tipped the informant, and the other men crowded into the carriage. My conscience told me to keep walking toward the park, but since the vehicle was headed in that direction, I climbed up and sat by the driver, an Arab who spoke French. My high school French was just sufficient for me to interpret that the female passenger was a "high class" French lady down on her luck and in need of income, which she earned in the world's oldest profession. Loud conversation, punctuated by female giggles, came from the carriage as the driver made several turns, confusing my sense of direction.

Visions of Parc Lyautey gave way to unpleasant views of littered streets as the horse galloped farther and farther from the city center. Without being told, I assumed that we were heading for the prostitute's home. Instead, when the carriage reached the outskirts of the city, the driver pulled up near a clump of trees. The other four sailors hopped out, ceremoniously helped down the lady—whom I saw for the first time—and the leader explained what the cost of our expedition, including carriage, driver, and service of the passenger, would be in French francs. My assumption was wrong again; instead of sex in the carriage, the prostitute pulled out a blanket and proceeded into a thicket, followed by our leader who, no more than ten minutes later, emerged from the bushes smiling and yelling, "Next!" I was petrified as the procession continued, each returning with a thumbs-up exclamation of satisfaction. If I had known where I was, I would probably have run away, and when I heard the command, "O.K., Jones," I almost blurted out that I didn't want to lose my virginity on a whore. But that would have exposed me as the wimp that I really was, a disgrace to my uniform. I have never felt more unworthy than when applause met my emergence from the woods.

When we returned to Place Lyautey, I had no more interest in sightseeing, so I followed the group to an improbably-named Charle's [sic] Bar on Rue Franchet d'Espéret. This time I needed no urging to drink, and as curfew hour approached, five drunken sailors stumbled back to the ship. The next day four of them graphically exaggerated stories of the afternoon; I was too mortified to corroborate any of them.

My emerging image among the crew—as a *real* gob—gnawed at my conscience both because it was deceptive and because I did not want it. If others viewed me as fitting in, I was beginning to feel out of place. My extracurricular interests lay not in drinking and whoring, which seemed to occupy the thoughts and plans of too many of the crew. I still possessed a college mentality, and I felt that my life in the Navy should represent more than debauchery. But living down my first two liberties would be difficult without earning a wimpy image and losing the "respect" so quickly and undeservedly gained.

For the next several weeks, to the extent possible, I consciously avoided more than cursory conversation with the Opera Bar Gang. I began spending more time reading and getting better acquainted with crew members who appeared to have interests more consonant with mine. Chief Miller, while not a college man, was wise, considerate, and respected. William E. Dauphenais, yeoman from Chicago, and John Frederick McLaughlin, radioman from Indiana, regularly shared liberty, read widely, and were good conversationalists. Michael Balog, gunner's mate from Pennsylvania, had a limited education but possessed admirable personal qualities. Walter Leo Marzean, electrician's mate from Philadelphia, a few years older than most of the crew, demonstrated a range of interests. Edmund Emil Runof, fireman from New Jersey, a blustery old salt whose vocabulary of profanity made us all appear juvenile, was the life of any conversation. John Stanley Hallas, motor machinist's mate from New York, was a fast-talking Yankee with a keen sense of humor. Lewis James Garvin, a carpenter's mate, was a serious, soft-spoken Floridian.

And then there was the radioman who greeted me at the gangplank on March 27, George Franklin Klumpp of New Orleans. He and I shared watch rotation and, since his bunk was directly beneath mine, we had ample opportunity to discuss our plans for the future. Both of us were determined to return to college and pursue a profession, and much of our conversation centered around future plans, his about as amorphous as mine. He was the first Catholic I had ever known, and I asked a thousand questions about his religion. He gave me a St. Christopher's medal which, perhaps just to show the broad-mindedness of a Primitive Baptist-turned-Methodist, I wore with my dogtag the remainder of the war. Without revealing my determination to avoid future shore liberties with the Opera Bar Gang, I found that George also felt a bit alienated from some of the crew — not from dislike but from the absence of common interests. Both of us avidly read everything available, including magazines to which I subscribed and books that George's sister Mary mailed to him. All three officers, soon promoted to lieutenant junior grade, perceived that Klumpp and Jones were a little different, and they were considerate in keeping us in the same watch section and liberty schedule. In July, Lieutenant Reece recommended both of us for the Navy's V-12 college training program, the completion of which could have led to a commission. Although we failed to gain admission to the program, the mere recommendation from our commanding officer boosted our self-esteem. For the next year and a half, George Klumpp and I seldom went ashore separately.

"Sightseeing" became our escape not only because it was a worthy use of time ashore but also because few other crew members sought to join us. My twenty-franc map and a few French-language guides were useful in orienting us to our new surroundings. We learned that the native Africans in Casablanca (*Dar-al-Baida* in Arabic; *White House* in English) had been under Portuguese and Spanish influence at various times in history before the country was formally occupied by the French in 1907. By World War II, the city was so heavily Europeanized that its administration and official language were French despite the much larger population of Africans, mostly Moslim Arabs. Except for its port, the city had suffered little from the invasion, and the European section was well-maintained. For example, a tall, impressive clock tower provided the focal junction for a half-dozen palm-lined streets radiating out from Place de France, where the invaders followed custom by planting a signpost pointing toward New York and other world cities (for example, "Berlin 2350 miles"). Modern buildings on three sides and along Boulevard de la Gare, Cours du Commerce, Avenue de la Republic, and several streets named for generals, gave the appearance of a typical French downtown. No doubt the Moroccans had their own names for the streets, but of course we could not have read the Arabic signs if they had been permitted by the French, who sought to impose their language wherever they went.

By 1943 Casablanca was a modern city superimposed on an ancient one originally called Anfa. The contrast between the two cultures was most startling within a five-minute walk from Bassin Delande, where the subchasers usually moored. There was irony in the name of the handsome divided street that led from the dock to Place de France: Boulevard du 4e Zouaves (Boulevard of the Fourth Zouaves), honoring a unit of the French infantry wearing brilliant uniforms and conducting quick-spirited drills. Algeria and Morocco traditionally provided troops for the Zouaves, whose colorful uniforms, including the felt fez — red, brimless, and tasseled — became recognizable throughout the world. In time, the Zouaves became the power with which the French governed huge native populations that were relegated to second-class citizenship in their own land. From the dock toward Place de France (since World War II called Place des Nations-Unies), the boulevard was divided by an island lined with palm trees and a virtual bazaar of peddlers, beggars, and dancing girls, all vying for the attention of the stream of passing American servicemen.

The avenue also divided two worlds: on the left, the world of the Europeans; on the right, the world of the Moroccans. The Ancienne Medina, the casbah of thousands of Arabs, was a sprawling slum surrounded by a masonry wall with an occasional entry gate. Inside the walls a maze of narrow alleys wound past dilapidated structures, mostly adobe, that we considered shacks, all providing cramped habitation and souks filled with an unimaginable array of goods from colorful clothing to trinkets and native herbs, all available through haggling. Forewarned of pickpockets, we were careful in crowds so thick with women in hijab and men in pantaloons that human contact was almost unavoidable. Children in rags crowded around westerners, begging for handouts. Wisely, military police were stationed at strategic locations, supplementing the local gendarmes. Many places, including of course the whorehouses, were posted off-limit to Americans. A tall tower — for calling the Muslims to prayer — cast a shadow across the vast area. One visit to the Medina was quite enough, although we returned from time to time for cheap souvenirs such as leather goods decorated with images of naked women dancing. My favorite purchase was a cedar trinket box, its hinged top featuring a crude hand-engraved and colored outline of the Medina's tower and the northwest African coast. A tooled leather billfold, colorfully decorated with scenes of Morocco, served the next year and a half as my billfold.

In sharp contrast to the casbah, the left (northwest) side of Zouaves exhibited the twentieth-century world more familiar to us. We were attracted by an American flag waving from a handsome building directly opposite the Ancienne Medina. Inside we were pleasantly surprised to find an enlisted men's club operated by the American Red Cross. The club offered comfortable lounges, refreshment rooms, meeting facilities, sightseeing tours, and services ranging from first aid to dancing with highly selected local females. Even I, who had been away from the United States only a few weeks, welcomed a Coca-Cola and a doughnut, but for all of us from *SC-525*, who had no onboard bathing facilities, the most welcomed service was the shower room with genuine hot water.[11] This reception center became our first and last stop on future liberties, and I soon came to appreciate the valuable facilities provided by the American Red Cross (ARC) and the United Service Organizations (USO) when they were established in Allied-controlled war zones. Equally appreciated was the Vox Theater, facing Place de France, also operated by the ARC and featuring American motion pictures and occasionally a stage show put on by visiting Hollywood or radio stars. Nearly seven decades later, I still remember how smitten I was by Lena Horne in *Cabin in the Sky* and *Stormy Weather*, and as a red-neck from the segregated south, I marveled that a Negro could look and sing so beautifully. I was reminded of how far both technology and culture had come since the Great Depression, when I saw my first motion picture on a white bed sheet hanging from a tree limb at Webb Yarbrough's Store, the image projected by means of a generator driven by the jacked-up wheels of a T-model Ford. Movies and minimal services were also available at NOB, and on August 17 we were treated to a hilarious real-life stage performance by comedian Al Jolson. I wondered what the Navy's mess attendants in the audience, mostly black, thought of Jolson's minstrel acts, which were reminiscent of those in which I performed in blackface at Cobb Memorial High School. Such experiences had lasting influences in altering my concept of human brotherhood.

George and I often rambled throughout the city, exploring and trying out our high school French. We found handsome government buildings, churches, and schools, often combining the Arabesque with modern European architecture. Palm trees were ubiquitous, and other tropical plants enhanced the cityscapes. The bell tower of Hotel de Ville (city hall) provided an elevated view of the city, including the harbor; it was a good place from which to get one's bearings and to take pictures. From there we could see El Hank, our landmark when on patrol, and we hiked the long distance to the site of the heavy guns that had bedeviled American ships before they were silenced. L'eglise de la Sacré Coeur was magnificently located among the palms. Then, of course, there was the Nouvelle Medina, which, as its name suggests, was newer and more substantially built than the original medina near the port. Both represented the French's way of segregating the living quarters of the natives from the upscale European sections. Despite better and more substantial structures, Nouvelle Medina retained the casbah atmosphere of warrens and frantic alley-vending. The usual prayer tower cast its shadow over a special area described amusingly in a broken-English guidebook this way:

> Tourists, amateurs in the study of morals, can from this place, enter in a few steps the closed section of *Bousbir*, the new Quarter reserved for prostitutes. Shut up between these impassable walls and evolving into a group which did not like romance, these last mentioned were none the less compulsory subjugated to constant and vigilant surveillance by the police and health services (free entrance granted to all visitors, not recommended to children or young girls).[12]

We of course could not pass up a "free entrance" to the *Bousbir*, although we refrained from accepting the more intimate invitations issued to two handsome sailors in their dress whites.

A few local bars and restaurants had been inspected and approved for patronizing by the American military. In addition to the Opera Bar, we sometimes stopped at Cafe-Brasserie de la Vallette on Boulevard Ney, and Grand Café Mers-Sultan, named for the avenue on which it was located. Mostly, however, we walked and took pictures with Stanley Hallas's camera. Naturally, we had to photograph the Anfa Hotel, famous for the Roosevelt-Churchill summit in January that challenged the Axis powers with the term "unconditional surrender." Nearby we ran into a youngster named Joseph Chocron, perhaps eleven or twelve, who had lived in Brooklyn, spoke English, and offered to introduce us to "pretty and clean" young girls. Although we declined his offer, Joseph did us the favor of snapping our picture together near the hotel. Somewhere around Place de France we had a pleasant conversation with a pretty Belgian, Luzette Baron, who spoke passable English.

Returning to the dock from one excursion, we discovered that the *Cinq-Deux-Cinq*—with only eight men aboard—had on short notice been ordered to escort a convoy out of the harbor, so our large liberty party, some of whom were inebriated, simply "crapped out" on *SC-519* and *-524*. Fortunately, my *Cinq-Deux-Cinq* only conducted the other vessels through the minefield, so she returned at 0045. The captain, seeing the miserable condition of his liberty crew, persuaded the base commander to allow us to remain in port the next morning. Occasionally I ran into old sound school mates such as Rickenback, Teel, and Wharton.

Escorting other ships to ports along the coast provided relief from the monotonous screening in the shipping lanes, and in one such assignment in particularly rough seas, *SC-525* provided antisubmarine protection for the French tanker *Melusine* to Agadir. The deck log recorded our sonar screening, alternating from the tanker's forward quarter to the stern, ordering zigzag courses, and eventually patrolling outside the harbor until the ship was safely in port. All hands were granted liberty—George and I for two straight days—and most of us headed to the casbah high up the hill. My second and third intimate experiences—both after a few drinks at the Atlas Bar—were less traumatic than the first time in Casablanca, but I still could not understand why sex was the all-consuming passion of some of my shipmates. It did explain, however, the skipper's requirement that men going ashore take along a prophylactic kit.

On our return from Agadir, we stopped at Safi, where the southern invasion forces in November (Operation Blackstone) overcame three days of Vichy French resistance. The visit at Safi was memorable because of its hot baths, a luxury enthusiastically mentioned in my diary. One crewman, however, remembered Safi because of another kind of bath. The "Old Tub," as we called the rusty and decrepit *Melusine*, broke down, and in exasperation the exec took Eddie Runof over to see if the two of them could be of help. When they were ready to return, Coxswain Millard Malone was summoned by semaphore flags, and he rowed over. Not finding the two men at the bottom of the gangplank, Malone dropped the line, climbed up, and brought the passengers down. To his horror, the dinghy was floating a hundred feet away. The exec's glare was sufficient to teach the coxswain his lesson, and, stripping to his underwear, Malone swam out and returned with the little pram. His face was not blue from the cold water; it was red from embarrassment. The crew never let him forget the incident.

A potentially serious but ultimately humorous incident occurred at Casablanca while the *525* was "playing buoy"—that is, serving as traffic control vessel moving slowly around Buoy Peter, directing ships through the swept channel to the harbor entrance. Soldiers on a large incoming troop ship, waving and observing that our little subchaser looked like a floating sardine tin, took pity on us and threw several cartons of cigarettes toward our deck. The pitches fell short, so two crewmen of our slow-moving vessel jumped overboard to retrieve the precious smokes. By the time they reached the cartons, they discovered that they could not swim fast enough to overtake the ship. Alarmed, other men on our deck threw over one of the liferafts but failed to release the line, which became entangled in the ship's screws. Lieutenant Waldron, though irritated by the carelessness, volunteered to dive in and untangle the line, but when he failed to surface in a reasonable length of time, Eddie Runof jumped in and swam under the stern. The officer quickly emerged unscathed and climbed back aboard, only to look back down for Runof, who was nowhere in sight. While the alarmed crew kept watching on the port stern, Runof swam under the ship to the opposite side, climbed back aboard, walked across the deck, elbowed his way through the crowd, and asked, "What you looking for?" From that time on, "What you looking for?" broke the seriousness of many bull sessions.

Our crew was often innovative and sometimes quite nervy. While in drydock in Casablanca, Promp, Schira, and Marzean struck up a friendship with the crew of a nearby French ship and, seeing a unique opportunity and taking advantage of international good will and generosity, untied the water barrels from our life-rafts, filled them with French wine, and lashed the barrels back in their normal positions. Their reasoning was that if a German U-boat should sink our ship, we would be a happy group of survivors. Sadly, the captain learned of a forthcoming inspection by a high-ranking officer with a persnickety reputation, and not wanting to stake his rank on the chance of getting caught, he ordered the barrels refilled with fresh water—but not before the crew had a hell of party.

Fairly often our ship protected vessels sailing northward to Fedhala, where the previous November the major force (Operation Brushwood) had landed before marching overland to occupy Casablanca. It was off Fedhala that the *Joseph Hewes* (AP-50), named for one of North Carolina's signers of the Declaration of Independence, had been sunk with the loss of over a hundred men. A memorable—and hair-raising—experience occurred in July when we escorted the *Melusine* via Fedhala to Port Lyautey (in Arabic, *Kenitra*), which was captured by the northern invasion force in Operation Goalpost. Named after French Marshal Louis Hubert Gonzalve Lyautey (1854–1934), the port town was the site of a modern airport several miles up the serpentine Wadi Sebou. The airfield and town were occupied after USS *Dallas* (DD-199) sailed up the river, silenced French guns, and landed a raider team. The river was still lined with several wrecked ships, perhaps some of them scuttled, but we were able to maneuver around them without getting our hull scraped. The docks were conveniently lined along the banks, adjacent to enormous warehouses from which Moroccan produce, brought in by train, donkey, and wagon, was shipped to all parts of the world. One of the warehouses was labeled "Algerienne de Meonerie, Cereales," for a railroad linked backcountry Algeria to the Atlantic port. Dual rows of trees lined the streets, once neatly kept, and Restaurant de L'Univers had reopened. Now, eight months later, except for the bustling air base, there was little to recommend the place to visiting sailors.

I had the good fortune to run into Wally DeMarquo, a radioman at Lyautey, with whom I had libertied while at Pier 92. George and I had an afternoon to kill, so when Wally told us that a swimming party was going by truck down to the popular Plage Mehdiya on the Atlantic, we grabbed our Navy-issued bathing trunks and climbed aboard. I described the experience in letter written fifteen years later:

> How well I remember the next hour or so! My friend, George Klumpp ... and I, with youthful daring, ventured further and further out into the ocean.... [T]he armed forces had put up long posts far out in the water and had strung barbed wire around the whole swimming area (whether to keep the men in or the sharks out, I do not know). Well, George and I went past the barrier, then realized too late that one of those typical Atlantic storms was a-brewing. We made it back to the barbed wire barrier, and then too exhausted to go further, hung on for dear life. The waves got larger and larger, and there we clung to the strands of barbed wire as breakers beat us against the wire. We couldn't turn loose and we were getting some nasty cuts from hanging on. To make a long story short, two lifeguards inflated a rubber raft, then pulling themselves hand-over-hand on the barbed wire, against the heavy breakers, finally made their way out to us. The results were the end of a swimming party for that day, a justifiable reprimand from all those on the beach, and two sailors ... with a lot of wire scratches.

That was not the end of the story. The remainder was told in an earlier portion of the same letter, written June 30, 1958. An abridged version: As we arrived at the beach and jumped out of the weapons carrier, I saw in the sand something shiny. I picked up what turned out to be an attractive gold ring with a puzzling design in its setting and, inside, the initials "E.J.McB." I showed the ring to everyone in the party, but it belonged to none of them. What does one do with a ring found on the beach and belonging to no one in sight? With little thought, I put it on my ring finger. It fitted perfectly. So when the lifeguards dragged George and me back to the beach, I was still wearing the new-found ring, which I jokingly called my "good luck charm." Our ship was ready to sail when we returned up the river, so I had no opportunity to locate a lost-and-found desk on the base. In time, I became enamored with the ring and wore it the remainder of the war. Years later I substituted my college ring, but from time to time I picked up my "souvenir" and wondered who "E.J.McB." might be. A member of a Sigma Chi chapter recognized the insignia as that of his fraternity, so in 1955 I wrote the national headquarters of Sigma Chi. The reply — "It would be impossible for us to determine to whom the ring belonged from just the initials"— was disappointing. Strangely, though, three years later I received a letter from E. Jack McCabe of Lafayette, Louisiana. He wrote, "My Sigma Chi Fraternity Hq. was kind enough to look up the initials on the ring you found and narrow the possibilities down to 2 people of which I was one.... I'm quite sure it must be mine, as I was in Port Lyautey from March to November 1943, and lost a ΣX ring there, I thought in the ocean. I was in the anti-submarine squadron of the Air Force."

I promptly mailed the ring to McCabe, with whom I carried on a cordial correspondence for several years. The *News & Observer* told the story under the title "Long Journey Ends: After 15 Years, Ring Back With Owner."[13] I had done a very good deed.

5

Closer to the Front:
Algeria and Tunisia

August–December 1943

At 0206 on August 26, 1943, I was awakened to conduct a sonar search of a suspect area outside the Casablanca harbor. In two hours of pinging, I could detect no echo suggesting a submarine, so *SC-525* resumed the normal Yoke patrol. Almost before I got back to sleep, however, the engines revved up and we returned to port. The captain, after picking up new orders from the base, gave virtually the entire crew shore liberty for the remainder of the day, arousing our suspicions that we would be leaving for another assignment. George and I rushed into the city and took advantage of the little 35-millimeter Kodak camera that I earned by selling magazine subscriptions in high school. Providentially, it had arrived in the mail that very morning. I recorded in my notes, "Probably last liberty in Casa[blanca]." On the base that night, we saw on the screen *Desert Victory* and *Rhythm of the Islands*. The next morning the captain confirmed our suspicions.

Late in the afternoon, we sailed out of the harbor and fell in behind a column headed by two fleet minesweepers, *Pilot* (AM-104) and *Prevail* (AM-107), and two wood-hulled motor (yard) minesweepers, *YMS-27* and *YMS-28*. Ensign McCormick wrote in the log, "Bound for Bizerte." From armed forces radio we knew that Bizerte, captured on May 7, was the nearest African port to Sicily, where the Allies had landed in July and where fierce fighting continued. There was a thrill, but also a little apprehension, in the thought of approaching the war zone. But Bizerte was days away, and we were scheduled to stop first at Oran.

As we sailed toward the front, we were thankful that no Sugar Charlie or Peter Charlie had been lost in Operation Torch and the succeeding nine months in the Moroccan Sea Frontier, but word had reached us that in June *PC-496* strayed from the swept channel near Bizerte, hit a mine, and sank with five casualties. We also received second-hand reports that our sister ships had been in the vicinity of other disasters and picked up survivors during Operation Husky, the July invasion of Sicily. Most disturbing was a report that *SC-694* and *SC-696* had been destroyed by bombs in Palermo just a few days before our departure from Casablanca. That news dampened the joy of the report that *PC-624* sank German *U-375* northwest of Malta on July 30.[1]

During the voyage toward the Mediterranean, the daily routine was somewhat relaxed, but the sonar and radar were continually trained to the port side as we remained within sight of the African coast. The five ships practiced several different formations, and the crew of *525* was kept alert by flag hoist and gunnery practice, and — remembering a paint-remover fire near the mousetraps on the forecastle earlier in the month — fire drills. The moment we entered the Strait of Gibraltar, however, the captain set two-section watches — four hours on, four hours off — around the clock. This added perceptibly to our vigilance. Furthermore, our hope to stop at Gibraltar was dashed as we passed through the strait with no more than a howdy.

Late on the 29th we arrived in the harbor at Oran (in Arabic, *Ouahran* or *Wahran*), Algeria. Like Casablanca, Oran had been captured by Allied troops in early November 1942. While the three-pronged invasion of French Morocco (at Port Lyautey, Fedhala, and Safi) utilized American troops directly from the United States, the multiple landings in Algeria were made by British troops and Americans trained in England. The ports of Oran and nearby Mers el-Kébir were the prime objectives of forces that landed at Mersa Bou Zedjar and Les Andalouses to the west and near Arzeu to the east. Allied forces overran French opposition and, in a pincer movement, captured Oran on the 10th. Upon their arrival at the harbor, however, even the toughest soldiers were sickened to discover that tragedy had befallen fellow invaders during the early hours of the operation. Afraid that the French might scuttle their fleet upon the landing of troops, and believing that the French naval commander would capitulate in the face of overwhelming force, the planners of Operation Reservist ordered HMS *Walney* and HMS *Hartland*, carrying Americans especially trained to prevent sabotage, to sail directly into the Oran harbor. The cutters broke through the protective boom, sailed in, and found themselves surrounded by destroyers, submarines, and torpedo boats. The effort proved disastrous, for the French ships and shore batteries opened fire and sank both vessels with the loss of several hundred men. Ironically, the two doomed ships, which in an earlier life operated as the United States Coast Guard cutters *Sebago* and *Pontchartrain*, flew large American ensigns, hoping to overcome the ancient antipathy of the French toward the English. The fierce resistance proved that loyal Frenchmen had not forgiven the British Navy's attack on the French fleet in the nearby port of Mers el-Kébir two years earlier to prevent it from falling into the hands of the Germans.[2]

As in the case of Casablanca, the American advance base units had performed remarkably, for when *SC-525* sailed into the harbor at Oran, there were few signs of the slaughter that had taken place the previous November. The harbor, hunkered beneath the heights on which the city rested, was a marvel of engineering. Its long jetty and protected mouth separated four massive moles from the Bay of Oran, whose waters were often turbulent. This port would be our refuge between sea patrols and escort voyages during the next four months.

The second major Mediterranean objective of the November invasion had been Algiers, the capital of the African nation that was, like French Morocco, dominated by the French, who treated the natives as second-class citizens. The capture of Oran and Algiers, and later Bizerte, provided essential port facilities for the huge fleet gathering in the Mediterranean to support the American and British forces in Sicily and, beginning in September, on the Italian peninsula.

Our shipboard activity at Casablanca had been fairly relaxed, so we were hardly prepared for the frenetic life that we experienced during our first ten days in Oran. Three hours after tying up beside *Pilot*, we were welcomed by an air raid lasting until midnight. The presence of the cruisers *Philadelphia* (CL-41), *Savannah* (CL-42), and *Boise* (CL-47), with their antiaircraft guns blazing, provided some solace, and apparently there was no damage to our fleet. The next day George and I hitched a ride on an army truck up the long, winding road to the city, where we found a welcome at the enlisted men's club administered by the Red Cross.

We had little time to savor our first liberty, however, for at 0400 the next morning, we were aroused to provide antisubmarine screening for the cruisers and destroyers as they left the harbor. For the first time, we felt the *genuine* importance of our little 110-foot wooden sub-chaser as we protected those powerful warships, which joined a larger convoy heading toward Sicily. After signaling the capital ships bon voyage, we returned to the harbor and learned that *SC-525* would not immediately proceed to Bizerte; we would remain in Oran as escort commander over *YMS-24, -29,* and *-30*.[3]

We had hardly tied up in the British trawler base when the captain received orders to sail with *YMS-30* to Nemours (in Arabic, *Ghazaouet*), a port about eighty miles west of Oran. Like other North African towns, Nemours, with its large port almost completely protected by breakwaters and connected to coastal communities by rail, was populated by Arabs but controlled by Frenchmen, now cooperating with the Allies. Colorfully set against coastal hills, Nemours had been chosen as the site for training William O. Darby's Ranger battalions, whose reputation would soon spread around the world. Along its main street were the "Cercle Civil" café with outdoor seating, a couple of bars, and a few shops. One local commodity especially interested the servicemen — vin blanc, vin rouge, muscatel, and anything else remotely resembling wine. Our first visit, however, was cut short, because that evening we rounded up a convoy of three Liberty ships and escorted them back to Oran, arriving the following morning. Several of us were given liberty that afternoon, but the crew remaining on the ship underwent another red alert and a call to general quarters. George and I had time to scout around and find a cold shower — a welcome discovery — in a base building. We were given about twenty-four hours before we beckoned the three minesweepers and sailed out into the Mediterranean to corral and escort into Oran a portion of a large convoy heading east. Frustratingly, about midnight the motor generator of my sonar gear broke down, and our ship accidentally crossed one of the "loops" — an underwater demarcation of the cleared channels. Still, we succeeded in bringing the tankers *Buffalo, Waller,* and *Palo Alto* safely into the harbor. Back in port, George and I had several hours' liberty, which was consumed by a haircut, shampoo, and movies at the Empire and Casino — theaters in town that featured English-speaking films. Returning to the ship, we learned with disappointment that the three YMSs had been given another assignment, and ours was the only small American patrol vessel attached to Oran. We were going to be busy.

This meant that *525* was the lone protector on a three-day escort trip with *Harpolyeus* and *Port Slave* to and from Beni Saf, another Algerian harbor about half way between Nemours and Oran. After directing the rustbuckets into the harbor, the captain acceded to my suggestion that we photograph *Cinq-Deux-Cinq* underway. So, while our wards proceeded to the docks in Beni Saf, the captain lowered the wherry, put Ensign McCormick, Signalman Cieslak, and me in it, then sailed the ship up the coast a mile or so and turned around. As our *SC-525* came barreling down the coast, the three of us clicked away. From amateur cameras and inferior wartime film, the resulting photographs were mediocre at best, but the three "wherry boys" never forgot the experience, for neither the captain nor we had given thought to the turbulence that the ship — sailing past at fifteen knots — would produce. The wherry surely would have capsized except for the ensign's presence of mind in turning the little splinter-weight boat bow-first into the waves surging out from the ship's wake. Perhaps for fear of criticism of higher-ups, the exec made no reference to the experience in the deck log. Even so, it was an exciting experience, and we did get rare — though very grainy — photographs of *SC-525*.

Slightly larger than Nemours, Beni Saf had a smaller harbor but a more interesting setting with good beaches nearby. Its artificial harbor had been constructed for the shipment of

Top: *SC-525* underway off Beni Saf, Algeria, September 1943. I took the photograph from the ship's oared wherry as the subchaser sailed by. *Bottom:* Another view from the wherry of *SC-525* with the captain, executive officer, and the chief boatswain's mate on the ship's flying bridge.

iron ore, and by the time we arrived, a substantial United States Navy contingent was stationed there. We tied up in the small harbor overnight, took more pictures, and all but a skeleton crew went ashore. L.E. Wynn (fireman first class), Virgil Anika (gunner's mate third class), George Klumpp, and I found a little bar, where I became too inebriated to stand my midnight watch after we staggered back to the ship. George, being from New Orleans, was better at holding alcohol (I never saw him drunk), so he took over my duty, and the officers, thankfully, never knew of my indiscretion. A friend in need is a friend indeed. Fortunately, we remained in Beni Saf another day, and crew members used better judgment as we explored the town, its beach, and its special attractions.

Or did we use better judgment? To accommodate the horny Americans, military and civil authorities had collaborated to provide a special service for the military contingents. Operated almost like a crude hospital, the "GI House" was staffed by carefully vetted and vaccinated prostitutes, whose services required registration and a condom for exactly fifteen minutes of pleasure in an assigned cubicle. Each customer exited through a lavatory, washed and gave himself a prophylactic treatment under the supervision of an on-duty medical corpsman. Only upon completion of the precise exercise was he allowed to check out by signing his name, rank, and serial number. This was obviously a very professionally run operation. Perhaps there were such extraordinary services in other Mediterranean towns, but if so, they escaped my attention and patronage.

Escorting *Harpolyeus* and *Port Slave* back to Oran, I listened extra carefully for sonar echoes, because an enemy submarine had been sighted from the air just after we passed Cape Falcon two days earlier. We never knew if the silhouette of *525* was caught in the U-boat's periscope. If so, perhaps we were too small to merit an expensive torpedo, the launching of which could have set off a wolfpack of Allied destroyers to track down the perpetrator.

Safely back at our home port, *SC-525* performed what came to be routine—escorting convoys leaving or entering Oran Bay. Fairly frequently, we had to swing the ship for compass deviation. Sometimes we served as duty messenger, with our captain transmitting instructions between commanders, going alongside to deliver top secret papers from one vessel to another.

Allied incoming ships were called "friends," and colored flares had particular meanings. Often we sailed toward targets, only to find that they were native fishing boats defying orders to remain clear of the sea lanes. Unclassified communications were transmitted by radio or by signal lamp. Boleslaus (mercifully shortened to B.L.) Cieslak was an expert at flipping the handle to flash messages in Morse Code. All hands were required to learn the code, and when no other vessel was in sight, I often practiced *dit-dit-dit/dah-dah-dah/dit-dit-dit* (SOS) and a few simple expressions. Fortunately, I was never called on to transmit official communications. Finally back in Oran's harbor, our groveling was rewarded when the skipper of the transport *Anne Arundel* (AP-76) allowed his mess attendant to share ice cream with our crew.

On September 8, we were up early to escort two merchant ships to Arzeu, east of Oran, from where we sailed alone to a smaller port, Mostaganem, the location on August 31 for a secret meeting between generals Eisenhower and Clark. That leg of the trip was interrupted at the Prime Meridian for a little ceremony during which several crewmen, dressed in poor imitations of pirate outfits, conducted a mock initiation. A colorful art certificate headed "IMPERIUM NEPTUNI REGIS" was designed by signalman Cieslak, who drew the image of Neptune, after which I typed the text. In addition to its novelty, the certificate taught us that we were located due south of London. Mine read:

TO ALL SAILORS WHEREVER YE MAY BE: and to all Mermaids, Whales, Sea Serpents, Porpoises, Sharks, Dolphins, Eels, Skates, Suckers, Crabs, Lobsters, and all other living things of the Sea. GREETING: KNOW YE: That on this 8th day of September 1943, in Longitude 00000 and Latitude 35-56-20 North there appeared within our royal domain the U.S.S. S.C. 525 bound east for Greenwich Meridian and for Mostaganem, Algeria. BE IT REMEMBERED: That the said Vessel and Officers and Crew thereof have been inspected and passed on by Ourself and Our Royal Staff. AND BE IT KNOWN: By all ye Sailors, Marines, and Land Lubbers and others who may be honored by his presence that Houston Jones, having been found worthy to be numbered as one of the Seahorses in the Solemn Mysteries of the Ancient Order of the Deep. [Signed by] Neptunus Rex, Ruler of the Raging Main [and] Davey Jones, His Majesty's Scribe.

At Mostaganem we picked up another vessel, then sailed back to Arzeu, where we were treated with another red alert. Bill Speckin, ship's cook second class, came aboard before we returned to Oran with two more ships. Over armed forces radio, we heard General Eisenhower report the capitulation of Italy, five days after British forces crossed the Strait of Messina. American forces went ashore at Salerno on September 9.

In subsequent weeks our ship regularly led Allied vessels out of or into the ports of Oran and Mers el-Kébir. Typically, we met large convoys (one of them contained eighty-seven vessels) that dropped off several merchant ships, which we led into Oran Bay, or we escorted ships out of the port to join larger convoys heading east or west. But there were also repeated escort assignments up and down the Algerian coast — to Mostaganem and Arzeu to the east, Beni Saf and Nemours to the west. Our wards ranged widely in classification and size; among them were *Gipp, Shiloh, Ticonderoga, Jonathan Worth, Stockton, Augustine Le Bourgne, Hebe II, Indiana, Gillis, Thaddeus Koscuisko, Lornaston, Marsa, William A. Richardson,* and vessels whose name we knew only in code or by sight. We sometimes wondered if personnel on those larger vessels realized that their safety depended upon the little wooden subchaser whose radar and sonar beams constantly scanned above and below the sea for enemy craft.

A rather scary situation developed on September 18 as we escorted SS *Huger* to Nemours. I was aroused at 0145 to investigate a sonar contact on our starboard bow, but I judged it not to be a solid object. Fifteen minutes later the gun stations were manned as we sped toward a radar contact on the port beam. The blip

I snapped this picture of Lieutenant (jg) Harry William Reece on the bow of *Cinq-Deux-Cinq* in Oran, Algeria, on the morning of his relief as commanding officer in October 1943.

turned out to be an uncharted tiny island. Then, before daybreak, the port engine "cropped out" and we limped into Nemours. Our talented machinist's mates made repairs, and upon our return to Oran we had nine precious days in port.

Command changed on October 13 when Lieutenant (jg) Harry William Reece was relieved by Lieutenant (jg) John Charles Waldron, both of whom had been promoted from ensign during the previous months. Simultaneously, Ensign John Underwood Barton reported for duty as third officer. The following day Lieutenant Reece gave his farewell address and posed for me on the forecastle, with the Oran base in the background. He graciously carried a roll of film back to the States and sent prints to my family. After his departure, life on the subchaser became a little more formal. I think most of the crew respected Lieutenant Waldron but did not feel that he was "one of us." In fact, Hugh McCormick, of the McCormick Spice family of Baltimore, who moved up to executive officer, was more popular among the enlisted men. Ensign Barton acted like the proverbial "ninety-day wonder," formal, exacting, less at ease; even his log entries were fuller and more formal. Bernard Pfau, pharmacist's mate, also came aboard on the same day; I did not know at the time how badly I would need his services three months later.

There was noticeably increased intensity in the harbors of Oran and MEK at mid–October. We welcomed back *YMS-24*, *-29*, and *-30*, which had been away several weeks, and soon we were joined by *SC-498*, *-515*, *-524*, *-526*, *-532*, *-561*, *-655*, *-666*, and *-695*, and *PC-546*, *-621*, and *-626*. Several of them had been with us at Casablanca, so we no longer felt lonely.

News from the Italian front was grim, even after the occupation of Naples the first of the month, so we were a bit unnerved when on October 19 four Nazi ships sailed into Oran's harbor — two transports of the Friegleit Lines, one named *Siniai*, and two hospital ships, one named *Aquileia*— for the purpose, we learned later, of carrying out an exchange of war prisoners.[4] Two days later we received the "honor" of escorting the Nazi ships out of the harbor, and on our return to the docks, general quarters was sounded and *SC-524* and *-525* sped out with *Bernadou* (DD-153) and *Cole* (DD-155), responding to a report from our sister *SC-515* that she had a sonar contact off Isle Habibas. Upon arrival in the suspect area, even after stopping engines to minimize screw noises, I could get no firm echo. All night we searched with negative results. A momentary panic occurred another day when two aircraft, plainly marked with the Swastika, approached the MEK anchorage; fortunately, gunners did not fire, for the planes were being escorted in by American fighters.

The war came perilously close to *525* in November. As we patrolled outside the harbor, our task was to challenge each approaching ship, "AA. AA." (Who are you? What is your code?) and, upon getting the correct response, report to the harbor operations master the admission of each "friend." This would have been a rather boring routine except for the realization that we were serving as a virtual policeman, controlling access to this key port in North Africa. Our puny guns would be little defense if an unfriendly vessel surreptitiously approached, but radio contact and our manual signal lamp could alert big sisters with their awesome armament. Escorting ships, either detached from or joining the many convoys sailing between Gibraltar and Italy, was more interesting. When the body of a convoy sailed close to land, we led the detached ships through the maze of vessels anchored in the harbor, my sonar head retracted; but to reach convoys far at sea, we became an escort, protecting the accompanying ships with sonar searches against submarines and radar scanning for enemy aircraft. Two episodes deserve a footnote to demonstrate how close *SC-525* came to tragedies while operating out of Oran.

Armistice Day, November 11, began normally as we patrolled across Oran Bay. *Yew* (YN-32) passed through, and *Trippe* (DD-403) sailed out to relieve our fellow patroller, *Dallas* (DD-199), which returned to the docks. A convoy began forming outside the harbor, ready to join a larger east-bound flotilla approaching from Gibraltar. At 1430, as the two convoys merged, *525* corralled three ships detached from the larger group and led them toward Oran. That assignment having been safely completed, we reentered the harbor, took on fuel, and looked forward to a quiet evening at the dock. Suddenly, at 2100, with a warning of enemy torpedo aircraft in the area, we received an urgent order to lead the French tug *Fort* toward a ship that was being attacked at a specified coordinate about ten miles at sea. We were hardly out of the harbor when a single glance at the horizon confirmed our worst fears: Several towering blazes pierced the night's darkness. We suspected the worst when shortly after midnight a countermanding message instructed us to return to patrolling, because the tug was no longer needed; the victim had sunk. After the war we learned that not one but four Allied ships were sunk by aerial torpedoes in the attack — three transports and a tanker. To this day I do not know how many Allied personnel died during that fiery night.[5]

Years later we learned the awful fate of another ship whose passengers waved goodbye to us. On Thanksgiving Day, 1943, nearly two thousand U.S. Army soldiers crowded aboard an Indian ship of Canadian registry, the troop transport *Rohna*, which joined Convoy KMF-26, headed not to Italy but through the Suez Canal to the India-Burma theater to fight the Japanese. Late the next afternoon off Bougie, Algeria, the convoy was attacked by a swarm of Heinkel-177 bombers. Confused by small planes approaching beneath larger ones, some eyewitnesses thought that the lower-flying planes were American fighters seeking to intercept the bombers. Instead, they were unmanned Henschel Hs-293 radio-controlled bombs, the lethal effectiveness of which had been proven three months earlier in the sinking of HMS *Egret* off the coast of Spain. One of the glide bombs hit and set *Rohna* afire. Within ninety minutes the transport sank with the heaviest loss of life — including 1,015 of the American soldiers — of any single World War II sea disaster The death toll would have been even greater but for the heroic action of the crews of USS *Pioneer* (AM-105) and HMS *Atherstone*. *Pioneer*, sister of vessels on which I served two years later, dragged aboard hundreds of soldiers, American Red Cross workers, and crew members of the lost ship. That was about five times the weight of the human flesh of *Pioneer*'s normal complement.[6]

Rough seas sometime rolled *Cinq-Deux-Cinq* to the extent that the sonar beam struck the bottom of the sea. From noon until midnight on 22 November, for example, an extract in the log read:

> 1200, Patrolling as before on courses 090 T and 270 T. Patrol shortened to avoid interfering with destroyer's search in same area. 0314, Investigated asdic [sound] crossing at MEK boom. Results negative and so reported. 1356, Returned to patrol. 1506, Destroyer patrolling inboard. Two P39s [friendly aircraft] in vicinity. Five ships entering harbor. 1558. Seven merchant ships, PC, and SC standing out. 1559, Three LSTs coming in. 2000, Patrolling as before. Sea rough, visibility very poor because of rain and fog. 2027, Changed patrol courses to 330 PSC and 140 PSC to avoid destroyer's patrol and to ride a bit easier. 2050, Used running lights [to avoid collisions in the fog]. *SC-651* patrolling inboard at 1500 yards. 2244, Investigated crossing of loops 3 and 4. Identified ships as friendly. 2325, Same investigation.

A few days later the raging sea was understated when Lieutenant McCormick recorded, "British Patrol plane identified himself as friendly. No further remarks as it was a very quiet watch, except for the seas." Security — or nervousness — led to frequent challenges of and by *SC-525*; if the proper code name was not radioed back and there was no confirmation as a friendly vessel, an attack was justified. One entry: "0735, Challenged by D153 [*Bernadou*] with 'Love.' This was wrong challenge. No reply was given. Told D153 her challenge was wrong." Mighty cheeky of a little subchaser correcting a mighty tin can! Crossing of the "loops" became monotonous when a French flotilla, under protection of the battleship *Lorraine*, came in. Lieutenant McCormick, disgusted at the inconvenience, wrote, "All these contacts were caused by the incoming French ships."

Life was seldom unemotional. Bloated bodies, routinely picked up at sea, were inspected to determine nationality. If American, British, or French, the body was taken ashore and turned over to base authorities. If German or Italian, it was usually tied to something heavy and jettisoned. We got rid of a broken toilet bowl by sinking one corpse. I made entries such as "*SC-515* picked up body of German aviator & brought it in. Most of meat eat[en] off by fish. Horrible sight." It was returned to the sea the next day. Another entry was simply "*PC-626* picked up German sub commander — dead."

In port, there was more than boredom. Usually accompanied by one of the officers, the radarman, and the radioman, I was a frequent visitor to the Attack Teacher, the sonar teaching device located on USS *Vulcan* (AR-5) at Mers el-Kébir.[7] We usually had to hitch a ride on a military vehicle for the seven or eight miles to and from MEK. There were few arranged sports for the fleet, and the good beaches were miles away. Consequently, George and I recognized our good fortune one day in being invited by lieutenants Waldron and McCormick and Chief Miller to accompany them on a bumpy truck trip to Ain el Turck, a splendid swimming beach west of Mers el-Kébir and not far from one of the invasion beaches. There we swam, sunned, and saw on a crude stage Hollywood comedian Sterling Holloway and an impromptu performance by a group of soldiers. The trip was doubly pleasant because we escaped the stench of sulphur that was sprayed in the sleeping compartments during the day, and when we returned, George and I simply spread our blankets on deck. Unfortunately, we soon attracted new roaches from other infested piers, and Lieutenant McCormick's taste for pancakes was irretrievably lost when, as he poured syrup from the gallon can, a struggling roach rode out on the first flow. Catsup, too, was served from gallon cans, which were opened by a one-twist gouge from a dinner knife. Emily Post and Miss Manners seldom visited a Navy mess hall.

Most of the crew played cards, but on a sailor's salary, the stakes were never high. Michael Balog and Eddie Runof spiked their coffee with cognac, and often one of the officers visited the aft compartment to order "lights out" shortly before ten. With early reveille the rule rather than the exception, each crewman was expected to keep himself in shape, even if there was no workout equipment or track aboard. My game was checkers, which did not require much exercise. On November 12, Lieutenant McCormick was duty officer and I was duty messenger on HMS *Scipio*, which meant that we were responsible for disseminating official messages throughout the harbor. I was kept on the run most of the time, delivering messages from ship to ship. George came up to defeat me three-to-one in checkers, but I had the pleasure of beating my executive officer and a British lieutenant.

We celebrated George's twenty-first birthday on November 20 by getting a haircut and seeing Irvin Berlin's great war movie, *This Is the Army*.[8] Our most memorable liberty, however, occurred November 29 when we rented Arab donkeys and rode them up Marabout Mountain to Fort Santa Cruz and the Santa Cruz Cathedral. There we joined a group of WACs (members of the Women's Army Corps). The view of the city and harbor was spectacular, but more interesting was our first ride on a stubborn camel. I had thought that all camels had two humps, but these dromedaries were built with only one, and I had difficulty trying to ride bareback, particularly when the critter kept turning its head and nipping my leg. I found the donkeys also quite stubborn but immensely more manageable than a camel that understood no English.

The trip up the mountain overlooking the city revealed to us the impoverishment of the Arab people, hoards of whom lived in tents and adobe huts worse than those we had seen in Casablanca. Women, their faces covered, used communal washing troughs and balanced loads on their heads; barefoot children in rags carried virtually naked babies; men took siestas on the ground; flies swarmed around everyone. The cemetery, with monuments in Arabic script and mosaics, was the oddly pleasant attraction of the trip. Yet, back in the middle of the city, the grand Intercontinental Hotel and other modern buildings, often flying flags of the Allied nations, suggested a city in prewar France. Several cinemas like the Casino, Collisee, and Empire, offered movies in English or with English subtitles and were frequented by military personnel fortunate enough to get into the city. A number of traveling shows, in both English and French, were brought in by the USO and were seen by thousands of soldiers and sailors stationed in the area. An enlisted men's club, administered by the Red Cross, provided welcome services. When in port, Lieutenant McCormick, Chief Miller, and I usually attended Protestant services either on the base or on one of the larger ships.

Our relationship with other crews was usually good. Fairly often liberty parties were left ashore when a ship was ordered out of the harbor on short notice, so crews of sister ships always tried to care for orphans, if only to provide a blanket for the night on deck. There was visiting back and forth, particularly between crewmen who had served together at a previous station, such as Pier 92. Officers had their own clubs ashore, and they often formed friendships. Our officers, for example, were well acquainted with *YMS-24*'s Lieutenant (jg) John Cox, who was better known as the Hollywood actor John Howard, and who would win the Navy Cross for heroism when his ship was sunk at Southern France the following August.[9]

Occasionally officers and crews of larger ships took pity on the sailors of the splinter fleet and shared such delicacies as they had. Bottled cola drinks were not among essential commodities shipped to war zones (but there was plenty of powdered Cool-Aid), so as a "cola-holic," I was always elated when a buddy on a larger ship allowed me to visit and share a scarce taste of Pepsi-Cola, a "dope" that originated as "Brad's Drink" in 1893 in New Bern, North Carolina. One of our few flaps between ships occurred when we cut the Liberty ship *William Patterson*'s stern line that threatened to break our jackstaff and radio antenna. The commanding officer, C.O. Sampson, became furious, but Lieutenant McCormick simply wrote in the deck log, "Was asked to slack off but paid no attention." Served him right.

There were, of course, other diversions and regular duties aboard ship, such as repairing equipment and weaponry, chipping paint and repainting various portions of the ship, scrubbing the deck with a holy-stone, airing bedding on good days, and joining work parties to unload stores from newly arrived ships docked at MEK. Our crew was quite adept at picking up any discarded object lying around the docks, always with an eye toward its adaptability for use aboard *525*. That is how we became one of the few small ships with a washing machine. Unfortunately, like Pepsi-Cola, washing machines were not given priority in war zones, replacement parts were as scarce as gold, and the jerry-rigged equipment was used sparingly and eventually abandoned for want of repairs.

The most unpleasant occurrence in Oran was the transfer to the brig of Noah E. Samuel, gunner's mate second class, to await a court-martial — the only major disciplinary action in my year and a half on the *Cinq-Deux-Cinq*. Edward Cain, an unpredictable motor machinist's mate second class, came close to a similar fate later.[10]

At both Casablanca and Oran, we looked forward to *Stars and Stripes*, the tabloid-size newspaper of the United States Armed Forces, published Monday through Friday in each occupied city. For a hundred francs, I was able to have the weekly edition mailed to my parents. The Oran edition of September 9 headlined, "Italy Quits!" and the issue included the schedule of the American Expeditionary Forces Radio. In addition to news and inspirational messages, the station carried entertainment such as "Yank Swing Session," "G.I. Jive," "Yarns for Yanks," and programs featuring Fats Waller, Fred Waring, Harry James, Bing Crosby, and Ella Fitzgerald. There was considerable excitement when on November 20 President Franklin Roosevelt disembarked in Mers el-Kébir on his way to the Cairo Conference.

The American Expeditionary Station, with its understandably biased reporting, was the chief means of disseminating information, for there was no general telephone accessibility, and television was still in the experimental stage. Mail, never far from our minds, was slow and sporadic — three weeks sometimes passed with no postal contact with the States. And when mail did come, it arrived in huge canvas sacks. In Oran I received twenty-two pieces at one mail call. Still, that was better than at Casablanca, for now we were on the direct line from the States through the Strait of Gibraltar to the war zone.

Although regular paper-and-envelope letters were never prohibited and could be sent via surface mail free (and via airmail if we applied a six-cent stamp), an alternative method of communication was introduced in 1943. To expedite messages to and from overseas personnel, and to minimize expense and space in transportation, the War Department introduced V-Mail ("Victory Mail"). The system was novel but simple: In the States, a message (limited to one side of a sheet) was written on a preprinted form that was folded twice, sealed, addressed, stamped, and mailed to our ship in care of the "FPO" (Fleet Post Office), New York City (or San Francisco). At the FPO the sheets were sorted by war zone, opened, flattened, and copied in miniature format on microfilm. The original manuscript was discarded, but the film was flown to the appropriate overseas processing center, where the image was enlarged and printed onto photo paper measuring about $4\frac{1}{4} \times 5\frac{1}{4}$ inches. The resulting V-Mail sheet was then folded into a small windowed envelope and eventually delivered to the addressee. The government claimed that 1,700 microfilmed letters would fit into a single cigarette pack. When the last V-Mail left New York on November 1, 1945, almost 1.25 billion — that's *billion* — had been sent to or from servicemen.[11] The Casablanca edition of the *Stars and Stripes* on July 11, 1943, reported that 50,000 V-Mails were processed daily at the Casa Signal Station, operated by the "ABS Signal Photo Mail Company" under command of the Signal Corps.

All mail sent back to the states was read by a censor (a commissioned officer) who excised any unauthorized information that might, if intercepted, reveal to the enemy information such as the writer's location and activity. Letters, properly addressed, were submitted unsealed to the censor, who, with razor blade or scissors, cut out prohibited information in ordinary letters or, in case of V-Mail, obliterated the information with censor's ink. The censorship stamp and the censor's initials were affixed before the letter could be accepted by the military postal service. A long list of prohibited topics was contained in a four-page document titled "Headquarters Administrative Order No. 1" issued by U.S. Naval Forces Northwest African Waters. In addition, all correspondence was required to be in English unless it could be proven that the addressee, a member of the family, was unable to read English. "Pen-pal" letters, described as "correspondence between postal acquaintances of no previous friendship," were to be "suppressed." The knowledge that someone else would read each letter no doubt inhibited many correspondents from expressing their genuine emotions and thoughts, but except for a few loose tongues, most censors took their responsibility as a necessary evil and respected the confidentiality of the correspondents. Even so, it is quite likely that an occasional writer planted subliminal (and sometimes graphic) messages for the sole benefit of the censor (who was usually his own superior officer). On a small subchaser, our officers probably read the pulse of the crew more distinctly through our letters than through direct conversation. So, even if wartime censorship guarded few military secrets from the enemy, it had other implications, some of them more beneficial than detrimental.

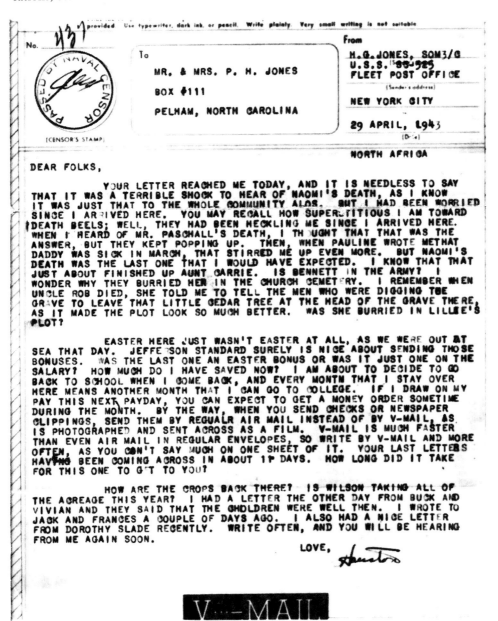

To save time and space, V-Mail was introduced in 1943. With this new technology, letters were microfilmed, the reeled microfilm was flown overseas, where photograph prints were made from the film and delivered to the addressee. Our executive officer, the official censor, initialed my letter attesting that I had given no information of value to the enemy.

Letters — whether via regular or V-Mail — and packages from home were eagerly received. My mother, with a fourth grade penmanship and spelling, tried to write twice a week, and in almost every letter she spent several lines complaining that she had not heard from me for a week or so and pleading to know how I was "getting along." She was a habitual worrier anyway, but now that her youngest son was in harm's way, she apparently spent much of her time — whether over a steaming cookstove or working in the field — imagining where I was and what I was doing. She of course had little understanding of geography and distances, so when a letter took two weeks to arrive, she assumed that I had gone farther away, but if it arrived in six days, she imagined that I must be back in the States. No matter how many times I explained that censorship prohibited divulging my location (except perhaps "Somewhere in North Africa"), she wanted to know, "Where are you?" and "Why don't you write often?" Actually, I did average writing once a week, but when a couple of weeks passed without receiving a letter, she almost panicked.

We reproduced on our stationery the insignia of *SC-525*, an image of a seahorse with a K-gun (depth charge) on its shoulder and a submarine gripped in its tail.

It was difficult for those of us serving overseas to understand the anxiety felt by our loved ones at home. Still, I eagerly looked forward to letters from my mother. (My father, insofar as I know, never wrote a letter; I saw him write only his signature and some simple figuring.) I also welcomed correspondence from my sister Pauline and sister-in-law Vivian (Buck, with a seventh-grade education, also did not write letters), for they tended to give me less hand-wringing and more real information. News of the family and neighbors was usually routine — for example, Uncle Bob and Aunt Nannie Willie visited last night, Buck is working in the mill, Daddy is helping at Mr. Tom Hodges's mule stable, Thomas Smith has been drafted, Edna Pettigrew has given birth to another boy, or the family attended the July 4th barbecue at Robert Smith's Store — but to me it was welcome information. There was much news about the crops — fixing the plant beds, watering and planting tobacco, shucking corn, picking and canning snaps, pulling watermelons — and, of course, the weather — too dry, too wet, too hot, too cold. These topics, while giving me a sense of nostalgia, reminded me over and over that I was glad to have escaped the farm. Even Navy service off Africa was better!

Despite wartime conditions, packages were allowed to be mailed via surface transportation, and perishable goods — for example, cakes — brightened the day for both the recipient and shipmates. Close quarters promoted sharing of perishable gifts, for surreptitious consumption was almost impossible. A favorite "party" in the mess hall sometimes featured "royal coffee," a treat from Eddie Runof and Mike Balog, who always seemed to find a crevice capable of hiding a bottle of hootch, usually cognac. Hester Fowlkes, Pelham's rural mail carrier, who had delivered wondrous packages to me when I was a child who spent his pennies on postal cards seeking free samples, exercised great patience in wrapping and mailing various gifts from my folks. For example, my mother mailed my Kodak and, for Christmas 1943, a shaving kit; and my sister sent a fruit cake. I asked my brother-in-law John to buy me a watch for not more than $40, but when the price of the Longines ran to $65, my father insisted on sending it to me as a gift, both for Christmas and my birthday two weeks later. That was probably the largest amount he spent on any gift in his life.

Wartime shortages back home became a recurring subject in correspondence. For example, pleasure driving was curtailed as gasoline rationing was instituted, and rubber tires were virtually unobtainable. Sugar and other products were limited. I caused my family considerable trouble when I made an innocent request for chewing gum, which was unavailable in military canteens overseas. I was embarrassed when I later learned the extent to which my brother Buck went to locate a whole carton of gum, which my mother mailed to me with great relief.

In my letters home, I tried to be upbeat, reporting for example, on the Memorial Day ceremony at NOB Casablanca honoring participants in Operation Torch; and for her birthday on June 7, I mailed an inexpensive handkerchief embroidered with a dancing Arab seminude. I also mailed a variety of cheap items, such as leather billfolds, silk scarves, and picture postcards. I did not realize at the time how much such simple gifts were prized by the recipients. I took greatest pleasure, however, in mailing back money orders from my monthly Navy salary, most of which was invested in war bonds. The savings were added to holiday bonuses sent by Jefferson Standard Life Insurance Company to military men and women who previously worked for the company. I wrote Mamma, "Every month that I stay over here means another month that I can go to college." In 1943, we could not have foreseen that a "GI Bill of Rights" would assist millions of veterans in gaining a postwar education.

I subscribed to the county paper, *Caswell Messenger*, and wrote Editor Erwin Stephens [March 29, 1943]: "Even though The Messenger is several weeks old when it reaches me, it is always interesting, and news from Caswell County is really precious here in Africa." And to *The State* magazine I wrote: "Here in Africa, where I am now stationed, we are beginning to realize just how much we appreciate the Old North State, and I know of no better way of keeping in touch with events happening from Elizabeth City to Murphy than by reading THE STATE weekly." *Jefferson Standard Life*, edited by Lois Fitch, kept me informed about my former colleagues in Greensboro and published several of my letters and photographs. Even at war, the printed word was magic to me.

On December 4, 1943, we received aboard twenty-seven field jackets. Ah ha! Field jackets were not needed in Oran. What's up? Shortly afterward, we entered Drydock No. 3: "High and dry-docked," the exec recorded in the log. Normally the crew performed the physical labor in scraping barnacles from our wooden hull, but this time Arab workers were hired by the Navy for the purpose. On blocks in the huge drydock with several other vessels, we fought a cat-and-mouse war with large rats that crawled along the dock and had to be driven off by force. We had less success in the battle against roaches, which found crevices that protected them from the fumigant expelled regularly in the compartments.

It was becoming evident that we were being prepared for combat duty. So on December 19, we waved goodbye to Oran and fell in behind *PC-626*. Our departure denied us the thrill of watching the New Year's day football "Arab Bowl" in Oran, in which the Army defeated the Navy 10–7. Except for an occasional suspicious sonar contact that proved false, identifying dozens of aircraft as friendly, and practice-firing our guns, the two-day eastward voyage was uneventful. Bypassing Algiers, we rounded Cape Blanc, the northernmost point in Africa, and on December 21 entered a long man-made channel running south from the Mediterranean Sea. We had arrived at the ancient Tunisian city of Bizerte (*Binzart* in Arabic; historic name, *Hippo Diarrhytus* or *Zarrytus*), now almost obliterated by war, located on the banks of a narrow neck of water opening the large Lake Bizerte into the Mediterranean. Farther down the waterway were located the wharves of Karouba and La Pecherie. Again American advance base forces had cleared out much of the dock wreckage caused by first Allied and later German bombings. Ships were constantly moving, some unloading, others loading, creating a beehive of activity. The wharves and piers extending out into the lake provided excellent docking facilities, and *SC-525* tied up at French Pier beside the familiar *SC-524*. I estimated twenty subchasers and patrol craft in the lake, but there were hundreds of other vessels ranging from seaplane tenders and destroyers down to tugs. Our SCs were nested—that is, one secured to the dock or anchored, with as many as six or eight others tied successively side by side. (Nesting required the starting of engines to move away when an inboard vessel was ordered to sea.) One midnight, an air alert sounded, but we saw no enemy planes. Early the next morning Ensign Barton took half of the crew to the port's chamber for gas mask instruction; the other half went in the afternoon; and the exec logged "Gas Detail aboard, instructions successful, no injuries." Things were beginning to look serious. We hadn't counted on gas warfare from the Nazis.

Meanwhile, at Bizerte we found ourselves in an entirely different Navy, subject to discipline that we had not practiced since boot camp. Base Commander H. H. Jalbert required newly arriving ships to shape up and conform to naval protocol. The dress code requiring whites ashore was strictly enforced, men were put on report for failing to salute, and the crew was put to work painting *SC-525* until every part of her sparkled. Captain's inspections were no longer perfunctory. Gangway watches were strictly observed; we provided sentry watch at the harbor gate; we were required to check lines every twenty minutes "as per night orders." Ships in turn stood visual signal watch for the entire SC nest. Hours were spent swinging the ship and running the degaussing range. Various equipment was checked by specialists from the base.

There was occasional liberty but virtually no place to go except to the Naval Operating Base, where everybody seemed to look alike, and into the devastated city, whose inner harbor was still littered with sunken ships and debris. George and I picked our way through rubble to a downtown theater that miraculously remained standing but in a very wounded condition. The roof and walls had lost their plaster, some of which crunched under our feet, but the projector still worked, and we watched Hedy Lamarr and Lana Turner in *Ziegfeld Girl*. But one trip into the devastation was enough, and thereafter we took every opportunity to go to the base for movies such as *Edge of Darkness*, *Apache Trail*, *It's a Great Life*, *The Hidden Hand*, and *Swing Shift Maisie*. My wish to visit historic Carthage across the lake was never fulfilled. So near, but so far.

After painting topside on Christmas eve and being surprised by Christmas greetings from much larger USS *Delta* (AR-9), I went to Protestant religious services in Hangar 3B, a very formal ceremony presided over by Chaplain M. J. Silseth. The hymns were familiar — like "O Come, All Ye Faithful," "O Little Town of Bethlehem," "Hark! The Herald Angels Sing," and "Joy to the World." There were two violin solos, a "brass choir," and a public confession, followed by Holy Communion. The next morning I returned for another Christmas service, less formal and more personal, and I preserved the mimeographed bulletin that covered both services. Back aboard ship, I enjoyed a good holiday dinner, the last one prepared by our cook, Alphonse Albert Le Riche. The next day he was transferred ashore for transportation back to the States; William V. Isaac, ship's cook third class, came aboard to replace him.

On December 30, we tied up alongside an LCI and loaded ammunition. The log read, "Took aboard 720 rds. of 20 MM. HEI; 360 rds. of 20 MM. HET; 160 rds. of 40 MM. AP(T) and 640 rds. of 40 MM. AA(T)."[12] By that afternoon a horrendous storm, including strong winds, made us nervous with all of that new explosive power aboard, but on January 2 we braved the waves to degauss the ship again. George and I continued to spend as much time ashore as possible, including attendance at a stage show, *Stand By for Action*, at the base. The title was prophetic. True to my old Boy Scout motto, "Be Prepared," I had used my ration card for a couple of extra mattress covers, T-shirts, and cartons of cigarettes before leaving Oran. Suddenly such items were more valuable than I could have imagined, for I found myself exchanging some of them to Arabs who were allowed to trade on the base. Mattress covers were particularly in demand, for with a couple of snips of the scissors, a white cover could become an Arab's outerwear. Like the French, of course, we looked upon the "A-Rabs" as a backward people incapable of adjusting to the modern world. We knew nothing of the high civilization of the Moors in the Middle Ages, and it did not occur to us that our occupying force might some day need the friendship and support of those from whose lands we were launching our battle against totalitarianism.

6

Agony at Anzio

January 1944

My birthday — January 7, 1944 — passed as pleasantly as the fevered activity in Tunisia's Lake Bizerte would allow. Bill Isaac, the new cook, scrounged a turkey from the NOB commissary and produced a delicious meal — including apple pie — that was devoured by the entire hungry crew. I was *the* man of the day. After nine months aboard *Cinq-Deux-Cinq*, I had overcome the anxiety felt during the first liberties in Casablanca and had become comfortable with most of my shipmates. I was on the verge of manhood, and I had finally found a home.

My premonition of imminent departure from North Africa was correct, for the day after I turned twenty, we fueled up, took aboard smoke pots, and — weighed down with antiaircraft ammunition and depth charges — sailed up the Bizerte Narrows and out into the submarine-infested Mediterranean. We were heading toward the *real* war. We joined *SC-639* and *-697* and *PC-556* and *-558* in corralling about twenty-five LCIs (Landing Craft Infantry) and heading northeastward. I watched passively as we met *LST-327*, returning from Naples with wounded troops, with no inkling that in less than three weeks I would be one of her patients. Our screening position was at the head of the convoy, which proceeded at about ten knots. That position was not always comfortable, particularly when we overtook two fleets of merchant ships and were forced to alter the course of our convoy. Furthermore, *525* experienced difficulties with both our sonar and radar gear, the former working only poorly, the latter sporadically. Those technical deficiencies caused anxious moments when *PC-558* sped off to investigate a sonar contact that, fortunately, proved negative.[1] We were further reminded on the first night of our vulnerability — and that of thousands of soldiers crowded onto the two dozen landing ships that we were guarding — when a floating mine was spotted and sunk by gunfire. Our warning message to the convoy commander was ignored, not a reassuring response in the face of danger.

The next morning we sighted the western tip of Sicily, and soon the island of Ustica off our port side; and before midnight we saw the red glow of an active volcano, probably Stromboli. At 0655 on the 10th, we followed the swept channel between the fabled Isle of Capri and Italy's Sorrentine Peninsula. Entering the cavernous Bay of Naples, we could see what appeared to be an enormous fleet at anchor and one continuous city onshore. Towering above this megacity stood, in its majesty, Mount Vesuvius, quiet and without even a whiff of smoke — so picturesque that I could hardly imagine how its lava, pumice, and ash had obliterated Pompeii and surrounding villages in 79 A.D. And of course I had no inkling of Vesuvius's behavior ten weeks in the future.

Instead of docking in the shadow of Vesuvius as we had anticipated, we led the LCI convoy about seven miles northwesterly to the little island of Nisida at the eastern edge of the Gulf of Pozzuoli. Nisida was what remained from an ancient volcano, the seaward side of its crater having been worn away, leaving high cliffs on which stood an ancient fort. The island gave the appearance of a pincer reaching out into a gulf that was filled with the largest armada that any of us had ever seen. The water was rough, but we were permitted to tie up on the protected side of a tiny artificial jetty that connected the island to the mainland. Unexpectedly, the captain allowed several of us to go ashore for a few hours, so we slipped into the industrial town of Bagnoli on the mainland, walking around and gawking at the devastation. Nearby was a large complex that had been converted into the 23rd General Hospital for the American Fifth Army, then fighting desperately less than a hundred miles away. I wrote, "Town pretty well bombed up. People poor — lots of bummers." We arrived back at the ship just in time to hear the sound of general quarters, but we saw only friendly planes in the sky.

Excitement increased the next morning when we learned that we were getting underway to practice an amphibious landing. At noon we joined a large flotilla of destroyers, patrol craft, LCIs, and LSTs that sailed between Cape Mesino and the island of Procida, then northward up the coast toward the mouth of the Volturno River. *525* screened the port bow of the landing ships to a point about thirty miles south of the battle line that stretched across Italy, and there on the night of January 11 we participated in our first "invasion." Let the log speak:

> 2000, In sight of our objective. Landing operations begun. 2136, DUKWs began heading for beach. 2240, Began rounding up stray DUKWs and inquired from each LST if their DUKWs were all in the water. 2325, Led last column of DUKWs toward shore to water depth of 17 feet. All engines ahead 900 RPM, heading seaward. 2347, Alongside *LST-348*, telling her to get underway.[2]

Shortly after midnight we screened ahead of the LST and, after being challenged by blinker ("AA. AA." meaning "Who are you? What is your secret call?") by a destroyer, we arrived back at Nisida at 0400. At daybreak we could identify sister subchasers *-515*, *-524*, *-534*, *-638*, *-649*, *-692*, *-693*, and *-978*. Happily, our crew was allowed to sleep late and to relax during the day.

Shortly after noon on January 13, *SC-525* and *-978* escorted *LST-348* and *-359* and several other landing craft southward for another landing practice. This time the site was along the coast near Salerno, the scene of the bloody Operation Avalanche less than four months earlier. Wreckage from that costly battle — battered, rusting Allied landing craft demonstrating the effectiveness of German shells and bombs — added realism to the simulated invasion. Again the log:

> 2000, Heading in toward the Red beach. 2110, Leading in second wave of LCVPs to 500 yards of the beach. 2200, Returned to *PC-627* to await sixth wave of DUKWs. 2230, Leading in sixth wave. 2330, Operations completed, heading back to *LST-4*, thence to Salerno. 2340, Changed speed to 600 RPM. 2345, All engines stopped. 2348, Laying to alongside *LST-4*, waiting for her to get underway. 0000, Continuing to await the departure of the *LST-4* for Salerno.... 0051, Alongside *LST-348*; told to get convoy underway.

As the convoy returned toward the Gulf of Pozzuoli, we detached *LST-4*, which proceeded into Naples; and upon arrival in the vicinity of Nisida, we tied up beside *SC-497* at the Bagnoli docks. We were in need of fuel replenishment, but during the day we began to feel like an orphan when our signaled requests to larger American ships were summarily turned down by each. It seemed inexplicable that in the practice invasions no "mother ship" had been designated to provide fuel and provisions to the individual subchasers and other small vessels incapable of distilling their own water or carrying large quantities of fuel. Not until late the next day were we able to obtain 1,850 gallons of diesel fuel from British *LST-322*. After that, we felt more kindly toward the "Limey" Navy. On Saturday and Sunday we moved from dock to dock around Pozzuoli, Bagnoli, and Nisida, carrying messages and taking on stores from the piers.

The bosun's high-pitched whistle sounded at 0530 on Monday, January 17, and within an hour we were circling the harbor notifying ships to get underway for yet another practice invasion at Salerno. This time we were in charge of an LCT convoy for a "dress rehearsal"— meaning that the next operation would be the *real* one, though we knew not where. By the time we left the gulf, the sea was so rough that it was difficult to keep the ships on course. In addition, confusion arose off Capri when our skipper had to order one landing craft back into the convoy lest it veer into a minefield.

The log recorded even more serious problems following the midnight rendezvous:

> 0000, En route to beach on Gulf of Salerno for invasion practice of full-scale operation. Secured Sonar. 0002, Observed flares from beach. 0055, LCT close aboard starboard side, lost from main group. Gave him the proper course to intercept. 0143, Changed course to 090 PSC. Observed tracer fire from beach. 0325, Nearing point Charlie, LCTs crossing starboard bow. 0545, All engines ahead 800 RPM, at beach, turning to seaward. 0600, Laying to off Salerno beach. 0700, Started search for assigned LSTs to supervise unloading. All engines ahead 950 RPM, Radar secured.... 1135, Sonar started. 1140, Taking up position astern of LCTs. 1200, Continuing to screen astern of LCTs on return route to Naples and Nisida.... 1655, Dropping back to pick up straggling LCTs.

As enlisted men, the crew had witnessed what appeared to be mixed signals and misadventures during this and the previous Salerno practice, but we had little knowledge of just how the operations should have gone. Consequently, when we returned to the Gulf of Pozzuoli, we did not know that the entire operation during the night of January 17–18 — appropriately named "Webfoot"— had been a frightening fiasco. In addition to the confusion among landing craft as they approached the coast, some transports unloaded troops so far at sea that their boats required nearly four hours to reach the beach. Rear Admiral Samuel Eliot Morison later wrote, "It was held on a night of very rough weather (17–18 January); the naval vessels did not close the beaches near enough, and forty dukws were swamped, with the loss of many 105-mm howitzers and a number of lives." Rear Admiral Frank J. Lowry, later in charge of landing the American 3rd Division at Anzio, judged "Webfoot" as "generously called unsatisfactory (actually it was terrible)."[3] It was too late, however, for another dry run. A simultaneous Exercise Oboe, conducted below Salerno by the British First Division, was also judged a fiasco.[4]

At that point we were only beginning to envision the complexity of an invasion of enemy-occupied territory by tens of thousands of Allied troops protected by several hundred vessels of all sizes. We had heard radio reports and read accounts of the Navy's role in previous landings, but not until we became full participants in the trials at Salerno did we begin to sense the enormity, intricacy, and danger of such an operation.

In the Moroccan and Algerian landings, soldiers had arrived from the States on large troop transports from which, several miles at sea, they climbed down rope ladders into 36-foot-long LCVPs, which carried them to the beaches.[5] Vehicles and weapons could be lowered into similar boats by davits. That traditional procedure worked satisfactorily in North

Africa because of the relatively light opposition by the Vichy French. But Nazi-occupied territory presented a far greater challenge, and in preparation for the invasions of Sicily and Italy, American shipyards rushed into production a series of much larger and more versatile beaching craft. The two largest were the 328-foot-long Landing Ship Tank (LST), capable of carrying 200 soldiers and 20 tanks, and the 158-foot-long Landing Craft Infantry (LCI), with a capacity of 188 men and their gear.[6] Both were equipped with navigational gear that enabled them to cross the Atlantic on their own bottoms, and both were capable of running upon a beach, dropping their ramps, and disgorging huge quantities of men, vehicles, or equipment.

Also introduced were the smaller 112-foot-long Landing Craft Tank (LCT) and the 31-foot amphibious truck with the acronym DUKW, nicknamed "Duck."[7] These arrived in the Mediterranean aboard LSTs or Liberty ships. The combination of large and small craft enabled the landing of tanks and anti-tank guns almost simultaneously with the troops and other equipment. However, the smaller craft were dependent upon escorts to shepherd them through the narrow channels previously cleared by minesweepers. As we learned in the practice exercises at Salerno, a subchaser, with shallow draft and short turning circle, served effectively as the mother goose to a "wave" of goslings — LCTs, LCVPs, or DUKWs — by leading them into shallow water, after which the escort returned to lead in another wave.[8] While marking time, the boats circled or lolled about like ducklings until the escort turned on her stern light and signaled for them to form either a column or a V-shaped echelon for the dash to the landing site. Thus a subchaser, upon reaching the anchorage prior to an invasion, yielded her customary position as perimeter antisubmarine escort to destroyers and destroyer escorts, which conducted sonar and radar observation while, simultaneously, when needed, shelling enemy sites on land and providing antiaircraft defense. In her temporary role, the SC, when not leading troops to the landing site, became a utility vessel close to shore, performing a variety of functions. Although surrounded by hundreds of ships, some of them many times her size, the SC's position put her in peril, for, within easy range of enemy aircraft and shore batteries, she was little more than a radar blip among scores of vessels racing, seemingly pell-mell, in all directions. The danger of a collision increased as blacked-out ships darted about at night, the smallest ones without radar. Virtual pandemonium sometimes prevailed during night air raids and on rough seas when men on deck were sprayed with shrapnel from bursting enemy bombs or shells. Equally dangerous was falling shrapnel from friendly antiaircraft fire.

Perhaps it was fortunate that my shipmates and I could not envision what was to come when at a meeting in the Gulf of Pozzuoli on Wednesday, January 19, the captains of the escort vessels and LCTs learned a few details of plans for the invasion for which we had been practicing. We knew that action was imminent, however, when *525* made a quick dash to Pier D in Naples to take aboard additional smoke pots, then sped back to Pozzuoli.[9] On the 20th, we filled our diesel tanks by courtesy of the same British LST that had accommodated us earlier, took on a thousand gallons of fresh water from the dock, and dropped anchor in the gulf. I recorded, "This Is It. Tonight Mr. Waldron told us that we were getting underway at 0300 for the invasion. It is to be at Anzio, 95 mi. up the coast, 33 mi. from Rome." Thus the word "Anzio" first entered my vocabulary, and I rushed to a map in the chartroom.

Since leaving Bizerte on January 8, we enlisted men had figured that *SC-525* would play some role in a military operation against the Germans, but until now the officers gave us no hint of its exact nature. Every man on the ship, whether or not he was conscious of it, anticipated some degree of peril, but we had only our individual imagination to conjure up images of what that danger might be. Early on, most of us assumed that our ship would help protect an invasion force by conducting antisubmarine screening along the fleet's rim, but our participation in those practice landings northwest and south of Naples confirmed that we would be called upon to perform a variety of functions unrelated to submarine warfare. Furthermore, we had learned from accounts of survivors of the landings in Sicily and at Salerno that submarine chasers could also be equipped as sweepers to clear mines within rifle-range of the shore-based enemy. *That* would be the worst luck of the draw, and we fervently hoped to avoid it.

Various scenarios ran through my mind: our ship torpedoed at sea, bombarded from the land, and bombed from the air; our landing craft shelled and strafed; our troops mowed down as they waded ashore. The ultimate image envisioned the evacuation of a defeated army, another Dunkirk. But what sobered me most during the captain's briefing was his suggestion that any crew member who owned real estate write out a will, which he offered to witness and put in the shore mail. Vague images of endangerment thus became real; our commanding officer was telling us that we might not return from the impending mission. Several married men followed the skipper's advice. Others hastily scribbled brief letters. I imagined how shocked a wife or parent would be to receive in the mail a will or note written on the eve of a dangerous mission by a loved one from whom there had been no communication for weeks. Faced with the greatest challenge of my young life, I went to sleep with a prayer on my lips.

* * *

To understand *SC-525*'s role among the nearly four hundred ships that participated in the invasion at Anzio-Nettuno, a brief summary of plans — unknown to us at the time — may be informative.

Following the invasion of Italy at Salerno, occupation of Naples, and drive across the Volturno River in the fall of 1943, Allied troops were stopped by determined German resistance in the mountainous terrain in the vicinity of Cassino. There, behind the Gustav Line, the Nazis repulsed repeated Allied efforts to break through to the Liri Valley, the way to Rome. As fortnights dragged on with the battle stalemated, British Prime Minister Churchill proposed a leap-frog landing behind the German lines near the ancient city of Anzio, about thirty miles south of Rome. Reluctantly approved by President Franklin Roosevelt, Operation Shingle was to be initially made up of the VI Corps, consisting of the American 3rd Division, British 1st Division, and several special forces. The landing was scheduled for 0200, Saturday, January 22, 1944. Generally a landing on enemy soil was preceded by a softening up of targets ashore by aerial bombing and shelling by large ships firing from the outer perimeter of the invasion force, but to maintain the element of surprise at Anzio, there would be no naval bombardment before troops were en route to the shore.

To land the troops and provide arms and supplies in Operation Shingle, Naval Task Force 81 was placed under command of American Rear Admiral Frank J. Lowry in USS *Biscayne* (AVP-11).[10] Merging convoys of several hundred Allied ships were to transport and land the combined forces in an effort to outflank German forces blocking Allied troops at the Gustav Line. "Peter Force," mostly British, was assigned to land several miles northwest of Anzio; a smaller group (TG-81.2)—composed of three battalions of Rangers, the 509th Parachute Infantry Battalion, the 83rd Chemical Battalion, and two evacuation hospitals — was to land just east of the Anzio harbor; and "X-Ray Force," mostly American, was to land in two groups, Red (TG-81.3) and Green (TG-81.4), just southeast of Nettuno.

SC-525 was one of six 110-footers and four 173-foot PCs to assist twelve LSTs, twenty-nine LCIs, and twenty-one LCTs in landing troops on X-Ray's Red Beach. We were to be supported by one each LCG, LCF, and LCT(R) (all three British), with two LCIs and one LCT as salvage units. My ship's specific task was to help land the 7th Regiment of the 3rd Infantry Division, United States Army. Our leader of TG-81.3 [LST Group Three] was Commander William O. Floyd in *LCI-233*. Other X-Ray special-purpose units were to be included in a follow-up group of sixty-five landing ships; an escort group of seven destroyers and two minesweepers; a sweeper group of eight fleet minesweepers, fourteen yard minesweepers, and one 110-foot subchaser; and a gunfire support group of cruisers and destroyers. Initially the three forces at Anzio on January 22 were to include 36,000 troops and nearly four hundred Allied ships ranging from cruisers down to PT-boats.[11]

As H-hour approached on January 22, members of our crew were privy neither to those details nor to Operation Shingle's intricate plans that called for each of the hundreds of ships to be located at a particular spot within the roughly twenty-mile arc that encompassed the invasion fleet and its supporting vessels. Only by later study of the invasion chart did we see that X-Ray Force was assigned a rectangular area about five by ten miles, pointing seaward from the Nettuno beaches. Shielded by four fire-support areas, a large transport square was drawn from which two boat lanes, Red and Green, ran to the beach. The troop carriers were to be crowded into the square for offloading onto landing craft, and it was at Point Charlie, on the shoreward side, that each escort (SC or PC) was to gather its wards (LCVPs, DUKWs, or LCTs) and lead them through the darkness to the appropriate landing beach. After passing Point Love about a half-mile out, the escort by megaphone or signal was to wish the troops godspeed, reverse course, and return to the transport square for additional duties.

SC-525 was to be only one tiny vessel among the more than 350 ships involved in the subsequent invasion at Anzio-Nettuno, and I was only one among nearly forty thousand Allied personnel, each of whom witnessed no more than a glimpse into the larger picture of the enormous, bloody, and lengthy Operation Shingle. Furthermore, I was spared intimate sight of the sacrifices ashore of the British and American troops who withstood a cruel winter siege before fresh reinforcements eventually broke out of the beachhead four terrible months later.[12]

* * *

At Nisida promptly at 0230 on Friday, January 21, 1944, reveille sounded, and thirty-two minutes later Lieutenant McCormick entered in the log, "Anchor aweigh, underway proceeding out of harbor. 'Shingle' operation begun." *SC-525* fell in astern of *YMS-226* and ahead of *YMS-34* as we sailed out of the Gulf of Pozzuoli, around Isola d'Ischia, and into the Tyrrhenian Sea, where we were joined by *PC-626*, *PC-1227*, and *SC-639*. We then took up our position on the port quarter of a mile-long convoy of LCTs, each loaded with up to four tanks and their crew. From the southeast toward Capri, additional convoys, escorted by destroyers and cruisers, were forming farther at sea. At noon west of Isola di Ventotene, our NAS-1 convoy could see on the horizon NAM-1, made up of LSTs and LCIs, screened by *PC-551* and *-1226* and *SC-497*, *-506*, *-534*, and *-692*. Throughout the afternoon each man had his own thoughts as the crew stood four-on/four-off watches. By early evening west of Isola di Ponza, the sky was clear, the sea was calm, and good visibility revealed blacked-out ships in all directions. Only the sounds of our screws and those of our wards — and Allied aircraft overhead — broke the silence, but by 2000 we could see flashes from the mainland battle front. Two red alerts were called, but we saw only friendly planes. Now, with the enemy at our back, we had reached the point of no return.

When I remember the approach of darkness on January 21 as we sailed along the Italian

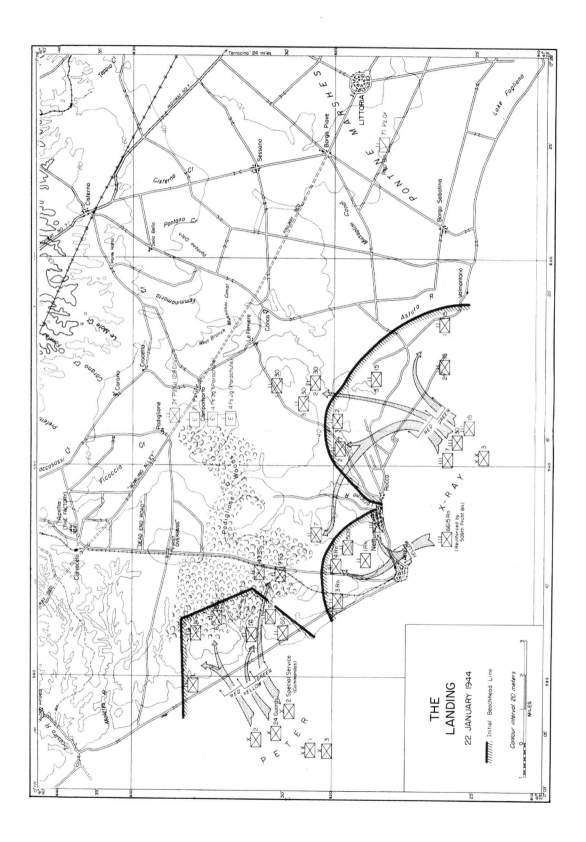

THE
LANDING
22 JANUARY 1944

////// Initial Beachhead Line

Contour interval 20 meters

MILES

coast toward an uncertain fate, I find the picture verbally captured by another subchaser's captain, who described a more serene cruise in more peaceful waters:

> The ship was darkened. Radio silence was in effect. Gun crews stood by on the 3-inch [on *SC-525* a 40-millimeter Bofors] forward and one of the 20-millimeters amidships. Another man stood by the depth-charge racks back aft. The sonar probed ahead with its long *piiiiing*. On each side of the bridge, lookouts swept the horizon ceaselessly with binoculars. Below them the helmsman kept the ordered course ... by the big, red-lighted steering compass just forward of the wheel, and to his right another man stood at the engine controls, where other red lights showed the ordered speed.... Abaft the two men and on the starboard side of the pilothouse, the chart was spread out on its table, with parallel rulers, pencils, dividers, and a stopwatch picking up the glint of the shaded red chart light on its gooseneck.[13]

Our armada moved at a maddeningly slow five and a half knots, but by midnight it was within several miles of our objective — the beaches both northwest and southeast of the twin towns of Anzio and Nettuno. Although the skies had darkened and every ship was blacked out, we could still see silhouettes of the awesome congregation of warships all around us. *SC-525* had by then maneuvered between the larger ships and the shore, so my sonar gear was secured and I had no specific battle station. Instead, I alternated between the crowded flying bridge and the equally crowded pilot house as lookout and ready handyman. We observed that the force was dividing as it approached land, the British group heading toward the beaches above Anzio and our American X-Ray Forces moving toward an area below Nettuno.[14] Lieutenant Waldron had not yet confided to the crew the *525*'s exact role except to explain that we were to lead a group of LCTs into Red Beach (to the left of Green Beach, where another force would land). We had surmised correctly that daring Allied minesweepers — twenty-three of them under direction of Commander Alfred H. Richards in USS *Pilot* (AM-104) — were surreptitiously sweeping a channel into each invasion beach.[15] We knew, however, that cutting mines from their moorings was only the first step; the live mines, whether submerged or floating, still had to be exploded lest they remain a deadly threat to the landing ships and their escorts.

The chronicler of the Navy's role in World War II, Rear Admiral Samuel Eliot Morison, described better than I those few hours as the darkened armada quietly inched toward hostile shores:

> There is nothing in warfare to be compared with the hushed tension of the final approach in a night landing. Everything ahead is uncertain. There is no sound but the rush of waters, the throbbing of your ship's engines and of your own heart. You can see nothing but the ship ahead and the ship astern. The shore, if dimly visible, is shrouded in darkness. A few mistakes on our part, or clever thrusts by the enemy, may utterly wreck a vast, long-planned effort. There can be no drawn battle, no half-success, in an amphibious landing; it is win all splendidly or lose all miserably.[16]

In real life aboard *SC-525*, the whole setting seemed surreal: Here we were within a few thousand yards of Nazi troops who were — we fervently hoped but doubted — unaware of the approaching hoards.[17] At 2002 Commander W. O. Floyd, leading Force X-Ray's Red Beach Group, sighted the flashing signal of William reference vessel; twenty-two minutes later the signal of Queen reference vessel came into view; and by 2250 our two columns had passed

Opposite: **The three landing areas at Anzio-Nettuno are shown on this map (left to right): Peter (British), Yellow (special forces), and X-Ray (American infantry). For nearly four months Allied troops seldom penetrated more than ten miles inland. No place on the beachhead or in the ships' anchorage was out of range of German guns (from *Anzio Beachhead*, Washington: Department of the Army, 1947, map 3).**

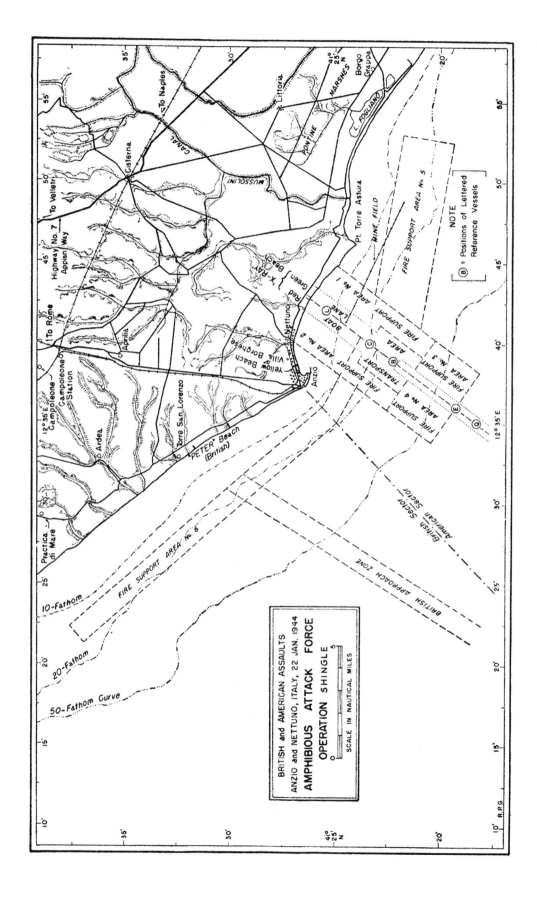

BRITISH and AMERICAN ASSAULTS
ANZIO and NETTUNO, ITALY, 22 JAN. 1944

AMPHIBIOUS ATTACK FORCE
OPERATION SHINGLE

SCALE IN NAUTICAL MILES

NOTE

Ⓑ = Positions of Lettered
Reference Vessels

both. All seemed orderly until suddenly, at 2335, an echelon of six minesweepers loomed ahead, crossing our path.[18] Entanglement was avoided when the tardy sweepers barely exited our path; our force flagship, for fear of fouling the sweep wires in her propellers, stopped engines until the trailing gear cleared. A potential betrayal of our secret approach had been averted by a matter of minutes. Instead of cussing the sweepers, however, we should have sympathized with the ships working in the dark as described later by Admiral Morison: "These three units, executing crowded sweep patterns in assigned areas, were like so many platoons of infantry trying to avoid collision in a darkened drill hall."[19]

At twelve minutes before midnight came the command "Stop!" We had arrived in the transport area within five nautical miles of the sandy beach below Nettuno. The sound of engines was replaced by the clanking of anchor chains, and the Red Beach scout boat was lowered from *LST-197*. By 0112, when the boat signaled that it was in position in the boat lane near Point Charlie, the LCVPs had been lowered by davit, and twenty-eight of them — each carrying three dozen members of the 7th Regiment of the 3rd Infantry Division — were speeding toward an uncertain encounter with the enemy.[20] Wave One was escorted by two PCs, two SCs, two LCSs, and one LCG. The other escorts stood by quietly and expectantly as successive waves were signaled. The next two hours would be among the most wrenching of my naval career as *SC-525* awaited the call for Wave Eight, scheduled at 0400. I had no way of knowing that the wait would be worse than the deed.

Any thought that may have been running through my mind was interrupted at 0149 when *LCT(R)-140* loosed her 798 five-inch rockets with their distinctive swish-swish launch and boom-boom landing, accompanied by a premature daybreak of orange and pink. The ear-splitting, ship-rocking sounds lasted for fifty seconds, almost simultaneous with deafening rocket explosions also on Peter Beach.[21] The aim of our X-Ray launcher was so accurate that only three rockets were reported to have fallen short — those too close for comfort to the crew of *PC-551* near which they fell. The invasion of Anzio was underway.

The first four LCVPs of Red Beach's Wave One landed undetected on a true beach one minute before the scheduled hour of 0200 on January 22, 1944, and the other two dozen landed within three minutes — a remarkable feat of timing.[22] Wave Two — twenty-two LCVPs led by *SC-692* and three other patrol craft and one LCS — encountered floating mines a mile from shore but landed safely ten minutes later, bringing the number of American soldiers on Red Beach alone to about 1,800.

Wave Three, consisting of twelve LCIs and two LCTs, beached by 0245, and all of them put their troops ashore and retracted within about an hour despite enemy machine gunfire from shore. However, six of them were so late in backing off that Wave Four (sixteen LCIs) was squeezed, helping account for one minor collision. *LCT-32*, one of Wave Five's four LCTs led by *SC-639*, became separated and did not beach until 0420, after eighty-eight DUKWs in Wave Six had begun landing. One DUKW foundered and sank, but its crew was rescued by another DUKW and put aboard *PC-1226*.[23] Further disaster was averted when Wave Seven (eight LCTs) proceeded on schedule without its leader, *SC-534*, which, after landing Wave One, failed to arrive in time to lead in the new group.

Opposite: **This map more clearly shows *SC-525*'s task during the invasion. We gathered our seven LCTs, loaded with men of the Seventh Regiment of the Third Division, at Reference Vessel Baker, then led them through the minefield from Point Charlie to Point Love. From there the landing craft proceeded independently to Red Beach. Our ship was then assigned to supervise the unloading of other LCTs (National Archives).**

Our moment with destiny had arrived. At exactly 0400, accompanied by *LCF-4, SC-525* began organizing seven LCTs — loaded with tanks and their crews — into a column for Wave Eight, and a half hour later we began leading them through the swept channel to within sight of the flashing lights of Red Beach. Suddenly, there was gunfire and confusion: Several mines, cut from their moorings by the sweepers but not yet detonated, floated into the swept channel, and nearby PT-boats began firing at them across our column. Without our captain's knowledge, our last two LCTs had been ordered by the wave control officer to hold up and await mine-clearance. This broke apart our column and forced *525* — after sending the first five landing craft onto the beach — to return through heavy traffic and mined waters to Point Charlie and round up the two detained vessels. Consequently, it was not until 0615 that the last of our seven LCTs beached. Lieutenant Waldron was furious, but he was completely vindicated by Vice-Admiral H. K. Hewitt, who later wrote, "... the Wave Commander should not have stopped the two landing craft waves from beaching because of the presence of floating mines in the lanes. Since the destruction of the mines was attempted by gunfire, the fire power from the landing craft would have been more effective than that from the PT boats."[24] Thus our skipper bore no responsibility for the delay in landing the last LCTs of the eighth wave. Wave Nine — the last to be assigned a definite landing time — also was held up by the control offer; consequently, two LSTs with pontoons (to be used as floating mobile piers or causeways) beached nearly an hour late. Fortune was with us, however, for if the machine guns that attacked Wave Three had not been silenced, the control officer's error could have led to a disaster.

Two tugs, HMS *Prosperous* and HMS *Thruster,* arrived about sunrise with the first follow-up convoy of four LCTs that landed on the beach and six LSTs that were unloaded by pontoon causeway. *SC-525,* after completing our original assignment, was put in charge of *LCT-32, -33,* and *-204* that were helping LSTs discharge their troops and tanks. Sandbars nearly 400 feet from the coast blocked some of the larger ships from reaching the beach. However, by "marrying" a smaller LCT to a stranded LST, men and vehicles could be transferred from the ramp of the larger vessel to the ramp of the smaller one. The LCT then backed off, turned, and carried its load to the beach, returning repeatedly for other loads. In this way on D-Day alone we participated in the unloading of 27,000 American and 9,000 British troops and 3,200 tons of vehicles, equipment, and ammunition at the beachhead.

Some of the tensions experienced during the ensuing dozen hours are documented by *SC-525's* selected log entries:

0815, Fired on floating mine. 0843, Enemy planes over beach.... 0930, Heading back to point 800 yards off shore to again supervise LCTs. 1035, Red alert. 1347, All clear. No planes sighted. 1438, Put in charge of LCTs while Comdr. Ritchie [of the Royal Navy] was at beaches checking progress of unloading. 1600, Lying to about one mile off beach just west of Red Beach. Sea calm, visibility good. Frequent sounds of gunnery inland. 1715, Informed LCTs that unloading would continue day and night. 1730, All hands at General Quarters. 1810, Started Radar. Position about 207 T. from Capo d'Anzio and 020 from top-heavy tower on beach. Depth of water, 30 feet. Ship being carried very slowly to sea. Keeping position on moored Liberty.

Between the same hours, Commander Floyd recorded a dozen red alerts, including these entries:

0818, Bombs falling in sea near Anzio. 0845, Fourteen Focke-Wulf-190s bombed Red Beach. Causeway unloading *LST-384* struck and several vehicles set afire. 4 Navy, 4 SeaBee and 24 Army men wounded. One plane shot down by the heavy AA barrage. Fires in vehicles quickly extinguished by fire party aboard *LST-384....* 1008, Enemy aircraft attacking Red Beach. Met by heavy AA fire. Several bombs fell in water.... 1043, Five aircraft bombing X-Ray beaches. One bomb struck *LCI(L)-20*, which was beached, near stern, starting oil fire which spread to after magazines.... 1208, Two ME-109s were met by heavy barrage.

The image of the German cross, painted under the wings of Nazi bombers, would be burned into our memories from that day forward. The commander's accounts, however, were limited to the landings at Red Beach; similar attacks were taking place simultaneously at Green Beach a mile or so to the southeast.

Activity all around us was so frenetic on D-Day that at 1010 Lieutenant McCormick failed to record in the log our role as stunned eye-witnesses to a tragedy of the first order. Only a few hundred feet from us, off Torre Astura, a submerged mine struck the stern of USS *Portent* (AM-106), sending up billows of black smoke and a 150-foot-tall column of white water. The ship quickly began to settle as several nearby small craft, including our sister ship *SC-692*, risked their own safety by speeding into the minefield to rescue the captain, Lieutenant Howard C. Plummer of Beaumont, Texas, and more than seventy-five officers and enlisted men as they abandoned ship. *SC-497* bravely exploded other floating mines while survivors were fished out of the freezing water. I stood on our flying bridge and watched helplessly as the smoking 221-foot minesweeper gently sank stern-first and, at the same time, slowly rolled onto her starboard side until the ship was literally upside-down. While the men in the water were being rescued, a lone sailor, presumably fearing the suction as *Portent* gradually went under, clung tenaciously to the twisting deck, then to the slippery port side, and finally to the keel of the down-turned bow. In effect, he clambered from the top of the ship to its bottom, which finally faced skyward. He clung there until a small boat came and plucked him to safety. It was a scene that I will never forget, and I regret that I did not have my camera in hand or make an effort to discover the name of the courageous sailor who pulled off the dangerous feat as if he were a circus performer. We were to learn later that eighteen men were killed, some imprisoned below deck. The protruding bow remained for days a visual reminder of the danger of mines even to the vessels designed to destroy them. Back in Washington, the name of the *Portent* was included in a short Navy Department release, dated March 31, announcing the loss of "eleven small U.S. vessels" in the Mediterranean. Small to the press, but large and special to us.

Naval personnel aboard ship knew little of what was going on ashore, but the continued pouring of troops onto the beaches emboldened us to believe that the invasion was going well. Beginning with machine-gun bursts that met Wave Three, the sound of explosions became more distinct after daylight. Smoke in the roadstead periodically cleared, enabling us to see puffs from artillery and bombs at the front. We also watched as colorful buildings disintegrated into clouds of dust as Kraut gunners found their mark, and we quickly learned the crying-cat sound of 88-millimeter shells hurled from beyond the limits of the beachhead. Only later we learned that within hours enough debris has been cleared from the port of Anzio to permit the first LST to dock, and that the three landing forces had pushed inland against weak opposition, forming oyster-shell enclaves. By that evening, the three forces joined, 36,000 Allied soldiers and 3,200 vehicles were ashore, and 227 Germans had been captured, all at a cost of 13 British and American Army men killed, 97 wounded, and 44 missing.[25] In the next forty-eight hours, the British advanced about seven miles, capturing the industrial complex of Aprilia (known by Allied troops as "the Factory"), and American forces approached the strategic city of Cisterna before being repulsed. The enemy had reacted with alacrity and immense force, and, unknown to us at the time, the beachhead would remain under siege for four bloody months. During that seemingly interminable period, our news came chiefly from

Allied radio reports, characteristically optimistic; word-of-mouth scuttlebutt transmitted between ships' crews, notoriously unreliable; and Axis Sally, whose contemptuousness increased as the weeks dragged on.[26]

In a letter home, written exactly two years later while returning from Japan on USS *Strive* (AM-117), I reminisced about D-Day at Anzio: "That day, more than any other in my life, stands out most clearly. That day, I saw a lot and learned more, probably than any other single day in the Navy. It is just as vivid as if it were yesterday." After describing the loss of *LCI-20* and *Portent*, I added,

> There were the humerous [sic] sights too — for instance when the SC sweeper *770* went into the breakwater to clear the entrance for troop ships. No sooner than she had streamed [minesweeping] gear, the Jerries started sending 88s out of the wooded yards of Villa Borghese and laid a half dozen of them right off her stern. I have never seen a little ship so wigglesome as the *770* was for the next few minutes. She made a complete circle in a third the diameter and took off like a bat from a hot chimney. And the old *Cinq-Deux-Cinq* did a little wiggling on her own during the night when those flares hung overhead and there was no way of getting out from under them.

The latter comment referred to parachuted flares and starshells released from German planes at night to light up the anchorage, exposing to their bombers and strafers the exact location of our ships. We hated the floating lights that seemed immune from the efforts of irritated gunners, who wasted an enormous amount of ammunition in a fruitless effort to shoot them down. Fortunately, barrage balloons tethered above many of our ships deterred enemy planes from flying very low, and after bursts of antiaircraft fire, a standard joke among gunners was "I may not have hit a Jerry, but I sure brought down one of those balloons." My reminiscence continued:

> I remember how we used to sit around the guns watching the bursting glow on the beach. Occasionally an ammo dump would go up and it looked like a giant fair with fireworks. The night ... continually burst into flame. Rarely did we realize that each of those bursts meant one or more less Germans or Americans or British. And no one can tell me that the Jerries suffered more heavily than we at the Beachhead. As I have mentioned before, our greatest threat, on the ship, was the 88s and larger shells that continually, for months landed in the anchorage, and the continuous air-raids, mostly with flares and starshells at night. There was little sleeping at Anzio, but I have always been thankful that I was on board ship rather than in a muddy foxhole or behind a stump. And another thing, if the Jerries had forced our troops into the sea, as seemed very reasonable at times during the January-May ordeal, we would be already on the waters headed for safe harbors.

During D-Day, as mentioned in my reminiscence, we lost a second American ship when a flock of Focke-Wulf fighter-bombers raided the anchorage. A 500-pound bomb made a direct hit on *LCI-20*, settling the craft on the sand. The British fighter-director ship *Palomares* hit a mine and had to be towed back to Naples. The invasion, which went so well the first few hours, was turning serious for the Navy. During ensuing days, the Nazis generally chose the hour before sunrise or sunset for their deadliest work, their aircraft coming in from the west in late afternoon or east in the morning. Gunners, facing the oncoming planes, had difficulty seeing them through the blinding backlit sun. Grave humor led us to describe the approaching sundown as "The Happy Hour."

D+1 (Sunday, January 23) was spiced up by seven Nazi air attacks, two of which materialized into bombs in the X-Ray sector. Of eight planes that attacked Red Beach in a single raid, one was shot down by *LCF-4*'s 40-millimeter guns. During the day *SC-525* was released to the Green Beach Group to supervise *LCT-32*, *-33*, *-34*, *-35*, *-203*, *-204*, and *-333* in unloading LSTs and merchant vessels. We went alongside *LST-327* for a bountiful supply of provisions without knowing that the generous Coast Guard-manned ship would enter my life again three days later. We narrowly escaped being rammed by an LCT headed directly toward us; only the sound of the danger signal saved us. Unanticipated enemies began to appear: German small boats variously referred to as E-boats, R-boats, S-boats, F-lighters, and 30-knot Italian MAS torpedo boats taken over by the Germans. Fortunately for us at Red Beach, the enemy boats were more troublesome to the Peter sector. We would encounter them later.

Almost simultaneously, to the northwest off Peter Beach, German HE-111 planes with radio-guided bombs and aerial torpedoes attacked two British destroyers, sending HMS *Janus* to the bottom with the loss of 159 officers and men and blowing off the bow of HMS *Jervis*. The irrepressible humor of fighting men even in the face of tragedy was exhibited when a whaleboat of survivors of the *Janus,* approaching their sister ship, burst into the saloon song, "Roll Out the Barrel."[27]

A dozen or so destroyers ("tin cans"), as well as the cruiser, USS *Brooklyn*, lobbed shells over the anchorage onto German positions resisting Allied troops. In return, ships offshore were constantly threatened by German gunners, for whom the anchorage was never beyond their range during the next four months. To sailors, this shelling was more nerve-racking than bombing; at least there was usually a "Red Anzio!" radio alert when an enemy plane was spotted, but whoosh-whoosh "Screamin' Meemies" from 150-millimeter six-barreled Nebelwerfer rocket launchers gave little advance warning but left an auditory reminder never to be forgotten. Still, naval invasion and support forces suffered less damage from land-based firing than from mines and bombs.

The weather deteriorated rapidly on D+2, Monday, January 24, when, inexplicably and despite illuminated markings to identify them clearly as hospital ships, three British humanitarian vessels were attacked by the Luftwaffe. *St. David* was sunk with loss of ninety-six lives,[28] and *Leinster* and *St. Andrew* suffered near-misses. During the day the cruiser *Brooklyn* also survived several near-misses. In the late afternoon and evening, about a hundred German planes of several types attacked the transport area, dropping flares and bombs. The destroyer *Plunkett* (DD-431) was struck with the loss of more than fifty men but stayed afloat, and minesweeper *Prevail* (AM-107) shot down three planes before receiving a hit that wounded thirteen. *Mayo* (DD-422), after shelling a military building on shore and shooting down a Jerry, struck a mine that killed several and wounded two dozen men, and the destroyer was taken under tow to Naples.[29] That night strong winds again played havoc with the landing beaches, driving several craft and causeways on the beach.

Unlike most warships, our small and fast subchaser could dart around the crowded anchorage, so during those first two days and nights *SC-525*, when not directing the unloading of other ships, served as a sort of water-taxi or communications vessel, carrying orders or personnel from ship to ship or just standing by for emergency action such as picking up survivors. One night we took a position along the swept channel so that LCVPs and other craft could be guided by our stern light, visible only seaward. Nearly every ship in the anchorage changed positions each evening to foil a small high-flying German plane that flew over at noon photographing locations of various vessels. We could do nothing to block the daylight view of the anchorage from the German observation posts high in Colli Laziali, which we called the Alban Hills.

In "Anzio: A Brief Memoir," written March 1 while I was recuperating in the 118th Station Hospital in Naples, I reminisced further about those first three days at Anzio:

There were many exciting moments when MEs & FW-190s & Stukas came right over us & missed us by a matter of yards. I proved to my satisfaction that there was something in me that I

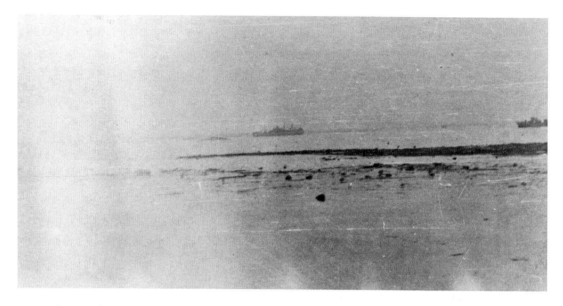

Only one of my photographs taken during the invasion of Anzio survived a Sicilian studio's disastrous processing — this badly fogged view of what I remember as the remains of *YMS-30*, which was exploded and sunk by a mine on January 25. Although this is the worst photograph in the book, it is also one of the most important because of the circumstances under which it was salvaged.

had doubted was there. Since we weren't using sound, I had no G.Q. station, so I took over the imaginary job of ship's photographer with my oft-abused 35 mm. Kodak. I hope some of the pictures are good.[30] I continuously ran from the gun deck to the flying bridge for shots at sinking ships, Nazis coming in, and tracer fire. I'll never forget the dogfight the night of Jan. 24 and then seeing the blazing JU-88 explode as it glided to earth. And those two Allied fighters — a P-40 & a Spit — which made a dive to earth after the pilots bailed out. It was a beautiful show.

In retrospect, "beautiful" seemed a strange adjective for such a dangerous engagement.

There was no respite on D+3, Tuesday, the 25th, as *SC-525* lay at anchor, attacked by shells from beyond Allied lines and strafing and bombing from the air. Lashed by increasingly heavy waves, we were also in danger of dragging anchor and being blown into mine-infested waters. That threat horribly manifested itself when *YMS-30* carried down its skipper, Lieutenant (jg) Thomas E. Garner (of Memphis), and sixteen members of his crew. In a re-sweeping operation to protect the heavy fire-support destroyers off Nettuno, the vessel struck a mine at about 1630. Commander Arnold Lott described the scene: "There was the usual fearsome blasts of flame and smoke, and by the time men on other ships turned to watch, all they saw was pieces of *YMS-30* tumbling back into the water. The explosion split the ship open like a pea pod...."[31] *SC-692*-and *YMS-62* and *-69* risked their own safety in rescuing survivors, but efforts to put the wounded aboard *LST-348* were delayed because of the vicious sea. The wood-hulled minesweeper had been under *SC-525*'s command during our first weeks in Oran, so we felt that we had lost members of our family. Saved by a piece of floating wood was a young man named Niles who would write letters for me when we shared a hospital ward in Naples two weeks later.[32]

Bombing continued throughout the day, and *PC-676* was damaged by a near-miss. Nearer to Naples the Liberty ship *F.A.C. Muhlenberg* was damaged by a near-miss that killed seven. During the evening of a bad day, the weather continued to deteriorate ominously; the winds grew stronger, the sea heavier, and the threat from the air no lighter. Ernie Pyle graphically described small vessels such as ours in similarly bad weather during the invasion of Sicily: "The little subchasers ... would disappear completely into the wave troughs as we watched them. The next moment they would be carried so high they seemed to leap clear out of the water."[33]

Other images and smells of those four days and nights remain vivid two-thirds of a century later. Under normal conditions, the umbrella of silver-colored barrage balloons floating above hundreds of ships might have resembled a twenty-mile-wide circus tent, but in fact the sky was filled during daytime with chemical smoke and at night by flashes from our own antiaircraft tracers and from exploding German shells or bombs. We seemed to live in perpetual twilight. Yet, at night the beachhead sometime resembled a rising sun. Black smoke, billowing from scores of generators operating onboard and pots floating nearby, sought to block the enemy's view of the fleet, but winds continually wafted the stifling stuff back into our faces and onto the decks. Most disagreeably, crews could not escape the acrid, greasy residue that penetrated our nostrils, eyes, ears, and hair. The stench seemed to permeate food, mostly sandwiches eaten on the run. For those of us on small vessels without fresh-water showers, the sleaziness was almost as unbearable as threats from enemy weapons.

Sleep was illusive also because the ship was never out of range of German gunners, and nearby airfields enabled enemy planes to swoop in at night with virtually no advance notice, thus eluding Allied fighters based a hundred miles away. Particularly unwelcome to the troops were "Popcorn Petes," the nickname given to Nazi bombers that flew over at night dropping thousand-pound bombs that exploded high up, expelling additional, delayed-action, antipersonnel grenades that detonated, like a string of Chinese firecrackers, just before hitting the ground.[34] During the first two weeks of the landings, the Luftwaffe conducted 277 raids on the port and roadstead, but Allied pilots shot down 65 planes to the enemy's 20 in the first ten days.[35] Even when occasionally the weapons were silenced and smoking abated, the dizzying movement and noise from scores of ships constantly moving around the anchorage made restful sleep extremely difficult. Smoke, tension, and exhaustion combined to weaken the very psyche, and the weather, so favorable for the initial landings, turned vicious on D+3. For the men ashore, conditions were much worse. For four months, the specter of a second Dunkirk lay in the back of many Allied minds.

The most memorable day of my naval career began at five minutes after midnight on the morning of D+4, Wednesday, January 26. George Klumpp and I, with virtually no sleep because of the tragedies of the day and the violent heaving of the bow, were a few minutes late for our graveyard watch. As we emerged from the forward compartment, Lieutenant Waldron, spying us near the bow anchor, yelled from the flying bridge, "Klumpp, Jones, hoist anchor!" That was an unmistakable, emergency order — petty officer rating notwithstanding — and we understood instantly that *525* was in danger of dragging anchor and perhaps colliding with a mine or another ship in the dark, raging sea. We knew the drill, so through the salty spray we fought our way up to the two-handled manual winch, released the lock, and began cranking. When the iron chain straightened and we felt the tug of the anchor as it separated from the sea floor, its weight seeming to increase with each wave that jerked the bow upward, we strained with every turn until one of us grunted, "Let's rest." George, sensing instantly that the safety catch had not engaged, jerked his hands back. Instead of letting go, I desperately tried to hold on. When a towering whitecap violently struck the port bow, the handles spun backward quicker than I could turn loose. Let the ship's log tell the story: "0030, Hand winch broke down, injuring JONES, Houston G., SoM3c, USNR. Both hands were broken when handles spun around to hit him."

My injury so unnerved the crew that it was thirty-five minutes before two strong-armed men succeeded in bringing up the anchor and enabling the ship to get underway to ride out the turbulence. By that time George Klumpp and Bernard Phau, PhM1c, had helped me to the aft compartment (I have no idea how they carried me down the vertical ladder) and given me the heaviest permissible dose of morphine in an effort to lessen the excruciating pain. Phau's preliminary examination confirmed that the left thumb was crushed and lying across the palm, and at least two metacarpels were broken in the right hand. Although "Pills" wrapped my hands, he made no attempt to set the broken bones, for he knew that was a task for a physician. Almost as bad as the pain was the nausea produced by the morphine and the constant pitching of the ship.

Although I was hardly conscious of what was going on beyond my ship, the 26th was another terrible day for the Allies at sea. *LCI-32*, now very familiar to us, went down with thirty men after hitting a mine. Ironically, she was attempting to rescue survivors from HMS *LST-422*, whose ammunition exploded following contact with another mine; 454 American soldiers, most of them from the 83rd Chemical Mortar Battalion, plus 29 British crewmen, were lost.[36] In a 30-knot wind, 35-degree rolls, and heavy sleet, about 150 survivors were rescued by the *Pilot* (AM-104), *Strive* (AM-117), and other vessels that braved the mine-infested waters. Even so, at daylight the rain-lashed waters were strewn with scores of corpses and a few freezing survivors. During the past two days, the violent storm had driven onto the beach one LST, more than a dozen LCTs, and several pontoon causeways. HMS *LST-366* and two Liberty ships — *Hilary A. Herbert* and *John Banvard* — were bombed.

Heavily doped up, I of course was oblivious of these additional tragedies, but my emotions burst forth during a noon air raid when I was told that I would be leaving my ship. The deck log read, "1400, Heading into Anzio Harbor to put JONES into the care of medical officer. 1425, Tied up alongside *LST-327* in harbor. 1438, JONES, Houston G., SoM3c, USNR transferred to *LST-327* for treatment and hospitalization."[37] Even under the haze of painkillers, I was crying within because I was leaving the twenty-six men whom I had come to consider my family. Watching my medical records handed to a stranger on another ship made me fear the future, for I had no assurance that I would return to *Cinq-Deux-Cinq* even if she survived the murderous Nazi attacks on the fleet at the Anzio Beachhead. I imagined the Krauts giving me a nasty send-off when two more air attacks occurred before either *SC-525* or *LST-327* could escape the confinement of the lethal little harbor.

Even if I had known that my commanding officer had taken the time that afternoon to make the following entry in my service record during the almost continuous air raids, I would have been in no condition to fully appreciate its meaning: "JONES, Houston G., SoM3c, V-6, USNR, Commended for duty well performed while actively engaging the enemy in establishing a beach-head near the town of Nettuno, Italy, during the period from 21 January 1944 to 26 January 1944."

7

"No-Hands Ward Ambassador"

January-March 1944

I have only a hazy memory of being assisted from *SC-525* onto the dock in Anzio harbor, through the febrile activity of unloading ships in the midst of still another air attack, and into the enormous open mouth of *LST-327*, from which tanks and fresh troops had just emerged. The down-ramp rested on the pier, giving off squawking sounds as the vessel rose and twisted with the waves. Records indicate that I was checked in and evaluated by Lieutenant W. E. McIlvain of the Navy's Medical Corps, who assigned me to an orderly and a bunk. Heavily sedated, I was in and out of sleep during the overnight voyage through the still-raging sea toward Pozzuoli, but I recall tender attention given every wounded man who occupied the bunks stacked one above the other. Most of the wounded were in much worse shape than I, and some did not survive the night. The soldiers just disembarked from this landing craft were already on their way to the bloody battle lines within earshot of the harbor, so, even in pain, I counted my blessings for being a sailor rather than a soldier.[1]

My conscience could hardly have borne the sadness had I known, that night, that some of the medical personnel who comforted me on the way to Pozzuoli would be among the twenty-one men killed and twenty-six seriously wounded when this Coast Guard-manned *LST-327* was torpedoed off Normandy exactly — to the day — seven months later.[2] I wish I had recorded names in addition to Lieutenant McIlvain's. My effort to communicate with any of them on the Internet more than sixty years later was unsuccessful.

Having been in Naples previously only long enough to pick up smoke pots at the dock, my thoughts rambled as we sailed along the morning of January 27: "I've always wanted to see Naples, but not like this." Despite grogginess, by the time *LST-327* docked at Pozzuoli, from where I had left in full vigor just six days earlier, I was ambulatory as long as someone went ahead to open doors. Instead of taking up ambulance space, several other walking patients and I were driven by army truck to Naples and through its narrow streets to the winding Corso Vittorio Emanuele. I had no sense of direction when I was admitted to the Army's 118th Station Hospital, a huge masonry structure, before the war an Italian military hospital with vaulted wards, some as narrow as tunnels, others as wide as basketball courts. Although the 500-bed hospital had been operated by the United States Medical Corps only since October 14, 1943, it appeared to be well-equipped and staffed.[3] Nor was I aware that a typhus fever epidemic was raging in the city and that a quarantine was in effect. That wouldn't have bothered me, because I couldn't go anywhere without a doorkeeper.

CITY OF ANZIO

CERTIFICATE OF HONOUR

TO
THOSE WHO FOUGHT SO VALIANTLY, WITHOUT FEARING FOR THEIR
OWN LIVES, ON THE BEACHHEAD DURING THE BATTLE OF ANZIO

LEST WE FORGET

Houston Jones

ANZIO BEACHHEAD RESEARCH AND DOCUMENTATION CENTER
ANZIO BEACHHEAD MUSEUM

The President
Patrizio Colantuono

ANZIO 22th January 2004

A certificate presented upon my return to the beachhead sixty years later bears a photograph of a landing ship docked in Anzio harbor. It was through the open ramp of *LST-327*, much like this one and near this very spot, that I was evacuated to the hospital in Naples on January 26, 1944.

The 118th Station Hospital, Corso Vittorio Emanuele, Naples, where I spent six weeks during the healing of hands broken during the invasion at Anzio. Each day from my ward, I looked out toward Mount Vesuvius, which erupted two weeks after I was discharged (Center for Archival Collections, Bowling Green State University).

My surgical ward, S210, with Captain Fuller B. Whitworth as ward surgeon, was lined with head-to-wall beds on two sides. In addition, a long twin row of head-to-foot beds, pushed closely together, extended down the center of the room. I was given one of the latter beds, Number 39, and with the help of sedatives I slept soundly, oblivious of the groans and moans that would break the silence of my days and nights for the next six weeks.

A poorly duplicated copy of my medical record, now on file with the Veterans Administration, reported the circumstances of the accident and described the examination:

Marked swelling of both hands with maximum tenderness right hand over base, 2nd and 3rd metacarpals, left hand tender over base of thumb and 2nd phalanx of thumb.... Radiographic examination of the bones of both hands reveal a chip fracture in the base of the proximal phalanx of the first finger left hand with a dislocation laterally and palmar of the first metacarpal of the left hand. There is a fracture, oblique complete, through the middle third of the shaft of the second metacarpal right hand and a fracture, oblique, complete through the lower third of the shaft of the third metacarpal right hand. There is a [___]iding of the distal fragment and [___]er displacement of the fracture of the third metacarpal.

The next day I was put to sleep with sodium pentothal, and the bones in my hands were straightened out and set by A. Lowell Randall, a thirty-two-year-old podiatrist from Marysville, Ohio. The left thumb, which had been forced over the palm, was wrested back into place, and the bones of the right hand were realigned but with a hump in the metacarpal leading to the index finger. Both hands and forearm were encased in plaster casts, and I was put back in Bed 39. Awake, I light-heartedly complained that it was just my luck to have my hands operated on by a foot doctor.[4]

As days passed and the pain lessened and my sense of balance improved, I began to feel guilty lying in bed, for I was a perfectly normal twenty-year-old with useless hands. Well, not quite useless, for the doctor, intentionally or not, had excluded from the cast the small finger on my right hand. I soon learned how much could be done — and could not be done — with a single finger. For example, in the latrine I could walk up to the urinal and open my pajama flap, and I could undo the string belt of my pajamas when I needed to use the commode; however, I could not pull up the garment or retie the knot. At first I was accompanied by an orderly, but it seemed demeaning for him to stand around while I had a bowel movement. The alternative was to ask for help from whoever happened to be sharing the latrine, but how embarrassing to ask a battle-scarred soldier or sailor to stoop down in front of my privates and pull up my pajamas for me! As humiliating as the quandary was, my handicap became a laughing matter when several of the other ambulatory patients with perfectly good hands were jokingly accused of volunteering for the arduous task for reasons other than kindness. Initially, such insinuative humor was not amusing to a sheltered boy from the farm, but of necessity I blushed, swallowed my pride, laughed with the troops, and threatened to devise a dollar-per-chance lottery to choose "handy" assistants for my latrine visits.

"Handlessness" had another unintended result: The name by which I have been called since 1944 was pinned on me by a tough Texas airman who occupied the bed pushed up against mine. Having noticed my full name, he played with my initials and exclaimed, loud enough for others to hear, "H.G.J. H.G.J. Hands Gone Jones!" With that quip, Houston became H.G. The airman's name was Joe H. Johnson of J-Bar-L Ranch near Guthrie, Texas. He was older and wiser and more wounded than I, but we developed a good relationship. The casts prevented me from dealing cards, but he figured that we needed a diversion, so he borrowed a chess board and put it over the crack separating our beds. I could pick up a light chess piece by gripping it between my single free finger and the right-hand cast. Joe had a poor student, but I accepted the challenge, learned the game, and endured defeat after defeat. Discouraged, I argued that he ought to build my confidence by letting me win occasionally, but he responded that to be successful, one had to learn to accept defeat gracefully. And he gave me repeated opportunities to yield gracefully. Maybe tomorrow, he'd promise. Tomorrow never came, but before I left the hospital he had taught me how to play a good game — even though he never gave me the pleasure of defeating him. From that point on, I enjoyed teaching other patients to play, but I was a little more generous than my teacher. That may explain why, when I eventually returned to the ship, I took such delight in defeating George Klumpp, Lieutenant McCormick, and anyone else who dared to take me on. Never having been an athlete, I had found a game in which I excelled. And I owed my prowess to an unmerciful cowboy-turned-airman from Texas whose life had been spared in a bloody aerial fight in Italy.

I was not the only sailor in Ward S210, but most of the patients were members of the Army or Air Force. Included were several members of the 509th Parachute Infantry Battalion who counted themselves fortunate to have reached the hospital. Despite its name, the battalion was not parachuted into Anzio Beachhead; instead, the men went into Yellow Beach with the Rangers as foot soldiers and in the next two months suffered tragically. For example, Jim Nixon was one of only twenty-three survivors of Company B of the 509th when the Germans overwhelmed and slaughtered most of the company near Carano.[5] The fact that I was among heroes added to my initial sense of inferiority.

All around me lay men horribly wounded, some without limbs, others with wounds that required dressing several times a day. Especially troubling were those whose physical wounds were coupled with hallucinatory images of their ordeal on the battlefield or in ship sinkings. Although the orderlies and nurses were attentive, there were too few helpers to promptly respond to every call. As I became more active on my feet, I developed a habit of walking around and chatting whenever another patient seemed to be in the mood to talk, for I saw that many calls were made less for medical attention than for conversation with another human. Those who were bedridden no doubt envied my ability and freedom to walk around, and it occurred to me that even without hands I could in many cases be of help. For example, if someone else placed a tray on my outstretched arms, I could take it to a patient and carefully slide it onto his bedside table. Or if magazines were stuck under my arms, I could walk them to another bed and drop them.[6] Soon, some long-timers seemed to prefer my help to that of the hospital staff. Combined, my freedom of movement and ability to be of help gave me enormous satisfaction, and instead of being inconvenienced when someone called out, "Hey, H. G., get your ass over here!" I felt that I really was performing a service. My role as "an extra hand without hands" came to the attention of the chaplain, Captain D.L. Ostergren, with whom I developed a warm friendship. He called me his "No-hands Ward Ambassador."

Yet, as independent as I was (except in the latrine), there were two additional tasks that I could not perform: I could not feed myself, and I could not write. The orderlies or other patients fed me and brought me liquids containing a straw, but for an inveterate note-taker, the second handicap was almost unbearable. However, I remembered the writing services that the American Red Cross offered in New York, Casablanca, and Oran. So, shortly after my arrival at the hospital, a young ARC representative named Helen Maier appeared and offered to help me contact my family back in the States. On January 30, I dictated to her a V-Mail message addressed to my parents; it read:

> I hope that my not writing in the past two weeks has not caused you any worry. We were out on some rather important operations and were unable to hit port. During these operations, I injured my hands and am now in a station hospital in Italy. It is nothing serious so there is no use worrying over me. However, I am unable to write for myself and it will be sometime before I'll be able to do so. Therefore, don't expect to hear from me very often for some time. This is a very good hospital and am getting fine care. Don't worry. Write often (same address). Lots of love, Houston (by Helen Maier, ARC).

Shortly afterward, I dictated and Helen sent a brief cablegram. There were no telephones and no telegraph delivery in my Caswell County farm community, so the message had to be mailed from the nearest Western Union office in Danville; consequently, it did not reach my family until February 7. My Red Cross friend also addressed to my parents a hand-drawn valentine, picturing a map of Italy partially hidden behind a double-paneled heart and the words "1944 Valentine Greetings." The card passed the army censor with no deletions, so folks back home learned that I was in Italy and correctly suspected that I had been in the invasion at Anzio.

My next letter was handwritten by a young sailor with whom I felt an instant affinity, for I *may* have seen him previously — from the flying bridge of my subchaser the day before I was injured. His surname was Niles, a motor machinist's mate second class, who had survived the sinking of *YMS-30*.[7] The explosion propelled him into the sea, and his unconscious body was rescued from a piece of floating wood. He had no memory from the instant of the explosion until he awoke near me, and thus did not know who had saved him. Although Niles had not been seriously injured physically, his conversation indicated that he had suffered slight brain damage. I spent many hours talking with him, trying to prompt him when he could not quite put into words what he wished to express. Still, on February 5, I dictated and he wrote for me a perfectly legible letter to my parents, reading in part:

> I am still in the army hospital in Italy. And I am getting along fine. My hands are still in a caste [*sic*] and they will probably remain in the caste [*sic*] for two more weeks. They do not bother me except for the inconvenience. We get good treatment here.
>
> My ship has gone back to Africa and I really miss the old bunch. However, they will be back to pick me up befor [*sic*] long. This letter will under go army censorship so I am afraid to say much about our part in the recent invasion. But, when I get back on the ship maybe I can write the whole story.

Captain Ostergren typed the envelope for my letter, signed it as army censor, and added a six-cent airmail stamp. Friends, life's most valuable assets!

Joe, my Texas bed-neighbor, though perfectly capable of writing his own letters, perceptively observed the pride with which my new friend had penned my letter, so he hinted that he'd appreciate a similar favor. Niles quickly accepted the invitation, and soon the survivor of *YMS-30* became a "secretary" for anyone needing a letter written. He called me his "agent," and the practice worked magically by occupying a mind that otherwise might have dwelt too heavily on his narrow escape from death in the freezing waters at Anzio-Nettuno. Instead of imposing on him, I had — quite unintentionally — done a good deed, and I was delighted to watch him become more alert and sociable as the weeks passed. How I regret not having kept in touch with this warm friend after leaving him in the hospital. We fool ourselves when we think that we will remember every detail along our road of life!

Weeks later I was crestfallen when a photo shop in Palermo fogged every image that I had taken during the invasion at Anzio — except one. The surviving light-streaked image shows floating debris from an exploded ship that I believe to be the remains of *YMS-30*, even possibly my letter-writer floating on a sliver of his ship's wooden hull.

Only a day after I entered the hospital, I received a shock. I was joined in Ward S210 by shipmate Eddie Runof, the iconoclastic motor machinist's mate first class on *SC-525*. The day after I was medivacced, Eddie was manning a 30-caliber machine gun when, according to the deck log, "0910, Attacked by enemy aircraft which dropped three (3) bombs, one 25 yards ahead, and two 50 yards on either bow. RUNOF, Edmund E., MoMM1c, USN was wounded by bomb fragments when one completely penetrated his right thigh." The log entry did not reveal three other circumstances later confided to me by our shipmate, John Stanley Hallas. First, the bullet went completely through Runof's thigh, and to clean the wound,

Pharmacist's Mate Bernard Phau ran a steel rod all the way through to clean the wound, then applied bandages on both sides. Whether old Eddie refused anesthesia, I know not, but he was a tough bird who taught me how to adjust to the cold winds when standing bridge watch: Breathe in the cold air and allow the lungs to adjust to the freezing temperature. (It worked!) Second, despite his toughness, Eddie often found an out-of-way place and read his Bible, and as he was being taken from the ship, he whispered that between the pages of his Bible were bills totaling two thousand dollars, and, that if he did not return to the ship, Hallas was to have the Bible and its contents. Third, inside the harbor, while Runof's stretcher was being raised up to the deck of the LST, a rope came loose, and strapped-in Eddie fell back down to the SC's deck. The machinist was doubly lucky because a guide wire prevented the stretcher from sending its patient into the frigid waters between the two vessels, and Eddie suffered no further injury when the assembly fell neatly on a flat surface.

Edmund Emil Runof— then about thirty-eight, an age that made him "old" in the eyes of teenagers — was one of the most interesting characters I have ever known. After seventeen years in the Navy, he had no home but the ship to which he was assigned. When he became eligible for transfer back to the States, he would not leave his "family." He refused to accept promotion to chief because that would make him assistant engineering officer, the very title of which he viewed as sissy. Typical of old salts, he had mastered the Navy's extensive vocabulary of profanity and upon the slightest provocation would sputter a line unfit for the ear of a sheltered farm boy for whom "drat" was a cuss word. A familiar name like "Eddie" just didn't seem to fit his iconoclastic nature, so most of the greasers called him "Rub." At first I think he looked upon me as effete, but once I adjusted to his language and showed admiration for the care with which he treated our ship's machinery, we became good friends. There was never a shipmate who would help another more quickly, and all of us proudly looked upon him as the fighting spirit of *SC-525*. One of his habits, however, appalled me. He loved escargots, plentiful in the Med but to me nothing but live, slimy sea snails. He delighted in going into a bar, ordering a bucket of live escargots, sitting patiently until a snail stuck its head out of the shell, then spearing it with a toothpick. Victoriously, he slurped the messy, wiggling creature from its shell, and sat back contentedly as if he had won a prize. Eddie had another peculiarity: He coined a different name for each of us — mine was "Hilary P.," from his favorite destroyer, the USS *Hilary P. Jones* (DD-427). In Ward S210, Runof regaled patients with his stories of experiences in the *real* Navy, and with "Hands Gone" Jones operating a two-arm/no-hands courier service, fellow patients heard a lot about our little *Cinq-Deux-Cinq*. Runof, however, refused to acknowledge my new nickname; I remained to him "Hilary P."[8]

Both Eddie and I were happily surprised on February 3 when George Klumpp, my liberty buddy, and Bernard Pfau, who had initially ministered to our respective injuries, rushed in for a few minutes while our ship stopped momentarily on its trip from Anzio to Bizerte. They brought along mail, and a few days later George wrote my mother reassuringly, "His doctors, I know, are the best because it seems that all the good doctors are in the service, and the poor civilians are content to take what's left."

The mail that Klumpp and Pfau brought was deliriously received,[9] but my hospitalization still was unknown at home. In fact, the cablegram had not yet reached home, and the letter written for me by Helen Meier would not reach Pelham until February 16. The first letter written by my mother after getting the cable was dated the 10th.

By February 18, the cast on the left hand had been removed, and bit of the one on the right hand had been peeled away, so I attempted to compose my first handwritten letter since the injury, complaining that the effort was "pretty tiring." Because of censorship, I still could not identify Anzio, but I was able to slip through the word "invasion" occasionally to give the secret away. I added, "After looking around me & seeing the condition of other soldiers & sailors, I am most fortunate in getting out so easily."

A few days later I was cheered by a long, witty letter from shipmate "Plump" Klumpp. It raised my envy because while again in Bizerte, he, Chief Miller, and Stanley Dauman had gone on liberty to the historic Tunisian city of Carthage, which I never was able to visit. Lieutenant McCormick, the censor, added a note in which he said, in part, "My big hope is that you are feeling quite spry again, enough so to half-way enjoy the change and the rest. We all realize what you must be enduring, but you will agree that the doctors are very capable. When your time is up, you can be very certain that we will be here to welcome you back with pleasure." It felt good to be missed.

By the last day of February, *SC-525* was back in Naples, Runof and I welcomed a visit from Chief Miller and Pharmacist's Mate Pfau; then the next day we were even more surprised when our captain and executive officer, Lieutenants Waldron and McCormick, accompanied by Klumpp and motor machinist's mate Stanley Hallas, came in. I wrote home, "They told me to stay in the hospital until they came back for me after they do some important work against the enemy." Of course, I knew exactly what that "work" meant — they were heading back to the fury of Anzio where German planes and shelling from behind the perimeter of the beachhead were taking a heavy toll on the fleet resisting the Nazi effort to drive the Allies back into the sea.

In a letter home, I reported having received about fifty messages since arriving at the hospital and promised to try to answer every one of them, now that the cast had been removed from my writing hand: "Both hands are very weak, but am regaining control of them. They will eventually be as good as ever, I think." I added:

> At last we can tell a little about where we've been, Africa, Italy, and Sicily. Casablanca was a beautiful city.... Bizerte has been completely destroyed by our own and enemy bombs & shells. That is the city I told you about in my Christmas letter. It was really an awful sight.... A visit to the Rock of Gibraltar was very interesting, but the Arabs of Algeria, French & Spanish Morocco and Tunisia, were the most interesting of all. I can't tell anything about Sicily & Italy for a while. But our ship has done her part against the Jerries and we're proud of her. By the time you get this, I will probably be out of the hospital, so don't be worried. This war over here won't be over this year, so don't get your hopes up to [*sic*] high about seeing me before Christmas. I am very well satisfied on the ship as long as the "hunting is good."

I reported that a fellow patient had told me that my cousin Edward Jones was at the front not far from my hospital — a sly way of revealing that I was in or near Naples.

Meanwhile, news from the beachhead arrived with the wounded almost each day, but we never knew who and what to believe. We also figured that the Mediterranean edition of *Stars and Stripes* (which sold for two lire but was free to hospital patients), the only English-language newspaper available on a regular schedule, gave the brighter side. For example, the paper repeatedly referred to the Anzio-Nettuno area as the "beachhead south of Rome." The headline of the January 26th issue read, "5th Widens Beachhead," and two days later, "Nazis Lose 25 Planes in Beachhead Battle; 12th ASC Units Chase Enemy Northward." The latter story included an interesting paragraph: "High on the victory list, with eight Nazi planes to its credit, was the 99th Fighter Squadron, which as the first American Negro fighter outfit to see combat, has fought in this theater for the last eight months." These were the Tuskegee Airmen. The January 29th issue boasted, "Germans Yield Below Rome; Allies Down 50 Enemy Planes."

THE STARS AND STRIPES

MEDITERRANEAN

Vol. 1, No. 61, Wednesday, January 26, 1944   ITALY EDITION   TWO LIRE

German Armies In North Russia Face New Threat

Soviet Offensive Aims At Clearing Out Wide Area

LONDON, Jan. 25—The battle of Leningrad has moved into a new and more critical phase for the Germans. A vast strategic plan aimed at destroying or driving from Russian soil the whole of the German northern armies from Leningrad to Novgorod, is apparent in the latest Red Army moves in the north.

Soviet field commanders have the Germans nearly to the point where, weakened and confused, they must face the dilemma that has hounded the Wehrmacht since the defeat at Stalingrad—whether to hold on and risk destruction or to withdraw and perhaps be overwhelmed in retreat.

The northern offensive has split into four distinct operations:

First, the struggle for control of the Tosno-Narva escape line to the west; second, the liquidation of the tough German salient between Krasnogvardeisk and Tosno at the eastern end of this line; third, the battle for the 50-mile German-held stretch of Leningrad-Moscow railway from Tosno to Chudovo on the Volkhov River and fourth, the outflanking drive from Novgorod aimed at the big German base of . . .

Stars And Stripes 2 Lire On All Days

The price of all editions of The Stars and Stripes in Italy is now two (2) lire. This includes the paper which contains the Readers Digest supplement. Distribution of the paper is free to patients in hospitals and rest camps and to all military personnel stationed in the Zone of Combat as defined by Army orders. Papers may be secured from the Special Service Office 5th Army Hq. or from Stars and Stripes offices in Naples and Foggia.

Vote On Pay Bill Expected Soon

By Sgt. DAVID GOLDING
(Stars and Stripes Staff Writer)

WASHINGTON—Final Congressional agreement on the scale of mustering-out pay for discharged service men and women is expected shortly now that an amended pay bill, passed unanimously by the House this week, is under consideration in joint conference with the Senate.

The House bill provides payment of 300 dollars for personnel who served longer than 60 days. It applies to all service men and women up to the rank of captain except those over 38 who applied for discharge to return to essential war industries and reservists whose full duty was passed in special school training. The 300 dollars would be paid in three instalments. A pay . . .

5th Widens Beachhead; Foe Sinks Hospital Ship

British Vessel, With Lights On, Hit Near Anzio

NAPLES, Jan 25—Three British hospital ships were subject to a prolonged bombing attack by the Luftwaffe off Anzio last night and one of them was sunk, it has been revealed by the Royal Navy.

The ships were a dozen miles off the coast and some miles from the concentration of combat vessels off the 5th Army beachhead when attacked, eyewitnesses said. The hospital ships were fully lighted and the red crosses brightly illuminated in the sky.

"It was a deliberate attempt to sink unmistakable hospital ships," said the master of one of them, Capt. C. W. Sanderson, of Goodwick, Pembrokeshire. "We could do nothing. We put on our lights, and that's our only weapon."

The bombers made two attacks, he said, and concentrated on the red crosses. The second wave of bombers came in low and dropped flares before making their bomb run.

"It was like daylight, and we were completely helpless," said Capt. Sanderson, who is master of the St. Andrew. She and the St. David and the Leinster had put to sea from the 6th Army beachhead area at dusk. They assumed . . .

Art Sent North, Rome Radio Says

LONDON, Jan. 25 — Radio Rome said today that 250 crates of precious art objects have been removed from Rome to storage places in Milan in the past few days. Books from the Academia d'Italia and the Monte Cassino library were among the art treasures transported to the northern city.

Rome Held Down With Iron Hand

By Sgt. MILTON LEHMAN
(Stars and Stripes Staff Writer)

WITH THE 5TH ARMY AMPHIBIOUS FORCES, Jan. 25 (Delayed)—A bad case of jitters is affecting the German troops stationed in Rome, according to Italian civilians who slipped out of the city yesterday and are now safely behind the new Allied frontline. News of the sudden landings on the beaches 35 miles south of Rome swept through the Eternal City like a whirlwind, they reported.

To counter the elation of the civilians the Germans have drawn a portion of guards around the . . .

Nazis Believed Shifting Troops To Guard Rear

ALLIED FORCE HEADQUARTERS, Jan. 25—American and British troops of the 5th Army have extended their beachhead south of Rome to a depth of several miles in some places and it was officially confirmed today that the seaside town of Anzio, just southwest of Nettuno, is in Allied hands.

Allied military observers, noting that German forces were forming some miles north of the 5th Army's advance elements, stated that strong enemy counterattacks might be expected within the next two or three days.

The German air force carried out extensive bombing operations last night against Allied shipping off the beachhead.

Fifth Army soldiers have driven the Germans back to the point where only long range enemy ar . . .

LONDON, Jan. 25—News of the Allied landings south of Rome was withheld from the German public for 26 hours, the . . .

Stars and Stripes, on the date of my injury at Anzio, fairly accurately described conditions at Anzio Beachhead three days after the invasion. The newspaper was avidly read by American servicemen in the Mediterranean.

Of course, not all of our new patients came from the Anzio Beachhead; one, Lane Wilkins of Lawndale, North Carolina, was a member of the United States Maritime Service from the *John Paul Jones*, a Liberty ship; others were brought in from the "Winter Line" along which, near Cassino, Allied and Nazi armies were in deadly combat. News reports repeatedly referred to German positions in or near the abbey at Montecassino, and if the decision made in February had been left to my hospital mates, Allied bombs would have rained down on the historic monastery in January.[10]

I was an eyewitness to history again on March 7. Patients in Ward S210 were in a dither over a rumor that we were to have special company. Orderlies tidied up, instructed bed-ridden patients to keep their covers straight, and assisted two patients on the western head-to-wall side to get up and put on their naval officers' uniforms. The leg-splinted officer was put in a wheelchair; the other one was able to stand and walk with assistance. Together they were ushered out onto the terrace where I often exercised with a view of Mount Vesuvius in the distance and the city of Naples with its steep funicular below. As an ambulatory patient with rapidly healing hands, and having won freedom of movement as ward ambassador, I followed them out, keeping a respectable distance and moving around to the side of several uniformed servicemen, who served as a sort of honor guard. I recognized Rear Admiral Frank J. Lowry, the commander of Operation Shingle. Then, from the other side of the terrace, a tall figure marched out in a field jacket, unmistakable from photographs as Lieutenant General Mark Clark, commander of the Fifth Army. Without introduction, he stood before the two naval officers and made remarks that I could not hear clearly, then bent down and pinned a decoration — soon to be identified as a Silver Star — on the officer in the wheel chair. The general repeated the ceremony for the ensign standing at attention. A photographer snapped pictures that were later distributed to newspapers by the Associated Press.

I slipped back and lay down on my bed just before the general and admiral, leaving the decorated officers on the terrace, were conducted into Ward S210 by the hospital commander. They paused and gave encouragement to several patients, then were led to the occupant of a bed adjacent to those of the two officers just decorated. After a few words, the general patted the enlisted man on the shoulder, then moved on to speak to and shake hands with a few other patients. I was both disappointed and relieved when the officers did not approach my bed, for I imagined that I might have cried out in pain if either had shaken my broken hand, still sore but looking perfectly normal. That would have caused a commotion: a third-class sonarman yelling at an Army general and a Navy admiral.

The officer-patients chose not to discuss details of the service for which they were decorated, and it was only later that the official story caught up with the rumors that trickled through the ward. General Clark, in his book *Calculated Risk*, gave a garbled version of the story. Before dawn on January 28, the general and several subordinate officers sought to slip into the Anzio Beachhead on tiny *PT-201* for consultation with General Lucas, commander of the landing forces. Seven miles south of Anzio, a challenge by USS *Sway* (AM-120) was correctly answered by blinker, but the minesweeper inexplicably opened fire with 40-millimeter shells, several of which hit the small boat. Realizing that the PT's signals were not being recognized, the wounded captain, held up by General Clark, ordered his ship to turn tail and speed seaward. Once out of range of the minesweeper's guns, the extent of the damage and casualties became evident. Two men had been killed and five — including the PT's captain and executive officer — had been wounded. More seriously wounded was the signalman, who had frantically sought to notify the *Sway* that it was firing on a friendly vessel. The companion *PT-216*, which had escaped the shells, sped alongside and put its captain in command of the damaged but still floating *PT-201*. General Clark later wrote,

> Our new skipper ... pulled up alongside the AM 120 and through a megaphone delivered an inspiring and profane lecture to the captain of the minesweeper, beginning with, "You just fired on General Clark!" and ending up with a great deal of strong but sensible advice. The flabbergasted captain said that the first rays of the morning sun had made it impossible for him to recognize our signals and that his crew had been quick to react because of reports of enemy torpedo boats in the vicinity.[11]

The officers whom I saw decorated by the general on March 7 were *PT-201*'s captain, Lieutenant (jg) George E. Patterson (a 1937 graduate of Duke University) of Macon, Georgia, and his executive officer, Ensign Paul B. Benson of St. Louis. The enlisted man — too badly wounded to leave his bed and whose name and picture never appeared in the papers — was the signalman, terribly wounded trying to save his ship and the life of the general. I wish that I had remembered his name, for I shall never forget the embarrassment as the officers showed their medals to the signalman and in unison expressed the wish that the petty officer had been properly honored also. Some of the other patients probably were reminded of the adage, "Officers get the credit, enlisted men get the shaft." The incident reminded me of a sad expression of a member of the 509th Parachute Infantry Battalion who commented to an admirer of his Purple Heart, "All I want is my arm back; you can have the medal."

Lieutenant Patterson and Ensign Benson became friends with Lowell Randall, who had put plaster casts on both them and me. Their story is perpetuated both in General Clark's book and a series of photographs that Randall sent back to Ohio and now reside in the library of Bowling Green State University. I hope the signalman's story, like mine, will be perpetuated also. For me, he was the real hero.

Having regained use of my writing hand, I penned on March 1 a five-page memorandum, some of which has been quoted in chapter 6, about the first four days of the invasion at Anzio. Here is another excerpt:

> We caught the Jerries by surprise — the rockets fired from LCTs shell-shocked those on the beach. But now after a month's fierce fighting, we have been pushed back from our original positions. Our troops are in a dangerous position, but I have faith that we will not be forced to evacuate. Those fellows from the 3rd Inf. Div., 504 & 509 Paratroopers Bn. will always be remembered. They lost heavily. Our air supremacy has given great aid to our troops. Offshore, U.S., British, French, Greek, & Dutch warships are continuing to shell the enemy positions along the coast.[12]

I interrupted my comments on Anzio with this parenthetical statement: "Here in this hospital where legless, armless bodies are frequently brought in, the accordion, which is now being played by one of the recuperated patients, makes sweet music.... How these fellows love the accordionist's version of 'Pistol Packin' Mama.'" In fact, despite the bad news from the Anzio beachhead and the Rapido-Garigliano river front and the sad condition of many of my wardmates, Captain Ostergren regularly cheered us up, and I came to respect him enormously. I think I attended every religious service that he held.

On March 9, 1944, Lieutenant (jg) F. P. Thomas entered in my medical record the words, "Discharged to duty this date." In just six weeks, I had found another home, and, though I looked forward to rejoining my shipmates, I was sad to leave Ward S210, where I had found companionship with men who had sacrificed much more than I for the sake of our country. That experience, and the influence of Captain Ostergren, rekindled in me a desire to survive the war and perhaps devote myself to the ministry.

That night, when I was unable to locate my old *Cinq-Deux-Cinq* in the teeming Naples harbor, I was reminded of my homeless night when I attempted to report aboard the ship in Casablanca a year earlier.[13] This time I found overnight shelter in a Navy hostel, then tramped around the docks the next morning, anxiously awaiting a familiar sight. Then, at 1223 on March 10, *SC-525* tied up alongside *YMS-78* in Naples harbor, and three men went aboard — Stanley Tokarz, a new motor machinist's mate third class, and two returnees, Charles E. Merckling, seaman first class, from Bizerte Sick Bay, and "Hands Gone" Jones from 118th Station Hospital. I was back on my floating home, almost under the shadow of what we all assumed to be a dormant Mt. Vesuvius. We would hear from that slumbering monster within a fortnight.

8

Cinq-Deux-Cinq *While I Was Away*

January 26–March 10, 1944

Only through accounts of shipmates, later confirmed by a reading of the ship's log, did I learn of the always dangerous and often exciting experiences of *SC-525's* crew during my absence from January 26 to March 10. My transfer to *LST-327* on the former date occurred during a bombing raid while both my old and new ships were most vulnerable—docked in the inner harbor of Anzio—and it was not until 2040 that night that *525* was able to leave the harbor and resume patrolling. The following day, waters still raged from the two-day wind and sleet storm, Boche gunners continued to shell the harbor area, and Eddie Runof was wounded by bomb shrapnel, necessitating a return to the vulnerable harbor for his transfer to *LST-321* during another horrendous bombing attack.[1] Again, *525* was imprisoned in the harbor for several hours because of repeated bombing and shelling attacks. The crew must have heaved a collective sigh of relief when the little ship finally was able to speed to the outer rim of the main fleet for, despite heavy seas that beached additional landing craft the ensuing night, they preferred defending the fleet from E-boats and U-boats to offering German bombers and gunners a sitting target in the harbor. During those hours, our sister ship, *SC-534*, was badly shaken by a bombing near-miss.

January 28 was stressful, but at least the dwindling food supply was replenished. Let *SC-525's* deck log speak:

> 0040–0143, Red alert. Flares and bombs dropped from enemy planes. 0400, Laying to off flank of anchored ships. 0702–0714, Red alert. 0735, Red alert. Attacked by enemy planes. 0800, Attack still in progress. 0845–0905, Red alert and General Quarters. 1030–1050, Red alert. 1135, Red alert. 1143, Attacked by FW-190s. 1335–1358, Red alert. 1418–1428, Red alert. 1514–1530, Red alert. 1610, Alongside *LST-348* to take on water and provisions. 1630–1643, Red alert. 1709, Alongside Liberty Ship to get report from LCTs.

January 29 was another very bad day, especially for the British Navy. During the morning, with Nazi bombers overhead, *SC-525* became a water taxi, carrying instructions among the fleet and racing to transfer wounded men from damaged ships to safer vessels. In the afternoon, she moved to the edge of the fleet. Log entries for the night read:

> 1645–1718, Red alert and bombs dropped. 1720, Underway to check on progress of [unloading] Liberty ships. 1745, Red alert. 1750, Attacked by bombers. 1752, British cruiser hit by glider bomb. 1810, Headed for cruiser to assist fire fighting. Attempted to swing stern of *LCI-219* nearer to blaze. 1923, Picked up one survivor. 1935, Discharged survivor to small boat, heading for

86

larger ship with medical facilities. 1940, Leaving scene. 2000, Laying to off convoy. 2200, Attacked by enemy planes. Hit made on Liberty ship which started to burn fiercely.... [January 30] 0307, Burning Liberty ship exploded at the stern. 0344, Bow of stricken ship blew up. 0400, Merchant ship still burning with ammunition going off spasmodically. 0710, Final explosion observed from Liberty as it slowly settled to the bottom.

The log did not tell the whole story. The cruiser was HMS *Spartan*, the target of enemy planes releasing glide bombs, one of which hit and set off enormous explosions and fires. The scene became more macabre as smoke filled the fading sky. Among the first of a dozen vessels to approach the doomed ship, *LCI-219* immediately sought to maneuver broadside against the cruiser's hull so that her water hoses could fight a fire near the aft antiaircraft guns. Caught in heavy waves, the LCI's skipper saw that the maneuver was not working, so he beckoned for *SC-525* to give her stern a nudge. In seeking to comply, our little wooden subchaser was caught in a deep trough, then hurled against the stern of the metal-hulled LCI. The crashing of wood was deafening, but there was no time to worry about the extent of damage, for by then *Spartan*, enveloped in fire and smoke, was beginning to sink. Both the LCI and SC — and several other vessels rushing to the site — were in danger of being sucked under with the capsizing cruiser, so all attention was turned toward survivors jumping into the angry waters where smoke and nightfall reduced visibility to only a few yards. Bodies were said to be floating like cordwood on an Oregon river. *LCI-219* took aboard ninety-five men, *LST-348* retrieved twenty-three, and several hundred other Britons were saved by similar small craft. Forty Englishmen went down with the ship. Aboard the armed trawler HMS *Hornpipe*, George H. Dormer described the scene: "'Spartan' lies on her side, the bilge just showing. A shattered Liberty Ship is still burning. In the approaches the sea was full of blackened bloated corpses [and] ... of petrol cans, which had bulged when their contents exploded, but which were still afloat."[2]

The Liberty ship mentioned in the log was *Samuel Huntington*, loaded with ammunition and gasoline; she was hit by another Hs-293 and settled in shallow water. Most of the men were taken off by *LCT-217* and *LCT-277*, but some gunners remained aboard and claimed to have shot down five planes before another bomb exploded the vessel the next morning. *ATR-1*, which had tried to assist *Spartan* earlier, fought *Huntington*'s fire until she suffered near misses from bombs. Fortunately, she had pulled away and was grounded before *Huntington*'s deadly explosion occurred a few hours later. Another Liberty serving as a troopship, *Alexander Martin*, was strafed and heavily damaged.

Of all the weapons that the Germans threw at the Allied navies at Anzio, the radio-guided bomb was the most feared. These unmanned winged bombs, developed as the "Fritz X," had been alarmingly successful at Salerno, where, among other targets, one exploded the cruiser *Savannah*. At Anzio, a more sophisticated version of the bomb, the Henschel Hs-293, damaged HMS *Jervis* on D+1 and now, on January 29, destroyed *Spartan* and *Samuel Huntington*. Twelve feet long, about a foot and a half in diameter, and weighing a ton, the winged bomb with a warhead of 660 pounds was powered by a rocket that fell away after launch from beneath the wing of a high-flying plane. Released as far as five miles from the target, the flying bomb was guided by radio frequency from the ferrying plane. Alarmed by the Salerno experience, the Navy equipped and stationed at Anzio two destroyer escorts, *Frederick E. Davis* and *Herbert C. Jones*, plus HMS *Ulster Queen*, with special frequency-jamming devices, but even they failed to prevent attacks that sank the British destroyer *Inglefield* and other victims. The air force tried to confuse enemy radar and radio frequencies by dropping over the roadstead "window," consisting of thin, narrow metallic strips of various lengths and frequency responses, but with only limited success.[3] Our best defense remained our own antiaircraft guns and Allied fighter planes. Probably untrue, but it was rumored that officers on capital ships encouraged SCs and PCs to fire on enemy planes to attract them to the flashes of their anti-aircraft tracers so that the guns of the larger ships could be directed toward planes attacking vessels other than their own.[4]

Despite being shaken up in the previous day's collision, *SC-525* resumed supervision of the LCTs in unloading Liberty ships.[5] That task was temporarily interrupted at 1145 on January 30 when she went alongside *SC-497* and took aboard the first mail to arrive since the convoy had left the Naples area nine days earlier. Members of the crew excitedly opened letters while, during "Red Anzios," *SC-525* became the anchorage's most popular vessel, running from ship to ship to distribute mail to other crews who were equally excited to see the scruffy canvas mail bags. The admiral and his flagship USS *Biscayne* had to wait until the next morning for *525* to deliver their mail — our captain's way of giving priority to the splinter fleet and other smaller vessels so regularly neglected. Another happy duty that day included procurement of meat and butter from *LCI-219*, a further example of the patrol vessels' dependence upon the kindness of friends, even one with which a collision had taken place the previous day![6]

Damage to the reduction gear resulting from the collision during the sinking of *Spartan* forced *SC-525* to leave the beachhead on February 2 and sail alone for repairs in Bizerte, with a stop at Nisida. It would be vain of me to suspect that I was the cause of the captain's decision to sail via Naples the next morning, but I was certainly the beneficiary of the detour, for it permitted George Klumpp and Pharmacist's Mate Pfau to visit Eddie Runof and me in 118th Station Hospital. Never were two familiar faces more welcome, for I had been in the hospital only a week and had not yet earned my status as the walking waiter and ward ambassador. The real reason for the detour became clear a day later when *525* was assigned to join USS *Sustain* (AM-119) in screening the port beam of a convoy of landing craft sailing for Bizerte. The trip was threatened by disaster when visibility decreased and the sea became extremely rough. *SC-525* suffered several forty- to fifty-degree rolls, and the LCTs and LSTs towing pontoons were forced to return to Naples. Equally serious, *525* began losing suction on the engines due to excessive rolling, and an LST put on her break-down light, requiring the Sugar Charlie to screen her in circles. This combination of weather and mechanical problems forced the convoy to alter course and to detour via Palermo. Eventually *Cinq-Deux-Cinq* reached Bizerte, and she went into drydock for extensive repairs at Karouba. Two 50-calibre machine guns were added, one on the stern and one on the flying bridge. I was pleased to later read in the log that, in the absence of his sonarman, the skipper sent several other men to train on the Attack Teacher. That was proof that the sonarman was being missed!

SC-525 left Bizerte on February 23, escorting USS *Narragansett* (ATF-88), which was towing a huge drydock. After a stopover at Palermo, the pair proceeded to Naples. The log is peppered with references to other ships sighted, some loaded with reinforcements for Anzio, others returning from the beachhead with victims of the ferocious German counterattacks.

On Leap Year Day, I was surprised when Boats Miller and Doc Pfau walked into 118th Station Hospital — and even more so the next morning when my captain, executive officer, and George Klumpp and Stanley Hallas rushed in before the ship sailed on to Pozzuoli. From there, the subchaser escorted five LSTs to Anzio, arriving at the beachhead on March 2 just in time to drop smoke pots during two air raids and begin searching for floating torpedoes dropped from German planes. The next day, while going alongside *LST-386* to pick up smoke floats, much of the beading along the starboard side was torn away. During the days and nights following, *SC-525* performed a variety of duties while dodging German 88s, firing on enemy planes, dropping smoke floats, searching for floating mines and torpedoes, screening the outer rim of the fleet, ferrying officers from ship to harbor, sinking a floating body by tying to it a 40-millimeter ammunition case, and going alongside USS *Steady* (AM-118) for orders. The vessel then escorted a convoy of LSTs and the crippled *ML-566* to Naples, passing at least two more convoys of landing ships with thousands of additional troops who would resist the determined German efforts to drive the Allies back into the Tyrrhenian Sea.

Near Anzio, while submarine chasers and other smaller craft were busy carrying out their specialized tasks associated with the landings, the cruiser *Brooklyn* (and later *Philadelphia*) lobbed shells onto German positions at the perimeter of the beachhead, and destroyers and destroyer escorts provided antisubmarine and antiaircraft duties in the roadstead. In addition to operating their jamming and decoying gear against radio-controlled bombs, *Frederick C. Davis* and her sister ship, *Herbert C. Jones*, joined in the fire-support for the ground troops. *Davis* was slightly damaged by a bomb from which shrapnel wounded one of her crew, but she remained at Anzio for months except for short trips to Naples.[7]

After my evacuation from Anzio on January 26, Allied naval losses associated with the beachhead had continued to mount. In addition to the American casualties previously mentioned, *LCT-220* went down in a storm on February 13; *LCT-35* and Liberty ship *Elihu Yale* were sunk by radio-controlled bombs on the 15th; *YT-198* was sunk by a mine on February 18; *LST-348* was torpedoed on February 20;[8] *LCT-26* foundered in heavy weather on the 25th; and *LST-349* and *LCT-36* were lost on February 26. Among warships damaged were USS *Ludlow* (DD-438) by shore battery on February 8 and *LST-197* by shelling on February 29. The minesweeper *Pilot* (AM-104), our partner in the Casablanca-Oran run the previous August, was damaged in a collision with merchant ship *Samuel Ashe* on February 20.[9]

A depth charge explodes two hundred feet off the stern of *SC-525*. Canisters could also be shot by K-guns off the side of the ship, and hedgehogs could be launched from the bow.

THE BEACH-HEAD

is going to be the big blow against the Germans.

Wasn't that the slogan when the Allied troops landed at Nettuno on January 21st?

TODAY

exactly three months of hard fighting have passed and you can now celebrate this event.

But it is still merely a beach-head, paved with the skulls of thousands of British and American soldiers!

The Beach-Head has become a Death's Head!

It is welcoming **You** with a grin, and also those who are coming after you across the sea for an appointment with death.

Do they know what they are in for?

Yes, they feel that they are landing on a

DEATH'S HEAD

AI · 065-4-44

Above and opposite: The Nazis employed propaganda warfare against Allied troops at Anzio. One of the most mocking was a two-sided broadside equating "Beach-Head" with "Death's Head" and featuring a skull superimposed over a map of the beachhead (courtesy 45th Infantry Division Museum, Oklahoma City, Oklahoma).

In capital ships, however, the British suffered even more heavily, for in addition to *Janus* and *Spartan*, a second cruiser, HMS *Penelope*, and the destroyer HMS *Inglefield*, were sunk on February 18 and 25, respectively. Both had assisted USS *Brooklyn* and several destroyers in shelling German positions as Allied troops sought to hold onto the tenuous beachhead the first month after the landings. "Pepperpot," as *Penelope* was called due to scars from a courageous record during previous operations, received two torpedoes from *U-410* and sank, carrying down her captain and more than four hundred men. The cruiser, sailing along at twenty-six knots, became the fastest-moving victim to succumb to a submarine torpedo during the war. C. S. Forester's 1943 novel, *The Ship*, was based on the real-life *Penelope*'s exploits in the Mediterranean the year before.[10]

Exactly a week later, an Hs-293 radio-controlled glide bomb sank HMS *Inglefield* off Anzio. Many of *Inglefield*'s crew were rescued by *LCI-12*, again demonstrating that American and British navies and armies shared both the glory and the agony at Anzio. Other British vessels sunk included *LST-305*, *LST-418*, and *LCI-273*. Not all of the action at sea was unfavorable to the Allies, however, for on March 10 off Anzio USS *Edison* and four British destroyers sank the German *U-450*; and on the same day off Sardenia, *Mull* sank *U-343*.

Bedeviling Allied forces — especially the Army — during the long stalemate at the beachhead was German propaganda. With her sidekick George, Axis Sally[11] broadcast daily from about 0600 until after midnight. The honey-toned propagandist called Anzio "the largest self-supporting prisoner-of-war camp in the world"[12] and described activities and movements of Allied troops so accurately that she seemed to be intercepting official communiques and watching from a perch in the Alban Hills. "Churchevelts," the propagandist charged, were conducting a "Jewish war but a Gentile's fight" against the Aryan race. Troops loved her inclusion of the universally favorite tune, "Lili Marlene," but they were less appreciative of her habit of playing "Happy Days Are Here Again" while reading the names of Allied soldiers claimed to have been captured that day. Although some of her reports were indeed uncannily correct, war correspondent Ernie Pyle was amused when Sally read off a list of ships claimed to have been sunk, for from his bunker on the beachhead he could plainly see those still-healthy ships flying their colors out in the anchorage.[13]

Bursting shells sent printed propaganda fluttering across the battlefield. One leaflet, depicting a skeletal Franklin D. Roosevelt raking a scythe across marching American soldiers, carried the president's promise of October 31, 1940, "I assure you again and again and again that no American boys will be sacrificed on foreign battlefields." Another, titled "Speaking of Time-tables," measured the rate of the Allies' advance at Anzio and concluded that it would be 1952 — if they survived — before reaching Berlin.[14] Typical of accusations of "two-timing" wives and sweethearts back home, "The Girl You Left Behind" was caricatured as bedding down with a 4-F rejectee. Wives of British troops were depicted as cohabiting with American soldiers back in England. More chilling was a leaflet titled "Beach-Head Death's Head!" the front of which superimposed a human skull on a map of the beachhead; the roadstead appeared as a bay of sinking Allied ships.[15]

In some respects, the Nazi propaganda hardly exaggerated. Anzio Beachhead, so easily established on January 22, was imperilled from the second day when German reinforcements rushed toward the invasion beaches. The advance of the British First Army to the edge of Campoleone on January 27 marked the Allies' deepest penetration until their troops eventually broke out nearly four months later. From the beginning, the Allies were besieged. Even after German offenses in February were repulsed and a draining stalemate developed in March, a Dunkirk-type retreat was avoided only because of the United States Navy was able to sustain about 100,000 soldiers in the beleaguered beachhead. In Naples, trucks were loaded with supplies and backed aboard LSTs, ready to roll onto the beaches; six of these large landing craft carrying a total of three hundred loaded two-and-a-half ton trucks arrived at Anzio-Nettuno daily. When unloaded on shore, the trucks returned aboard the LSTs, often carrying Allied sick and wounded personnel or German prisoners of war. In addition, fifteen LCTs arrived weekly and four Liberty ships each ten days.[16] Without a serviceable airfield at Anzio, only this naval sealift furnished the lifeblood of the beachhead and enabled the Allies to cling to the precarious enclave and eventually break through German defenses in May.

The tenuousness of the beachhead was probably not understood by most soldiers who lived under miserable conditions and were concerned primarily with avoiding death. The Nazi caricatures, therefore, were received by most Allied personnel as nothing more than propaganda. We have no evidence that Axis Sally's colorful verbal contrast — between life in a freezing beachhead foxhole and allegedly humane treatment of captured prisoners in historic Rome's comfortable accommodations — adversely affected morale. In fact, both printed and broadcast "news" sometimes distracted listeners from their unhappy circumstances and may have provided an unintended benefit to the GIs and Brits, especially those who appreciated the recorded American music, including the melodious voice of Bing Crosby. Even so, propaganda — including that of the Allies — proved to be a prominent if not decisive weapon during the war.

In retrospect, *SC-525* had been extremely fortunate during the first six weeks of the Anzio struggle. Only two of the crew — Eddie Runof and I — had suffered bodily harm. And the little subchaser, although threatened by mines underwater, near-misses of bombs from above, shells from ashore, collisions with sister ships, and ravages from rough seas, had survived to reach Naples on March 9. I was excited when I was mustered out of the hospital that morning and began searching for my ship among the hundreds of vessels in the huge harbor. Unknown to me, shortly after *Cinq-Deux-Cinq* settled alongside *SC-771* that day, Lieutenant Waldron ordered that lines be cast off. "Oh, no, not again!" the crew moaned, suspecting another assignment to Anzio — or if more fortunate, to Palermo or Bizerte. Instead, there was great relief and joy as *525* set a course for the Isle of Capri for well-deserved overnight liberty.

Thus, while I chafed in a spartan hostel in Naples, my shipmates were carousing across the bay in the fabled prewar resort. But they had earned that reward. The ship's log is silent on the crew's behavior that night, but by noon the next day *525* was speeding at fifteen knots back to Naples to pick up a very important personage — Sonarman Jones, now insisting on being called H.G., not Houston, in remembrance of hospital

At Anzio, I earned the first of five battle stars, shown here on the European-African-Middle Eastern campaign bar. I am also wearing the official sonarman rating badge that replaced the "lefthand quartermaster" patch.

wardmate Joe Johnson, who gave me, if not a change in identity, a new name. Within two hours of my return to my floating home, we headed back to sea behind *YMS-36*. Twenty-four hours later in Palermo, a drydock lifted our battered wooden hull out of the water for extensive repairs and mechanical and electrical updating. For two weeks we heard of Anzio only from *Stars and Stripes*, Armed Forces Radio — and, of course, from Axis Sally, who taunted us with not-too-exaggerated descriptions of the true-life struggle going on at the beachhead.

9

Back Aboard, Back to Anzio

March 10–July 1944

SC-525 remained in and around Palermo for about two weeks in March carrying out Dog Patrol, challenging approaching ships and reporting them to the harbor master, conducting firing practice on all guns, swinging ship, and dashing out to investigate radar targets near the coast.[1] Most of the targets turned out to be local fishing boats, but we couldn't take any chances in light of the mosquito fleet that the Nazis launched against the Salerno and Anzio invasion forces. We simply could not afford to give the benefit of doubt to our erstwhile enemies, almost none of whom spoke English (and we had no one aboard who spoke Italian). In retrospect, the civilians were simply attempting to find seafood for survival, for the war had left them destitute, and they were, as so often is the case in war, victims of military madness. Sometimes there were so many boats to be taken in tow that we strung them one behind the other.[2]

Back in port, there were domestic duties such as scrubbing clothes, for we couldn't trust our duds to locals who might abscond with them. Trust is an early victim of war. Only officers had regular access to base laundries. (Remember, this was long before the introduction of the corner coin laundry!) White T-shirts and nainsook skivvies soon turned gray. A standard procedure for washing dungarees was to soap them down, spread them flat on the clean wood deck, and scrub them with brushes or holystones. At sea, the crew often attached dungarees to a line, threw them over the stern, and allowed the wake of the ship to produce the "streakedy" appearance that became trendy among civilian kids a half-century later. We could not have imagined that one day teenagers would actually pay manufacturers to tear or wear holes in new clothes and sell them at premium prices. Whether in port or on the water, subchasers often looked like Chinese junks with clothing hanging on yardarms and every available line and railing.

Cleanliness is an inevitable casualty of war, but on a vessel with no facility for the desalination of sea water, the problem was exacerbated by the absence of a even a salt-water shower for the crew. The ward room contained a tiny shower head, but the officers were forbidden by higher authority to use fresh water except when a replenishment supply was available (e.g., in port). At sea, our fresh water was such a precious commodity that its use was limited to cooking, drinking, brushing teeth, and face-washing. In those circumstances, only sea water could be used for bathing, and so-called "salt-water soap" produced more grease than suds. We almost forgot what a hot shower, wash cloth, and sudsy soaps felt like, and a first inquiry upon the arrival at a new port was, "Where can I get a shower and wash my clothes?" Even ashore, we learned the meaning of the economical "navy shower"—one douse, then soap, and a final douse to rinse off. George Klumpp and I became rather adept at scouting for base facilities, and if we found none, searching other sources of running water. In Palermo, for example, by following a water pipe in a bombed building, we were able to find a headless shower, something like a lawn hose without a sprayer. Our skin turned blue from the cold, but at least we had a *shower* with brineless water.

Sick bay inoculations were required for typhus, typhoid, and some diseases that I'd never heard of; they were certainly not one of our favorite pastimes. Otherwise, this duty in Palermo was rather lackluster. Life became so routine that Boats broke the spell by buying from a soldier a motorcycle, the usefulness of which was problematic on a deck cluttered with armament and assorted stumbling blocks.

The presence of such a useless vehicle on a 110-foot vessel spawned endless jokes and gave Boats opportunity to create colorful stories of imaginary daily trips. He was always ready to answer our question, "Where'd you go today, Boats?" Another crewman bargained for a child's tricycle, but the captain intervened to keep *525* from becoming Palermo's ship of fools. We took wagers to determine with whom Suzie, the ship's little brown terrier of unknown heritage, would sleep. Companionship was that desirable.

Exploring Palermo's historic sites, viewing movies on the base and aboard larger ships, and writing letters provided welcome diversions. Bill Speckin, our ship's cook, was transferred to *LST-387*, and he was replaced by Robert J. Clarkson just in time to join the entire crew (minus Lieutenant McCormick and Ensign Barton) on March 25 for a group photograph, posed on the dock. Every enlisted man was decked out in dress blues—probably the only time all of us were together in full dress during our entire Mediterranean service. The photograph remains one of my most prized possessions because it keeps fresh in my mind the countenances of my shipmates.

Lying awake amidst the sounds of wounded wardmates while in the hospital in February, I had begun to think

Fellow crewmen Hallas, Clarkson, Isaac, and Runof posed in the "uniform of the day" with *SC-525*'s 20-millimeter Oerlikon antiaircraft gun in the background. Neatness and cleanliness were virtually impossible on a ship without water distillation equipment.

The crew of *SC-525* dressed up for this picture on March 25, 1944, in Palermo, Sicily. Kneeling is Lieutenant (jg) John C. Waldron (commanding officer), and standing, left to right, are Millard Malone, Otto Promp, John Schira, Stanley Hallas, Stanley Tokarz, Walter Marzean, Robert Clarkson, Virgil Anika, William Dauphinais, Lewis Garvin, Lewis Miller, Stanley Dauman, William Isaac, Michael Balog, Albert Price, Paul Hedrickson, Boleslaus Cieslak, Houston Jones, Bernard Pfau, George Klumpp, Charles Merckling, John McLaughlin, and Edward Cain. Lieutenant (jg) Hugh McCormick and Ensign John Barton were absent when the photograph was made.

about my future — if I should live to be a civilian again. My original expectation of assignment to clerical work when I joined the Navy had been frustrated when a boot camp naval officer detected what he thought was a "musical ear," and I was detoured to Fleet Sound School in Key West to earn a rating of sonarman. More than a year later, with occasional access to the radioman's typewriter (with only capital-letter keys), my ambition was reinvigorated, so on March 23, 1944, I had a frank discussion with the skipper. Lieutenant Waldron agreed that there would be no objection to my enrolling in a Navy correspondence course for yeoman. I had no idea that I would be half-way around the world, in the Pacific Ocean, before my ambition was fulfilled, but the extensive study and tests relieved me of many hours of boredom at sea during the coming months. The executive officer was so cooperative that he decided to give me a new assignment — typing the daily deck log from manuscript entries made for each watch by the officer on duty. Yeoman Dauphenais was perfectly delighted to be relieved of the tedium.

Shortly after the picture of the crew was taken, we returned to our grungy dungarees, started engines, and began screening *LST-197* to Naples through a very rough sea. As we entered the swept channel between Capri and the Sorrentine peninsula, we ran into an eerie darkness. Although we had heard by radio that Mt. Vesuvius had exploded earlier in the week, its first major eruption since 1872, we assumed that it had quieted down. Instead, the skies —

clear when for weeks I gazed at Vesuvius from the veranda at 118th Station Hospital — were now roiling with smoke and ash varying from white to jet black. Visibility was so poor that we used the radar to find our way through the fleet to our assigned dock. Safely moored, we found the air so stifling that we covered our nose and mouth with cloth, and the water hoses were kept running to prevent accumulation on surfaces of the ship. Although we were witnessing the still-smoking volcano from the west, it was not until later that we learned the extent of the property and human cost to San Sebastiano and several other small towns. More serious for the war effort, winds blew hot ash outward and caused severe damage to the American 340th Bombardment Group, which lost eighty-eight B-25 Mitchell medium bombers, whose fabric surfaces and plexiglass were burned off.[3] Our short time in the stifling atmosphere was an exciting but miserable experience, and we were not saddened when *SC-525* was ordered the next morning to get underway and lead *LST-394* to Bizerte. Thus, my first liberty in Naples was thwarted by Vesuvius's rude behavior. On the way to Africa, all hands turned to and scrubbed volcanic ash from exposed surfaces.

While in Bizerte, Albert Price, motor machinist's mate, left us to return to the States, and Lewis Garvin had an emotional reunion with his brother. A prized moment occurs in combat areas when, usually by happenstance, a relative or friend or an acquaintance from back home is encountered, and in this case we all shared the joy of a brotherly reunion. Although the showing of emotion between men — even brothers — was viewed as unmanly in the 1940s, even the toughest old salt accepted a hug on such an occasion.

On the 31st we began escorting *LST-394* and *John M. Harlan* back to Palermo, meeting, as usual, additional convoys returning to Africa from the beachhead. We sailed near the watery location of a tragedy two days earlier when HMS *Laforey* was hit by a torpedo from *U-223*. USS *Kearney* (DD-432) and USS *Ericsson* (DD-440), plus patrol craft, rushed to *Laforey*'s aid, and one of them succeeded in depth-charging the submarine but not before the U-boat fired another torpedo that sank the British destroyer with which we had become familiar during the initial invasion at Anzio.

From Palermo we continued with *LST-394* to Naples. One night we manned the 20-millimeter guns before discovering that the two radar targets were friendly. In Naples, Eddie Runof rejoined the ship on April 3 just in time for another overnight visit to Capri and a welcomed liberty. This, my first landing on the fabled island, was soured by mothers holding their daughters in windows, offering them, for a price, for the pleasure of the sailors. Under the strain of war, I had little sympathy for a destitute people, whom we still viewed as enemies.

Some members of the crew were in pretty bad shape when an hour after midnight we were roused with orders to get underway and speed with *SC-532* toward Isola d'Ischia, where a submarine had been detected. Fortunately, I had not taken a drink, so at least the sonarman was at his best; but try as I might, I was not able to confirm a sonar contact with a sub. As I had done on previous occasions, I cursed the elusive U-boat for not giving me a chance to become a hero. After the disappointingly negative search, we went into Naples harbor, still gritty from the volcanic eruption, and met the paymaster before rushing on to Pozzuoli. There we took on more fuel and water and, with *SC-526*, began organizing a convoy of twenty-one LCIs for still another cruise to Bizerte. About the only excitement of the trip was the discovery that the "mine" on which we so vigorously fired was no more than a floating barrel. We were in Bizerte only long enough to pick up our new pharmacist's mate, Stuart J. McBride, then sailed alone for Palermo again. We thought we really had a Nazi target that night when we scrambled to general quarters and headed for the "enemy," that, to our astonishment and no little embarrassment, turned out to be our sister ship, *SC-693*, which had not replied properly to our challenge. Luckily, our gunners restrained their fingers.

For three weeks we again performed routine duties in and outside Palermo — patrolling, communicating entry of ships, investigating the increasing number of local fishing boats approaching dangerous mined areas, furnishing electricity to sister ships in port, attending gas mask and aircraft recognition instruction, compensating the compass, and holding ship materiel inspection. Seaman Robert D. Behm reported aboard. On April 9, Miller, Hendrickson, Marzean, and I went to Easter services and communion at the amphitheater. Among ships berthed near us were old friends, *Ericsson* (DD-440) and *Brooklyn* (CL-40), both taking a breather from Anzio. On April 15 George and I walked through the Catacombs, the most bizarre experience of our Mediterranean service.[4] On April 16 Boats Miller and I went to religious services at the base, and George and I visited the barracks and beach. The next day, we went to *Philadelphia* (CL-41), also recently at Anzio, for a movie, and the next day to 10th Port Theater to see William Powell and Myra Loy in *Shadow of Thin Man* and to the

When my most frequent liberty mate, George Franklin Klumpp (left), and I could not afford the cost of separate portraits, we had one made together in Palermo, Sicily, following my return to the ship from the Naples hospital.

MacKenzie (DD-175) to see Bob Hope and Betty Hutton in *Let's Face It.*

Pain had persisted in my right hand after reporting back aboard, so on April 20 I went to the sick bay in Palermo for an X-ray. The doctor discovered a fracture that had escaped previous examinations, and the bone was reset; fortunately, a cast was not required, and the hand was only strapped. Although I had an excuse to avoid heavy work for a few weeks, I was still able to turn the sonar handle with my left hand. Climbing ladders with only one hand was challenging, but I remembered my embarrassing condition two months earlier — with no hands at all — and did not complain. For the next two days we went to sea and practiced dropping depth charges, shooting mousetraps, firing all guns, and swinging ship.

During these blasé weeks, I took four more progress tests on my yeoman's course, leaving one, plus typing. We heard over the radio that thirty or forty German planes attacked Naples on the

25th. The next day George and I, decked out in our dress blues, went to a studio to have formal photographs made. When we learned that the cost of separate portraits exceeded the sum of AMC in our pockets, we simply posed together. After a ship's inspection, we took thirty-four books to the base library as a gift. On April 29, we sailed again to Bizerte, where Coxswain Millward Malone left the ship and Seaman Bernard Long reported aboard. On May 1, we had a special "birthday" lunch commemorating the second anniversary of the Philadelphia launching of *SC-525*. Three-quarters of that time had been spent in the African-European theater of operations.

Five days later we took the port beam of another convoy from Bizerte to Naples, over which Vesuvius stood quietly. There we took aboard a smoke generator for the fantail and many twenty- four-ounce depth charges before proceeding to Pozzuoli. Back in those familiar waters, we fueled and set out for Anzio again, screening a tug, HMS *Frisky*. When we reached the Anzio roadstead on May 8, naturally we were welcomed with a "Red Anzio" and an attack by about thirty Jerry planes. Just like old times. These encounters were becoming increasingly exasperating. The next day off Torre San Anastasio we loaded fog oil from *LST-174* before being attacked by a dozen more German planes. Not a single bomb found its mark. Ashore, many of the handsome buildings that survived the initial landings at Anzio and Nettuno were now in rubble, victims of German bombs and shells since my departure on January 26.

We were greeted also by what I initially assumed to be scuttlebutt from the crew, even a fairy tale—a report that the Germans had moved to the front a giant artillery piece that lobbed bullets large enough to be seen by the naked eye as they sailed toward Anzio, emitting sounds of a freight train.[5] During the very first night, I learned that this was no exaggerated claim. I had been taught in sonar school to distinguish between sounds emitted by approaching and receding objects, and I gave thanks as I heard this one—just like a train—come toward us ("up doppler"), pass over, recede ("down doppler"), and splash into the sea outside the anchorage. The unwelcome visitor left its audible calling card during subsequent nights. Had we known at the time the full story of the giant gun, we might have been even more anxious, for it was only after the war that we learned the nature of what we called "Anzio Annie" or "Anzio Express." Actually the Germans moved not one but *two* huge railroad guns into the Alban Hills, where they were backed into tunnels, emerging at night to shoot their almost unimaginably large projectiles—563 pounds each—toward the anchorage, which was easily within the weapons' range of 38 miles. Statistics on the 5K(E) guns named by the Germans "Leopold" and "Robert" are staggering: caliber, 280-millimeters; weight, 214 tons; overall length, 135 feet; barrel length, 70 feet; muzzle velocity, 3,700 feet per second.

Unlike the six-barreled 150-millimeter Nebelwerfer's "Screamin' Meemies" and the highly effective 88s, "Anzio Annie" and "Anzio Express" were more effective as weapons of fear than of actual damage. Still, fear itself is a demoralizing weapon, so there was hardly a lax moment in the Anzio-Nettuno area after the introduction of the monsters. Moreover, while they sank no ship, they kept us unnerved, destroyed some buildings in Anzio and Nettuno, and on the battlefield tore earthen holes large enough to swallow a boxcar. By rolling out of the tunnels only at night or during bad weather (when they could not be spotted by Allied planes), the heavy monstrosities escaped damage from our bombers and were captured by the Allies at Civitavecchia only after the breakout from the beachhead in late May. After the war, "Leopold" was taken apart and reassembled at Aberdeen Proving Grounds in Maryland, where it continues to be visited by Anzio veterans, each of whom can tell a unique story of the terror that led to the "Anzio Stoop"—an instantaneous reflex when the swooshing sound of a quarter-ton "up doppler" projectile was heard.[6]

Smudge pots were set off upon radio notification of "Red Anzio," and the smoke generators were turned on during actual attacks. However, smoke-laying was effective only when the winds were favorable, so we often repositioned our ship to get windward of the fleet. The greasy-smelling smoke sometimes was so dense that we protected our nose and mouth with a cloth, which, when removed, exhibited three black spots. Later I wondered if some of our men contracted black lung disease.

Smoke, however, provided little protection from German long-range guns beyond Allied lines and from the German and Italian "mosquito fleet" at sea. The latter included variously named "E-boats," "F-lighters," "Schnellboots," and "MAS-boats." In April, American PTs sank several F-lighters and at least one corvette. On May 13, I made the following entry in my notes: "*PC-627* sank a German E-Boat on Peter Patrol at 0110. Heard her reports over radio. Five of her [i.e., enemy boat's] crew injured. She picked up injured enemy survivors. E-Boat out of action 15 minutes after contact and remained afloat for one hour. *PC-626*, also in the area, contacted and engaged two other E-Boats and chased both away. Several raids tonight." Later in the month, *626* damaged and captured an Italian speedboat. And my ship's log on May 12 recorded, "Germans shelled harbor area for entire watch, firing 2 or three shells every 15 minutes."

During this latest assignment at Anzio, the crew learned the purpose of those mysterious pound-and-a-half depth charges picked up in Naples. The Germans launched about thirty experimental Neger midget "submarines," essentially human torpedoes. The shell of one torpedo was modified to accommodate a motorized propeller and a pilot's seat with plastic observation dome, and beneath was slung an armed torpedo. The entire contraption weighed nearly three tons, moved at only about three or four knots, was difficult to steer, and left a tell-take wake on the surface. It was not designed as a suicide weapon, but its firing procedure threatened the pilot with death or capture. At Anzio, Negers caused temporary panic among the fleet and demanded increased vigilance. Sonar was only minimally effective in detecting the approach of what was essentially a surface craft, so at night small depth charges were dropped periodically as a deterrent. In April, *PC-591*, *-558*, and *-626* and *SC-651* encountered and sank three midgets. The nuisances were ineffective against the American fleet, but they did provide a rocket-boost for the political ascendancy of one junior-grade American lieutenant, whose ship, *SC-651*, helped destroy one of them.[7] The Negers were soon improved to enable them to submerge to a depth of ten feet, and several, renamed Marders, were credited with sinking or damaging Allied vessels during the Normandy invasion. In Operation Dragoon, the invasion of Southern France in August, they were worrisome but caused little damage to the fleet.[8]

At Anzio, or in connection with the defense and resupply of the troops, Allied ships continued to suffer from mines, submarines, and shore batteries after my reboarding on March 10. That month the Germans increased their aerial mining of the sea lanes, but equally as dangerous were mines that had escaped the earlier work of Allied minesweepers. Some were still anchored below the surface; others lost their anchor and bobbed to the surface when stirred by the wake of passing ships. Elsewhere, in March, *LCI-277* was damaged by a bomb, and *PT-207* was a victim of friendly fire, always a danger from itchy fingers when scores of ships were congregated. In April, *PC-621* was hit by an aerial mine; and *YT-207* and *LCI-34* were victims of shells from behind enemy lines.

Damage or loss of warships was widely reported through scuttlebutt and occasionally in official communiques, but the loss of troop and supply ships was seldom publicized. Battles could not have been won without these unheralded vessels that delivered the enormous loads of troops and materiel and supplies required by the troops. Among such vessels, the real work-horse was the "Liberty ship," nicknamed "Ugly Duckling," officially identified as "EC2" (meaning "Emergency Cargo Size 2"). Between 1941 and the end of the war, 2,751 Liberties were built, including many by the North Carolina Shipbuilding Company in Wilmington. The average cost of the vessels was $2,000,000, so any group that sold that amount in war bonds was allowed to suggest a ship's name. More than a score of vessels were commissioned with North Carolina names, a record of which Tar Heels can be proud. Approximately 440 feet long, 56 feet wide, and draft of 27 feet, a Liberty was capable of carrying nearly 10,000 tons of cargo — or, in terms of shipping space, 2,840 Jeeps, 425 2½-ton cargo trucks, 156,000 cases of 50-caliber ammunition, or 430,000 cases of C rations.[9] Each Liberty carried a crew of Merchant Mariners, augmented by Navy-trained Armed Guards that accounted for the downing of scores of enemy aircraft. In addition to losses of Liberty ships already mentioned in the text, at least eleven others were sunk or damaged in the Mediterranean area in support of Operation Shingle from January through May: *Edward Bates, George Cleeve, Peter Skene Ogden, Daniel Chester French, Virginia Dare, Clark Mills, William B. Woods, Meyer London, Thomas G. Masaryk, James Guthrie,* and *Paul Hamilton*. In terms of lives lost, the sinking of *Paul Hamilton* from an aerial torpedo off Algeria on April 20 was the worst — 47 crew, 29 Armed Guard, and 504 Army Air Force. During the same period, at least ten Liberties received damage from enemy mines, bombs, or shelling: *Alexander Martin, Richmond P. Hobson, F. Marion Crawford, Samuel Johnston, James Guthrie, Jared Ingersoll, Charles Piez, Alexander Graham Bell, Stephen F. Austin,* and *John Armstrong*. The *James Iredell* was damaged by weather; *Horace H. Lurton* was shelled by friendly fire; and several others suffered from various incidents. Of special interest to me were *Alexander Martin, Virginia Dare, Samuel Johnston,* and *James Iredell*, names associated with my native state of North Carolina.

There was little let-up in the naval war in May. *PC-556* was damaged by a bomb on the 11th, but the most serious loss came two days earlier in an enemy attack upon an Allied convoy north of Palermo. Escorts *PC-558* and *-626* detected two Marder human torpedoes and sank both, capturing the pilot of one; but early the next morning, a full-size submarine, *U-230*, attacked the PCs. *558* was torpedoed and sunk with considerable loss of life. *PC-1235* also became involved in the battle, evaded three torpedoes, returned to pick up three dozen survivors, sped to Palermo to unload them, then returned to the scene to continue *558*'s patrol pattern. Inexplicably, *1235*'s skipper was called to a Board of Enquiry to defend his decision to pick up survivors while an enemy submarine was possibly still around.[10] There were a few more Allied victories — for example, *PC-627* sank a MAS mosquito boat on May 14; *PC-545* sank an E-boat on the 19th; and *PC-626*, then back at Anzio, captured a speedboat and its crew.

Enemy air power, so anemic in the early stages of our invasion and never in command of the skies, levied a toll on Allied navies which, while not inconsiderable, paled in comparison with the death and suffering rained upon the troops ashore. On D-Day our first acquaintance was made with German fighters, Messerschmitt-109s and Focke-Wulf-190s, several of which were blasted out of the sky by Allied antiaircraft fire. The greater danger to the fleet, of course, came from the bombers, particularly the Junker-88s, Heinkel-111s, and Dornier-217s. However, no Nazi plane left so vivid an impression upon me and many others as the Junker-87, the *Sturzkampfflugzeug* (dive bomber in English), which we simply called the Stuka. Looking and sounding like a screaming vulture, the propeller-driven Stuka exhibited none of the sleek lines of the ME-109 as it descended almost vertically, slanted just enough to allow a bomb to clear the propeller blade. The single-engine craft featured an inverted gull wing with fixed wheels, to each of which was attached a powder charge so that if one was shot off, the other one could be blown away to permit a belly landing. Like "Anzio Annie," the Stuka may have been more a weapon of fear than of actual harm. Still, many veterans of Anzio remember the angst of the sight of the ugly craft, its V-shaped wings suggesting the word "vulture."

An epic naval battle occurred on May 3 north of Algeria when *U-371* attacked, and was attacked by, Allied warships. The submarine's new skipper, twenty-five-year-old Oberleutnant Horst-Arno Fenski, had already compiled a remarkable record as commander of *U-410*. Before being sunk near Toulon in March, *410* counted among its victims one Norwegian vessel, five British ships including the cruiser *Penelope*,[11] American Liberty ships *Richard Henderson* and *John Bell*, and, most recently, *LST-348*.[12] Having survived the loss of *U-410* and now commanding a different sub, Fenski had his chance to claim another victim. On May 3, *U-371* torpedoed USS *Menges* (DE-320), killing thirty-one and leaving the destroyer escort without a usable stern but still afloat.[13] The following day other Allied ships — including USS *Joseph E. Campbell* (DE-70), *Pride* (DE-323), and *Sustain* (AM-119), HMS *Blankney*, and French vessels *Sénégalais* and *L'Alcyon* — arrived on the scene and began underwater and surface attacks against the sub. *Sénégalais* was torpedoed (but remained afloat), but after *U-371* surfaced for air, gunfire forced the German crew to abandon ship. Forty-eight of them were rescued by the Allies. Oberleutnant Fenske, an authentic German naval hero, was the last man to abandon *U-371* before she finally flooded and sank.

Aboard *SC-525* on May 12, Stanley Dauman, one of my favorites among our crew, was hit by a 30-caliber bullet, but the culprit was not the enemy; it was an errant shot from the friendly shore. He was transferred to *LST-263* for medical attention. Thus, Dauman, S1c at the time, joined Runof and me as the third casualty aboard *SC-525*. Three days later, amidst still another air raid, we sped up to twelve knots to overtake and escort *LST-174* and a Liberty ship sailing for Naples. Just when we thought we had escaped the Nazi threat, we encountered another red alert in Naples, a sign that the Luftwaffe could not be ignored south of the battle front.

Undaunted, and not knowing when the opportunity might present itself again, George Klumpp and I rushed off for a long-awaited exploration of Pompeii.[14] Dauman rejoined us from the hospital, and Gerald M. Schaefer, an S2c fresh from the States, reported aboard on May 19, in time to share with his new shipmates an overnight liberty at the Isle of Capri. Again, despite a yellow alert, many of the crew boozed and whored up, only to be aroused early in the morning for a rushed trip, in company with *SC-691*, to Salerno, where we briefly conducted another practice invasion with LCVPs. We returned to Naples on the 20th, but before nightfall we stocked up on provisions and, screening a convoy of LSTs and a Liberty ship, headed for *525*'s fourth tour of duty at Anzio. Gerald Schaefer did not have to wait long for his baptism of fire.

Back in the familiar anchorage in sight and sound of fierce fighting ashore, *LST-394* became our mother ship, supplying fuel, water, and fog oil, as we carried out Jig Patrol southwest of Torre Astura, smoking around a French cruiser and two destroyers that were shelling across the battle line. The Frogs' fire was returned by the Germans, but their crews and ours watched with relief as the shots splashed down half a furlong beyond us. At night, we intermittently dropped small charges (too many of them duds) to warn off any Negers or Marders still around; repeatedly repaired balky radar, sonar, and fog gear; shielded capital ships with smoke; and performed messenger and courier duty between ships. Tying up alongside a bobbing vessel during heavy seas sometimes results in disaster, but fortunately we suffered only minor damage in one of our encounters with *LST-394* when we dropped a drum of fog oil in the water, then, while attempting to retrieve it, snapped three lines and bent the mizzen-mast and boom. From time to time we joined other patrol vessels in an endless smoking chain ("necklace") that encircled the cruisers and destroyers. A bit farther at sea, the cruiser *Philadelphia* (CL-41), fresh from shelling German positions, collided with destroyer USS *Laub* (DD-613) on May 23, and the next day, *PC-626* engaged an E-boat for thirty minutes before capturing it.

By mid–May, Allied troops for four months had held onto a sixteen-mile-wide beachhead, never more than ten miles deep, against a powerful German army that had reacted swiftly to the invasion and rushed up reinforcements with surprising speed. Every inch of that soil, plus miles of sea covered by the Allied fleet, had been within range of German artillery since January 22.[15] Soldiers or sailors knew not where the next shell or bomb would fall. When repeated Nazi offensives in February and March were staved off in bloody fighting, both sides dug in for what essentially became a stalemate of human suffering. Those of us who slept in warm, dry beds aboard ships never forgot our blessings when compared with the plight of soldiers suffering "Anzio Anxiety," even dying, without cover or food only a few miles away, some of them within sight of our floating home. Each warm meal, even in the midst of threats from mines, bombs, and shells, reminded us of our good fortune, and I wondered how many and how often soldiers ashore looked out and yearned to be on our little *SC-525*. So near but so far, we wished that we could share our warm bedding and hot food. Later, the dire condition of troops was captured poetically by a soldier quoted by Audie Murphy:

> Oh, gather 'round me comrades; and listen while I speak
> Of a war, a war, a war, where hell is six feet deep.
> Along the shore, the cannons roar. Oh, how can a soldier sleep?
> The going's slow on Anzio. And hell is six feet deep.[16]

Spirits began to rise with the initiation of Operation Diadem in mid–May along the Cassino front and with concerted shelling of German positions near Formia and Gaeta by *Brooklyn*, *Philadelphia*, *MacKenzie*, HMS *Dido*, and other naval vessels supporting the soldiers on land. Spitfires, spotting for the ships' gunners, were sometimes joined by an L-4 Grasshopper observation plane launched from an LST converted to a landing strip by means of a metal grill laid from wheelhouse to stem. This operation along the coast assisted in the breaching of the Gustav Line and was followed by Operation Buffalo, the code name for a major offensive to break out from the beachhead. We rejoiced on May 25 when the Allies captured Terracina and the two armies linked up in the Pontine Marshes, a short distance from where we plied the waters of the Tyrrhenian Sea. On the same day, bloody Cisterna fell, and the VI Corps turned in the direction of Rome. The war — even the war in Italy — was not over, but despair gave way to optimism when on May 28 we concluded our role at Anzio, where *SC-525* had spent thirty-nine days of endangerment, coming away with only three human casualties but many scars to our personal psyches and our ship's wooden hull. Our departure preceded by only one day the parting fury of the Nazis, whose "Anzio Annie" and "Anzio Express" blanketed the beachhead with 609 shells, signs that although they were yielding in the battle for Rome, they were not giving up Italy.[17] In fact, Nazi troops were still in the Italian north when the Germans finally surrendered a year later.

For the ships remaining, however, danger still lurked; our cruisers and destroyers continued to shell as far north as Civitavecchia until Rome was captured; and Germany's U-boats, Mickey Mouse surface vessels, mines, and Luftwaffe remained threats. In heavy air raids on

June 10, USS *Symbol* (AM-123), *LST-211*, and *LCI-41* were damaged, and as late as July 9, USS *Swerve* (AM-121) went down after hitting a mine off Nettuno.[18] Thus, just as the first ship sunk at Anzio (*Portent*) was a minesweeper, so was the last one. Six months later, when I joined the Pacific minesweeping fleet, I would remember that little statistic.

After the war, Allied casualties incurred in the Anzio operation were totaled, and those of us who served in the Navy were again reminded of our blessings. Figures can lie, and even official sources are misleading and often contradictory, but Rear Admiral Samuel Eliot Morison, the nearest thing we have to an official naval historian of World War II, recorded U.S. Navy losses as 160 killed and 166 wounded and U.S. Army losses as 2,800 and 11,000, respectively. Her Majesty's Navy losses (366 killed and 63 wounded) similarly contrasted to those of the British Army (1,600 and 7,000, respectively). A half century later, Barbara Brooks Tomblin gave combined Allied casualties as Navy, 562 killed and 229 wounded, and Army, 4,400 killed and 18,000 wounded.[19] The figures for the physically wounded do not include thousands of service personnel who suffered mental and psychological scars and those injured in performing regularly assigned duties (such as hoisting an anchor).

Of *SC-525*'s casualties (Jones, Runof, and Dauman), only crusty Eddie Runof was counted in the official figures because his wound came directly from an enemy bomb and therefore earned him a Purple Heart.[20] Our crew suspected that, when the medal was offered to the motor machinist's mate, Eddie told the officer where to put it. Dauman and I shared virtual ignominies: He was shot by one of our own soldiers, and I was afflicted by a winch. Seeking a more sympathetic explanation, I concocted a story that I did not receive a Purple Heart because Lieutenant Waldron couldn't spell — that the log recorded that I was wounded by a "wench." I was disappointed when decades later I obtained a copy of the *525*'s log and found that the skipper had correctly spelled "winch" — a most deflating bit of information to one who returned from the Mediterranean with only a swinging dogtag as his "medal."[21]

Those of us who served in our narrowly circumscribed capacities at Anzio could not have known that, following the war, self-proclaimed military "experts" would vigorously disagree over the conduct of Operation Shingle, and, in fact, over whether it ought to have been conducted at all. My job, and that of my shipmates, was to fight the enemy, and we went wherever our military leadership chose to send us and did whatever we were assigned to do. Of course, we bitched incessantly, complaining about everything from "ninety-day-wonder" officers to "not-fit-to-eat" food. And we had our individual opinion on just about every subject. But we did not know that postwar critics, in their ivory towers, would question whether we should have been at Anzio. That the operation was not a complete success is evident to all. For example, Prime Minister Winston Churchill, who strongly advocated the leap-frog invasion, later complained, "I had hoped we were hurling a wildcat onto the shore, but all we got was a stranded whale."[22] But Marshal Albert Kesselring, whose troops resisted the invasion forces for four months, said "if you had not pitted your divisions in the Mediterranean, as at Anzio-Nettuno, you would not have won the victory in the West."[23] Kesselring also said that the Allies avoided being driven back into the sea because of "the excellent coordination of the enemy air force and navy gunfire with the forces on land [that] created a decisive effect."[24] Well, with only 40- and 20-millimeter guns, our little subchaser couldn't inflict much injury on the Kraut army, but our underwater sonar and depth charges helped protect the ships that provided gunfire support and landed 110,000 troops and 500,000 tons of weapons and supplies from H-Hour through May. More than a half-century later, I am not bothered by the controversy about which I knew little at the time, and I find silly some of the "what if?" scenarios. History is what was, not what we wish it had been. Plans

Above and opposite: Three of my photographs taken in Civitavecchia in June 1944 graphically reveal the destruction of a city: a street scene showing a bank and the facade of the Cathedral of St. Francis of Assisi; Stanley Tokarz (left) and Otto Promp standing near the cathedral's altar from which precious objects had not been removed ten days after the Allies captured the city; and an example of other gutted buildings nearby.

are made on the basis of information available at the moment of decision, not on that revealed afterward.

Oblivious of future judgment of our part in the Anzio-Nettuno landings, *SC-525* left the beachhead anchorage on May 28 to screen the starboard quarter of an LST convoy heading to Pozzuoli, but we continued on to Naples and tied up to *YMS-21*.[25] After only eight hours, during which time we unloaded the fog generator and many drums, we rushed out with *SC-666* and *-691* and *YMS-37* and *-43* to screen another convoy to Bizerte. The base in Tunisia had changed since our last visit, and again we were subjected to strict naval rules. Reveille was regulated, morning muster was called, watches were tightened up, inspections of the ship and crew were stepped up, and the crew was required to wear whites after 1630 each day. Personnel-wise, we transferred Michael J. Balog, GM1c, and Lewis J. Garvin, CM3c, for transportation to the States; and Edward J. Cain, MM2c, was committed to the base brig, charged with insubordination — our second disciplinary problem. Repair personnel swarmed the ship, supplies and ammunition were loaded, and we added the mount for another 20-millimeter gun. We thought little of these omens when on Sunday I went with Boats to services at Resurrection Chapel, La Pecherie/Karouba. The next day we were excited by the news of the capture of Rome; on the 6th we listened anxiously to radio reports of D-Day in Normandy; and soon we heard that the important seaport of Civitavecchia had been taken. These were heady days!

We remained at French Pier, Bizerte, until June 10, enough time to allow Cain to serve his five-day brig sentence and return aboard, and for Edward A. Soto, S1c, and Hamilton Allen Knowles, S2c, to report aboard for duty. We steamed alone to Palermo. On one watch, I thought I had a contact, but it turned out to be the wake of a fog-bound destroyer. In Palermo, inexplicably, a barge came alongside and hoisted off the 20-millimeter gun mount from the after platform. The next day another was brought out to replace it. Oh well, just another snafu. We returned to Fox Patrol and tested our antisubmarine armament by firing the 40-millimeter and eight mousetraps and rolling off four ashcans, two of which failed to explode. We were becoming increasingly suspicious of the quality of our depth charges.

On June 15 we set out with *LST-141* for Naples. When on June 17 we took aboard a Besler fog generator and eighty one-and-a-half-pound depth charges, we used language even shocking to a sailor, for we just *knew* that we were heading back to Anzio. In fact, we did escort a convoy up the familiar coast but, happily, during the night we "detached" a Liberty ship at the Anzio-Nettuno anchorage, then continued to Civitavecchia.

The scene outside the harbor of this main seaport for Rome was similar to that at Anzio two months earlier except that the number of ships was not as large and, despite red alerts and periodic antiaircraft fire, we did not undergo a real bombing raid during our two weeks there. Our assignment also was familiar, for we joined *SC-503, -524, -535, -655, -1029, -1030,* and *-1044* in protecting the large warships from underwater and surface attacks by continually patrolling, smoking, and serving as a water taxi to other ships. My own professional duty was frustrated by repeated malfunctions of the sonar, and for many hours we dispensed with pinging, instead simply echo-ranging with the head as a hydrophone. We did investigate a number of sounds, particularly on June 26, when an enemy attack was predicted, but no submarine was detected. The radar equipment also was balky, and technicians from larger ships failed to solve the problem. On several occasions we tied up inside the wreck-riddled harbor, and one day Otto Promp, Stanley Tokarz, and I picked our way through rubble to conduct a photographic tour of the dead city. The most poignant scene was that of the bombed-out Catholic cathedral with some of its sacred treasures still on the roofless altar.[26]

While the Allied armies drove the Germans north from Rome, swimming parties over the side occasionally broke our monotony. Again, it seemed surreal to be cavorting within fifty miles of the battle front. One of the supply ships in the anchorage was *David L. Swain*, but except that its namesake was a North Carolinian, it did not mean much to me in 1944, the one-hundredth birthday of the North Carolina Collection which Swain founded at the University of North Carolina and for which, thirty years in the future, I would be named director. Our favorite ship in the area, however, was USS *Barricade* (ACM-3), from which we drew welcome fresh food and supplies. On July 1, relieved by *SC-978*, we sailed alone for Naples, giving a final wave to Anzio, the scene of so much drama and pain the previous twenty-four weeks. The next day we first tied up to *YMS-21*, then to USS *Achelous* (ARL-1) for the repairs of the starboard beading torn off at Anzio. Ironically, during the next two days of rough water in the harbor, our port side was battered even more as it rubbed up and down the side of the iron-hulled *LCI-948* to which we were moored. We seemed destined to be an ugly duckling.

10

Attacking the "Soft Underbelly of Europe"

July–September 1944

On July 6, 1944, *SC-525* loaded up with vegetables and got underway from Naples for practice landing operations at Salerno in preparation for what we knew not. On the first day we led in the second wave — a half-dozen LCVPs with men from *LST-602* — after which we discharged fresh provisions to USS *Planter* (ACM-2). We berthed in Salerno harbor beside *YMS-24*[1] but were promptly called out to join *PC-625* in escorting *LST-76* and *-210* from Salerno to Palermo. However, the next day we sailed back to Naples with *210*, which had been unloaded and reloaded overnight. Within an hour of arrival back to the shadow of Vesuvius, we started engines and again sped toward Salerno and tied up alongside *SC-535*. Ours being the outboard ship, we stationed an anti-limpet watch.[2] For three consecutive days, we led waves of LCVPs into Yellow Beach. We were becoming real buddies with the troops who, bearing their heavy backpacks and weapons, repeatedly waded ashore during these rehearsals. We did not envy their role, for once in each "Higgins Boat," sometimes for hours, three dozen battle-ready soldiers stood like closely planted corn stalks, one body bumping against another, as the whitecaps tossed them up and down and sideways. Every one of those Thunderbirds envied our place aboard what must have appeared to be a huge ship in comparison with their little plywood craft. By now we recognized some of these two hundred or so men by face and nickname, and when the sea was calm we delighted in yelling greetings, sometimes sharing a joke or an insult.

After overnighting again in Salerno harbor, on the 14th we rushed out to overtake a convoy of *LST-210*, *-394*, *-602*, and *-365* (the last one British) heading for Palermo. Sharing the screening duty with *PC-559* and *SC-1044*, we were getting tired of these back-and-forth jaunts with hardly a day for walking on terra firma. Even so, we could not complain when we thought of the men crowded into the LCVPs.

Consequently, we welcomed more than two weeks in and around Palermo, a dizzily busy port, an intermediate stop between the war front and the supply and reinforcement depots in Algeria and Tunisia. Inside the harbor, we were haunted by the memory that two of our sister ships, *SC-694* and *-696*, had been destroyed there at the dock by German bombs the previous August. As usual, one of our patrol assignments was to challenge, identify, and report the approach of ships to the harbor master. Too much of the time was spent in the demeaning task of chasing fishing boats and arresting Sicilians violating the territorial integrity of what was supposed to be secure waters. This was boring duty, but after the thunderous and nerve-wracking experiences at Anzio, we did not complain. Besides, occasional days spent in the harbor enabled the crew to explore the heavily bombed city and to enjoy the R & R facility at Mondello.[3] Not surprisingly, Boats Miller had found his motorcycle of no use aboard the ship, so he sold it to an army man with his feet on the solid ground. I thought Boats, normally a very shrewd fellow, had made a fool of himself until I discovered that he doubled the original purchase price and pocketed the profit.

After boarding more provisions, ammunition, fuel, and water, *SC-525* sailed solo for Naples, passing active Stromboli. On July 30 we again took aboard the Bessler Fog Generator and SGF oil, plus many cases of 40-millimeter AA and 20-millimeter HEI and HET ammunition, then sailed for Salerno.[4] We spent two nights there before moving to Vietri Beach near the bottom of the famed Amalfi Drive, where we anchored for several peaceful, delightful nights. Swimming over the side was permitted, and some lovely ladies from the town swam out and, rather remarkably, were allowed aboard during daylight hours. For a few nights, the war seemed far away.[5] George and I took the opportunity to explore the city of Salerno and photograph natives and their activities, including a traditional Italian funeral procession behind a glass-sided, horse-drawn hearse.

On the night of August 6, we threaded our way through a vast number of ships heading in different directions as we moved back to Pozzuoli, barely escaping a shell that landed a hundred feet off our port bow, and another astern, both apparently fired accidentally from the direction of Naples harbor. Just before midnight we sortied with an LCT convoy and sailed

In a photograph taken from *SC-525*, LCVPs loaded with Thunderbirds of the 157th Regiment, 45th Division, wait for us to lead them into the beach during a practice invasion at Salerno. Thirteen days later, we escorted these same infantrymen to the beach in the Baie de Bougnon during the invasion of Southern France.

by Ischia toward Salerno for yet another practice landing, this time leading in LCVPs, then returning to lead in the twelfth wave. Neither we nor the troops knew at the time that this was a final dress rehearsal and that we would lead these exact same men from the 45th Infantry Division into a real-life invasion beach just nine days later. In the afternoon, we screened the convoy as it returned to Baia, west of Pozzuoli, then docked that night in Naples harbor for radar repair. We moved back to Baia the next day and served as communications vessel, scampering around the bay to deliver messages and passengers, but in the evening we sailed again for Salerno, then at 0305 returned to Pozzuoli with *SC-530*. We suspected that we were on the verge of another venture — one that we hoped would not be as traumatic as our experience at Anzio.

*   *   *

The nature of the forthcoming venture would be revealed to us piecemeal. Long before the June cross-channel landings in Normandy (Operation Overlord), plans were underway in the Mediterranean for an invasion of the "soft underbelly of Europe" along the coast of either southern France or northwest Italy. Initially the operation was planned to approximately coincide with the Normandy invasion, but it was delayed because most of the landing craft utilized at Anzio had been required in the cross-channel attack. Prime Minister Winston Churchill

SC-525 (noted with arrow) was dwarfed and virtually hidden by LSTs loading equipment at Nisida in preparation for the invasion of Southern France in August 1944. Trucks were backed into the vessels for rapid exit when the ramp hit the invasion beach. Barrage balloons deterred low-flying enemy planes (National Archives).

strongly opposed the plan, preferring instead an invasion of the Balkans. According to Mediterranean gossip, when the Côte d'Azur was fixed as the invasion site, the name of the operation was changed from "Anvil" to "Dragoon" to reflect the minister's belief that he had been "dragooned" into accepting it.[6] Although the new invasion was to be carried out largely by American personnel, the British and French would have significant naval presences, and Free French troops were designated — for reasons of morale and sentiment — to capture the ports of Toulon and Marseilles. Canada was represented by two transports and some commandos, and several other nationalities were represented, including one Greek naval vessel.

Only high-ranking military officers were knowledgeable about the overall plan for the landings, which would be carried out by nearly 900 ships plus smaller craft along thirty miles of French beaches reaching from St. Raphael westward toward the great naval base at Toulon.[7] Under the designation "Western Naval Task Force," Vice-Admiral H. Kent Hewitt in USS *Catoctin* (AGC-5) was to land three divisions of Lieutenant General Alexander M. Patch's United States Seventh Army plus several special forces, the entire operation to constitute the VI Corps under Major General Lucian K. Truscott, Jr., familiar to us at Anzio. Diversionary expeditions and special force attacks both east and west of the main landings were scheduled for pre-dawn hours, but H-Hour for the main landings was set for 0800, August 15, when three army divisions — the 3rd, 45th, and 36th, designated respectively as Alpha Force, Delta Force, and Camel Force — would begin landing. Alpha (Task Force 84), under command of Rear Admiral Frank J. Lowry (who had been in charge of the previous landings at Anzio), in the Coast Guard Cutter *Duane* was to put ashore the 3rd Division in the Baie de Pampelonne and Baie de Cavalaire southwest of St. Tropez; Delta (Task Force 85), commanded by Rear Admiral Bertram J. Rodgers, was to put ashore the 45th ("Thunderbird") Division — made up of many Apache and Cherokee Indians — along three miles of beaches in the Baie de Bougnon (known to us as La Nartelle); and, on the far right, Camel (Task Force 87), under Rear Admiral Spencer S. Lewis in *Bayfield*, was to beach the 36th Division near St. Raphael in the Gulf of Frejus.[8] Each force was further divided into assault groups named for the particular section of beach (Red, Green, Yellow, Blue) on which each wave was to discharge its loads of soldiers.

Of the huge armada, Delta Force was assigned 211 vessels of all kinds, including the flagship *Biscayne*, eight troop transports, more than a hundred landing craft, two battleships, six cruisers, eight destroyers, and assorted landing, escort, and mine vessels.[9] We would learn later that *SC-525* was to be a part of Delta Force's Red Beach Assault Force under command of Captain R. E. Parker, charged with landing the Thunderbirds of the 3rd Battalion, 157th Regiment, on a beach extending about three miles between Pointe des Sardinaux and Pointe de la Garonne, east of St. Maxime. Our Red Beach Group included ten LSTs, six LCIs, seven LCTs, one LCG, four LCSs, two LCM(R)s, two LCCs, one LCM, and one additional subchaser.[10] My ship's specific responsibility was to corral and lead toward Red Beach two waves of LCVPs, into which soldiers had scrambled from troop carriers. With the successful landing of the twelfth wave, we were to lead the empty boats back to the staging area, after which we were to patrol the waters against submarine and air attacks and to be ready for special assignments such as smoke-laying, mine-shooting, and rescue of survivors.[11]

Preparations for the landings had been preceded by ten days of intensive bombing by Allied planes for a hundred miles along the French and Italian coast, and, still unknown to us, the operation had actually begun on the night of August 14-15 with diversions and commando raids near Hyères to the west and Cap Roux to the east.[12] Then at 0315 on D-Day, 5,000 paratroopers were dropped north of our landing beach, followed by troop-laden gliders, and before daybreak minesweepers began clearing channels in preparation for land-ing craft.[13] Between 0550 and 0730, more than a thousand land-based Allied planes roared over the silent armada and bombed gun emplacements and saturated the landing beaches with bombs that produced clouds of smoke and dust; then shortly after 0600, a naval bombard-ment began, ranging from shells from the familiar cruiser *Philadelphia* to rockets from LCTs converted for the purpose, one of which —*140*— we considered our "security blanket" because we had escorted her to Anzio and again to Southern France. Just before the landing craft started in, unmanned drone ("Apex") boats were sent in to blow up underwater obstacles.[14]

During the wee hours of the 15th, hundreds of ships silently and slowly sailed into their assigned waters in the thirty-mile width of what at H-hour, 0800, would become a new war front. Each force designated staging areas in which troop transports and landing craft were crowded in preparation for the landing. LSTs and LCIs, which required no escort, were at the ready, but soldiers on troop ships had to climb down cargo ladders into LCVPs and other small boats that, without independent knowledge of the swept channel, required shepherd-ing through the cleared minefields to the shore. Ships of Delta Force gathered in two trans-port areas, one seven and a half miles and the other ten miles from the beach at La Nartelle. From there, the Delta wedge narrowed to a width of about three miles by the time it reached the beach. The stage was set for *SC-525*.

*   *   *

Back at Pozzuoli on August 9, *SC-525*'s crew conducted another gas mask drill and pre-pared for a second invasion of enemy-held territory. In the evening we sailed around Capo Miseno and joined LCT Convoy SS-1A, abeam of the familiar and comforting rocket ship *LCT(R)-140*, heading for the island of Corsica, already in Allied hands. We dogged the watch,

British *LCT(R)-140*, with her 798 rockets, is being escorted by *SC-525* to the invasion of South-ern France, August 1944. In the background, left to right, are an LST, a destroyer, and a PC class of subchaser. More than 800 ships participated in Operation Dragoon.

and the radar again malfunctioned. The trip was slow — about five knots — and the course was zigzagged to avoid being caught in the trough of the rough sea. As we passed through the Strait of Bonifacio separating Sardinia from Corsica, our task, in addition to guarding against U- and E-boats, was to keep the LCTs in the narrow swept channel through the heavily mined area. A few feet too far to port or starboard could lead to disaster. The log noted "considerable interference with sonar of other escorts," the radar malfunctioned, and numerous meteorites fell — a bad omen? At midnight, the officer on duty reported, "Investigating straggling rocket barge on starboard quarter of convoy. She said she was not lost." The officer responded, "If you hit a mine, you will be!" Before noon, we entered the harbor at Ajaccio and tied up at St. Joseph Pier. Men from Admiral Lowry's staff came aboard to check on needs in each department.

The deck log entry for Sunday, August 13, is missing, but by early Monday we were sailing northward at only four knots along the coast of Corsica, screening off the port beam of *YT-196*, the last ship in first column of the convoy. At 1455 the log read, "Received message stating that landing east of Toulon would take place at 0800 on 15 August 1944. All craft congratulated on excellent performance to date." Until then, crew bets were on San Remo or Genoa; now we envisioned pink buildings, high surf, and French bathing beauties. However, two words, "to date," sounded ominous, and we were not reassured by several floating mines that were spotted and sunk by gunfire. The chill of mined waters forced the captain to assign a bow watch, perhaps the most hazardous duty a sailor is called upon to perform. My sonarman's status spared me from the assignment, but we knew that if the bow struck a mine, we'd all go into the drink together, regardless of rank. We hoped that nearby our minesweepers had done their work. Overhead soared an occasional aircraft, and our itchy-fingered gunners, continuously at their stations, had to be warned to fire only if we were attacked.

Shortly after 0300 on D-Day, August 15, our convoy abruptly changed course to 300° and the navigator entered, "All quiet so far." An hour and a half later we reached the first transport area and at 0500 we were in the second transport area nearer to the beach. The sea was almost blanketed with vessels from transports to small landing craft, and the danger of collision appeared as much of a threat as the enemy. As dawn approached, we were within seven miles of the German army. At 0600 Allied planes began bombing the beach; shells poured from the cannons of battleships, cruisers, and destroyers; and thousands of rockets sailed over our heads and burst upon the beach. The intensity of the concussions was most evident when the legs of our dungarees slapped our thighs and a sudden whoosh hit our cheeks. Within a half hour, *SC-525* was corralling our Wave Three LCVPs and heading for Oboe reference vessel between the transport area and the beach. Mist and dense smoke from the bombing and shelling threatened to obscure the beach, but a red alert lifted our eyes upward, and we were glad to see only Allied planes, dropping "window" anti-radar strips.

Our time had come, and my mind flashed back to the mines that had interrupted our eighth wave at Anzio. Had the AMs and YMSs been thorough in their sweeping this time?[15] But there was no time for second-guessing, for, as the log recorded, "0755, At 'Charlie' reference vessel. Opposition seemed to be light and destroyers were standing off beach and firing at point blank range. 0800, Proceeding in from 'Charlie' reference vessel with LCVPs of Wave Three toward beach. 0805, Held correct heading for wave to pass." As each LCVP passed, noise from its motor and planes overhead probably drowned out our cheers of good luck to these men, but they certainly returned our signals of thumbs-up. I had a lump in my throat, for these were the men with whom we had practiced landings at Salerno, and they had become "our" soldiers. They had christened us Honorary Thunderbirds, and we had symbolically

At 0800 on August 15, 1944, *SC-525* led the third wave of LCVPs, loaded with infantrymen of the 157th Regiment, 45th Division, to the beach in the Baie de Bougnon at La Nartelle. The 20-millimeter Oerlikon antiaircraft gun is pointed westward, from where a German air attack was anticipated but never materialized.

inducted them into the Donald Duck Navy. Now they were rushing into harm's way with only their backpacks and weapons, while we remained fairly secure on our floating home.

For several minutes we watched as the little boats became visibly smaller on their way to the beach, then *525* reversed course and sped back toward "Charlie" to assemble Wave Twelve. From the flying bridge, with no battle station except as lookout, I could hardly distinguish these 3rd Battalion Thunderbirds through the haze as they sloshed ashore against rifle fire. They were quickly out of sight, heading uphill toward the resort town of St. Maxime, searching house to house for Nazis.[16]

I can amplify the log entry with a personal observation captured in a photograph snapped from our flying bridge. Just to the left of our Red Beach, where the land curves southwesterly to form Pointe des Sardineaux, stood a large, handsome building, probably once a resort hotel. The scene seemed contradictory: American soldiers, perhaps heading for death in battle, scrambling ashore almost in the shadow of a luxury hotel. So I framed the view to include the contrast. Just as I snapped the picture, a shell or bomb blew the building apart, sending up a tower of dust and smoke. At almost the same time, *Montcalm* set off a thunderous shelling toward St. Maxime, knocking out an anti-tank barrier.

As we headed back for our next group, the fourth wave landed successfully on Red Beach at 0824 in the face of artillery fire, and seven more waves followed. Our log continued: "0854, At 'Charlie' reference vessel, 12th wave standing by. 0900, Heading for beach with 12th wave. 0917, Red Beach well secured. 0930, 12th wave into beach. 0935, Section Baker on watch. 1014, Red alert." We had performed our assignment by safely leading in two columns of LCVPs carrying more that four hundred Thunderbirds, who were already picking their way

I snapped this photograph of a large building exploding just as the third wave of 45th Division troops hit the beach at La Nartelle in the Baie de Bougnon. A Sicilian photograph processor badly scratched the emulsion on the film.

up the hills to face the formidable German army. Later we were relieved to learn that our entire 3rd Battalion, 157th Regimental Combat Infantry, waded ashore with only one man killed by shell fire. By the time we had Wave Twelve safely ashore, the LCIs, each with about two hundred fresh troops, were touching the beaches.

We did not know at the time how effectively Allied bombs and shells had protected us and our wards as we approached Red Beach. To the west, Point de Rabiou on Cap de St. Tropez was honeycombed with underground trenches webbing out to six 155-millimeter guns recessed into a hillside, the easternmost of which were within range of our boat lanes and landing beaches. More frightening would have been 75-, 65-, and 81-millimeter cannons at Point Sardineau; an 88-millimeter at Yellow Beach; and a 75-millimeter at Point de la Garonne, which together could have covered the landing area from three sides. Pre–D-Day bombings had destroyed some of these large guns, and only a few of them were turned upon the landing forces. The destroyer *Hambleton* knocked out two of the weapons on Point Sardineau just before the first wave headed for the beach, and it was discovered that others had expended their rounds toward the fleet rather than toward our boat lanes.[17] Our timing had been almost perfect. Equally fortunate, a French 220-millimeter field gun (ironically, marked Bethlehem Steel, 1918), capable of reaching every transport ship in the fleet from Point Issambres, had been knocked out by pre–H-hour aerial bombs, which, according to Admiral Rodgers, "left the muzzle pointing impotently earthward." Kraut gunners, who had not been killed in the aerial and surface bombardment or picked off by landing troops, surrendered. That was not the case of more than thirty machine gunners along the coast for several miles; those not hit by rocketry had to be taken by the Allied troops. Both we and the troop-laden Higgins boats had been spared possible annihilation by the accuracy with which bombers and naval firepower had wiped out these major threats.[18]

My sonar gear was useless in the midst of hundreds of ships extending as far as the eye could see, so, as at Anzio, I was a free hand, prepared to take the helm or any other assignment. In fact, most of my time was spent watching the skies for airplanes and worrying about a collision between the tightly bunched vessels scooting in all directions. One of my vivid memories was the sight of an F6F5 spotting plane crashing into the sea near Point Sardineau at about 0930. I was relieved after the war to learn that the flyer, Lieutenant (jg) Francis R. Roberts, survived when his F6F-5 plane clipped one of the ubiquitous barrage balloons suspended above the LSTs. The plane, from one of the covering light aircraft carriers, USS *Tulagi* (CVE-72) and *Kassan Bay* (CVE-69), was a total loss, but Lieutenant Roberts suffered only leg wounds and was rescued by USS *Murphy* (DD-603). My little Kodak 35-millimeter camera dangled from my neck as I alternately moved from the deck to the flying bridge, but the accident happened faster than I could think, and I did not get a picture of the incident.[19]

The troops for which we had been responsible were ashore in Delta Red Assault Area, so it was with tremendous relief that *SC-525* at 1105 joined *PC-1596* in running a five-mile, back-and-forth, nine-knot patrol of Sector I. Just what we were patrolling for was not evident; my sonar was useless with ships all around us, and we could have watched the sky while at anchor. However, a stationary target is more inviting to the enemy; furthermore, while in motion we could more quickly pick up survivors or rush to the aid of a troubled vessel. By evening, we witnessed anti-aircraft firing on the beach, and *PC-545* joined us in patrolling. Later, we saw a large fire on the beach, and one enemy plane was seen to release a radio-controlled bomb during a raid.[20] For our crew, this had been an unexpectedly good day. Perhaps the contributions of *SC-525* had been only modest on this D-Day, but by midnight of August 15, our Delta Force had landed 33,000 troops and 3,300 vehicles from 11 transport and cargo vessels, 30 LSTs, 41 LCTs, and 36 LCIs — all without a single Navy casualty in the actual landing process and "but few casualties to the Army assault forces."[21]

At sea, however, the day had not been without loss to the Navy. *LST-282* was sunk, with forty casualties, by a glide-bomb off Cape Dramont in Camel Force. *LCI-588* and *-590* were damaged by mines in Alpha Force, *LCI-592* was hit by mortar fire, and the freighter *Tarleton Brown* was near-missed by a bomb over toward Toulon, still in Nazi hands. On the plus side, USS *Somers* sank the German *Escaburt* and captured and scuttled a corvette.

Units of the 45th Division, with the loss of only 109 men in our entire area, had by nightfall made contact with units of the 3rd Division. Admiral Rodgers credited much of the success of the "Delta Plan" to the rehearsal at Salerno on August 8, which, with the same personnel and vessels, was a mirror image to the actual landings at La Nartelle/Bougnon.[22] Nevertheless, significant casualties would have occurred had not aerial bombardment and naval gunfire neutralized powerful guns overlooking the landing beaches. Characteristically, American and British minesweepers bravely swept boat lanes in the face of enemy fire from ashore; and landing craft, converted into rocket launchers, like our friendly *140*, silenced many machine guns and blew up coastal obstructions just prior to the landings.

For several ships — including my own — good luck ran out on D+1. At 1135 on August 16th, while steaming in the Gulf of St. Tropez at normal speed to make way for a convoy of large ships coming into the anchorage, *SC-525*'s port propeller shaft broke forward of the forward strut, allowing the screw to slide aft and jam the rudder. The captain, finding no volunteer to go over the side but not wanting to order an enlisted man to do so, personally

Following the ramming of *SC-525* by a British merchant ship on D+1 in Southern France, the captain, Lieutenant (jg) John Charles Waldron, personally swam under the vessel to inspect the damage.

went down to inspect the damage. Answering our call for assistance, *PC-1596* came alongside with block and tackle and diving gear, but all efforts to fix the problem failed. On radioed instructions, *525* started toward our old friend, USS *Narragansett* (ATF-88), near Delta Beach, using only the starboard engine. At 1614, as we held a steady course — flying appropriate international signals on both starboard and port yardarms to signify "maneuvering with difficulty" — a British merchant ship, *Empire Gawain*, bore down toward our port side. Cieslak frantically blinkered the approaching vessel and the captain ordered full rudder and sped up the engine. It was not enough; we were rammed hard enough on the port side to throw men to the deck. The bow of the freighter hit near our life raft, splitting the wooden frame about fifteen feet and damaging the beading and rubbing stroke. *SC-503* rapidly closed in and stood by in the event that we started to take on water, but a quick inspection below deck revealed no leaks. Using the starboard engine, we were able to maneuver alongside *Narragansett*, whose repairmen began diving to determine the full extent of the hull damage and the cause of the broken shaft. Just as the divers went down, enemy bombers roared overhead, so the inspection was quickly suspended. We cast off, got underway, but, on one engine, found evasive action virtually hopeless. No bombs hit near us, and after the raid subsided, we returned to *Narragansett* but were instructed to anchor until daylight. We spent an uncomfortable night. The next morning, according to the log, the Eighth Fleet salvage officer, Lieutenant (jg) Ernest Winkler, accomplished a temporary repair: "Screw cut from shaft; shaft pulled loose from hull. Loose shaft wedged into fore and after struts. Repairs constituted an emergency measure which would enable us to proceed under own power to a repair base." In other words, we were afloat on borrowed time.

A much graver tragedy occurred that day a few miles away in the Camel Force area, where the bow of *YMS-24* hit a mine, the circumstance compounded by its gruesomeness. The explosion threw the anchor onto the bridge, virtually decapitating the captain, Lieutenant (jg) Samuel R. Pruett. Without her bow, and her rudders out of control, the remainder of the doomed ship made two complete circles before her engines failed and she began to sink. Although himself wounded, the executive officer, Lieutenant (jg) John R. Cox, Jr., gave orders to abandon ship, then jumped into the sea to assist wounded crewmen, courageous action that led to the conferral upon him of a Navy Cross and French Croix de Guerre. Lieutenant Cox was better known to millions of Americans by his stage name, "John Howard," Hollywood actor seen by millions in *Lost Horizon*, the Bulldog Drummond mysteries, and other motion pictures. War respects no distinction between class or status.[23]

The loss of *YMS-24* was very personal to us, for we had worked with her many times and knew her crew, some of whom were rescued by *YMS-63*, whose bow struck another mine. The calamity was cruelly compounded when Royal Navy *ML-563* came to help and was herself exploded by a mine and began sinking. The resulting commotion attracted the notice of German shore batteries in the hills, and they began firing on the tragic scene. In turn, the enemy guns drew shells from Allied fire support ships, some of whose shells meant for the Germans fell near the stricken ships and their survivors.[24] On the same day *PT-202* and *PT-218* strayed into a minefield off Frejus, vainly searching for a tanker to replenish their nearly empty fuel tanks; both hit mines and sank. *LCI-951* was damaged by a mine. A day later (August 17) British *YMS-2022* was mined and sunk in the same area, and the cruiser *Tuscaloosa* suffered a near-miss from a shore battery. Almost simultaneously, our warships continued to repulse attacks by a motley assortment of enemy surface vessels. Together, *Aphis, Cormick, Endicott, Frankford, Harding,* and *Scarab* disposed of a half-dozen German small craft. Two more were dispatched by *Charles F. Hughes* and *Hilary P. Jones* (the latter, the source of the nickname that Eddie Runof coined for me). As long as unswept mines littered the sea and the Germans controlled the mountains above the Riviera and the ports east of Monte Carlo, the naval vessels sailing along the coast remained at risk.[25]

A tragedy of monumental proportions may have been averted aboard USS *Catoctin* (AGC-5) on August 18 when six of her crew were killed and 31 wounded by shrapnel from a bombing near-miss. Just two days earlier, Secretary of the Navy James Forrestal, Major General A.M. Patch of the Seventh Army, and Contre–Amiral Lemonnier of the French Navy had been with Admiral Hewitt aboard the flagship.[26] Timing controls much of life's experiences.

We counted our blessings: We had put our troops ashore safely; we had not been shot up by shore batteries; we had spotted and exploded by gunfire several floating mines; and, though crippled, our ship still appeared to be seaworthy. Nevertheless, on D+2 (August 17), the captain was summoned to the flagship *Biscayne*; upon his return he took over the conn, revved up the engines, and turned the ship toward Corsica. We had lasted only two days at the Côte d'Azur but had participated in and survived another lifetime of experiences. Unlike at Anzio, our crew was unscathed, and the following citation was added to my service record: "JONES, Houston Gwynne.... Commended for duty well performed while actively engaging the enemy in establishing a beach-head in the Gulf of St. Tropez Southern France, during the period form 15 August to and including 17 August 1944." I also affixed a second star to my African, European, and Middle Eastern theater service ribbon.

YMS-43 began escorting us to Corsica; now the escort was being escorted. The sea lanes were filled with ships going to and returning from the war zone. We arrived in Ajaccio on August 18, but USS *Achelous* (ARL-1) could not perform necessary repairs on *525*, and we would have to limp on to Naples. Exasperated, the skipper announced liberty for the crew and headed for a stout drink at the officers' club. The eggheads — George Klumpp and

I—first sought out the birthplace of Napoleon Bonaparte and then found that the faithful American Red Cross could arrange a trip to the top of the most prominent mountain, on which was located the castle of Count Borga. Actually, the trip up and back, on a narrow, steep, crooked road, was more memorable than the building itself.[27] The following day, as if we were being neutered, our depth charges and hedgehogs were removed. Then we limped out and joined a small convoy and proceeded with great anxiety, noting nervously in the log that "weak port side shows no sign of undue strain from increasing sea." As if misery loved company, SC-1029, badly damaged on D-Day by an explosion of a runaway "Apex" drone boat, was towed along by YMS-43. At least we were under our own power, and we were comforted to see so many hospital ships moving in both directions as we negotiated the channel through the heavily mined Bonifacio Strait. If we or the 1029 sank, help would be near for us cripples.[28]

On the 22nd, as we tied up in Naples harbor, our bad luck continued when LCT-152 scraped our bow, splitting the bow stem. Then we were dumfounded by the news that, yes, there were two propeller shafts ready, rushed up especially for us from Palermo, but Naples did not offer facilities for installing them. Well, by now we had become accustomed to running back and forth, so with YMS-43 watching over us, we sailed on to Palermo, arriving on the 25th for four days in the drydock. With our ship high and dry on blocks, the entire crew went to work scraping and painting the hull (in the prescribed "haze grey") while workmen carried on the repairs necessary to make 525 seaworthy again. My hands had by then healed, so my rank did not spare me from attacking barnacles with long-handled scrapers. While in drydock, we slept without running water, so an enterprising crew member cut out a hole in a plank and placed it between two supports extending out over the water. Voila, a "back

Damage during the invasion of Southern France forced SC-525 back to a Palermo drydock for repairs. Here, my hands having healed, I am scraping barnacles from the hull of the wooden sub-chaser. A good sonarman had to be versatile.

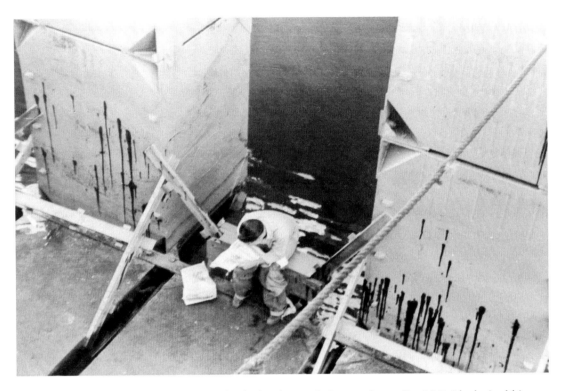

With no other toilet facilities on the drydock, pharmacist's mate Stuart Jay McBride devised his own. Fortunately, there was no health department in Palermo to inspect the facility.

house" just like on the farm. My photograph of "Pills" McBride sitting on our new privy suggests that the rickety one-holer would not have passed a health department examination.

There was ample time for shore liberty in and around Palermo, and I picked up a few more crude souvenirs, such as stitched pillow covers depicting the outline of the island. Before leaving Naples, I had run ashore and sent an EFM cablegram to my parents, assuring them that I had survived another unnamed "adventure," but, still under censorship regulations, I was unable to describe overtly our recent experiences. During those days La Nartelle seemed far away until the week-old August 17 Rome edition of *Stars and Stripes* jogged our memories with headlines like "Riviera Coast Secure" and "Churchill Sees Landing from British Destroyer." In a story headed "Navy Clears Way Before Doughboys Pile Ashore," the paper claimed that "The infantry came ashore at 0800 hours this morning [August 15] and scarcely got its feet wet"—certainly a little hyperbolic. We chuckled at Bill Mauldin's cartoon, "Up Front," depicting a foot soldier aboard a ship telling a sailor, "You fellers oughta carry a little dirt t'dig holes in." We smiled as we read comic strips like "Donald Duck," "The Flop Family," "Major Hoople," and "Blondie," and listened to Armed Forces Radio programs. We were, however, rather startled by a headline in the August 23 Naples edition of *Stars and Stripes*, "War's End 'In Sight,' Monty Tells Troops." That prediction from Field Marshal Bernard L. Montgomery up in Normandy sounded recklessly optimistic for those of us who had been at the "Soft Underbelly" of France, where our seamen were daily warring against mines, explosive boats, and shells from the mountains above Monte Carlo.

If we thought that our front-line service was history, we were rudely disillusioned when *525* was lowered from drydock. She moved to Dog Berth, and a crane tied up astern and put aboard a smoke generator and an arsenal of ammunition. Eddie Runof was not the only gob spouting colorful oaths when at noon on August 30 we set a sea detail and began a two-day nonstop sail back to Southern France at a thousand RPMs (about 12.3 knots). Our solitude was broken only by the sight of south-bound convoys, a colorful show put on by a Corsican volcano, and a puzzling floating object described in the ship's log as a "Long, thin pole, about 15 feet long, with flag." Suspecting that the contraption might be booby-trapped, and refusing to fire on a flag, we gave it a wide berth and continued northward.

Upon arrival in the Delta Force area, the captain reported to Lieutenant Ostrum aboard *SC-503* and the operations officer on *Biscayne* (AVP-11) and learned that our assignment was to patrol the Gulf of St. Tropez. The next nine days, duties — like challenging ships as large as French cruisers, escorting Liberty ships through cleared channels, distributing provisions and mail to other vessels, dropping and hoisting the anchor, and scampering to general quarters — were not very exciting, and pods of porpoises played havoc with my sonar.

The monotony was broken on Sunday morning, September 10, when we docked in St. Tropez. Presumably because we were the only men who made special efforts to attend religious services whenever available, Lieutenant Waldron granted shore liberty to Lieutenant McCormick, Chief Miller, George Klumpp, and me. Thankful for having survived another invasion, our party sought to locate a church in the resort community. Finding no English-language service in St. Tropez, we bummed a ride on a weapons carrier, whose driver scared the daylights out of us by taking shortcuts across fields clearly marked *Achtung: Minen*. We crossed the 43rd parallel and ended up in the beautiful little town of Ste. Maxime on the north shore of the gulf, almost overlooking the beach at La Nartelle, where we had landed the 45th Division Thunderbirds the previous month. If there was a Protestant church in Ste. Maxime, we could not find it — after all, France was a heavily Catholic country — but we did get a warm reception from the local populace, impressed by our neat dress whites. We also experienced the feel of a quaint and colorful French coastal town and brought back picture postcards of prewar scenes. We watched the time and caught a ride back, by crowding into one of those ubiquitous Jeeps,[29] arriving in St. Tropez just before our liberty hours expired. A chill came over us as we looked around the docks and found no sign of our freshly painted haze-gray ship. Nervous, high-pitched inquiries solved the mystery: In our absence, *SC-525* had been ordered by the *Biscayne* to rush toward the Italian border for a special mission, the nature of which was not revealed. So there we were, stranded in a bombed-out French harbor. My mind flashed back to the day in Casablanca when I arrived at the dock to board my new ship and discovered that she was at sea. On that occasion I had slept on the deck of a friendly sister vessel. Now, a year and a half later, in company with our executive officer, I was again shipless. Fortunately, naval hospitality came to the rescue, and we were offered the deck of *SC-503*. Many years later — after St. Tropez, the playground of Brigitte Bardot, became the toniest resort on Côte d'Asur — I wondered why I was so apprehensive about being left ashore there. Luckily, before nightfall as we prepared to bed down on the deck of another vessel, the unmistakable *525* rounded the breakwater. Our party eagerly jumped aboard. Shipmates who had been denied liberty that morning made us the butt of jokes, but the quartet counted our blessings for an exciting day ashore. We learned that six hours and many miles eastward, *Cinq-Deux-Cinq* had received a radio message countermanding the special order, so the ship reversed course to pick up the church party. We immediately proceeded to Canebière Bay and resumed our monotonous patrol duty.

While *525* was carrying out routine patrols and messenger services in the Delta area, other vessels were conducting dangerous missions near the Franco–Italian border. As Allied troops pushed the Germans eastward toward Menton, capital ships were called upon to shell Nazi positions in the mountains overlooking the coast. Minesweepers — AMs, YMSs, and VPs (the latter LCVPs equipped with sweeping gear) — sought to clear minefields so that firepower ships could be brought closer in. The sweepers faced three threats: undetected mines, shells from shore gunners, and attacks from surface craft — E-boats, torpedo boats, explosive boats, and Neger/Marder semi-submarines. For example, on September 5 a dozen "human torpedoes" sought to slip past *Incredible* (AM-249) on their way to attack the larger warships, not wanting to waste their explosive load on minesweepers. The AM's skipper wrote later, "They cruised with the torpedo under water and with just the head of the pilot in a glass dome above the water. We all fired at them and I'm sure my ship hit at least two of them." Shortly afterward, the Perspex domes began to appear near the French cruiser *Le Malin* and American destroyer *Ludlow*, and a spirited battle ensued during which at least three of the weird craft were put out of action. Captured, the talkative eighteen-year-old pilot of one of them admitted that he was aiming for the cruiser that flew the hated French flag; he also assured his captors that many more "wonder weapons" were ready to emerge from the port of Menton, just east of Monaco. And indeed they did appear. On September 9 and 10, more were engaged and repulsed by destroyers and minesweepers dodging shells from mountain gunners.[30]

We were congratulating ourselves on having been spared German shells off Monte Carlo and Menton when on September 14, passing our old cruiser friend *Brooklyn* in the Camel Force area, we were signaled by USS *Mainstay* (AM-261) to take station on her starboard beam as she sped eastward. We were heading for our most dangerous mission of Operation Dragoon. Before nightfall, we wished we were back at our lackluster job of patrolling the gulf.

It sounded like a normal job, for by then we were accustomed to operating around the sweepers. Under orders from *Mainstay*, we sailed eastward and screened AMs and YMSs within sight of Monaco and — more significantly — in sight of Boche gunners in the mountains behind Monte Carlo and nearby Menton. Passing within two miles, we had a marvelous daytime view of the fabled city from the sea. Although I had read about Monte Carlo, at the time I knew little of the glitter of pre-war Monaco and simply admired from offshore the handsome buildings that had escaped the war. Prince Louis II had supported the Vichy government, but Italian troops, then Germans, occupied the little country, and there they were, lobbing shells at our American ships.

Our detail was to lay smoke to obscure from German gunners the activity of several sweepers, including *Mainstay, Implicit* (AM-246), *Incredible* (AM-249), and *YMS-250, -359,* and *-373*. Our *525*, of course, was unprotected from German binoculars in the hills; our job was to obscure their view of the sweepers. In other words, we were expendable. On the first day, as the deep-water sweeping gear cut loose mines that floated to the surface, we exploded three with gunfire and helped the YMSs kill three more. The underwater explosions resulted in spectacular photographs. The photos, however, concealed the real-life danger from the German shells and from cut mines that could, in the roily currents, bobble up against the hull of our — or any other — ship. Somewhat amusing only in retrospect, we also sank a paravane lost by one of the sweepers. The day's operation went so well that we were rewarded with an overnight in Nice beside *SC-651*. There was time only for a quick walk around Vieux Nice to see the exteriors of multicolored boutiques and baroque churches with their red-tiled roofs. St. Nicholas Cathedral with six onion-shaped domes, a vestige of Russians who once used Nice as a retreat, was the most spectacular. Despite the war, Promenade des Anglais and the waterfront of the Bay of Angels retained their attraction.

Early the next morning we sailed out again, this time to the French-Italian border, with

Lieutenant (jg) Hugh P. McCormick, executive officer, primes and drops a smoke pot to screen minesweepers from German gunners in the hills above Monte Carlo.

instructions (as if we needed them) to beware of mines, one-man submarines, and German gunners in the hills. On the way, we scrambled to general quarters and manned our guns as several torpedo boats headed straight for us. Fortunately, Cieslak was able to read their friendly signal, but we did not let down our guard until they were close enough to be recognized by eyesight. We stationed a bow lookout, and we exploded eight Type 82–5 contact mines and helped *YMS-359* sink another. Again we overnighted in Nice between *YMS-359* and *-373*. Another quick walk ashore in the strangely dead but beautiful city, and exchanges of "what if's" with men on the sweepers, preceded a good night's sleep.

On the third day (September 16), hell broke loose. Enemy shore batteries opened up shortly after the YMSs streamed gear near the coast, so we ceased smoking and turned seaward at full speed. It would have been ridiculous for us to have fired our guns, the largest being a 40-millimeter. On the way we exploded two more mines and left one floating. In the early afternoon we sneaked back to our screening and smoking position, but the Krauts spotted us and again fired, scoring eight near misses. Later in the afternoon, we formed up to make another run along the beach. The log reads: "1709, Started smoking. 1730, Shelling began, seven or eight shells landing close to AM-246. 1810, Stopped smoking after making run to cover YMSs [with smoke]. Began shooting at mines." As night fell, we screened the sweepers west past St. Raphael and anchored in the Gulf of Frejus, not conscious of the fact that more than two hundred mines had been swept earlier in this Camel Force area.

The 17th brought relief; we sailed around the gulfs of Frejus and St. Tropez, ferrying Commander Brown and going alongside sister subchasers for deck-to-deck messages. Relief, however, was short-lived; late that night we took aboard three more cases of smoke pots. Then at 0545 in the morning, we sped back to the pregnant waters off Menton, where, at 0925, general quarters was called in anticipation of enemy shelling. Two hours later came a welcome surprise: "Operation cancelled. Heading back for Camel Area. Secured from General Quarters." Before night, we had sailed all the way back to St. Tropez, going alongside several ships for reasons the crew knew not. Something was up, but what?

Our hair-raising experiences off Menton, Ventimiglia, and San Remo in support of Mine Squadron 11 had lasted only three days, but that was long enough for *Cinq-Deux-Cinq* to become a specific target of enemy gunners and to learn the terror of many "near-misses." We had been fired on specifically; there within sight of Monte Carlo, lobs with our name on them carried no return address. That must have explained why Lieutenant Commander Harold Brown, ComMinDiv-32, came aboard and personally thanked the crew for our performance. Our whaleboat then delivered him to the cruiser *Philadelphia*, which again cast its enormous shadow over our little subchaser in the Gulf of St. Tropez.

From the operations just concluded, *SC-525* earned a rare mention in a book detailing Operation Dragoon. Commander Arnold S. Lott, in *Most Dangerous Sea*, recorded:

> Sweeping off Menton, only a mile west of the Italian border, commenced September 10. Besides clearing 48 mines, the sweepers had several bouts with German shore batteries, and sunk [*sic*] or captured some German "human torpedoes" and explosive boats. Particular credit was due the Menton sweepers—*Implicit, Improve, Incessant, Incredible, Mainstay, Pinnacle, YMS's 17, 164, 179, 250, 359,* and *373,* plus *SC 525* (smoke layer)—because all of them were new arrivals in the area. None of the ships and only a handful of their personnel had ever before swept mines under enemy fire.[31]

German gunners high above Monte Carlo shelled the waters in which minesweepers, with *SC-525* as protective smoke layer, sought to clear the sea lanes. This was one of our many near-misses during the operations near the French and Italian border.

Moored alongside the jetty at St. Tropez on September 18, we had chance for reflection about events beginning August 15. Judged at the end of the first month, the invasion of Southern France had been highly successful, for Allied losses had been mercifully fewer than military authorities had predicted. Admiral Morison opined, "It [Dragoon] may stand as an example of an almost perfect amphibious operation from the view of training, timing, Army-Navy-Air Force coöperation, performance and results."[32]

Still, the cost had not been inconsequential to the United States Navy. The unwanted distinction of the first naval loss during Dragoon went to *LST-282*, which was hit by a glide-bomb and sunk with forty casualties on D-Day. The sinking of two other ships was very personal for the crew of *525*. The tragic loss of *YMS-24* off Frejus has already been described[33] but off Toulon on September 1, *YMS-21* also struck a mine and sank after *Planter* (ACM-2) helped rescue thirty-one survivors. *SC-525* had operated with both of these craft many times the previous year, and their loss, coming only a few months after we saw *YMS-30* go down at Anzio, deeply upset our crew. Our kinship was deeper than personal acquaintance with the men, for, like our subchaser, each yard motor minesweeper was wood-hulled. At 136 feet long with a complement of about thirty-two, she was designed with an eight-foot draft, speed of fifteen knots, and a tight turning curve, enabling her to clear mines closer to the shore than could the larger 221-foot, steel-hulled fleet minesweepers (AMs). YMSs proved their splendid worth in all of the North African and Mediterranean operations, and we felt a close affinity to their sailors, who, like ours, were cramped into tiny spaces on a bucking ship with minimal amenities.

As in Shingle, so in Dragoon enemy surface craft were little more than nuisances to Allied vessels. The pestering came from a few MAS boats, corvettes, torpedo boats, one-man submarines, and strange little "explosive boats." Among American ships that dispatched gnats along the French Mediterranean coast were *Harding* (DD-635), *Cormick* (DD-223), *Satterlee* (DD-626), *Charles F. Hughes* (DD-428), and *Hilary P. Jones* (DD-427). USS *Ludlow* (DD-438) and the French *Le Malin* helped destroy a number of Neger/Marders off Monaco on September 5, and the human torpedoes' base was eradicated near Ventimiglia. Skirmishes between Allied and German surface craft continued until near the end of the war, however, for as late as March 1945 several enemy torpedo boats were destroyed. Still, not a single Allied ship was sunk by this motley assortment.

On the other hand, mines — which recognize neither truce nor surrender — remained lethal threats for years. Only three weeks before Germany surrendered the next year, the American *MTB-710* was sunk by a mine.[34] Nevertheless, Allied commanders concluded in the fall of 1944 that the enemy mines could remain along the Franco–Italian coast, a wise decision because German artillery in the mountains high above Menton, Monte Carlo, and San Remo remained a threat until the surrender the following May. Furthermore, the Allies placed a higher priority on driving Nazi troops from other sections of Europe. Consequently, mountain gunners and mosquito-size boats along the Riviera continued to threaten Allied shipping from their lairs, and as late as February 11, 1945, a shell from above San Remo damaged USS *McLanahan* (DD-615), killing one man. The war in the Mediterranean was not over in September 1944, but the attention of the United States Navy was now directed toward the Pacific, where the battle against Japan was at a crucial stage. I would be given the opportunity to see the faces of other enemies.

11

Another Side of War Ashore in Sicily, Italy, Corsica and France

January–September 1944

Awaiting me when I rejoined the crew on March 10, 1944, was so much mail that I could hardly believe it was all mine, and as *SC-525* followed *YMS-36* from Naples toward Palermo, I eagerly devoured news from family and friends in the States. Many of them assumed that I had been wounded critically, and I felt alternately amused and a little embarrassed by their profound concern. Having grown up in a family that seldom showed solicitous emotions, I was not accustomed to sympathy so intimately expressed. For several weeks I sought to respond to every message, and I spent many of my off-duty hours writing letters with my right hand, by then healed enough for writing and light work but too tender to steer the ship in rough seas.

Among my most loyal non-family correspondents were Julia Wright, Dorothy Slade, Myrtle Carter, Evelyn Zimmerman, Arthur Turner, Barbara Simpson, and Lois Fitch. In high school, I had a crush on Julia, whose family was generally recognized as the "upper crust" of Caswell County. Despite the two-step difference in our economic and social status, Julia treated me as an equal, and we confided with each other as extremely warm friends. Had the war not intervened, I suspect our relationship would have matured into a serious romance, but that eventuality aside, she became a faithful correspondent both before and after she entered college. More than anyone else's, her letters kept me abreast of the activities of my age-group — what was happening in the community, who had died, who won the latest athletic contest, who was dating whom, who was volunteering or being drafted for military service, and who was stationed where. She had an uncanny resemblance to Susan Anne Womack, a Reidsville girl with whom I was also enamored but who did not become a regular correspondent. Judy, on the other hand, proved to be a real patriot by organizing her fellow students at Stratford College into a special club whose members regularly corresponded with servicemen from the Caswell and Pittsylvania counties.

Dorothy was a more mature local intellectual who taught at Cobb Memorial School, and her letters were always newsy and light-hearted. When I sent her a five-franc note from Africa, she claimed it was greater than her monthly salary. And when she learned of my injury at Anzio, she wrote,

> Listen, you mug! When I sent you after Adolf, I didn't think I needed to tell you to keep out of the way of the Huns and their ambassadors of ill-will torpedoes, bullets, and such. (The "and

such" includes whatever hit, bit, or otherwise afflicted you.) Hope you are getting along all right. Will you be out soon, or do you have a pretty nurse?

Dot worked tirelessly in coaching students who competed in the school's annual public speaking contest, to the winner of which, beginning in 1942, I furnished a sterling silver cup in commemoration of my bi-state championship the year before.

In my senior year at Cobb Memorial, another girlfriend was Myrtle Carter, whose framed color photograph accompanied me throughout the war and whose letters were eagerly awaited. Evelyn Zimmerman was class valedictorian, and though we were never particularly close, she was a faithful letter-writer from East Carolina Teachers College. Arthur Turner was a friend from Locust Hill Methodist Church; he escaped the draft but dedicated himself to the war effort on the home front, including writing to men in uniform. At Lees-McRae, Barbara Simpson was so "forward" with me that I was more than a little apprehensive around her, but her genuine warmth was shown in her correspondence, which was sometimes jazzed up with artistic drawings. Lois Fitch, editor of *Jefferson Standard Life*, regularly sent news about my former colleagues at the insurance company. In turn, she published several of my letters and in the January 1945 issue reproduced five photographs that I snapped in the Med.

My heart was warmed by so many friends — and some correspondents whom I did not know — who felt it a patriotic duty to show their concern for me and other service men in combat areas. I appreciated every letter and sought to answer each one. Letters informed us at the front that life was also increasingly difficult back home, where gasoline, sugar, rubber, and many staples were scarce, some of them strictly rationed; yet complaints were muted. Reports of deaths and tragedies reminded us that we were not the only unfortunates in the world. For example, a sad letter from Miss Alison Stirling described the disastrous fire that gutted Lees-McRae College's library, in which I had worked as her assistant for four months in 1941. Of course, communications from the war zone were eagerly anticipated at home by family and friends. I learned later that some of my letters were circulated around the community, and several were printed in the *Caswell Messenger*, for which I had been an occasional "freebie" community correspondent before the war.

My own letter-writing was sporadic but certainly more regular than that of some crew members who had become strangers to their blood relatives and looked upon their fellow sailors as their only family. The ship's officers encouraged their men to write, and they appear seldom to have taken offense to complaints and criticisms that inevitably crept into correspondence — perhaps the most stinging references being to "ninety-day wonders." As censors of outgoing correspondence, Lieutenants Reece, Waldron, McCormick, and Barton certainly understood that complaining (we called it "bitching") was a necessary relief during periods of anxiety, and that some men served best after "blowing their stack." Other members of the crew may have approached the offense under occasional circumstances, but Noah Samuel and Edward Cain were the only two to actually serve time in the brig for insubordination.

The United Service Organization (USO) and American Red Cross encouraged servicemen to keep in touch with the homefolks, and sometime they provided printed greeting cards with complimentary mailing for men in a hurry. Some religious organizations also produced cards in English. For example, I mailed home a white folded card containing a drawing of a cross and a golden lamb and the printed words "Signum Praecepti Paschalis" and "Wishing You a Happy Easter." The inside message read: "Sicily 1944/Here's a little/Easter message/With love in every line/And a happy wish/Between them/For you." Perhaps in Italian, the lines rhymed. A more colorful folded Mother's Day greeting from Sicily did indeed rhyme: "No wish could ever tell you, Mom/How much you've meant, it's true/But, on this 'Mother's Day,'/I pray to be much nearer you!"

We were permitted to identify our location as "In the Mediterranean," but censorship regulations forbade naming the country except when mailing preprinted greetings such as those just mentioned. The regulations, however, did not prevent me from developing devious ways of outwitting the system. For example, when a letter from home revealed that a neighbor was believed to be in Italy, I wrote (September 11, 1944), "I might run into Thomas Smith sometime when I go ashore." When my folks asked me if I had been in the invasion at Anzio, I wrote back, "You asked me a question in your 16th letter about my travels. Well the answer is yes." And in my letter to Uncle Will (September 10), I wrote about the thrill of seeing places that I had studied in school, including "those that have been uncovered after hundreds and hundreds of years of darkness under the earth."

There were, of course, diversions aboard ship in addition to letter-writing, bull-shooting, and card-playing. For example, Joe Johnson would have been proud, for his repeated skunking of me in chess in 118th Station Hospital had not gone to waste. Now that the checkmate master was back at the battle front, I considered myself an heir to his prowess as a player. Surprisingly, few of the crew knew the game, so George Klumpp and I took over the board and managed to play nearly every day. Between the inauguration of our first series on March 21 and our last games six months later, I kept a meticulous record proving that I won 83 to his 53. I felt that I had become the master of *something*.

I continued to attend religious services when convenient. For example, on June 4, 1944, while we were back in Bizerte, I attended Protestant services at the RecWel in Karouba and heard Chaplain Jamison preach on "The Life Unseen," after which I took communion. In fact, throughout my year and a half in the Mediterranean, I continued to think that I might eventually enter the ministry, and at 118th Station Hospital the idea was strengthened by the friendship that I developed with Chaplain Ostergren. The army chaplain defied stereotypes of a minister; in appearance, he looked more like a professional football player. But the gentle giant, as strong as an ox, was as gentle as a lamb. A Swedish Lutheran, he comforted a Catholic in the absence of a priest as quickly as he softly prayed with a dying Protestant. Fairly often he and his assistant brought a portable organ into the ward, distributed song books, and led in singing both familiar hymns and popular American songs. When I turned my hands-in-cast into a walking waiter service, the chaplain found a willing helper, and I felt a sense of worth in carrying papers, magazines, and trays of food to the bed-ridden. Never having undergone a scriptural epiphany and having little real knowledge of the Bible, I began to see that a minister was not limited to preaching the Gospel; he could live by its teachings too.

Through my liberty mate George Klumpp, I got to know Father Preyer, the priest at the base at Bizerte, and I learned that Catholics did not wear horns. And on Sunday in several ports, I joined my executive officer, Hugh McCormick, and my fellow Tar Heel, Boats Miller, in paddling the little wherry over to a capital ship for services conducted by its resident chaplain.[1] I shared the disappointment of Stanley Dauman, one of my favorite members of the crew, that there was no Jewish "church" for him aboard the ships.

From April through June, I spent much time studying for and taking examinations in the yeoman's course, conducted by correspondence through the Navy Department. Of the fourteen assignments, I failed four, which I retook in June and passed. My final score was 3.5 out of a possible 4.0, with a typing score of 3.6. My certificate was dated September 19, 1944, although my reclassification was not effected until May 1 the following year, by which time I was on the USS *Speed* (AM-116) in the Pacific.[2]

I also occupied myself in jotting down what — because of military prohibition against diaries — I called "notes," including meticulous accounts of expenditures and savings during my first fifteen months in the Navy. As a recruit, my salary was $40 per month, but that was boosted to $70 as a third-class petty officer, and there was a $10 raise in July. Jefferson Standard Life Insurance Company commemorated holidays by sending a $25 war bond to each former employee serving in the military. From enlistment through August 1944, I had received $1,807 in salary and $225 in war bonds, and of that I had saved $1,289.45 for future college expenses. In 1944, that was enough to pay for two years at Lees-McRae College.

The absence of banking services in occupied Africa and Italy led to the compensation of military personnel in $1, $5, and $10 paper bills that were almost indistinguishable from regular 1935a silver certificates except for the color of the Treasury Department's seal. These "yellow seal" bills served as a precaution against an enemy's seizure of vast quantities of American paper money; in such an event, the currency could simply be nullified, just as Confederate money was repudiated by the Federal government a century earlier. In addition, however, with the invasion of Italy, the United States issued proclamation money called "Allied Military Currency," pegged at 100 Italian lire to the American dollar. Notes of 50 lire and higher were approximately the dimension of the American paper dollar, with the denominations written in English and Italian. The one lira and two, five, and ten lire notes were half-size.[3] The reverse of all notes carried the words "Allied Military Currency" and enumerated the Four Freedoms, as pronounced by President Franklin D. Roosevelt. We could convert our yellow-seal dollars to AMC notes and spend them on whatever was for sale locally. In addition, however, the military postal system sold money orders, and that was the means by which I sent savings back to the States.

My expenditures through August 1944 included repayment of Uncle Kester's loan of $50 (plus $5 interest), a gift of $50 to my sister Pauline, and $75 in donations to Locust Hill Methodist Church. Most of my other expenditures paid for subscriptions such as *The State*, *National Geographic*, and the *Caswell Messenger*, the latter often arriving in tatters weeks late. Still, any reading material was welcome overseas, as I explained in a letter published in *The State* Magazine on May 13, 1944: "Here in the European theatre, where I am now on duty with the Navy, a magazine like *The State* is just what the doctor ordered. I ... am looking forward to continued enjoyment of future issues. But I hope it will be unnecessary for all of them to come across the Atlantic to reach me."[4]

Back in the States a new invention called "television" was barely in the experimental stage (visual signals could be sent "line of sight" only about fifty miles), but for those of us fortunate enough to be near a radio receiver in the Mediterranean, the Allied Expeditionary Service provided an auditory peek into the outside world — the other battle fronts and the home front. The AES usually began broadcasting early in the morning and ended at 2200 (thus not keeping troops awake too late). Programs previously seen at home were rebroadcast, interspersed with news from the British Broadcasting Company. Programs included the Lux Radio Theater, the Aldrich Family, Red Skelton, and Yarns for Yanks. Comedians like Jack Benny, Fred Allen, and Fibber McGee and Molly were great favorites. More importantly, AES helped answer our yearning for music. Myrtle Carter kept me informed by mail of the most popular tunes back home.[5] But the titles meant less than the rebroadcast of the actual tunes, and we especially looked forward to hearing the "Lucky Strike Hit Parade," the Fred Waring Show, and Tommy Dorsey's Band. AES also played patriotic songs like "The White Cliffs of Dover," popularized by fellow Tar Heel Kay Kyser's "Kollege of Musical Knowledge," and "When the Lights Go On Again All Over the World," by Vaughn Monroe and his orchestra. The lyrics of the latter reminded us that the coast of our home country also was blacked-out at night. Music with messages reassured us that we were not forgotten by non-combatants back home.

While we were cheered by reports of victories on the war front, we were wise enough to suspect exaggerated claims of friend and foe alike. We especially learned to take the boasts of Nazi radio broadcasters with more than a grain of salt. While our compatriots in England and France were treated with radio programs from Berlin by one Axis Sally — the turncoat American, Mildred Gillars — we in the Mediterranean had our own "Axis Sally," whose programs were beamed out from Rome before its capture in June. *Our* Sally was in reality Rita Luisa Zucca, a native of New York who, while visiting Italy before the war, renounced her American citizenship and became a propagandist for Mussolini. With background music of "Between the Devil and the Deep Blue Sea," her nightly broadcasts started with the greeting, "Hello Suckers!" She then interspersed exaggerated claims of Nazi victories, taunts to our troops, and nostalgic songs such as "Moonlight Serenade." Like Berlin's Sally, ours sought to depress morale by portraying Allied soldiers' wives and sweethearts as being unfaithful back home. For example, she warned that Yanks stationed in England were having their way with two-timing wives and girlfriends of the Brits fighting alongside us at Anzio. With her partner, known only as "George" (who spoke impeccable English), the Roman Sally was a thorn in the side of Allied forces at Anzio because she seemed to know more about what was going on in the beachhead than those of us at the scene. On several occasions, she broadcast the names of captured Allied soldiers, adding an invitation for her listeners to join their colleagues in a nice, safe prisoner of war camp, where they could enjoy the luxury of a warm bed, hot meals, and humane treatment — much better, she and her sidekick suggested, than dying in Anzio's icy foxholes in what the propagandists called the "world's largest self-sustaining prisoner of war camp." For four months, Axis Sally's description of Anzio was not far off the mark.[6]

We also occasionally picked up the Nazi station, Radio Belgrade, which at 9:55 each night played the one German tune that we all loved — "Lili Marlene," made famous in English by Marlene Dietrich.

A second means of disseminating news in the Mediterranean was *Stars and Stripes*, the official newspaper of the United States Armed Forces, printed in several editions (e.g., Casablanca, Oran, Naples, Rome). Our Italy edition was produced, usually in eight pages, six days a week, by its own staff in Naples. A tabloid (11½ by 16½ inches), the woodpulp paper looked much like a hometown newspaper, its banner printed over an image of American flags tilting to the left and right. The headline usually reflected the latest news releases from combat areas. For example, the issue for January 26, 1944, carried the headline, "5th Widens Beachhead; Foe Sinks Hospital Ship," and gave a generally realistic report on the landings at Anzio-Nettuno, including the correct names of three British hospital ships, one of which, the *St. David*, was sunk. In addition to news stories, sports, opinion columns, and an official warning that the blackout hours in Peninsula Base Section for the week were 1740 to 0651, the issue contained two humorous cartoons by Sgt. Gregor Duncan; a cartoon strip called "The Sad Sack" by Sergeant George Baker; and Al Capp's comic strip, "Li'l Abner." The January 28 issue carried a column, "Puptent Poets," containing several poems by soldiers, none of them — particularly a GI's paean to his shoes — award-winners. The favorite columnist was, of course, Ernie Pyle, who better than any other war correspondent captured the authentic flavor of combat; he was viewed as a folk hero for, as young people used to say of North Carolina's Thomas Wolfe, "he *understands*."

For the British fighting forces, *Union Jack* provided similar news coverage. In the February 18 issue, shortly after the Allied bombing of the monastery at Monte Cassino, a front-page story began,

Preceded by strong artillery fire, German troops have resumed their heavy attacks against Allied positions in the northern part of the Anzio beach-head. Latest reports show that heavy fighting continues. Enemy aircraft are busy bombing and strafing, though heavily out-numbered by Allied planes, while shells from long-range guns are falling into our lines. Fierce tank battles are being fought.

A sober report by newpaperman J. M. MacLennan described the status of the invasion forces: "There are no safe base jobs in this theatre of war. For that is what the Anzio beach-head is to-day; a self-contained zone of operations in which a separate campaign is being fought by Allied troops who have no direct contact with the outside world."

Yank, the army's magazine of humor, with the forlorn "Sad Sack," provided hilarity to readers in Italy. Nearly every copy was passed around so frequently that the pages containing "cheesecake" photos of females quickly became tattered. Another popular publication was *Time* Magazine's "Pony Edition," printed on thin 6 × 8½ inch paper in 34 pages per issue. For $3.50 per year to APO and FPO addresses via first class mail, I subscribed and shared my copies with my shipmates.

Shipboard life deprived Navy men of much of the humor, ribald stories, and claims of sexual conquests typical of army camps. But we did share some of the humor, including poems playing upon place names. Each man made up his own corny version of "Dirty Gertie from Bizerte"; mine went like this:

> Dirty Gertie from Bizerte
> Wore a mousetrap 'neath her skirtie,
> Strapped it to her knee-cap purty,
> Baited it with Fleur-de-Flirte,
> Made exploring fingers hurty,
> Made all the boys alerte!
> She was voted in Bizerte
> Miss Latrine for 1930.

Another literary gem was published in the Mediterranean edition of *Stars and Stripes*:[7]

> We've had Stella the Bella of Fedela,
> And Gertie that wench from Bizerte,
> And fat, filthy Fannie from far-off Trapani,
> And other girls not so alerte.

Between January 8, 1944 — when we first left North Africa for Italy — and her decommissioning in Toulon the following September 21, *SC-525* went through two invasions and crisscrossed those waters more than a dozen times. The "Milk Run," the signalman from Wisconsin called it. We sometimes felt like a perpetual ferry, a shuttle, for although we were frequently in sight of land, we seldom had time to test our sea legs. Furthermore, many of our port calls were limited to taking on ammunition, provisions, water, and fuel, leaving no time for shore liberty. We were elated, therefore, when opportunities allowed us to see and learn more about the lands that we were seeking to free from Nazi oppression.

In January 1944 the *Caswell Messenger*, my home county newspaper, published part of one of my long letters:

> here in this new country, where we have been only a few days, there are many interesting and historical sights [*sic*] to be seen and I am looking forward to liberty in order to take in some of them. The war has destroyed many of these places that would be interesting. For the past month, every port in which we have stopped has been battered and in some of them, large cities before the war, hardly a building stands intact. The sad part of it is the realization that we did much of the damage ourselves. Churches, schools, homes, nothing held sacred.

Then, becoming an advocate, I continued, "Right here I'd like to put in a 'plug' for the American Red Cross. It is the best organization that the American people are called upon to support.... Every occupied city ... has a club set up, which offers numerous types of entertainment to the troops, from dances and stage shows to just talking to an American in civilian clothes."

We had observed in French- and Arabic-speaking Africa that many of the locals found it advantageous to learn a few words of English, and sailors often reciprocated by adopting simple native words and phrases, particularly when on liberty. However, my own first attempt to help win the war against Hitler by exercising my high school French proved embarrassing. Shortly after I boarded the subchaser in Casablanca, the captain asked me to translate instructions from the French pilot who was directing *SC-525* past sunken ships toward a lowered drydock. Each time I asked the pilot "gauche?" (left?) or "droite?"(right?), he repeated, "juste." When he realized that I did not understand the word, he pointed gauche, then droite, and then emphatically dead ahead with a loud "*juste!*" With reddened face, I realized he meant, as we said in the Navy, "steady as she goes" (that is, straight ahead). Linguistically challenged sailors found that there was such an English-speaking presence in large port cities that we had little incentive to learn much about the native tongues. However, at 118th Station Hospital I was given a sixty-two-page booklet titled *Italian: A Guide to the Spoken Language [Introductory Series]*.[8] The phonograph platter accompanying the booklet was quickly lost because there was no record-player on the ship. Still, I prided myself in learning a few signs, numbers, and such useful terms as "KO-may see KYA-ma?" (what is your name?), "GRAHTS-yay" (thank you), "KWAHN-to KO-sta?" (how much does it cost?), and "TROHP-po KA-ro" (too much). At bars and cafes, we played loose with the language by giving curt orders like "paisan, veni qua" (meaning venite qui or venire qua, come here) and "adanta via" (meaning andara via, scram). Civility always suffers during war, and we gave little thought toward winning friends among those who had been our enemies a few months earlier.

The remainder of our crew had been in Palermo twice previously, but the March 1944 assignment afforded me my first landing in Sicily. Facing the Gulf of Palermo, the city was founded by Phoenicians perhaps as early as the eighth century B.C. Surrounded on three sides by hills and with a heritage combining that of Greeks, Arabs, Byzantines, Romans, Venetians, Normans, and Spaniards, the city presented interesting contrasts between the ancient and the modern. Its location on the northwest corner of the island made it a natural stopover for seagoing vessels in both ancient and modern times, and Palermo eventually became Sicily's largest and most important port which, when captured in July 1943, provided the Allies an enormous military asset. Despite heavy bomb damage, the city was still filled with interesting sights that had escaped a bewildering number of wars over the centuries.

Shortly after *525* went into drydock at Palermo to repair the sonar hoisting mechanism and damaged hull suffered at Anzio, I rushed out with George Klumpp for my only real liberty since we left Oran the previous December. First, we located the Enlisted Men's Club for Coca-Cola and refreshments. Then we joined a tour — by means of a 1920s-model bus — sponsored for servicemen by the American Red Cross, and we spent Sunday taking in sights both of war damage and of surviving cultural institutions. Structures near the harbor had been pretty well destroyed by first Allied and later Nazi bombing, but new facilities had been built quickly by American forces, and the harbor had been made fully functional by the advance base units. Little restoration had been undertaken in the residential and business area, however, and bombed-out buildings occupied both sides of Via Francesco Crispi and many other streets. Begging children seemed to emerge from every alley, and only occasionally was there evidence of business recovery. I photographed one example — a man who proudly posed with his artistically arranged but limited quantity of fruits and vegetables brought in from the countryside. There appeared to be many admirers but few buyers along the rubble-filled street. Other scenes in Palermo were haunting: a donkey cart and hand-pushed organ-grinder, a few bedraggled pedestrians, teetering buildings, bombed-out Fascist Party headquarters, an occasional shop with a few items for sale.

We visited many historic sites in and around Palermo, including the city's monuments that had escaped bombing—such as Il Duomo, the impressive cathedral, consecrated in 1185, with its much-later, incongruous cupola; the Norman Palace, its grounds and Arabesque Capella Palatina; Piazza Bellini; Villa Tosca; Chiesa di Matorana and San Cataldo; Teatro Massimo (opera house); and Fontano Pretoria (the "fountain of shame") with its Renaissance nude statues. We of course couldn't resist taking each other's picture with hands on intimate parts of the nude marble statues.

Certainly the outstanding experience was a visit to the Benedictine Cathedral of Monreale, located a few miles outside Palermo. The overpowering structure was built on a hill in the twelfth century during the reign of William II ("William the Good") of Normandy, and eight centuries later it gives the appearance of a three-dimensional illuminated medieval manuscript. Blending several architectural styles, the church is massive—about 330 feet long and 130 feet wide—shaped as a Latin cross with three apses. The columns and capitals were taken from even older buildings in Sicily. In the central nave forty-two mosaics represent episodes in the Bible, and in the lateral naves the miracles of Christ are depicted. Over the apse, gold, glass, and small stones of myriad colors form a gigantic figure of Jesus extending his blessing, claimed to be the largest such image in the world. Below, the Virgin Mary holds the infant Christ on her lap, and to the right of the altar King William II is represented as offering the church to Mary.[9] Outside, columns shimmering with gold mosaics form an Arabesque courtyard of almost indescribable beauty. My black-and-white photos could not capture the sparkling colors of the cathedral.

A contrast to the grandeur of the Cathedral of Monreale was the simple beauty of the Church of San Giovanni degli Eremiti (St. John of the Hermits), so hidden that all of its five red domes could be seen simultaneously from only a few locations. Built by Moorish architects during twelfth-century Norman rule, the little church stands as a gem among Palermo's more recent buildings. The cloister and garden feature palm, orange, and pomegranate trees and flowering roses and jasmines—a little haven of peace in the teeming city. The black-and-white photo that I snapped is only mediocre, but I was fortunate to purchase an original watercolor, signed by the artist Tearotini, showing four of the red domes.

An even greater contrast to both Monreale and San Giovanni was found beneath the Capuchin Monastery where were displayed mummified bodies of thousands of prominent Sicilians, some of the corpses four hundred years old. As early as the 1530s, Cappuccini Friars discovered that bodies of their monks—placed in crypts dug out of the dry limestone beneath the monastery—underwent a dehydration process that significantly slowed decay. The discovery led to experimentation in mummification that offered more prolonged preservation. It also led to interest among the wealthy and influential, who sought immortality for themselves and their families. The penurious order, probably seeing dual opportunities (to accommodate wealthy Christians and to attract financial support) began admitting bodies of laymen to the limestone crypts, more of which were excavated as needed. The process became rather sophisticated with the excavation of crypts accommodating the bodies of families of professional and social classes, to which relatives or friends might come to visit, commune with, and pray for the dead. As demand increased, more excavations eventually led to large rooms in which shelves and niches were carved out, permitting an artful display of the corpses, sitting, lying, standing, or hanging. A traveler, John Lloyd Stephens wrote in 1837, "in the vault of the convent at Palermo I had seen the bodies of nobles and ladies, the men arranged upright along the walls, dressed as in life, with canes in their hands and swords by their sides; and the noble ladies of Palermo lying in state, their withered bodies clothed in silks and satins, and adorned with gold and jewels."[10] And in 1853 John Ross Browne wrote that the dead were visited by relatives once a year "to pray for the salvation of their souls, and deck the bodies with flowers."[11]

By the time George and I joined other American servicemen being conducted through the spooky vaults (for a fee, of course), the scene was macabre: Most of the bodies were little more than skeletons covered by dry skin and rotting clothing, some with ghoulish expressions mimicking every imaginable emotion from pain to exhilaration. Among the best preserved was the corpse of one of Garibaldi's associates, General John Corrao, who was assassinated in 1863. Although mummification was officially ended in 1889, additional bodies were admitted for several more decades. A process was improved early in the twentieth century by a Sicilian, Professor Alfredo Salafia, and in 1920 he apparently prepared the corpse of a young girl named Rosalia Lombardo, for on March 12, 1944, the girl's body was so well preserved that it looked like a sleeping child.[12]

On subsequent dockings in Palermo, George and I discovered the pre-war ocean resort of Mondello, separated from the big city by Monte Pellegrino. In most occupied cities, the armed forces quickly established an officers' club, leaving the welfare of enlisted men to the American Red Cross and the USO. Mondello, the most welcoming facility that we found in Europe, was unusual in that it served all ranks. In addition to a beautiful cassino built on stilts in the Gulf of Palermo, there were luxurious dressing rooms, recreational facili-

Just as George Klumpp snapped this picture of me showing off my "new" hands at Mondello, our captain, Lieutenant (jg) John C. Waldron, right, emerged from the pavilion, which sported a huge V for victory sign. This may have been the only R&R spa at which officers shared facilities with enlisted men.

ties, refreshment stands, and bicycle rental. A military band often played, and female members of the armed forces, plus a few local señorinas highly selected by military authorities, were often available as dance partners. The dual role of the resort was documented in a rare photograph. I was sitting on a railing in front of the cassino (which was decorated with a huge and colorful letter V), proudly showing off my "new" hands, when Lieutenant Waldron, our captain, stepped out of the building just as George snapped the shutter. Sixty-one years later the prized picture was reproduced on the cover of Mary Best's tribute to World War II veterans, *North Carolina's Shining Hour*.[13]

Another highlight of our meanderings in Palermo was the discovery of a secluded cold shower in one of the base buildings. We made good use of the spigot and shared the secret with several of our favorite shipmates. Later, while *SC-525* was getting repaired from the pounding at Southern France, I attended Protestant services at the Naval Operating Base and heard Chaplain Ivan B. Bell preach on "Taking Life Apart and Putting It Back Together Again." Among the hymns was "Onward, Christian Soldiers," which seemed particularly appropriate as we engaged the Axis powers and their diabolical dogma

My shipmate Stanley Hallas remembered better than I the details of a visit aboard *525* by two pretty Army nurses, escorted by a mysterious American male driving a fancy Ferrari and lugging a motion picture camera. Lieutenant Waldron was suitably awed by his visitors, so he sought to impress them with the capabilities of his fierce warship. On a pretext of perhaps swinging the ship or of testing depth charges, the captain sailed *525* far out into the Gulf of Palermo to demonstrate the awesome power of his intimidating subchaser. The guests were treated to gunnery practice and various maneuvers, but the pièce de résistance was a simulated attack upon a submarine. The crew rushed to battle stations, and depth charges were set for a deep-water explosion. Two cans were pushed off the fantail, K-guns boomed other charges to port and starboard, and we began ticking off the seconds. Suddenly — far too quickly — one of the rolled-off charges detonated when only about twenty feet down, and the thunderous explosion blew the stern of the *525* out of the water, knocked several crew members to the deck, and evoked a collective bellow, "What the hell... !" Of course, our crew recognized the snafu — one canister had been set incorrectly or had exploded prematurely — but the captain cleverly concealed his chagrin. The visitors, greatly impressed by what they assumed to be a well planned attack on an imaginary submarine, went away comforted that our little ship was manned by tough old salts capable of taking on the entire Kraut U-boat fleet. We thought the explosion had thrown our little dog Suzie overboard, but hours later the pup sneaked out from her hiding place and from that time on was happy to serve as a lap dog. After the war Hallas encountered the nurses' mysterious escort, who revealed that in fact he had been an intelligence officer with the OSS, and he was simply on a lark with his female friends. Regrettably, none of the crew ever saw the movies that the visitor shot during *525*'s only depth charge attack with females onboard.

Sicilians did not like to be called Italians, and the souvenirs available to Allied forces often reflected pride in their island and its culture. For example, I purchased a marble ashtray representing the shape of the island, with the names of major cities inscribed. I also mailed home several silk pillow covers and a table set, all embroidered with the outline of the island. The needlework was amateurish, but in each instance the seamstresses appeared in dire need, so I considered each purchase an act of charity to the destitute. Of course, for all that I knew, the women may have been working for the Mafia, but I came away feeling good.

If in 1944 I had known more about the heritage of the intriguing area bordering the Bay of Naples, I would have come away with a more profound understanding of those ancient lands whose recorded history and lore date back thousands of years. In high school I studied geography, but my textbooks paid little attention to the history and natural features of the Mediterranean that intrigued me when, three days after my twentieth birthday, I put my first foot ashore in Italy upon our arrival at the island of Nisida in January 1944.

Future dockings in the Gulf of Pozzuoli gradually opened my eyes to the uniqueness of this northeastern edge of the Bay of Naples. I began to understand why Pozzuoli appeared to literally spring from the sea, for some ancient buildings — including the Temple of Serapis (euphemism for the ancient marketplace) — did indeed rise from the sea. Other structures, including the nearby ancient Roman Port Julius, were completely covered by water. At first I assumed that the sea had gradually risen over thousands of years, but I learned that the entire quarter-moon-shaped area from Posillipo to Monte di Procida — Campi Flegrei, known in literature as the Phlaegrean Fields — sits above a vast subterranean sea of magma, produced by colliding tectonic plates and causing the land to rise or fall several feet per decade. To better understand the phenomenon, on June 17 George and I rode a Red Cross truck to La Solfatara, a huge hell potted with cauldrons of sulphur fumaroles and thermal springs surrounded by odd-shaped mountains of tufa and signs reading "Pericola." Dirty steam and mud gurgled and bubbled through scores of vents in the earth — a process called bradiseism — giving off what to us was an objectionable rotten-egg odor. The scene was surreal, however, for a few locals, apparently familiar with the fickleness of this natural phenomenon, dared to mud-bathe in one of the steaming pools. The mountains all around were products of volcanos, one of them — Mount Nuovo — having completely obliterated the town of Tripergole in 1538.

Pozzuoli had a history for other reasons. It was founded by the Greeks in the fifth century B.C. and the apostle Paul stopped here on his way to Rome. In the second century A.D., the Romans displaced the Greeks and changed its name to Puteoli, meaning in Latin "little wells" — a comment on the hydrothermal vents. Among the impressive ruins was the amphitheater that once provided 20,000 seats above its elaborate underground system from which gladiators and their victims emerged. (Only toward the end of the twentieth century did archaeologists begin excavating ruins of Rione Terra at the acropolis above Pozzuoli.) Of many craters in the area, Lake Averno was described by the Roman poet Vergil as the "foul-breathing" entrance to hell. To the west, an even earlier Greek settlement at Cumae, around the peninsula facing the Gulf of Gaeta, is noted for the cave from which Sibyl, the priestess of Apollo — according to Vergil's *Aeneid* — issued her prophecies and led Aeneas down into the underworld.

Nisida, the pincer-shaped vestige of a volcanic cone between La Gaiola and Bagnoli, came to feel like home during our many cruises around Gulf of Pozzuoli. High atop the island, where his wife Portia committed suicide, Marcus Brutus plotted to kill Julius Caesar and afterward consulted with Cicero over the future of Rome. From there, one could see in all directions, a perfect spot from which to view on a clear day the multiple cities around the Bay of Naples — or to keep in eye on the hundreds of Allied ships that filled the entire bay prior to the invasions at Anzio and Southern France. An official Navy Department photograph captured *SC-525* tied up alongside LSTs being loaded just before we sailed toward the invasion beaches of Côte d'Azur in August.

From January to early March, my view of the sprawling city of Naples, with Mt. Vesuvius in the background, had been limited to what could be seen from the veranda of 118th Station Hospital, located near one of the funiculars high up on Corso Vittorio Emanuele. Immediately after I was piped back aboard on March 10, *SC-525* sailed to Palermo, and our return to Naples fifteen days later had been so marred by the stifling atmosphere of erupting

Mt. Vesuvius that we remained only overnight. Other stopovers also had been brief, so it was late May before George and I could really explore the city and its historic environs.

When hardened Allied troops broke through the Chiunzi Pass from the Salerno beachhead and captured Naples on October 1, 1943, they were shocked by the degree to which the retreating Germans had destroyed the city, blown up its water and sewer system, and left its factories and infrastructure in shambles. The following spring I was introduced to the pathetic story by a little pamphlet, *Soldiers Guide to Naples*, published by the Special Service of the Metropolitan Area Peninsula Base Section. It began:

> Today Naples is a bombed, sacked and gutted city.... The Naples of pre-war days is gone. It will be impossible for you to visit that Naples — it may never exist again — but some of the old city still remains, some escaped the ravages of war, and while you can you should see as much as possible in order to visualize the days that were and realize better the vandalism of the sacking, destroying Germans.

George and I obeyed the advice. Naples (originally *Neapolis*, later *Napoli*, meaning "new city" in English) had undergone sieges and changes of masters many times since its founding by the Greeks 2,500 years ago, and more recently it was the capital of the Kingdom of the Two Sicilies. In 1861, following its capture by Garibaldi's army, Naples was absorbed into a unified Italy under King Victor Emanuel II, and it remained the chief city south of Rome. Its harbor was important commercially, but in the twentieth century Naples became popular as the seaport for the rapidly developing tourist destinations of Capri and the Amalfi Drive. German efforts to make the harbor useless to the approaching Allies ultimately proved futile, because American advance base personnel quickly cleared wreckage from the docks and readied the bay as the rendezvous for the hundreds of ships supporting the invasions at both Anzio and Southern France. The Allies also made rapid progress in reestablishing essential utilities, opening railways and public thoroughfares, and reestablishing civilian authority (albeit subservient to heavy military influence). More sadly, the civilian population had been left destitute — beggars, thieves, prostitutes, and black marketeers almost indistinguishable from proud and patriotic citizens anxious to restore civility in their city — all this despite the employment of many locals by Allied authorities in the restoration projects.

Boys, ranging from age 6 to 16, called *scrugnizzi*, roamed the streets stealing, scrounging, trading, and pimping with questions like "Hey Joe, you sleep my little sister? Virgin." One tyke, when ordered to scram, grabbed his crotch and with raised eyebrow asked, "You like Italian boy?" Everything seemed for sale, and the street boys had learned that soldiers' tastes were eclectic. At nearly every restaurant licensed by the Peninsula Base Section, scrugnizzi congregated outside, badgering uniformed men as they entered, pushing noses to the windows, and sidling up to departing customers. Owners of the establishments kept an eye out for quick-footed youngsters who rushed in, grabbed food from the table, and disappeared into the crowd. Some of the urchins made it a game with the expectation of getting a meal in a detention camp if caught.

Driven by the need to survive, Neapolitans were resourceful, an attribute described this way in an irreverent map folder simply titled *Napoli Compliments of the American Red Cross*:

> The war has cost Naples her factories, her rail and trolley system and many of her proud buildings. Thus you have come to a city of jobless men and women.... Nobody's making anything ... so everybody sells. The good citizens of Naples will sell you anything from a bogus oil painting to their daughter's last pair of silk bloomers. But, whether it's a cameo or a dinner, they'll ask three times what its worth.

I saw no silk bloomers for sale, but I saw much in the way of cameos, jewelry, glass, porcelain and shell curios, pottery, and gloves. I was particularly proud of my purchase of

pair of white kid gloves for my mother. When years later I read Norman Lewis's *Naples'*
44,[14] I felt absolutely confident that the gloves had been made by Liana Pagano, a thirty-two-
year-old widow living at Aniello Falcone 32, described so vividly by the author. Most of the
other "souvenirs" purchased on the streets of Naples have been lost over the years, but one
still hangs over the head of my bed — a fringed tapestry showing a steaming Mt. Vesuvius.
The view, in a silk wall hanging, is from approximately the location of my hospital on Corso
Vittorio Emanuele, and it evokes memories of good and bad times. At Pompeii I purchased
from Tallo Giovanni a lovely watercolor depicting a smoking Vesuvius as seen from the excavated ruins; and a street artist named Vittorio drew a remarkable charcoal-and-crayon likeness of my sailor-capped head.

Naples in 1944 was a city of contradictions. Despite Allied bombings and Nazi sabotage,
some stately buildings stood with their historical and architectural aura casting shadows over
devastation and squalor. The sole standing hotel, however, was the Miramare on Via N. Sauro;
it served as the American consulate. Few public utilities had been restored, so the function-
ing communal fountains were shared by scrubbing washwomen, nude children, roaming
dogs, and pigeons. In a city virtually without porches, front doors opened directly onto steep,
narrow, crooked streets and alleys, over which clothes lines were habitually strung. The only
motor vehicles belonged to the military, so hand wagons, an occasional horse-drawn car, barefoot women, and street urchins were
common sights. The main street running
north from the center of the city was
called Via Toledo, then Via Roma. On it
were located the best sales shops, particularly in the Galleria Umberto, which
had been spared bombing by the Allied
planes and in whose arcades servicemen
could find artwork, cameos, bracelets,
and collectibles favored by troops looking for mementos to send home. Slant-
ing off Via Roma, however, were scores
of alleys into which careful troops would
venture only for sexual release.

Particular progress was made in providing facilities for American and British
military personnel, including at least four
station hospitals (70th, 103rd, 106th, and
118th). An Army Exchange Store (PX)
was open at the corner of Via Roma and
Via Arnando Diaz, and an enlisted men's
club nearby offered a lounge, showers,
and refreshments. The Merchant Seamen
had their own club, and there was even
a Christian Science Service Center.
Officers were better cared for, with three
clubs and four messes. Seven locally
owned restaurants — Ursini, Ciro, Da
Giovanni, Zi Teresa, Bersagliera, Gio-

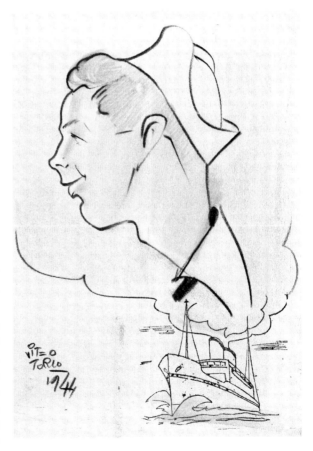

I was twenty when Vittorio, an itinerant Italian caricaturist, drew this likeness of me in Italy.

comino, and Umberto—were approved for Allied military patronage; the price of a regular dinner was fixed at fifty lire. Also approved were three baths and ten barbershops (four lire for a shave, six for a haircut, and ten for a shampoo) with the admonition, "Towels are to be changed with each customer." Ubiquitous facilities—fifteen "Pro Stations"—sought to shield Allied troops against venereal disease—a commentary on the prevalence of prostitution, the only means of income for some Italian women. For horny troops arriving from the front for "I and I" (intoxication and intercourse), opportunities were ubiquitous. Vino ran like water, and soldier-driven "passion wagons"—army trucks serving as portable whore houses—were easily recognizable.[15]

Among eight theaters approved for service personnel were the Red Cross Theatre on Via Roma and the famous San Carlo Opera House, at which GI presentations were free and operas required a "slight charge." George and I were fortunate to obtain tickets to a performance of *Rigoletto* at San Carlo, the architectural wonder of a people for whom music is the "red wine" of their culture. Our tickets were in the nose-bleed gallery, because the orchestra was packed with full-dressed, beribboned officers, often escorting aristocratic Italian ladies who remained above the common folk even in their country's defeat. Even so, it was an unforgettable experience for one whose musical heritage had been pretty much limited to hill-billy tunes over Nashville's station WSM. Protestant church services in English were offered at four places, Catholic at five places, and Jewish at two, but we could scarcely afford time for religion in such a history-rich part of the Mediterranean world.

An enormously important electronic service available to Allied personnel in Naples was "EFM," a canned type of message, that permitted a soldier or sailor to send home a cablegram containing prepared text in a choice of wordings. I was happy to pay the sixty-lire fee to send a cablegram to my family on August 24, about the time they were reading newspaper accounts of Operation Dragoon and wondering if *525* had been involved. The American Red Cross, of course, arrived on the heels of the liberators, and from the enlisted men's club on Armando Diaz, its staff, largely female, provided a homey feeling to tens of thousands of lonely Americans and Brits.[16]

Before the war, Mussolini was hailed for "making the trains run on time," and, despite the mayhem inflicted upon it by the Germans as they fled, the rail system was up and running again only a few weeks after the Allies occupied the city. Surprisingly, the trains of the Naples Cumana Railway to Pozzuoli ran every thirty minutes, and those of the Naples Circumvesuaviana Railway ran hourly during the day. The military fare for third-class round-trip tickets from Naples to Pompeii and Vesuvius was twenty lire and to Pozzuoli only four—real bargains since the exchange rate was a hundred lire per one American dollar.

George and I purchased tickets for a number of city tours led by local guides approved by the Red Cross. In addition to knowing how to negotiate the rubble-strewn streets and avoid teetering buildings, each native guide tried to protect his wards by shooing away the hoards of peddlers, urchins, and beggars. Castel dell'Ovo (Old Castle), dating back a thousand years, was a good starting point because of its location near the harbor. To the surprise of those who thought history began with the discovery of America, Castel Nuovo (New Castle) actually dates back to the thirteenth century. Nearby the Royal Palace, extending 800 feet along the waterfront and dating from around 1600, was once the king's residence and home for the National Library, but it lay in ruins. Another royal palace, Capodimonte, far north of city center, fared better. Many of the rarities from the Museo Nationale, including ancient murals from Pompeii and Herculaneum, had not yet been returned from hiding, so we could see only the outside walls of the museum. Sixteenth-century Castel San Elmo towered over the city, providing an unexcelled panorama of Naples and the smaller cities around the bay to the south. The nearby Museo di San Martino was closed. Of the 257 churches and 57 chapels in Naples, most impressive was the San Gennaro Duomo, built in the thirteenth century and containing the tomb of the patron saint who lived in the fourth century and is credited with saving the city from famine, war, plague, and the fire of Vesuvius. Two vials of his dried blood are said to liquify when Naples and its environs are endangered. Of more immediate emotional appeal to us was the ceremony attending the raising and lowering of the American and British colors in front of the modern, gleaming post office building that reflected the Fascist taste in architecture.

The highlight of my land excursions in Italy, of course, was a visit to Pompeii. I had watched Mt. Vesuvius day by day during its dormancy while I was in the hospital on Corso Vittorio Emanuele, and I wanted to get closer to it. However, the eruption just before the arrival of *SC-525* in late March was not what I had in mind. Wearing cloth masks for breathing and keeping the water hoses going day and night to prevent our ship from being enveloped in pumice, we were happy to return to sea the very next day — but not before I took photographs to document the experience. For a week, local residents and thousands of service personnel stationed in the area were afforded no such escape, but fortunately the volcano slowed its vomiting prior to our arrival, and only by radio we heard about the devastation of villages on the northwest side of the mountain. Characteristically, our armed forces rushed to the aid of the threatened citizenry. According to *Time*,

> One night Allied military trucks chugged up the mountainside, began the evacuation of some 17,000 people. From San Sebastiano, Massi de Somma, and Certola, the homeless and their meager belongings were carted downslope to emergency shelters and food. In the lava-lit darkness, while grimy soldiers struggled to unsnarl traffic, an air raid alarm sounded. Men doused lights, but Vesuvius paid no heed.[17]

Now, seven weeks after the March eruption, we saw not even a whiff of smoke from Vesuvius when we docked in Naples. George and I rushed to the Red Cross, paid our twenty-lire round-trip fare to Pompeii, and headed for the Staziono Circumvesuviana, where we found ourselves in a chaotic crowd storming the train before incoming passengers had dismounted. Seeing men crawling through barred windows, I snapped a picture and realized that we would not get aboard unless we joined the shoving crowd. Once inside the standing-room-only car, we watched disbelievingly as more Italians clambered atop or hung onto the sides of the cars. Apparently this was an accepted procedure, because our tickets were not taken up, and the train stopped at the entrance of a tunnel to allow the hangers-on to jump down. Wedged in the crowd, we could see little as the train skirted the bay at the base of the towering volcano, but somewhere along the way I was able to stick my camera toward the window to snap a picture of the now-serene Vesuvius. It was hard to imagine that even at that very moment the potential for another disaster lay beneath our rumbling train.

We were unaware that we passed near San Sebastiano, devastated only weeks earlier, and Ercolano, under which lay the buried city of Herculaneum, whose population met death on the night of August 24, 79 A.D. — about seven hours before the residents of Pompeii were asphyxiated. I probably had never heard of Herculaneum, whose fate was virtually ignored in the pre-war textbooks. One name was indelibly associated with Vesuvius's eruption early in the Christian era, for there had been a witness whose letter to Tacitus guaranteed that the story of Pompeii (originally Greek *Pompeion*, meaning emporium) would survive. From Misenum, on the peninsula southwest of Pozzuoli near where we often anchored, Pliny the Younger, nephew of Pliny the Elder (commander of the Roman fleet), described how his uncle set sail in the direction of Vesuvius when he saw a giant umbrella-shaped "fearful black cloud" spreading up from the summit, enveloping the cities with the obscurity of a tempestuous night. The commander reached Stabiae (now Castellammare di Stabia) but died when deadly flames and fumes destroyed the town. Back in Misenum, his nephew remained a horrified spectator as the volcano lit up the sky during a night from which there was no dawn on the 25th. Modern science reveals that Herculaneum was buried beneath more than sixty feet of solidified ash, and Pompeii by nine feet, fatal to every breathing creature.

Pliny's description of the terror might have been considered fiction but for accidental discoveries of subterranean ruins by diggers in the eighteenth century. Treasure seekers eventually were supplanted by serious archaeological researchers, and by 1944 a substantial portion of Pompeii had been excavated and opened to the public. The entrance fee was five lire for enlisted men, who took some satisfaction in noting that civilians and officers paid twice that amount. George and I, joined by three American soldiers, wore ourselves out walking the cobblestone streets, hopping the drains, climbing into the amphitheater, viewing temporary museum exhibits and plaster molds of human bodies, marveling at the multiplicity of Roman deities, and photographing many of the sites. Pompeii is more than a ruin; we felt that we were walking past roofless and crumbled buildings whose residents were on a journey and would face a huge task of restoration upon their return. There were hovels of the slaves as well as grand homes of the wealthy, temples for favorite deities, and houses of prostitution.

No doubt anticipating heavy visitation by Allied forces following the occupation of Naples, the director of excavations at Pompeii, Amedeo Maiuri, rushed into publication an illustrated paperback guidebook titled *A Companion to the Visit of Pompeii*,[18] a copy of which I purchased for sixty lire and was able to review only cursorily before meeting the guide at Porto Marina. Even so, its map gave George and me a sense of direction, and its text provided more reliable information than that imparted by our heavily accented local historian. Most interesting was the Forum, a rectangular piazza roughly 125 by 465 feet, surrounded by the remains of the Basilica, where Roman justice was meted out; Temple of Apollo, with its reproduced statues of Apollo and Diana (both deities represented as archers); Temple of Jupiter, from the ruins of which was recovered a giant head of Jupiter; the building of Eumachia, representing the corporate community; and the Macellum, the public market. We walked the stone-paved streets to the extremity of the ruins and were amazed at the size of two amphitheaters — the larger one capable of accommodating nearly the entire population of first-century Pompeii. In area, Pompeii was also much larger — two miles long and covering more than 160 acres — and historically and architecturally more diverse than I had expected. Typically, we servicemen were intrigued by the public baths and particularly the house of prostitution, which left little to imagination with its physical arrangement for different classes of debauchery and its obscene graffiti and paintings. A stranger in Pompeii could easily find the Lupaner by following the directions pointed by penis-shaped carvings on corner buildings. Clearly, sexual depravity is not a modern phenomenon.

I was impressed most by the well-preserved mill and bakery. Raised on a masonry base, each mill consisted of two parts in volcanic stone. The conical lower stone, called *meta*, served as an axle, and the biconical hollowed upper stone, called the *catillus*, turned by a wooden frame and long handles pulled by asses, ground the grain into flour. Though shaped differently, the two-thousand-year-old mill was as efficient as the water-wheel contraption that ground meal and flour at Womack's Mill near my childhood home. I went away reminded again that all progress did not begin with my generation.

I snapped this photograph of the Temple of Apollo in Pompeii during an excursion with George Klumpp and a group of soldiers in May 1944. The bawdy paintings on the walls of the den of sexual pleasure had not yet been opened to the public.

The March eruption had blocked the route up to Vesuvius's crater, so even if there had been time, we could observe the crater only from photographs. I did, however, bring back a vial of the 1944 pumice and a watercolor view, by Tallo Giovanni, of a smoking Vesuvius with Pompeii in the foreground. The excavations at Herculaneum open to public view were minimal, so we did not stop. Sixty years later, when I returned to see what I had missed, I found Herculaneum more archaeologically instructive than tourist-crowded Pompeii.

The Salerno that we visited during our practice invasions had escaped the savage devastation that the retreating Germans inflicted upon Naples, so we saw relatively little damage to that city. Actually, the main American landings that made Salerno's name a household word the previous September had occurred some twenty miles south of the city near the ancient remains of Paestum, and much of the fighting had been done in the hills east of the beaches. Furthermore, we knew only what we had read in *Stars and Stripes* or heard by radio. Only later did we learn the more complete story of Operation Avalanche, during which associated naval losses had been substantial from submarine attacks, newly introduced glide bombs, and shelling from ashore. Among the losses had been American destroyers *Bristol, Buck*, and *Rowan*, the minesweeper *Skill*, a tug, and six LCTs. The British lost minelayer *Abdiel*, the hospital ship *Newfoundland,* and five LCTs. As in virtually all battles, however, the army bore the heaviest cost in human lives, the British suffering the largest number of casualties. And as in the case of Anzio, Americans back home sometime were not fully conscious that the war in Italy was an *Allied* operation in the fullest sense of the word.

George and I spent a pleasant afternoon strolling through Salerno and found it the cleanest town we had seen in the Mediterranean. Shops were open, roller-skaters were out on the streets, and civilians mixed with servicemen. An oddity — a CPO (chief petty officer) Club — was provided for U.S. Navy personnel. George was second class and I was only a third class petty officer, but we were welcomed in for refreshments. We also attended a movie at the Cinema Teatro Impero, but our most memorable experience was to witness a funeral procession following a glass-windowed, horse-drawn hearse. Here we were looking at a tradition quintessentially Italian, a survivor of many conquering armies.

Vietri sul Mare, where we anchored several times during the practice invasions, occupied a picturesque coastal terrace near the bottom of Chiunzi Pass, through which American Rangers fought their way across the Sorrentine spine and opened the drive to Naples, which fell on October 1, 1943. As we frolicked in the waters once frequented by the jet set from around the world, we, of course, were oblivious of the carnage that occurred in the mountains just above us. Furthermore, if the term "Amalfi Drive" had meant anything to us — Vietri is considered its "first pearl" — we would have had neither time nor vehicle to follow its circuitous route upward. Nor could we have predicted that Vietri earthenware — majolica, produced in this quaint little town — would become an international collectors' item a half-century later. With limited knowledge of where we were, we simply enjoyed the moment in company with the Italian women who welcomed us as conquering heroes who had freed them from German rule.

My shipmates had raved about their previous visits to Capri, so I was excited when finally, on April 3, SC-525 made another call, my first. Regrettably, we arrived so late that our carousing was limited to the harbor area. Besides, we were routed out just an hour past midnight to undertake an antisubmarine search off the island of Ischia. We had much better luck when on May 18 we docked at Capri for eighteen hours. Eschewing female companionship and venereal disease available for a fee around the Marina Grande, George and I — at least on this occasion — took the high road; we made our way to the mountaintop village of Capri which, even in wartime, provided breathtaking beauty and views. We discovered that most luxurious facilities had been reserved for commissioned officers, so we enlisted men saw little of the glittering interiors pictured in slick magazines. Still, the panorama was spectacular toward Amalfi Drive, Sorrento, Naples, Pozzuoli, and the islands of Ischia and Procida. Mount Vesuvius, which had behaved since the March eruption, stood quietly as a distant sentinel. The view also impressed upon us the paramount importance of the Bay of Naples in prosecuting the war. Ships of every variety, as far as the eye could see, seemed to fill the horizon.

Piazza Umberto lived up to its reputation as a town square lined with cafés and bars offering plenty of vino but little food. We walked along Vittorio Emanuele but due to darkness could not get to the Certosa di St. Giacomo, the fourteenth-century Carthusian monastery noted for its alluring perfumes. And, of course, distances were too great for us to reach Villa Jovis, where in the first century A.D. Tiberius ruled the empire and kept his stable of cherubic boys; and an excursion to Anacapri or the Blue Grotto was out of the question. Still, I fell in love with Capri and knew that, if I survived the war, I would come again. I could not have imagined that my return would be delayed sixty years. During the interval, I prized a five-inch conch shell, cut in half, bearing the inked legend "Ricordi di Capri" and an image of the Blue Grotto hand-painted in its concave center. I bought the souvenir for an ashtray at the harbor village, where most of the crew spent the night servicing mothers and daughters who outnumbered the crews of our fleet of subchasers. Such overnight stops by Allied vessels probably contributed more to the economy of local residents than their trinket market and fishing fleet.

Naturally, nearly every Allied serviceman in Italy was familiar with the song, "The Isle of Capri," and I was so enamored with it that I had my high school classmate Myrtle Carter send me the lyrics. Like many servicemen deprived of musical knowledge, I at first assumed that the song had been written especially for us during the war — that is, until I discovered that the lyrics by Jimmy Kennedy had been set to music by Wilhelm Grosz and made famous by Ray Noble and his orchestra when I was only ten years old.

My first step ashore at Anzio on January 26 was one that I would never want to repeat. Our little 110-footer must have looked like a rowboat, and the captain must have worked a bit of magic to gain permission to sail *SC-525* into the crowded port, muscling past much larger ships nervously awaiting their turn to dock and unload their men and equipment — all of this in the midst of another air raid. With both hands in splints and still under the influence of morphine, I felt like a zombie as I was removed from *SC-525*'s aft compartment. I cannot remember how I was maneuvered up the ladder, onto the deck, onto the dock, and into Coast Guard–manned *LST-327*. I remember only the scene of scores of wounded men, nearly all soldiers, some on stretchers, others, like me, being led by corpsmen. I must have cried, not from pain but from sadness, not knowing whether I might see my subchaser and shipmates again, but I also was conscious of how fortunate I was compared with many of those whose moans and groans I heard through the overnight voyage toward Naples. Following my transfer, *SC-525* remained at Anzio Beachhead until February 2 and returned for the week of March 2–9 while I was still in the hospital. After I reboarded, we served two more sentences at Anzio — from May 8 to 15 and 21 to 28 — giving *Cinq-Dux-Cinq* a total of five weeks in the bloody fray. We also eerily eyed the miserable site on our way to and from Civitavecchia the following month.

Anzio (originally Antium) dates so far back that two thousand years ago the Roman poet Horace dedicated the town to the Goddess of Fortune. It was frequented by Augustus and Cicero, and Nero and Caligula were born there. It was where Nero built his favorite palace and a grand harbor. With the decline of the Roman empire and its sacking by the Saracens, however, fortune deserted the area, which was virtually abandoned until it was reinvigorated by Pope Innocent II, under whose auspices about 1700 a new harbor was built. With papal blessing, Anzio and its beaches became a favorite retreat thirty miles from the Vatican. In time, Nero's grand structures were neglected, and they eventually crumbled. In the twentieth century, Anzio became a popular Italian coastal resort community and fishing port with ferry connections to the Pontine islands.

Before the invasion, the Germans had forced out many of the residents of Anzio and Nettuno, and following the landing, the Allies evacuated most of the remainder to the Naples area. Consequently, the beachhead was little more than a giant military battleground. German shelling wreaked extensive additional damage upon the town, so when *SC-525* returned for our third assignment on May 8, most buildings near the harbor were in crumbles. It was as if the Boche had taken delight in inflicting damage upon their erstwhile allies, the Wops (or Dagos), as both we and the Germans contemptuously called the Italians. By then, the beachhead appeared secure and German firepower was concentrated at the front, but walking outside the secured area was still chancy because of tottering buildings, unexploded mines and ammunition, and shells from the German railroad gunners in the Alban Hills. Sightseeing, therefore, was an on-the-run activity, but at least I was able to see close-up the stubby lighthouse on which our navigator had fixed our position in the roadstead and which had survived nearly four months of war. Most interestingly, the Phare d'Anzio was located at what once was Villa di Nerone (Nero's Palace), now hardly recognizable except for projecting walls and the remains of an ancient amphitheatre. Still, the ruins, which give an idea of the extravagant tastes of Roman leaders, have yielded several important pieces of art, including the

Borghese Gladiator, now in the Louvre. Portions of the Neronian jetties could be seen underwater, though many of the boulders were utilized in the creation of the new harbor to the east. The location of the Temple of Fortune had not been identified.[19]

Remarkably, Villa Borghese, built in 1674 by Cardinal Costaguti between Anzio and Nettuno, escaped much damage and served Allied officers during the invasion. Sitting on high ground, surrounded by trees and gardens, it commanded a spectacular view both toward and from the Tyrrhenian. Today it is a popular public park.

Nettuno, named for the Roman goddess of the sea, was founded by the Saracens in the ninth century A.D., thus making it a young sister to Anzio, which the same Saracens virtually abandoned. Little remains of the Moslem era except a few remnants in the Borgo Medievale with its narrow streets and small squares. Like Anzio, following the landings Nettuno was a ghost town except for the presence of Allied forces. By far the most spectacular site was Fort Sangallo, completed about 1503 under Pope Alexander VI. The massive structure, facing the sea and surrounded by a moat on three sides, featured four interesting heart-shaped corner bastions. Interior colonnades and an incongruous four-level tower were capable of protecting warriors and townspeople.[20]

Several miles down the coast, beyond the beaches on which we had helped land thousands of soldiers, stood Torre Astura di Neptune, which, like Phare d'Anzio, had been a prominent landmark by which ships determined their positions in an era before global positioning had been imagined. The existing structure, quadrangular but with a pentagonal tower, was begun in the twelfth century. It sits on an island but is connected by a colonnade to the mainland. It has seen several masters in its eight-hundred-year existence.

Our June assignment at Civitavecchia taught me two lessons: (1) the degree to which an entire city can be destroyed in modern warfare, and (2) that in Italian a "c" is often pronounced "ch" and "ch" is often pronounced "k." I soon learned that rules in the Italian language are as fickle as they are in English, but the scenes of a devastated city were permanently etched in my mind. The harbor had been bombed repeatedly by Allied planes even earlier, but the town had been shelled in January in an effort to make the Germans believe that the gathering armada would land troops in that vicinity. There is no evidence that the Nazis had been fooled, even though they were taken by surprise at Anzio. Additional bombings and shellings at Civitavecchia during the deadlock at the beachhead, designed to make the Germans think that the Allies might attempt another leap-frog landing, also appear not to have been taken very seriously by the Nazis.

We arrived ten days after Civitavecchia was captured by the Allies, and the city gave us our most vivid understanding of the war ashore. None of the African, Sicilian, and Italian cities that we had seen were so utterly destroyed as this seaport thirty miles northwest of Rome. The harbor, begun in the second century A.D. by Emperor Trajan, was littered with bombed and shelled ships, and our advance base forces had cleared only a couple of docks for Allied vessels. Together, the retreating Germans and the attacking Allies had sentenced the city to death, and virtually its entire surviving population had been driven into the countryside. Boxcars sat as splintered skeletons on their tracks; oil storage tanks appeared as collapsed mushrooms; hardly a piece of unbroken glass could be seen.

Even the ancient Fort Michelangelo lay in ruins. This massive structure, overlooking the harbor, was constructed in the sixteenth century by order of Pope Julius II della Rovere. The names of its original builders were overshadowed by that of the man who completed the "donjon" (the central tower)—the versatile Italian painter, architect, sculptor, and poet, Michelangelo. The fort is quadrangular with round turrets at the corners—each named for a saint — and the octagonal donjon at the center front. It sits on ruins of earlier centuries and is virtually a city within itself, even with its own chapel. A tunnel connects it to the city, thus providing protection for a portion of the population in case of an attack.

When Otto Promp, Stanley Tokarz, and I went ashore by whaleboat and picked our way through rubble-filled streets, we found utter devastation, hardly a building standing undamaged, some in danger of toppling from the mere clomp of our footsteps. During several hours ashore, we encountered only one civilian, dazed and disbelieving as he staggered through the ruins of the once-flourishing city that before the war was home to perhaps 30,000 of his fellow citizens. Portions of a few buildings had withstood the repeated bombings and shellings; for example, the handsome facade of the Banca Nationale del Lavoro, with its iron balcony, masked the wreckage of its rear. Virtually every standing structure was bereft of glass windows.

The sight that moved us most was the Cathedral of St. Francis of Assisi, built in the eighteenth century facing Piazza Victor Emanuele. The ornate Baroque tower stood out majestically from the rubble that covered its marble steps, fan-shaped to extend to the street the entire width of the building. Miraculously, from high above the entrance, two large statues — St. Francis of Assisi on one side and St. Anthony of Padova on the other — continued to beckon worshipers. As Otto, Stan, and I climbed over the debris and entered the sanctuary, we were showered by sunlight, because the roof lay in a contorted pile on the floor. Even so, we could imagine what the interior looked like as described for tourists: "the temple appears beautifully shaped, high, long and with only one aisle, decorated on both sides by symmetric chapels hollowed into the background, alternated by pillars that, with their bases and rich capitals, look like they are holding up the majestic royal dome that covers the entire premises." Making our way over the fallen dome, now neither majestic nor royal, past a triumphal arch separating the presbytery, we came to a beautiful altar made of precious metals, jewels, and marbles. Behind the altar two columns supported a gable, above which rested the statues of Justice and Hope. Below, framed in gold stucco, was a fresco painting of St. Francis by Antonio Nessi. Like the altar, columns, and statues, the fresco was so pockmarked from shrapnel that it provided a heart-rending background for the photograph that I took of Stan and Otto. One could hardly stand in this holy place, so horribly disfigured but retaining its aura of the sacred, with dry eyes. We were incredulous that the gold icons and precious objects had not been scavenged. Then we were reminded that we were in a ghost *town*, not a ghost *cathedral*, and neither an itchy-fingered souvenir-collecting American nor a starving Italian would dare desecrate the House of the Lord.

My only souvenirs from Civitavecchia — found among rubble of other buildings — were a letter handwritten in Italian to a soldier, Carlo Rocco, and a Fascist Party membership card of one Millefiorini Ulisse. Unlike some of our earlier exploits, this shore liberty left us in a somber mood. More than a half century later, black-and-white photographs keep alive my memory of this melancholic experience.

The harbor at Ajaccio, Corsica, had become an important staging area for Allied forces since its liberation from German and Italian invaders in September 1943. *SC-525* limped into the port nearly a year later with visions of being patched up by the experienced crew of USS *Achelous* (ARL-1) so we could return to the battle zone in Southern France. However, when he learned that our wounds could not be healed by the tender, and that we were destined to sail on precariously through the minefields of Bonifacio Strait and Tyrrhenian Sea, our exasperated skipper announced liberty for the crew. George and I first sought out the birthplace of Napoléon Bonaparte on Place Letizia, named for the emperor's mother. Except for its height — six floors — the shuttered building, facing a narrow alley, looked like the remainder of the neglected row houses, all sadly in need of revitalization. A simply engraved marble slab between two windows revealed the distinction of the structure. A waif, an old man with a cane, and a lone donkey ambled down the street. On that Friday, Napoléon seemed to be only on the minds of inquisitive American servicemen, and I wondered about the coincidence of dates—our invasion of Provençal occurred on Napoléon's one hundredth seventy-fifth birthday. We later learned that the local youngster who became emperor of France was not Corsica's favorite son, even though Ajaccio's main street was named Cours Napoléon. In addition, the huge equestrian statue of the emperor, in Roman garb, was commissioned by Napoléon III in 1865 and is derisively called locally "L'Encrier" ("The Inkstand"). The museums were closed, as were many of the commercial outlets. The harbor was filled with warships, but there simply was little to see or do in wartime Ajaccio except walk the dreary and virtually deserted streets.

Luckily, we fell in with several soldiers, and the faithful American Red Cross arranged a trip for us to the Punta di Pozzo di Borgo (usually called Le Chateau de la Punta) atop the most prominent mountain in the area. In my letter home, I described the hair-raising trip: "the road leading to it [the chateau] is about seven feet wide and the mountains in American States have never seen such a crooked road. Sometimes the bus had to back up three times in order to make the curves; besides that, it was almost straight up. It took us nearly two hours to go the ten miles up to the chateau."

The frightening ride was rewarded by my first step inside a European castle, albeit a modern one by continental standards. In Corsica and France, the Pozzo di Borgo family was famous—or, to some, infamous—because Count Carlo Andréa Pozzo di Borgo (1764–1842) was a fierce opponent of Bonaparte and his successors. Ironically, the two men were born only a few blocks apart in this remote part of Corsica, but they were miles apart in politics. Even though the chateau was built four decades after the politician's death, its location was chosen deliberately to overshadow the Bonaparte descendants' country estate, Les Millelli, which sits surrounded by olive groves on a nearby promontory. The insult was compounded because the exterior building stones came from the ruins of Napoleon's residence in Paris—Les Tuileries—which burned in 1871. In fact, the Punta di Pozzo di Borgo is virtually a replica of one of the pavilions of Les Tuileries. The Pozzo di Borgo family thus rubbed salt into old wounds by imitating great castles of France a short distance from the less grand Les Millelli. During World War II, however, the estate was neglected, and when our party of servicemen visited the four-story Pozzo di Borgo chateau, the windows were shuttered and the sumptuous furnishings and paintings looked drab in the darkened Renaissance interiors. Even the mountainside had been deprived of its beauty by a fire that burned many of the trees. Still, the view of the surrounding area, including Ajaccio and its busy harbor and rugged terrain, was spectacular, and the afternoon trip gave us respite from the experiences of recent days.[21]

Our penultimate liberty in the Mediterranean—at St. Tropez—has already been described.[22] True, we had a few nights in Nice and St. Raphael, but those evening hours hardly counted. Toulon, then, provided my last step upon the continent of Europe for nearly sixty years. There, on September 21, George and I crossed USS *Barricade* (ACM-3), to which we were tied, and made our way through the dockside rubble into a portion of the city that had sprung back to life after its liberation. Not knowing what the future held and thinking how cool it would be to brag that we got our last haircut in France, we visited a local barber, who welcomed us as conquering heroes and taught us how quickly we had forgotten our high school French. Our status as liberators did not exempt us from the barber's usual fee, which we paid with some of our last occupation money. We next stopped by a fashionable stationer,

Montbarbon, Papeterie, at 29 Rue d'Alger, where for the French equivalent of sixteen dollars I bought a handsome ink pen mounted on a brownish marble base. The pen served me well in college and, though disused since, it remains a prized souvenir, a daily reminder of my emotional goodbye to *Cinq-Deux-Cinq*, my home for a year and a half while an adolescent was growing into a man.[23]

12

Back to the "Good Ole U.S. of A."

September–November 1944

By the middle of September we had begun to detect a restlessness among the fleet, and rumors began circulating that our days in the Mediterranean were limited. After the ports of Marseilles and Toulon were captured and Allied troops moved into the interior, the threats along the southern coast were reduced to mines, a few desperate torpedo craft, and the mountainside gunners. From the Nazi standpoint, the Luftwaffe was needed elsewhere, for the sinking of an occasional ship would do little to defend the homeland. And from the Allied standpoint, why keep a large fleet in the Mediterranean, especially when it was needed in the Pacific? And of what value would scores of small American patrol vessels be even if they safely negotiated their way back across the Atlantic?

The solution came as a jolt, but when revealed to the crew, the plans for our splinter fleet sounded perfectly reasonable: Our ship—along with forty-nine other American subchasers and a number of yard minesweepers and other small craft—was to be turned over to the French Navy, and half of each crew would be held aboard for a few weeks to train the Frog personnel. That meant that the other half of our American crews would be transferred immediately to other duty stations. As rational as the plan was, mixed feelings followed official word that we would be leaving *SC-525*. Consequently, exhilaration vied with sadness when on September 20 we sailed into Toulon, another picture of utter destruction. George and I rushed ashore and bought a few souvenirs, and upon our return, I had the presence of mind to persuade Lieutenants Waldron, McCormick, and Barton to pose in front of my Kodak for a parting memento. The three officers exercised their best judgment in selecting crewmen for the "First Draft"—that is, the first half of the crew to be transferred. George and I were chosen to leave the very next day. We were surprised only until we realized that there were so few German submarines left in the Mediterranean that the new crew needed neither a sonarman nor radioman with only a high-school level of the French language.

The deck log for September 21 read:

1305, Tied up alongside *PC-625* and USS *Planter*. 1340, Men leaving on draft took gear to *LCI-42*. 1420, The following named men were detached this date from duty aboard this vessel: Lt. (jg) John U. Barton; Boleslaus L. Cieslak, SM1c; Edmund E. Runof, MoMM1c; John S. Schira, MoMM1c; George F. Klumpp, RM2c; Edward Cain, MM2c; Robert J. Clarkson, SC2c; Stanley Dauman, RdM3c; Houston G. Jones, SoM3c; John S. Hallas, MoMM3c; Charles E. Merckling, S1c; Bernard N. Long, S1c; Hamilton A. Knowles, S2c.

On September 21, 1944, I was among the half of the crew transferred from *SC-525* for transportation back to the States. With my old Kodak, the lens wet from sea spray, I posed the three officers in Toulon for one last picture. From left are Lt.(jg) Hugh P. McCormick, executive officer; Lt.(jg) John C. Waldron, commanding officer; and Ensign John U. Barton, third officer.

The log continued, "The following named French Navy men reported aboard for duty: LeBorgne, CBM; Mattia, S/M; Fouasson; Geoffroy, Q/M; Volle, Q/M; Gorry, G/M; Goureous, S/M; F. Moal, M; Owen, S/M; Guyomaid, Q/M; Gibajo; Bonnans; G. Moal."

Each of us who walked off *SC-525* on September 21, in accordance with Escort Sweeper Dispatch 191127A, was ordered to leave behind — for use by our French replacements — our mattress and a blanket. In return, each was given an order, signed by Captain W. L. Messmer, Commander Escort Sweeper Group, that authorized any Navy supply officer to issue a new mattress and blanket at no charge.[1]

Having left behind our bulky mattress and hammock, each of us in the first draft carried our belongings in a seabag, but I cheated a bit by sneaking a few of my most prized possessions, including photographs and notes, in a small satchel picked up in Italy. Tired from struggling across the pier to *LCI-42*, my heart felt that it was in my throat when, at 1830 on September 21, I watched my former floating home sail out of Toulon harbor, leaving me and a dozen of my shipmates on a strange ship. That would be, I presumed, my last sight of *SC-525*, my *Cinq-Deux-Cinq*.

My one night aboard *LCI-42* reminded me again of how fortunate I was to be in the Navy. The huge, stuffy, smelly sleeping compartment was equipped minimally for troops, and I realized that the previous occupants, all foot soldiers put ashore earlier in the day, might already be in battle against the Germans. I longed for the bunk on which I had slept for eighteen months—the one adjacent to the one-holer serving sixteen men. Homesick, but also feeling alternately happy and guilty for being on my way home, I slept poorly.

I never thought the time would come when I would long for Boston baked beans or flap-jacks—about which I had so often complained on *525*—but K-Rations on the LCI changed my mind. More than ever, I empathized with soldiers and marines who were forced to sub-sist, sometimes for weeks on end, on prepackaged victuals that included hard-tack biscuits, canned meat product, compressed cereal bar, instant coffee or cocoa, sugar tablets, chewing gum, a can opener, and a swab of toilet tissue. Named "K" for its creator, Ancel Keys, the rations were developed for use in the field where cooking was not an option.[2] Dinner (lunch) and supper (dinner) packages varied a bit from the breakfast pack, but each sought to pro-vide a high-calorie diet. One day on K-Rations was a sufficient reminder of how fortunate we had been with *525*'s piano-sized galley, from which "Cookie" fed twenty-seven men, each of us complaining about the "rotten" powdered eggs, "tasteless" dehydrated potatoes, and "bilge water" coffee.[3]

On September 22, *LCI-42* sailed from Toulon to St. Raphael, where we were to board our transport. It was discovered, however, that—oops—in the fast-moving actions and deci-sions the previous day, our officers had overlooked a little detail: the transfer of our pay records. Fortunately, *SC-525* was still in the gulf, so she was summoned to come alongside. The records were pitched over, giving me one last chance to greet and wave goodbye to my old ship and mates. In the meantime, while we dilly dallied, the convoy on which we were to sail had already left, so the LCI set out at full speed to overtake *LST-691*. The sea was choppy but not angry, so we were able to pitch our seabags across and then jump from one bobbing vessel to the other—a new meaning of the expression "jumping ship."

We had a slow, rolling, three-day trip during which time we repeatedly thought of the soldiers who had occupied the LST bunks on which we lay. We also remembered our berths back on *SC-525*, on which now lounged our successors, French sailors. The voyage was uneventful, for, though a couple of German submarines may still have prowled the Mediter-ranean and remained a threat to Allied shipping, our convoy was not challenged. Upon arrival at Oran, Algeria, we were taken by truck to the United States Naval Receiving Station at Tent City, near Arzeu. The "station," to which we were assigned, was really a camp consisting of Quonset huts lined up on a dirt field with a mosque in the background.[4]

George Klumpp, Stanley Dauman, Stanley Hallas, and I were assigned to Hut 60, in which my "home" from September 25 to October 13 consisted of a space about five-by-seven feet—just enough for a folding wood-and-canvas cot and a seabag. From the upward-curv-ing wall a string held my towel, washcloth, and metal meal tray. This claustrophobic scene was captured in a picture taken of Dauman and me sitting on my cot. In my lap sat a very large dog of indeterminate breed, which had become a camp pet and reminded me of my early farm experience with animals, a companionship that I had missed in the Navy. There was no lounge, so except for the washroom and head, this hut was simply a place for several dozen sailors to sleep. And in the next couple of weeks, we did a lot of that. Nevertheless, even with no privacy, we felt fortunate to have survived two bloody invasions and to be on our way home. In times of reflection, I wondered how many of the sailors I had known on other ships and bases had been sacrificed in the Mediterranean. On a more cheery note I wrote, "Movies daily, chow O.K., no work, liberty 2–1, everything fine." In other words, with vir-tually no duties, we lolled around, sleeping, playing cards, and keeping company with my adopted dog; on several occasions we did go into Oran and Arzeu for liberty. Try as I might,

Stanley Dauman (right) and a canine friend sat with me in our cramped living space in the Quonset hut at Arzeu, Algeria, while we waited for transportation back to the States. Clothes and eating utensils hang from cords strung along the curved walls.

however, I did not get to Mostaganem. In Oran, considerable progress had been made in cleaning up bomb damage, and we particularly appreciated the improved enlisted men's Continental Club.

*   *   *

While our half of the crew waited impatiently at Arzeu for transportation to the States, Lieutenant Waldron and the other half were training our French successors aboard *SC-525.* Four hours after those of us in the "First Draft" boarded *LCI-42, Cinq-Deux-Cinq* sailed for St. Raphael for three days of exercises. Apprenticeship continued on a voyage to Palermo as escort for *LST-1012.* Upon her return to Southern France on September 30, the little vessel hugged up against the *Brooklyn* and the *Philadelphia,* both comforting behemoths remembered so gratefully for effective shelling of Nazi positions at Anzio. Even if only for the transfer of aviation gear from one to the other, this contact was a reaffirmation of the usefulness of a 110-foot wooden patrol vessel in a war in which the capital ships received almost all of the public recognition.

From the Gulf of St. Tropez, *SC-525* again sailed to Toulon where, the log noted, "Work [is] continuing in preparation for transfer of ship to the French." The final English-language entry was made by the captain, Lieutenant (jg) John C. Waldron, at 1100, Sunday, October 8, 1944:

Decommissioning and transfer party aboard to transfer to French Mandle [*sic*] the USS *SC-525.* Party consisted of:

   1. Capt. W. L. Messmer
   2. Capt. B. H. J. Bourgeaius
   3. Lt. R. Belknap
   4. Lt. B. Walker

Upon completion of exercises, F. Petit, EVI assumed command. Mr. Waldron formally relieved. Thus is written "finis" in the U.S. history of a fine little ship. JCW.

But that was *not* "finis" to the wooden vessel that for a year and a half served as my floating home. Commander Theodore R. Treadwell, author of *Splinter Fleet*[5], the best account of wooden subchasers in World War II, traced the transfer of the fifty SCs to the French. He discovered that *SC-525* was redesignated as *CH-102* and served the French Navy through the war. In 1951, her designation was changed to *P-691* and later to *M-691*, with service as a training ship for Ecole Navile. Finally, on May 18, 1972 — thirty years after her commissioning — she was given the designation *Q-499* and stricken from the French Navy's list of commissioned vessels. Commander Treadwell wrote me, "I have nothing to indicate her fate after that but most were stricken and sold to private parties. A few were demolished. For all we know your *525* might still be afloat somewhere in France."[6] Indeed, she might be. If so, I hope her French owners are sensitive to the heritage of *SC-525*, which served valiantly in the war that restored the independence of their motherland.

*   *   *

On October 12, 1944, seabags in tow, my fellow crewmen and I were trucked from Arzeu to Oran harbor to board USS *General M. C. Meigs* (AP-116).[7] The fast troop carrier, capable of transporting 5,100 men at twenty-five knots per hour, was named for the Union quartermaster general, Montgomery Cunningham Meigs. Although only four months old when we boarded, *Meigs* had already crossed the Atlantic several times, on one trip transporting to Italy the first Brazilian troops to fight the Germans. Unlike *John Ericsson* on which I sailed to Africa, *Meigs* was built for troop transport and exhibited no signs of opulence.

The several thousand soldiers and sailors on the nine-day crossing were so excited to be returning to the States that we mostly talked, played cards, slept, and imagined our first restaurant meal and encounters with American "civilians," our term for anyone not in uniform. Anticipation increased as *Meigs* approached New York City, and every able-bodied man (and a few women) donned military dress and fought for a place on deck to get a first glimpse of the skyline on a clear morning. Imagination outran reality, and there were several premature cries of "There it is!" I held my old Kodak as I climbed upon some life-rafts, ready for the first *real* sight. Once we had arrived near the mouth of the Hudson River and maneuvered around milling ships, thousands of eyes began searching for a statue, the symbol justifying our battle against the Axis powers. Again, there were premature exclamations of "There it is!" As the Statue of Liberty finally emerged from the morning haze, my snapshot captured the scene: Over the heads of sailors and soldiers, who weighed down the bow of *General M.C. Meigs*, appeared Bartholdi's "Liberty Enlightening the World," a gift to the United States in 1886 by the Franco–American Union. Now, for the second time in the twentieth century, we Americans were repaying our French allies by freeing their country from German oppression. We were back in the "Good Ole U.S. of A."

Anticipation again gave way to reality, however, when *Meigs* tied up to Pier 51 on October 21. There were no brass bands, no excited sweethearts or wives with babies, no familiar faces to meet the returning soldiers and sailors. Even near the Statue of Liberty we were still

Hundreds of sailors aboard the troopship *General M.C. Meigs* eagerly searched for the first sight of the Statue of Liberty upon our entry into New York harbor on October 21, 1944.

at war, and the movement of large bodies of troops was a tightly held secret. Instead, we were met by a sea of busses that would take us to various bases for further assignment.

My shipmates and I were taken to Long Island, the location of the Advanced Base Assembly and Training Unit, Naval Training Center. My orders read, "FFA CSFLANT," meaning for further transfer to Commander Surface Fleet Atlantic. We took temporary residence in a large barrack adjacent to the luxurious Lido Beach Hotel. As soon as George and I could get permission, we went to Rockville Center, purchased servicemen's half-fare tickets, and rode the Long Island Railroad to New York City. Our next stop was the Pepsi-Cola Canteen in Times Square, which served as our rendezvous for the next several weeks. My gratitude for safe return to the United States was expressed in my first purchases — a snow globe and a pillow cover, both with a likeness of the famous statue on Bedloe's Island.

George looked up his friend in the city, Virginia Rogan, who introduced me to her pal Miriam, and the New York natives led us on several sightseeing tours. Despite wartime restrictions and shortages, the city teemed with humanity, and the subways were still running. In Times Square, a large billboard called attention to the ruins of an enemy plane and the campaign of thirty-one agencies soliciting funds for the Allied war effort. In lower Manhattan, I photographed Wall Street and surrounding landmarks such as Delmonico's Restaurant and Trinity Church; and in upper Manhattan we visited Central Park and the Bronx Zoo. Throughout the city, fascinating sites offered surprises to a boy from a tenant farm.

While waiting for our records to be reviewed at Lido Beach, George and I made several more trips into Manhattan, but on October 25 we were given thirty-day rehabilitation leaves. We left our gear in the Lucky Bag for safekeeping but, instead of going directly home, we checked into the Navy YMCA at 167 Sands Street between the Brooklyn Bridge and the Brooklyn Navy Yard, and remained for more sightseeing and shows in New York City. On October 28 we attended the Army-Duke football game at the famous Polo Grounds. It was a great show with the West Point marching cadets performing smartly in formation; their team performed as smartly also — winning 27–7.

My last action in Africa had been to send an EFM telegram to my parents: "All well and safe. In good health. Best wishes to all at home." I wanted my return to be a complete surprise, so I had planned to arrive in Reidsville completely unannounced. However, from Brooklyn I did send a post card to my Uncle Kester, thinking that he might come to see me in North Carolina. Instead, he wired right back, "Come this way. Will take you home." Obediently, I bought a bus ticket to Steubenville, Ohio, and visited with him, Laura (née Laura Ieropol), and their daughters Frances Jane and Jackie. That night I was paraded around Steubenville in my dress blues, complete with sonarman's badge and European service bar with two battle stars. I felt like a mobile exhibit as my relatives proudly showed me off. Most effusive were the members of Aunt Laura's family, particularly her father, a first-generation Italian-American haberdasher, who had given me my all-time favorite necktie for high school graduation. The next day Kester and I started south, overnighting in Frostburg, Maryland, but not before obeying my uncle's command that I wire my sister Pauline. He was afraid that my sudden appearance might be too much for my mother who, at age 61, had not been in good health. The message was simple: "Kester is driving me home. Arriving late tomorrow. Please inform mother."[8]

It was 2015, Wednesday night, November 2, when Kester's headlights shone on the humble four-room house in which I was born. The light from the single bare bulb in the "front room" was hardly visible through the window, but a honk on the car's horn was followed instantly by another bare bulb lighting the little front porch. The first person to burst out of the house and grab me was my cousin Nancy Fowlkes, always an emotional girl. My immediate family was more reserved; we were unaccustomed to hugging or even shaking hands, so it was a little awkward when my brother William (Buck) next approached me with the usual country greeting, "Hey!" I am not sure, but perhaps I shook hands with him and my father and I probably hugged my mother and sister Pauline for the first time since I was a baby. Uncle Bob Fowlkes and Aunt Nannie Willie were there for support. Although Uncle Bob was the only large landholder in the family and lived in a big painted house on a paved road and drove a Dodge, he was always solicitous of my mother, his only full sister, who married a good but very poor farmer. So I had been met by family members closest to me.

My presence in the county was modestly announced in the *Caswell Messenger* on November 12: "Houston Jones, of the U.S. Navy, is spending a thirty-day furlough with his parents, Mr. and Mrs. P. H. Jones. Houston served over seas the past two years."

My diary revealed a whirlwind of visits during the next twenty-three days. My father proudly took me to Yanceyville to show me off, in uniform, to the elite of the county — Dr. Houston Lafayette Gwynn, for whom I was named; Dr. L.G. Page, the dentist; Johnny Gunn, the Ford dealer; Sam Bason, the banker; Erwin Stephens, the editor; and others. The day ended at Uncle Bob's, whose children several years earlier had broken me out of my shell and encouraged me to associate with young people from a higher social level and to join Locust Hill Methodist Church. On consecutive nights, just about all of the relatives and neighbors crowded into my little home's front room, which served dually as my parents' bedroom and the only sitting room in the house. I caught up on news — good and bad — and the neighborhood gossip.[9]

The two years of my absence had not been kind to my family and friends. Cousins Cecil Jones and Charles Fowlkes, Jr., both airmen, were missing in action in the Pacific and European theater, respectively. Another cousin, Jimmy Harrelson, was a prisoner of the Germans; and high school classmate Larry Lovell and friend Herman Moore had been killed in battle. Childhood playmate Thomas Smith was recuperating from wounds in France. Happily, cousins Billy Jones and John Fowlkes, who had been stationed near Pearl Harbor during the initial Japanese attack, were safe on Saipan; and friend Hulon Briggs had returned safely to the county after flying forty-three missions over Germany. I was surprised to learn that Chaplain/Major Wilbur Kenneth Anderson of the First Armored Division had been at Anzio, where he baptized dozens of soldiers in the Tyrrhenian Sea, possibly in sight of my subchaser. I wondered how many other relatives and friends might have been involved, unbeknownst to me, in that four-month quagmire. The *Caswell Messenger* noted that the V.W. Webster family had five sons in the war, equaled by the R.N. Whitlow family, which had three sons and two daughters in service. A large portion of the paper was devoted to news of service personnel — including reports of wounds, citations, promotions — and letters from them, some graphic in their description of military action, and some, ironically, trying to cheer up the home folks.

My furlough coincided with big news in the local paper — the launching of the USS *Caswell* (AKA-72) at the North Carolina Shipbuilding Company in Wilmington. Mrs. Walter Williamson, a leading light in Locust Hill Methodist Church, christened the attack cargo ship that, unknown at the time, would participate in the invasion of Okinawa the following April and operate in the vicinity of the two minesweepers on which I would serve during 1945. The editor promoted the use of V-mail for speed and economy in communicating with overseas personnel and urged readers to subscribe to war bonds. I marveled at the news that the citizens of my poor Locust Hill Township had purchased $26,000 in bonds that fall. Volunteers and inductees were categorized by race, as were lists of families in dire need of food and clothing. For some, the Great Depression hung on despite wartime employment.

A few draft-age men still in the neighborhood seemed to exhibit an inferiority complex, particularly those classed as "4-F." Conversation almost inevitably turned to wartime shortages and the rationing of scarce goods. Erwin Stephens, the diligent editor of the *Messenger*, apologized for the sparse news coverage because he was able to find neither help nor replacement parts to keep his press running properly. There was gossip that some families, with political "pull," had finagled more than their share of ration coupons for various products in short supply.[10] Several people were charged with counterfeiting ration coupons, not an easy task before the invention of computers and scanners. The *Messenger* carried one particularly discordant note: A young man, claiming conscientious objector status, was sentenced to eighteen months in jail.

At home, I found another discordant note. My father, never a supporter of the New Deal's "socialistic" crop control program, for the first time in his life was threatening to vote for the Republican candidate, Thomas E. Dewey, in the November election. This was a shocking sentiment, because since the Democrats disfranchised blacks in 1900, the Republican Party had been shunned by most southern whites as the "Nigger Party." It was even more surprising because Daddy had been such a strong "Yellow-Dog" Democrat that he voted for a Roman Catholic in the presidential election of 1928. In retrospect, his aberration should have been no more shocking than my own political transformation since that juvenile outburst in 1941 when I blamed the war on President Roosevelt.[11] Whether I succeeded in changing Daddy's mind, I will never know.

The weeks at home gave me my first opportunity to get to know my nieces and nephews.

Buck and Vivian's Joseph, Marie, and Judith, were five, four, and two years old; and Pauline and John's Ronald was three. Never comfortable around children, I spent as much time with them as my patience would permit. Elsewhere in the rural neighborhood, now grandly called "Jones Community" in cousin Lillie Jones Walker's weekly who-visited-whom column in the local paper, population growth seemed unaffected by the war.

Not a day passed without my receiving visitors or my visiting others. It would have required two me's to accept all of the invitations that I received, and I was conscious of my father's meager gas-ration coupons and the condition of his black 1937 Ford two-door. Still, I did a lot of traveling, and my rehabilitation order contained a rubber stamp from the Caswell County War, Price and Rationing Board No. 45–10, reading "30 gal. gas issued 11-3-44." Kester remained in the county for a week, and it sometimes appeared that I was his son rather than my parents'. (Perhaps I was the only debtor who had repaid his loan from the battle front, and with interest.) One night I dated Janie Ruth Pleasant of Topnot, and Kester and Cousin Nancy joined us for a bowling trip to Danville. One day was spent with my father at the tobacco auction in Danville; and Armistice Day was spent in Durham with my brother Buck and neighbor Steve Smith to watch Duke defeat Wake Forest in football. I attended services at Locust Hill and also at my sister Pauline's Greenwood Presbyterian Church. In Greensboro I visited former co-workers at Jefferson Standard Life Insurance Company and my former landlady, Mrs. Marjorie Feree, all of whom made me feel right at home. I returned to Greensboro on the 22nd for a company party; it must have been an unusual experience, for I wrote, "What a time! Girls, Girls, & Girls. Carried 3 out, brought 5 back. Went to see 'Arsenic & Old Lace' at midnight. Back at 0300." My parents got not a wink of sleep before I returned. On a date with Myrtle Carter, we took pictures in Ballew's Park, went to movies, ate at Franklin's (a favorite restaurant in Danville), and visited the Wrenn sisters — Susan, Frances, and Mary. A visit with Julia Wright gave me an opportunity to thank the Stratford College girls for their faithful letter-writing to men in service overseas. And, of course, a visit home would not have been complete without a basketball game; on the 17th, I cheered as Cobb Memorial boys defeated Bartlett Yancey 58–27 — a rare triumph over the much larger and better-funded school, the only one in the county with an indoor court.

I wanted to return to Banner Elk but could not in good conscience consume so many gasoline ration coupons. It would have been a sad trip anyway, for several of my former school-mates, including Ray Aheron, Bruce Black, Keith Blackwelder, Billy Buchanan, James Cokalis, Fred Reid Jones, and Charles Wetmore, had been killed in action.

On November 25, shipmate George Klumpp stopped in Reidsville on his way up from New Orleans, and we borrowed my brother-in-law John's beat-up Chevrolet and, decked out in our Navy uniforms, badged and beribboned, we visited Myrtle Carter and friends in Danville. After the experience of anonymity among the throngs of servicemen in New York, I was surprised at the warmth with which we were greeted in Reidsville and Danville. We were treated like honored guests, and everybody seemed to want an explanation of the serv-ice bars on our uniforms. No doubt our stories of experiences at Anzio and Southern France grew more fanciful with each telling.

My New Orleans buddy had often asked about my "hometown," so I drove him to Pel-ham to prove that the unincorporated place really existed. One photo showed the solitary building that housed the store and post office downstairs and residence upstairs; the other showed the entire "town" — i.e., the aforesaid building plus a tiny shed that served as the sta-tion at which, if flagged down, a Southern Railway train might (or might not) stop. George, a big city boy, laughed, but he would have been more incredulous if I had taken him to my humble farm home, the inconveniences of which would have made our one-hole toilet facil-ities aboard *SC-525* appear luxurious.[12]

That night we caught the train to New York and again took a room at Brooklyn's Sands Street Navy YMCA. On November 27th, we reported to ABATU at the pink Moorish-style Lido Beach Hotel. George was soon transferred to New London, Connecticut, and I learned that my next duty station would be USS *Speed* (AM-116), a 221-foot fleet minesweeper that we had often encountered during our Mediterranean service. My boarding date, however, was delayed a couple of weeks, so George and I continued to meet for dates with Virginia and Miriam and to enjoy other grand experiences in New York City, where uniformed per-sonnel were allowed reduced-price tickets for stage shows, exhibitions, and movies. The most memorable performance was by a bean-pole of a youth from across the Hudson River. His name was Frank Sinatra, and between motion pictures he sang with Raymond Paige's orches-tra in front of screaming and swooning girls at the Paramount Theater on Times Square. I took a picture of the marquee advertising the movie ("Our Hearts Were Young and Gay") and exhibiting a huge caricature of the young crooner from New Jersey, whom I suspected to be just another fly-by-night bobby-sox idol. I did not have the nerve to join George when he lived out his fantasy by skating on the outdoor ice in Rockefeller Center. We of course toured most of the historic museums plus other sights that we had missed earlier. An instruc-tive experience was a Circle Line boat ride around Manhattan Island, for it allowed me to again see my old haunts, USS *Prairie State* and Pier 92, and to gain a better geographical per-spective of Manhattan.

I had always been a wall-flower, never a dancer, and I was embarrassed by my social backwardness, which I concealed as best I could. As a stranger in the Big Apple, I felt that I might, surreptitiously, remedy one aspect of my social inadequacy, so on December 9 I began a series of lessons in Dale's Dance Studios, 745 Seventh Avenue. My attractive dance partner threw many compliments toward me, but I judged progress by the degree of my confidence, and I came to the conclusion that the compliments far outweighed my progress. That being the case, I did not begrudge the twenty-dollar expenditure but consoled myself by foresee-ing few opportunities for dancing in the Pacific war zone, to where *Speed* would be heading within a few weeks.

The dance lessons were held in the mornings, but I had afternoons and evenings free for other activities. For example, I paid three dollars for a Madison Square Garden ticket to see Western Michigan defeat Brooklyn College and Valparaiso defeat Long Island University in basketball. The next night George and I slept in St. George's Church at 16th Street east of Third Avenue, and the following morning I heard the famed theologian, Dr. Ralph W. Sock-man, at Christ Church Methodist. We made the Pepsi-Cola Canteen — strategically located in the triangle formed by Broadway, 7th Avenue, and 45th Street — our home away from home when in the city. In that respect, we were just two of hundreds of thousands of serv-ice men and women who carried home after the war a high opinion of the patriotism of Pepsi-Cola, a soft drink that had its beginnings as "Brad's Drink" in New Bern, North Carolina. For veterans, the names of the United Service Organization, American Red Cross, and Pepsi-Cola are remembered as World War II "good guys."

As the youngest child in a family with two older brothers who paid little attention to the "kid" of the family, I had been deprived of a close brotherly relationship. And, although I had friends among classmates and shipmates, I remained pretty much a loner who guarded his secrets and avoided close personal relationships. In high school I had warm friends like Julia Wright, Myrtle Carter, Peg Watlington, Joseph Hasty, Buster Payne, and Billy Neal, but at Lees-McRae College, a volatile friendship with Haywood Meeks taught me to be careful, to withhold expressions of familiarity. I kept up my guard and bottled up my feelings. Aboard *SC-525*, mutual interests, especially in book-learning and in our further education, led to my liberty partnership with George Klumpp. Although he was Catholic and I was Protestant, we both were religiously inclined, and we talked frankly and debated spiritedly — sometimes heatedly.[13] Despite an occasional lapse in discretion, neither of us was addicted to alcohol and dirty language, and of all members of the crew, George's interests more nearly paralleled mine. Our compatibility was recognized by the officers, who arranged for our return to the States together, and we enjoyed liberties in New York, where his girlfriend, Virginia Rogan, "fixed me up" with her pal Miriam. Now, in November 1944, our paths were to diverge, but I still wore with my dogtag the St. Christopher medal, a safe-journey icon that George gave me in Casablanca when I joined the crew. At the time, we assumed that we would remain in touch, attend the same college, and serve as best man in each other's wedding. But that was not to be, for, as Haji Abdu El-Yezdi wrote in *The Kasidah*,[14]

> Friends of my youth, a last adieu! haply
> some day we meet again;
> Yet ne'er the self–same men shall meet;
> the years shall make us other men.

When I left New York for Norfolk to board a new ship headed halfway around the world to fight another war, George and I were spared knowledge that we would never see each other again. The years did indeed make us other men. George Franklin Klumpp, together with two granddaughters, died in a tragic boat accident near New Orleans on December 15, 2001.[15]

13

Stateside Interlude: Norfolk and Panama

December 1944–March 1945

As mid–December approached on Long Island, I again hoisted my seabag and headed for the Naval Receiving Station, Norfolk, to await boarding my new ship. Several forgettable days in a barrack — near where I had gone through boot camp two years earlier — allowed a few trips into Norfolk, teeming with other gobs. Then, on December 16, I reported aboard USS *Speed* (AM-116), a "Two-Twenty" attached to Mine Division Seventeen, Mine Squadron Six, United States Atlantic Fleet. At 221 feet, the steel-hulled fleet minesweeper was twice the length of *SC-525*, and at 890 tons with a 32-foot beam, draft of 9½ feet, and speed of 18 knots driven by General Motors diesel engines, this was a *huge* ship for me. Her armament was proportionately heavy; in addition to a 3"/50-caliber gun forward, she was loaded with two 40-millimeter and several 20-millimeter antiaircraft guns, plus an impressive arsenal of depth charges — two rails and five projectiles for launching. The complement was 105 men, and that included three sonarmen, two of them outranking me. Of course, I hoped that, having passed my examination for yeoman, I might soon be approved for a change in rating from SoM3c to Y3c. However, I had been assigned as a sonarman, so any change in rating would have to wait until I could win support from my new officers, of whom there were about a dozen, all strangers to me.

Speed had earned a meritorious record during her twenty-one months in the Mediterranean, and I had seen her on many occasions without suspecting that I might some day sail on her. Built by the American Shipbuilding Company in Cleveland and commissioned October 15, 1942, *Speed* reached the Atlantic by way of the Lakes Erie and Ontario and the St. Lawrence River. After shakedown cruises off Boston and Norfolk, she departed New York on March 19, 1943, for the Med, arriving at Cape Ténès, west of Algiers, three weeks later. On July 5, she departed Mers el-Kébir, Algeria, with Vice Admiral H.K. Hewitt's Western Naval Task Force for the invasion of Sicily. Off Scoglitti, she served as a control ship during the amphibious assaults, then swept Sicilian waters and escorted convoys between North Africa and the war front. A few days after *SC-525* arrived at Oran in late August, *Speed*, as a unit of Rear Admiral H. L. Hall's Southern Attack Force, sailed for the invasion of the Italian mainland. While off Salerno on September 25, she helped rescue survivors of her sister ship, USS *Skill* (AM-115), which was cut in half by an enemy torpedo.

I served on USS *Speed* (AM-116) from December 1944 until September the following year, participating in minesweeping operations around Okinawa and in the East China Sea. On May 1, my rating was changed from Sonarman to Yeoman.

For the next nine months, *Speed* conducted minesweeping and antisubmarine patrols and escorted convoys from North Africa to Italian ports. While steaming from Oran to Bizerte in April 1944, she witnessed a major German air attack that sank three Allied ships, including *Lonsdale* (DD-426) and troop transport *Paul Hamilton*, the latter carrying down more than five hundred soldiers on their way to Anzio Beachhead. *Speed* was present with my *SC-525* in the practice invasions in the vicinity of Salerno in early August and escorted an LCI convoy to Southern France, where she participated in the Camel Force landings near Frejus and St. Raphael. Several weeks later, while *SC-525* was dodging German shells off Monte Carlo and Menton with newer minesweepers, *Speed* was clearing the sea lanes westward toward Toulon. With the Mediterranean under Allied control, *Speed* sailed from Oran and arrived at Norfolk on December 11 for an overhaul in preparation for action against Japan. She became my home five days later.

To me, everything aboard the ship was new except the sonar gear, so I was disoriented for several days while simply trying to find my way around. There would be time for that, however, for *Speed* and her sister ships were undergoing substantial repairs, renovation, and modernization at the Norfolk Navy Yard, St. Helena Annex, on the east side of Elizabeth River. So I faced quite a few weeks before resuming my role as ping jockey. Many members of the crew rushed off for rehabilitation leave, and little activity was required for those of us aboard except to stay out of the way of the shipyard workers, most of them seemingly mechanical and electronics specialists. Even as a new arrival, therefore, I was given shore liberties. On December 21, for example, I attended services at the Navy Yard Chapel, Portsmouth, and I went into Norfolk a couple of afternoons. My hope of getting home for Christmas was thwarted by the absence of more senior crewmen, but I was promised a three-day New Year's leave. I wired Reidsville, "Delay Christmas Dinner until January 1." So I attended Christmas services at the Marine Barracks in Portsmouth and on New Year's Eve caught a bus to Reidsville, thence to the weatherboarded log room in which I spent my first seventeen years.

For the next three wintry nights, sleeping on a straw tick upstairs without heat, I was reminded of how accustomed — in two years — I had become to modern conveniences such as running water, central heat, and indoor toilets. The mice seemed more active than usual between the chinked logs and the sheetrock, and, unlike in earlier years, I did not have my favorite gray-and-white "Kitty" to share my bed, ready to pounce for her favorite fresh meal. I almost wished to be back in my warm canvas-bottom pipe bunk on *SC-525* where, when nature called, I would not be forced to go downstairs, through my parents' bedroom, and into the dark cold night for relief. Thankfully, there was no snow during my visit.

The waking hours were filled with neighbors dropping by, for, to conserve my father's precious, limited supply of gasoline ration stamps, I drove only a few miles. However, it was obvious that my mother had used some of her sugar ration coupons in the pies and cakes with which she celebrated my brief homecoming.

My name again entered *Speed*'s log on January 3 when I reported back aboard at St. Helena Annex. The ship's own machinery had been disabled, so water, steam, and electricity were piped aboard from the Navy Yard. The makeup in the crew was in flux, and there was much going-and-coming from men on leave, men being transferred "with bag and hammock" to other posts, and others being transferred onto *Speed*. Several of the crew were recorded as absent over leave (AOL). Lieutenant Commander Raymond C. Dryer, of Glen Cove, Long Island, returned aboard on January 6 following his rehabilitation leave, and I was immediately impressed by his gentlemanly dress and demeanor. However, I quickly learned that he was no patsy, for he was hardly back in the wardroom when he held a captain's mast and gave a one-step reduction in rate to two seamen for having been AOL for more than three days, then transferred them to the Naval Station. He also restricted to the ship for ten days a steward's mate for being "found on the streets after 0100." This was not a captain to be taken lightly. Meanwhile, two of the sonarmen, Alfred Raymond Bishop and Clarence Michael Lickfield, were transferred to the Fleet Sound School in Key West, so I knew that there was a place for me on the bridge.

During the next several days, Horace Albert Clabaugh, Luke Joseph Jolicoeur, and Alexander Watson, Jr., returned from leave; they would become three of my closest friends when we reached the Pacific. But the development of friendships aboard would be delayed, because on January 14, along with Louis J. Gnecco, William Mason Reid, Coward Harmon, and Willie Frank Jackson, Jr., I was ordered to CIC Training School at Little Creek, Virginia for "temporary additional duty." Little Creek was known for its specialization in the study of minelaying and sweeping, and I was introduced to a type of warfare that I had witnessed only as a scared spectator when the lethal weapons sank our ships and threatened all of us at Anzio and Southern France. Except for a reunion with old shipmate (and hospital mate) Eddie Runof,[1] I remember little of the four-day training exercise, but I received a certificate reading, "Completed a special course of instruction in C.I.C. and A.S.W. at the Minecraft Training Center, Little Creek, Va." I proudly sewed on my left sleeve — above my sonarman insignia — a colorful patch picturing a black mine on a yellow background with three lightning bolts on the sides.

In fact, my certificate was not merited, for my group did not "complete" the course. At breakfast on January 18, I saw a headline in the *Ledger-Dispatch* (Norfolk) which blared, "Navy Yard Annex Fire Damages Two Piers And Ship; Eight Men Hospitalized; 100 Others Given First Aid." Accompanying the story were photographs of an awful conflagration engulfing a pier and a ship identified only as "a minesweeper." A quick glance at the text under the photograph identified Pier 3, and I knew that there was only one AM — mine — moored at that pier. Another photograph showed the unmistakable shape of the starboard side of the bridge of a fleet minesweeper, almost certainly mine. The report continued, "Heavy black smoke boiling up from the creosoted pilings of the piers, and fanned by a brisk north wind caused most of the casualties," which included four servicemen and several workmen and firefighters. I wondered which of my shipmates were among the casualties.

Confirmation that the minesweeper was indeed my *Speed* was not long in coming; our party was summoned by the public address system and told that we were to immediately return our still-smouldering home. Quick transportation was arranged, and at 1100, arriving at Pier 26 in Portsmouth, we were puzzled to be directed to board a huge seaplane tender, USS *Barnegat* (AVP-10). At the top of the gangplank, we were escorted across the deck and there, below us, seemingly not seriously damaged, sat our *Speed*. That first view of the port side was deceptive. Once on deck, we were able to peek around to the starboard side and see that the paint was burned off as if the entire forward half of the ship had been skinned.

Rumor outran factual accounts among both the crew and the press. However, Lieutenant (jg) S.L. Cohen, the officer on duty, provided concise details of the fire in the ship's log:

> 1436, Fire broke out in water between dock and starboard side of ship forward. (Exact origin under investigation.) Notified fire department and commenced fighting fire. 1438, Cast off sludge barge YSR No. 1. 1445, Crane placed brow on fantail. Evacuating yard workmen and personnel not engaged in fighting fire. 1451, Yard tug came alongside fantail to port to assist in fighting fire. 1455, Observed first fire truck on scene. 1504, Commenced cutting stern lines to dock. 1514, All lines clear. Underway in tow of tug clearing Pier 3.... 1520, Moored port side to Pier 4.... Small fires still existing in radar shack, ward room, and electrical store room. Fire trucks assisting in fighting fire. 1525, Fires in radar shack and ward room extinguished. Small fire still smoldering in electrical store room but under control.

A few minutes later, *Speed* was lashed to the side of her sister ship, USS *Sustain*, and the twins were towed first to Berth 1, Portsmouth. Finally, at 2255 *Speed* was moved to the starboard side of *Barnegat* at Berth 26, by which time the onboard fire had been extinguished. Meanwhile, at the original site, dynamite had broken the burning Pier 3 away from the face of the dock.

When my Little Creek party returned aboard on January 18, we were given time only to gather up our belongings and stuff them into our seabags. The metal ship, still warm from the fire, was now uninhabitable, so the crew was billeted in a large St. Helena barrack with row after row of bunks, somewhat reminiscent of the 118th Station Hospital. Even in January, the quarters were so warmly steam-heated that we lived with the windows open. For the next month, we were landlubbers at St. Helena, because *Speed* was off-limits while scores of Navy Yard personnel and contractors sought to restore her to seaworthiness. Sanding and painting the exterior were easy tasks; much more complicated was stripping out and replacing the electronic equipment that made the vessel a warship.

Hundreds of feet from the stricken ship, we listened to different stories on the origin of the fire. The most plausible theory blamed it on a lighted cigarette carelessly thrown into a trash can, after which a passer-by saw paper burning and instinctively picked up the can and threw the contents into the water between the ship and the pier. The burning debris fell on an acetylene line, setting off a fire that spread quickly to the creosoted piles, the wooden pier, and back to the starboard side of the ship and thence into the electrical compartments. The *Speed* had no defense; her utilities had previously been severed, she received water and power from the dock, and even her engines had been disabled. I am not sure if the Navy ever pinpointed the "someone" whose impulsive act probably ignited the fire.

Nevertheless, there remained some apprehension aboard, for this was not the first fire suffered by *Speed*. On January 9 a workman's cutting torch damaged an officer's blanket, bedspread, and pillow case. And only two days before the disaster a motor machinist's mate was given ten days' restriction, charged with negligence of duty while on fire watch.

We were not always idle in the barrack, however, for there were military lectures, tests, movies, demonstrations, and musters. For example, this entry was made in my service record for February 5: "Night Vision tested this date with Radium Plaque Adaptometer and PASSED." There were also outdoor exercises and games, at none of which I excelled. Evenings gave us time for shooting the bull, and I became best acquainted with the men who sacked near my bunk. Four of them became frequent liberty mates. William A. Green, yeoman first class from Washington, D.C., and Addison F. Kingston, storekeeper third class of Delanco, New Jersey, shared my clerical interests. I especially buddied up to Green, who had the job to which I aspired, and over the next several months he allowed me access to the yeoman's shack, which led to my acquaintance with the skipper who later recommended that my rating be changed from sonarman to yeoman. Kingston was old enough to permit us to call him "Pop," for anyone thirty-some years old seemed to be ancient to us just-turned-twenties. John C. Larson of Enterprise, Kansas, and Don R. Latta of Corning, Ohio, were both seamen, so we had little in common except that both were just plain joes with none of the affectation that exhibited itself in some of the crew. Although we were not teetotalers, the five were more interested in cultural sites and activities than in bars, and we attended services in the Yard Chapel and Wright Memorial Methodist Church in Portsmouth, and a plainly named Memorial Methodist Episcopal Church in Norfolk.[2] I could write back to the Reverend Joyce V. Early that I was still a good Methodist. Well, at least a Methodist. On February 16, I was granted another three-day leave in North Carolina, and again I visited and was visited by relatives and old friends, and at night slept on the no longer beloved straw tick with familiar sounds in the walls. When I returned to Norfolk, I did not know that fifteen months would pass before I would sleep cold again.

Back "on board"—which meant in our land-based quarters—all was not harmony. Some of my shipmates had mistaken the lax discipline at the barrack as license in the city. The most common offense was not jumping ship but overstaying leave. A few examples: On February 7, the log recorded that a steward's mate "returned aboard under guard after being over leave eight days five hours and fifteen minutes. [...] held aboard ship as Prisoner-at-Large by order of the Commanding Officer." Two days later at a captain's mast, the man was reduced in rating one grade. At 0250 on February 8, a motor machinist's mate returned aboard under guard after his arrest by the Shore Patrol for violating ComFive Order 28–44 (on the streets after 0100). The captain found extenuating circumstances (the man had lost his ID and had been attempting to retrace his steps to find it), so he was simply given a warning. At captain's mast on February 20 several seamen were convicted of being absent over leave; two were given extra duty of ten and fifteen hours, and another was restricted to the ship for twenty days. A month later, one of the same seamen was convicted for being absent over leave six additional days and was confined for five days on bread and water with full ration on the third day. Significantly, most of the men with egregious offenses were transferred to other ships and stations, a pointed message that our skipper wanted a crew of sailors who knew and followed regulations.

Speed changed piers several times as the restoration and repairs proceeded, and on Feb-

ruary 24, she got underway on her own power for a trial run near Thimble Shoals in the
Chesapeake. By that time part of the crew had moved back on board. A couple of days later,
we made a post-repair trial run at Hampton Roads and moored at Craney Island while receiving GSK supplies. On the 28th, at the Norfolk De-perming Station we had our coils energized, then moored at Convoy Escort Pier 21, Naval Operating Base, Norfolk. We knew that
we were getting ready to return to war when we took on an arsenal: 326 rounds of 3"/50-
caliber, 3,920 rounds of 40-millimeter, 17,640 rounds of 20-millimeter, 108 rounds of impulse
charges, 6,030 rounds of small arms ammunition, and seven boxes of pyrotechnics. One thing
for sure: Fire prevention was henceforth to be a prime concern.

On March 2, we sailed to the State Port Ammunition Barge at Hampton Roads and took
aboard underwater ammunition, thence to lower Chesapeake to stream, adjust, and repair
magnetic minesweeping gear. After recovering the gear, we anchored off Wolfe Trap magnetic
range. For the next several days we streamed O-type gear,[3] went through the degaussing range,
calibrated the radio direction finder, compensated the magnetic compass, and commenced
pulsing to adjust the magnetic panel board. On the 7th, we conducted exercises with USS
Intrigue (AM-253) and USS *Opponent* (AM-269); and for two days we carried out antisubmarine warfare practice with USS *Heroic*.

There was considerable excitement on March 10 as we conducted gunnery practice in
northern Chesapeake Bay and proceeded to Baltimore, Maryland, for the night. This was my
first liberty in Baltimore, but there were only a few hours for sightseeing, and I was disappointed not to get over to Fort McHenry, which we could hardly see in the blacked-out harbor. More exercises on the way back to Cape Charles the next day confirmed that *Speed* was
both seaworthy and ready for action, so on March 13, ComServRon-5, Captain Wertz, held
a satisfactory departure inspection of personnel and materiel. The crew did not realize at the
time that *Speed* would require further extensive modernization when she reached the west coast.

When on March 15 we got underway from Norfolk for the Panama Canal Zone in company with the stores ship USS *Yukon* (AF-9), the captain was at the conn and the navigator
was on the bridge. One shipmate missed the sailing; he had been convicted at a deck court
martial for being absent over leave six days, reduced to the lowest rank (apprentice seaman),
and put ashore "complete with bag, hammock, records, and transfer papers." Having shed
some of our unwanteds, we were off to the "other" war, and there would be no slackers aboard.

I went back to the familiar sonar gear, pinging away, with full knowledge that German
U-boats still roamed the east coast, where they had done great damage to American shipping
the previous three years. General Quarters was sounded so often that we became proficient
at getting to our battle stations on the double. There were frequent inspections, gun practice,
flag hoist drills, and an assortment of duties to keep us busy.

Cruising at an average of twelve knots, we passed San Salvador Island to port on March
19, and four days later fell astern of the *Yukon* as we approached the isthmus, where we docked
alongside USS *Dour* (AM-223) at the U.S. Naval Base at Coco-Solo, Panama Canal Zone. A
USO representative greeted our ship and gave each crewman a useful little pamphlet titled
Panama in Your Pocket containing intriguing bits of information: That the canal [in 1944] was
50 miles long, cost $380 million, lifted ships 85 feet above sea level and brought them back
down again (in three steps up and three down), required an average of six hours for a crossing, and shortened the distance by water from San Francisco to New York by 7,873 miles.
Most remarkable of all, the pamphlet claimed that the Pacific entrance to the canal was twenty-
five miles *east* of Caribbean entrance, which meant that this was the only place in the world
where the sun rose in the Pacific and set in the Atlantic. The booklet also reminded us that

the Canal Zone, with a civilian population of 60,000, was an entirely United States government community associated with the operation of the Panama Canal. There was no private enterprise or home ownership of any kind. The zone was limited to a strip of land extending five miles on either side of the canal, but with the specific exception of Colon and Panama City, which remained under the jurisdiction of the Republic of Panama.[4]

Located a few miles west of Coco-Solo on Manzanillo Island was a rambling city named for Columbus — Colon (the Columbian name) or Cristobal (the Spanish name). We were given shore liberty, an opportunity for us to see a little of the life of a Spanish-culture area of Central America. I apparently had not learned my lesson at Casablanca, for, instead of going ashore with Green, Kingston, Larson, and Latta, I fell in with another bunch, none of whom I knew well, and we took a horse-drawn "carromata" to Colon. We were impressed by the Hotel Washington, the monuments, and Mount Hope Cemetery, final resting place for many who died during the digging of the canal. I found the street architecture interesting, particularly the open porches on nearly every building, and wanted to see the sights, but the others opted first to sample the local cuisine. We had lunch at a rather ordinary place called "Restaurante U.S." at the corner of Bolivar Avenue and 11th Street. Obviously, the business had only recently changed ownership, because a tape reading "U.S." had been pasted over "Olympia" on the face of the menu. The prices were steep for the time — for example, fried chicken cost $1.45. Remembering that every hundred dollars saved equaled the cost of a month in college, I took the chicken chow mein at 85 cents and splurged for home-made pie at ten cents additional. During lunch, the waitresses flirted with the sailors, and the conversation gradually got around to the presumption that *Speed* would go directly to the Pacific war zone. A whispered conversation between the head waiter and one of our group set off a succession of suggestive winks and a sudden but silent consensus of how we should spend the afternoon: bar hopping and whoring. For the first time since Africa, my willpower failed me, and a couple of drinks weakened my resistance. Besides, the bordello was fairly well kept, and the women appeared to have met the city-ordained health standards posted on the wall at the entrance. This was obviously an establishment sanctioned by both naval and municipal officials to operate for the pleasure of the many American servicemen stationed at this strategic location of the Western Hemisphere — though perhaps without the strict rules of the pleasure house at Beni Saf. I was certainly a reluctant companion — but "when in Rome, do as the Romans do." After all, I had not yet earned a reputation on *Speed* comparable to the one my subchaser shipmates had bestowed upon me many months earlier.

On the morning of March 25, after taking aboard two dozen seamen for transportation across the Isthmus, *Speed* entered the Gatun Locks that lifted us to the surface of Gatun Lake, through the Gaillard Cut to Miraflores Lake, thence down the Miraflores Locks toward the west coast. It seemed absolutely bizarre that, though we had passed from the Atlantic to the Pacific across the Continental Divide, we were *southeast* of our starting point. At 1945, the OOD, probably oblivious of the irony of our location, simply entered in the log, "Standing out of Panama Canal at various courses and speeds into the Pacific Ocean." And, he might have added, into another war.

14

Hiatus: California and Hawaii

March–June 1945

Even the air smelled differently as we sailed along the Pacific coasts of Panama, Costa Rica, Nicaragua, Honduras, El Salvador, Guatemala, and Mexico. The equatorial sun beamed down on the ship's metal hull, making life on deck uncomfortable during the day, and there was little cooling at night. Still, training exercises increased, and on the assumption that *Speed* was heading for new battle experiences, our officers did not allow the crew to loll in the tropics. In fact, there were more soundings of general quarters, musters at battle stations, drills — fire, rescue, overboard, abandon ship — and daily inspections of magazines, smokeless powder samples, and watertight compartments. On the second day out, the starboard rack of depth charges was released and two "K" guns were fired to a depth of 400 feet; and on April 2, off Baja California, coastal Mexicans must have imagined a great sea battle when we fired additional depth charges and every major gun on the ship, including 3"/50-caliber starshells and more than two dozen 40-millimeter projectiles.

The only real excitement of the voyage occurred on March 30. Let the ship's log tell the story: "1823, Reed, Jesse Francis, GM3/c ... was cleaning a .30-calibre rifle. The rifle had been used, not fired, during exercises on afternoon of 30 March 1945. Rifle accidentally fired penetrating patient's left big toe. Negligence not apparent. Treatment administered by Norton, J.J., PhM1c, on board this vessel." Naturally, many of us initially suspected that the gunner had staged the incident to avoid going back into battle, but upon second thought, why would anyone shoot his toe off in Mexican waters when we were within four days of California? Regardless, the injury was painful and possibly infectious, so radio contact was made with the United States Naval Liaison Officer at Manzanillo, Mexico; he instructed the ship to detour to that harbor. We arrived in complete darkness and apparently undetected by the Mexican military, for when daylight arrived, we found that *Speed* had woven her way between several other ships to reach the inner harbor. As we anchored and sent Reed ashore by small boat, we remarked how easily a Japanese submarine could have, with immunity, attacked a large North American city. I never saw Reed again, but I wrote home on May 23, "One fellow did shoot off his big toe and that left him behind, but I think I'd just as soon keep my big toes and go look over the Japanese homeland."

We passed through San Diego's antisubmarine net early on April 4 and moored to USS *Dour* (AM-223) in a nest containing the seaplane tender USS *Gardiner's Bay* (AVP-39). Fairly promptly the Shakedown Training Group of the Western Sea Frontier came aboard for arrival inspection. Within six hours, the Commandant of the 11th Naval District ordered *Speed* out of his harbor. Initially stunned, we learned later that the inspection party found our ship so unfit for battle that we were ordered to proceed to Alameda for major corrections. So much for our looked-for liberty in San Diego and a side trip to Tijuana, seemingly every sailor's paradise.

Two days later we passed Farallon Islands and Mile Rock Light, through the antisubmarine nets, into San Francisco Bay. Although I had occasionally been at the helm while alternating with sonar duty earlier in the voyage, I was elated to be at the steering wheel again as we approached and passed under Golden Gate Bridge. However, my good luck prevented me from taking pictures until we were well into the bay. Consequently, by the time I was relieved, my first photograph showed Golden Gate fading into the background as we paralleled Fort Mason. I then turned the camera southeastward and captured the Coit Tower on Telegraph Hill. Only then did I realize that we had passed the downtown area, which I framed with the tower to the left. It occurred to me that the absence of New York–style skyscrapers was explained by the earthquake and fire that had devastated the city thirty-nine years earlier and that remained a threat as the tectonic plates rubbed beneath California. I was so enthralled by the fascinating skyline that, except for the exclamation of shipmates, I would have failed to get a fine photograph of the local attraction about which I had read most — Alcatraz. Within a few minutes, we sailed under the Bay Bridge and past busy wharfs along the 'Frisco waterfront, thence southward to anchor off Hunter's Point. The next day we sailed for Alameda, where *Speed* was neutered with the removal of depth charges before proceeding to a pier operated by General Engineering and Drydocking Company, which had previously built from scratch a dozen minesweepers. So *Speed* was in good hands, and we learned that our ship would undergo a lengthy overhaul — a fate that brought glee to the sailors who knew something of the wonders of San Francisco. Since I had heard little about the west coast, I wondered what all of the fuss was about.

Again, the ship's water, electricity, and steam were furnished from the dock, and *Speed* was treated as a hospital case. But the crew was not inactive, for we were forever mustering by sections on the dock for calisthenics and make-work assignments. We knew little of what was being done to the ship, which became peripatetic as it was jostled around in the labyrinth of GEDC. On April 19 *Speed* was towed to Drydock #1, pushed onto a marine railway, and lifted on blocks in "drydock position," meaning high, dry, and vulnerable. By that time the crew had been moved into a barrack in Alameda; we were again landlubbers. But the officers did not forget us, for they devised time-consuming inspections, and once, on May 1, there was a full-scale captain's inspection, which culminated in a ceremony at which Commander Dryer presented to William J. Dempster, motor machinist's mate, a Navy and Marine Corps medal for heroic action in the Med.

Meanwhile, I had learned why so many of my shipmates had been excited about our visit to San Francisco, for our compulsory layover in the bay area provided me one of the most interesting months of my naval career. During the hiatus at Alameda, the crew was generously granted liberty an average of two of each three nights, and there was good transportation across the Bay Bridge into San Francisco. My first stop in the big city was the Pepsi-Cola Center for Service Men occupying a handsome building on Market Street. Like the Times Square center in New York, this one was heavily patronized by men of all branches of service. In response to my question about an inexpensive hotel, I was told that the city had constructed at Civic Center, on the grounds of City Hall, a battery of two-story wooden barracks with overnight bunks for transient servicemen. It was there in Bed 145, Dormitory G, that I

I joined my frequent liberty partners, Alexander Watson, SM1c, left, and Luke J. Jolicoeur, QM1c, right, in San Francisco's Golden Gate Park while *Speed* was undergoing repairs in the Alameda Shipyard.

spent my first night in the city, and I returned from time to time to partake of the patriotic generosity of the city. Adjacent, just off Market Street, was a free dispensary for service personnel. I was indeed impressed by the spirit of Californians who were no longer afraid, as they had been three years earlier, of an attack from the Japanese. Innocents like me could not distinguish national origins of the ubiquitous Orientals we encountered, but we were assured by the government that dangerous resident Japanese were securely detained in internment camps.

After my four months aboard *Speed*, new friendships had begun forming, and it was natural that I came to know best the men with whom I was in daily contact on the bridge. My most frequent liberty buddies while in California were Willard Green, the yeoman ("Yogi") from Washington; Luke Jolicoeur, the "Frog" quartermaster ("Spokes") from Quebec City; and Alex Watson, the signalman ("Flags") from Pittsburgh. Together, we sight-saw most of the tourist spots and dozens of movies and shows, the most memorable of which was the stage performance at the Geary Theater by Helen Hayes in *Harriet*, the moving story of Harriet Beecher Stowe. Our favorite daytime destination was Golden Gate Park with its art museums, planetarium, aquarium, arboretum, stadiums, and outdoor concerts. Especially intriguing to me was the Japanese Garden with its tea house, pagoda ponds, bridges, bonsai, and flowering cherries. The irony of the internment camps did not occur to me at the time.

On April 15, I attended services at First Presbyterian Church in Alameda, heard the Reverend John A. Glasse preach on "Human Scaffolding," and remained for a bountiful lunch offered to all servicemen among the worshipers. My attendance was documented by a picture postcard addressed to my parents by Ralph L. Thomson, the church's service personnel officer, who assured them that I was "looking very well indeed." The following Sunday I attended Dr. C.S.S. Dutton's special "United Nations Conference Service" at the gothic vine-covered Unitarian Church at Geary and Franklin Streets, San Francisco. (I would remember the latter experience when, after the war, I joined the Unitarian Church of the Larger Fellowship, a mail-order membership from Boston.) At a nearby corner I snapped a picture of "Myrtle St." impressed in concrete, and sent it to my friend Myrtle Carter back in Caswell.

All was not happiness in the bay area. I remember the exact moment when, on the dock at Alameda, I heard the numbing news that President Roosevelt was dead. Perhaps I took it harder because of my hot-headed and ill-advised blurt, just after Pearl Harbor, that the president's policies had forced the Japanese into war, an accusation for which I never forgave myself. Now, on April 12, 1945, I again held some views that I would soon repudiate. I wrote home,

> The news of President Roosevelt's death just reached us an hour ago over the radio. It was a great shock and everyone shows it. Even the most ardent Republicans on the ship are wondering how the problems of peace can be worked out after his death. Certainly Truman is not capable of the type of leadership we need. If Wendell Willkie had lived, now would be the time for him to be useful. In my opinion, Willkie, Roosevelt, and Hull were the only ones suitable for the presidency at this time; now two of them are dead and Hull is in the hospital. We were looking forward to seeing the President here at the San Francisco Conference on the 26th. His death will not hinder the war — or even slow it — but it certainly leaves us without a man to lead us toward peace.

So much for the political sagacity of one only three months beyond the voting age of twenty-one. However, I was not the only American pleasantly surprised by Harry S [without a period] Truman's able postwar leadership.

The reference to "San Francisco Conference" was to the birth of the United Nations Organization (UNO, as it was originally called), which took place in the Civic Center during our presence. A beautiful floral welcome was planted on a grassy bank in Golden Gate Park. In many colors, the words reading "San Francisco Welcomes United Nations" overlay a shield, in the center of which appeared the national eagle. Unfortunately, I had no Kodachrome film (which still was in its experimental stage), so my black-and-white photo does not reveal the message's full floral beauty.

The conference brought big names from around the world, so it was an exciting time in San Francisco. One of those big names — Senator Tom Connally of Texas, chairman of the Senate Foreign Relations Committee and vice-chairman of the organizing committee — made more news than he intended when in an interview he implied that the Germans were suing for peace. The resulting headline in the *San Francisco Examiner*, "NAZIS SURRENDER," so excited Luke, Alex, and me that we took a room at Hotel Crane and photographed ourselves holding the front page announcing the claim. We failed to note that just above the bold headline was, in much smaller type, a line reading "High U.S. Official Says" The senator, predictably, claimed that he had been misquoted. Regardless, the false report was premature by only a few days, for on May 8 San Franciscans joined the remainder of Americans in a huge celebration of V-E Day.

Meanwhile, back in Alameda, discipline was eroding. A motor machinist's mate was sentenced to thirty hours of police duty for intoxication, public disturbance, and striking a shore patrol; and an apprentice seaman was given the same sentence for intoxication and possession of three I.D. cards — two for himself and one for another sailor. At least four men were

The United Nations was formally organized while *Speed* was in the San Francisco area. I snapped this floral tribute in Golden Gate Park.

restricted to the ship or given extra duty for failing to salute a commissioned officer. More severe punishment was meted out to one of my CIC-Little Creek partners; he was reduced to the next inferior rank for insolence toward a commissioned officer and refusing to obey an order. The boom was lowered on one seaman. Assessed thirty days' confinement for being absent over leave for more than two days, he simply jumped ship. Before we left the bay, he was declared a "straggler" from the vessel, and his records and effects were transferred to the Navy Receiving Station at Treasure Island. But we would hear from that obstreperous seaman again.

Thirty-two months after I joined the Navy with high expectation of being assigned clerical work, my ambition was fulfilled on May 1, 1945, when Commander Dryer's recommendation for my rate-change was officially approved by the Bureau of Naval Personnel. Instead of Sonarman Jones, I was now Yeoman Jones; instead of a ping jockey, now I was a "yogi" or "feathers" (referring to the cross quills of the rating badge). Actually, I had spent much of my time in the yeoman's shack after settling in on *Speed*, for Willard Green was happy to have me as an assistant, and the skipper and his executive officer, Lieutenant Avery, were satisfied with my competence and trustworthiness.

On May 6, back aboard ship, we lit off the main engines, stationed a special sea detail, cast off, and sailed under the Bay Bridge and conducted a sonar check near Red Rock. That exercise completed, with a pilot at the helm, we conducted an exciting full-power run — the first one since Norfolk. I was again impressed with the get-up-and-go of my ship. We returned toward Treasure Island for runs through the degaussing range before again sailing under the bridge to anchor overnight near South Beach. The next day we compensated the compass, swung the ship, then sailed up San Pablo Bay to Vallejo and moored near the cruiser USS *Pensacola* at the Mare Island Naval Ammunition Depot. Ominously, we brought aboard an arsenal of depth charges, ammunition for all guns, and a Mark 104 demolition outfit. On the 8th, we sailed back to Treasure Island, calibrated the pitometer, ran the measured mile, and returned to Anchorage 12 off South Beach.[1] I was among the lucky ones given liberty on this, the officially proclaimed V-E Day, but by the time we got into the city, some of the day's festivities were over. We had, however, experienced three memorable events during our stay in the bay area: the death of President Roosevelt, the birth of the United Nations, and the celebration of victory in Europe. I took time to send a Western Union telegram to my sister reading, "Leaving Frisco. Will write later[.] Everything is fine. Don't worry. I am still in the States."

I suppose it was because I had become something of a bridge rat during the voyage from Norfolk, but for whatever the reason — even though my rating had been changed to yeoman nine days earlier — I was given helm duty when on the afternoon of May 9 we weighed anchor in South Bay and and steamed toward the Bay Bridge. Commander Dryer was on the bridge, along with the OOD, Lieutenant J. R. Beasley, Jr., so I felt flattered to be in their presence as helmsman, and I wondered if it was just a coincidence that I was the only man among our crew of more than a hundred to be given the privilege of steering *Speed* both *into* and *out of* San Francisco Bay.

On entering the bay on April 6, I had been relieved after steering the ship under the Golden Gate Bridge, giving me time to photograph sites around the bay, including the underside of the Bay Bridge. Now I was content to glance at the city as we passed it to port, but there was little of interest to view before reaching the bridge. The effect of the undertow on my steering into the bay had been noticeable but not erratic, but it was considerably stronger as we cruised up from South Bay. Our course toward the Bay Bridge was at an oblique angle, but we were to change course toward the northwest to follow the channel for a perpendicular approach to the bridge. Following orders, I dutifully sang out, "Aye, aye, sir, left to 345," then, when the ship came around, "345, sir," to which the captain responded, "Steady as she goes." Once in the channel, I felt that the rudders were not responding as tightly as usual, for I repeatedly turned the wheel, sometimes to the port, sometimes to the starboard, to keep the king-spoke upright. This was not unusual in huge San Francisco Bay, where the sea tides met the onrushing rivers. But as we neared the bridge, the current became perceptibly stronger, and I worked hard to keep the heading within two degrees of 345, which would carry us just starboard of the mammoth central concrete anchorage that tied together the pair of two-tower suspension bridges connecting San Francisco with Yerba Buena Island. Within minutes, maintaining course became more difficult as the current pushed the ship to port even as I maintained a heading close to 345. I must admit to momentary panic before the captain recognized the steady drift and barked out "Right to 350!" Even so, we cleared that monstrous concrete pier by perhaps a hundred feet — too close for a ship loaded with ammunition meant to be expended against the Japanese. Since that May day in 1945, I still cringe when I hear of problems with the Bay Bridge, such as earthquake damage, for if we had collided with the concrete supports, *Speed* might have brought the entire west portion of the bridge down upon her. I mused that no one would ever have known that I was "driving" the ship that caused the calamity because so little evidence would have survived.[2]

I was "relieved to be relieved" from helm duty as *Speed* bade farewell to the beautiful city of San Francisco on the afternoon of May 9. We sailed into the sun, passing through the Golden Gate into the Pacific. It was no secret that we were heading for another exciting city —

Los Angeles, or at least its port, San Pedro. We arrived on the 11th and moored at Cerritos Dock, Terminal Island. However, without getting ashore and after spending the next day on various drills at sea, we sailed to Santa Barbara and spent the next day conducting single-ship sweeping exercises for moored and magnetic mines in nearby waters. The following day we joined USS *Refresh* (AM-287) and *YMS-146* and *-301* in streaming gear in sweeping formation with "O" type gear. That night I went ashore in Santa Barbara but remembered little of the experience. After another morning with the three ships, this time streaming magnetic mine gear and recovering dan buoys, we sailed back at sixteen knots to San Pedro. On the 16th, *Speed* rendezvoused with *PC-811* and *YP-645* for noisy artillery exercises, firing on a towed sleeve. The training experience was expensive for the taxpayers — 60 rounds of 3"/50-caliber, 432 rounds of 40-millimeter, and 4,800 rounds of 20-millimeter ammunition. We returned to Terminal Island for the night.

Apparently, we had been given the seal of approval by the naval powers, for on the 18th we were admitted into San Diego harbor, out from which we had been contemptuously kicked in April, and, after first mooring at the West Coast Sound School, returned to sea for a degaussing run and the calibration of all coils. Two consecutive nights of liberty enabled several of us to explore a bit of San Diego. There followed two interesting days of antisubmarine maneuvers with *PCS-1442* and USS *Iris*, using *SS-34* as the quarry. That evening we joined USS *Lofberg* (DD-759) for night steaming, steering various courses and speeds to maintain visual distance. Interestingly, *Lofberg* had been commissioned only a month earlier at the Bethlehem Steel Company in San Francisco, so *Speed* was probably her first "partner" in a sea exercise. Years later, the destroyer would earn seven battle stars for action in the war with North Korea.

Our last two days in San Diego were quite eventful — and might have been more eventful for me had not my rating been changed from sonarman to yeoman just three weeks earlier. The Navy decreed that sonarmen who attended sound school prior to November 1943 should return for advanced training. I might have fallen in that group had I remained classified as sonarman. Instead, I stayed aboard while our two second class ping jockeys, William M. Reid and Lawrence J. Fournier, were shipped over to the West Coast Sound School, San Diego. To replace them, we welcomed aboard W. R. Kelly and Robert E. Perry, both SoM2c.[3]

Luke, Alex, and I were given shore leave on the 19th and enjoyed enormously a dinner at the Downtowner, a simple restaurant that, in serving fried rabbit and buttermilk, rekindled childhood memories for me and provided a new experience for the city slickers, who gobbled up the food reminiscent of the American South. We toured San Diego and saw Spencer Tracy and Katharine Hepburn in *Without Love*, which I characterized in a letter home as "very good but it's about the craziest picture I've ever seen." It was 0230 before we signed in — stone sober, to the surprise of the officer on duty at the gangplank.

Three days later, I was given the melancholy task as special messenger to deliver the proceedings of a summary court-martial to the district legal office. Remember the "straggler" left ashore at Treasure Island? Well, he was apprehended, brought back to *Speed* under guard, charged with being sixteen days AWOL, made a prisoner at large, and given a summary court-martial on May 21. The verdict was sealed, and the sentence was not entered in the log, but the man was transferred under armed guard on the 22nd to the Receiving Station at Camp Elliott. Radarman Vernon Paul Geiger, soon to become a member of my liberty party at Okinawa, delivered the troubled seaman to the detention center.

With four hours to kill after delivering the document, I returned to the Downtowner for a big steak. I was up early again on the 23rd, excused from muster with orders to pick up guard mail from the naval district building. I took the opportunity for a doughnut breakfast ashore — my last stateside meal for eight months. In fact, I had to eat fast and rush back to the ship, for promptly at 0904 we cast off and sailed westward to another war. I sat down at the Underwood typewriter — the one whose carriage rose and fell with heavy waves, interspersing capital letters in strange places — and described the moment:

> There wasn't a single man below decks this morning unless his station was there, who came up one time or the other; everyone was up to say goodbye to the rugged CALIFORNIA (a big wave just went under) coast and the small islands close by. We are alone now; steaming independently, and all land has been lost over the horizon. What lies ahead, none of us know; but even the new men who had never been to sea before are in a surprisingly good spirit and there isn't a man on board who shows any outwardly [*sic*] sadness over leaving. All I have to say is, I might as well see the world on Uncle Sam while he'S [*sic*] got me.

The latter remark reminded me of the attitude of our gunnery officer, Ensign Richard L. Graves from Martinsville and Leaksville: "I wouldn't go over if I didn't think I'd come back."

It was everyone's guess that our first stop would be Hawaii, so we anticipated at least a short hiatus before encountering Japanese subs and mines. Alone, we sailed on a zig-zag course at fourteen knots, occasionally at full speed. The crew was kept alert with frequent musters on station, general quarters at dawn and dusk, daily inspections of magazines and smokeless powder samples, antiaircraft exercises, and every imaginable drill — fire, collision, opening/closing watertight compartments, man overboard, rescue, and abandon ship. Even so, it was a leisurely eight-day cruise, during which I typed in carbon copies — there were no instant copiers during World War II — a descriptive circular letter. For example:

> This trip is giving me the first time in two months to do much writing. I have plenty of time to waste at sea; but not so in port. Don't get me wrong; I am not killing myself at work, but we keep regular hours (normally 0800–1130; 1300–1700) in the office and after eating and washing up after chow, there usually is an odd job to do such as washing hats and sox. Lights are out at 2200 and I normally hit the hay pretty soon after that. Only when there is more work that Jones and Green can do during the regular hours do we have work to do at night.

I added,

> there are about a half-dozen of us who usually make up some sort of combination and make liberty together. They are [Willard] Green, my boss, from Washington, D.C.; [Addison] "Pop" Kingston, the Storekeeper from Delanco, New Jersey, a fellow who everyone likes for his humor, seriousness, friendliness, and intelligence; [Alexander] Watson, the Signalman from Pittsburg [*sic*], a quiet but swell fellow; [Luke] "Frog" Jolicoeur, the Quartermaster Frenchman from Canada and the Bronx, a fellow who gets a laugh out of everything whether it's funny or not, especially when it pertains to the French; John Larson, Fireman from Enterprise, Kansas, a serious and well-liked fellow; and [Horace] "Clay" Clabaugh, Electrician from Chicago, a swell guy and good friend. The funny part of the group is the range of ages. When you put a bunch of fellows into sailor's garb, it is almost impossible to distinguish the ages apart. In civilian life there is always a barrier in ages, but in service age is completely forgotten. Some of the fellows of 17 act older than others of 40. Of our liberty group, Frog and Pop are 36, Green 25, Larson & Watson 24, and Clay is 19.

Our dress code at sea was very relaxed — blue cotton shirts, denim trousers, and white Dixie Cup sailor's hats — but we did receive instructions to dye our shipboard hats blue. From the air, a white hat could easily be sighted, whereas a blue one would blend in with colors of the ship. The order reminded me that if we should go ashore in Hawaii, I would be out of uniform in my white jumper with its sonarman rating patch on the left arm. I picked up yeoman patches in Diego, and when I learned that Frog had been a tailor in civilian life, I took advantage of his talent. He did a fine job of sewing the patch on the sleeve, but when he handed the garment to me, I realized that the patch had been sewn to the inside rather the outside of the sleeve. The error was my fault, for I had turned it inside out for rolling, and I had not reversed the sleeve before handing it to Luke. He joined me in a big laugh, and I wrote home, "We're always pulling jokes on Frog and he never gets any rest when any of the bridge gang is around."

The slow pace aboard gave me time for more reading. My favorite war correspondent, Pulitzer Prize–winner Ernie Pyle, had been killed on Ie Shima northwest of Okinawa while we were in San Francisco, so I had purchased a copy of his *Here Is Your War*. Aboard, Pop Kingston owned *Brave Men*, which I liked even better because it caught the drama of our Mediterranean experiences. Pyle had a knack of making interesting an otherwise boring story. For example, by studying the defenses of the common fly so ubiquitous in North Africa, Pyle concluded that the insect became airborne in reverse. Consequently, he determined that the way to swat a fly was to aim two inches *behind* the insect rather than in front of it. (My own attacks on Pacific flies proved that either Pyle was pulling his reader's leg or that African and Pacific flies used different modes of liftoff.) I also read *Combustion on Wheels*, by David L. Cohn, which was written while the author was a house guest of the Poteat family at Forest Home in my native Caswell County.

It fell my pleasure to type into the service record of every crew member on May 27 the statement, "Serving outside continental limits of the United States this date." That meant a pay increase, but there was more excitement because we anticipated that we would soon have liberty in Hawaii. We entered Pearl Harbor at night on May 31 and tied up at the Destroyer Escort Dock. The destruction wrought by the Japanese on December 7, 1941, had been pretty well concealed, but we knew that our ships and our sailors still lay beneath the waters.

If we expected to sleep late and go on liberty the next day, we were sadly disappointed, for within eight hours we were steaming out of the harbor for four days of intense exercises with *Ptarmigan*, *Seer*, *Sway*, *Swift*, *Symbol*, and *Threat*. The trials in Area C-7 west of the island of Lanai encompassed almost every imaginable engagement against mines of all kinds, as well as against enemy airplanes, submarines, and surface vessels. *LSM-386* joined us to launch a drone for firing practice.

Upon returning to Pearl Harbor, our initial disappointment was assuaged when the crew was given generous alternating shore liberty in Honolulu for six straight afternoons. Four of my mornings were spent at Mona Loa learning more about radar, resulting in this entry in my service record: "Completed four (4) days temporary duty under instruction in operation of SL Radar at Radar Operator's School, Pacific Fleet Schools, Pearl Harbor, T.H." Of my three afternoons in Honolulu, the first was least satisfying because Frog, Alex, and I only explored the downtown where streets were narrow and drab, food was unpalatable, and the citizens seemed unfriendly to the thousands of military men whose presence made the place seem like an occupied territory. In company with Pop Kingston and Vernon Geiger, my second foray gave me a different view, particularly of Waikiki Beach, about which I wrote home,

> Now that is the place to go while in Hawaii. We went to the Royal Hawaiian for our swimming and what beautiful surf! I don't think I've ever enjoyed swimming so much. The Royal Hawaiian is one of the most beautiful hotels in existence and is built right out on the beach, with the entrance covered with palms, banana trees, coconut trees, and native flowers.

But my third liberty, in company with Frog, Alex, Clay, Larson, and Harry Lee — the latter an addition to our gang — was the best of all. I purchased some Kodachrome film and documented our attendance at a concert at the beach by the Royal Hawaiian orchestra, our lounging in the spacious gardens of the pink hotel, and the splendid view of Diamond Head. Only at Waikiki did I see the Hawaii pictured in travel literature, and I fondly hoped to visit again.[4]

No doubt thinking about my welfare as we moved closer to another shooting war, I spent my last morning in Pearl Harbor at divine services in the new chapel at Destroyer Escort Docks and listened to Chaplain Fred E. Robb preach on "Follow Thou Me," accompanied by a trumpet solo by another yeoman, John R. Killman, of *YT-633.*

15

Bloody Okinawa

June–August 1945

The good times could not last, and on June 11 *Speed* steamed out of Pearl Harbor, escorting MS *Pennant* toward our next island, Eniwetok (later spelled Enewetak) in the Marshall Islands. Three days and a thousand miles farther, I wrote home, "Today is Sunday; yesterday was Friday. Today is the day after yesterday, but somewhere along the line we lost Saturday. It's strange to go to sleep on Friday night and wake up Sunday morning." The anomaly was explained in the ship's log: "2200, Crossed international date line. Change[d] day and date from Friday 15 June 1945 to Saturday 16 June 1945." For a crossing ceremony, performed on the bow, several men had their heads shaved by Charlie Bolton, the congenial electrician's mate who doubled as ship's barber. Recognizing a unique opportunity, Ensign Bernard Cole, ship's service officer from Massachusetts, broke out his motion picture camera and persuaded five shave-heads to allow him to paint letters on their respective bald pates, then posed them together to spell "S P E E D." Then he posed the shiny head of Gregory, our black cook from Gaffney, South Carolina, while Seaman Joe Viera of Boston bounced the end of a broomstick off the bald-headed "8-ball." Even our most straight-laced officers enjoyed the shenanigans. Greg good-naturedly took a lot of kidding about being "blackballed," then cheerily prepared a tasty evening meal.

I added in the circular letter, "The crew — officers included — looks like a baseball team now. We were issued caps like the one that Admiral Mischer [Mitscher] always wears and it's now difficult to tell whether we're marines, soldiers, sailors, or baseball players. Nowadays, we wear as few clothes as possible and even that is too much." After tight discipline enforced on the continent, we enjoyed the loosening of both regulations and clothing in the tropics.

Except for an engine breakdown by *Pennant* that left her dead in the water for a short while, the nine-day cruise was uneventful; of course, the usual musters and drills kept us sharp. Our radar and sonar gear — on which I voluntarily took turns even though my new rate of yeoman was already official — were the objects of concentration because submarines roamed the seas, though we doubted if our "Two-Twenties" would be their prime target.[1] And we never knew where a carrier-based aircraft, decorated with the Jap pilot's score-card, might be prowling. Mainly, though, when not in the yeoman's shack I hung out on the bridge watching the seemingly infinite blue surface of the broad Pacific, amused by porpoises that playfully led us westward. The sea acted up a few days, and some of the crew carelessly became sunburned. Our ears to the world were the armed forces radio stations beaming from Eniwetok, Kwajalein, Guadalcanal, and Saipan. We had few movie reels on the ship, so boredom was a chief enemy. Some of my waking hours were devoted to teaching Alex Watson to play chess. He learned too quickly for comfort, and I had to muster every trick to defeat Lieutenant (jg) Jack Euphrat, the engineering officer. I wrote, "I'm hesitating to play him again, because he's the toughest player I've run up on so far." Still, Texan Joe Johnson would have been proud of my continued prowess in the only sport that I ever mastered.

Reaching the Marshall Islands on June 20, I wrote, "At first sight, you'd wonder why any nation would sacrifice the lives of hundreds of men for these little dots of islands and coral reef known as Eniwetok." The atoll, roughly elliptical, consisted of about forty small, low-lying islets surrounding a lagoon about fifty miles in circumference — the rims of an ancient volcano. The total land mass was less than five square miles, but on the larger island — Eniwetok proper — an airfield, built after the island's capture by Americans the previous year, played an important role in the war against the Japanese. The islets and underwater rims acted as a buffer against rough waters and, except during typhoons, provided an exceptionally protected roadstead for the fleet.[2]

Mail had preceded us to Eniwetok, and when I read a letter from Myrtle Carter giving me the name of the ship on which her brother Lewis was serving, I was surprised to see that very ship anchored about 300 yards from *Speed*. I sent a message by blinker and hoped to get over to see Lewis the next day, but that plan was ended when we were ordered out to rendezvous with ComCortDiv-11 for a "Hunter Killer Mission" against a submarine that had sunk an LST and a Liberty ship. For two days we conducted the search with USS *Parks* (DE-165)

Lookout duty was a serious responsibility because of threats — kamikazes in the air and mines in the sea. Mines cut by the sweeping gear often bobbed to the surface and had to be exploded by gunshot. Here off Okinawa I am spottig mines and directing sharpshooters.

Minesweepers also conducted antisubmarine warfare; shown are a K-gun and rack of depth charges on *Speed*'s fantail. The mystery of a solid contact between Eniwetok and Guam was never solved, and we could not prove a kill.

before being joined by *Levy* (DE-162) and *Wintle* (DE-25). Judging the hunt unsuccessful, *Speed* was detached on the 24th and ordered to proceed independently to Guam in the Mariana Islands.

We were sailing solo on June 25 when, according to the log, "1121, Made sound contact on bearing 140°T, distance 2200 yards ... prepared for hedgehog attack, c/s 10 knots (197 RPM). 1125, Sounded general quarters, set condition 'AFIRM.' 1159, Fired and expended 24 hedgehogs, no results. Steering various courses and speeds investigating contact." Dissatisfied, the captain ordered a second run on the contact. This time we dropped one depth charge set for 200 feet; it exploded, but there was neither oil slick nor sign of wreckage. So at 1246 three magnetic controlled charges were dropped. Two of them exploded at 660 feet, but there still was no confirmation of wreckage, so the attack on the mysterious contact was abandoned and we resumed our zig-zag course. The mystery was never solved, but it furnished *Speed*'s first hair-raising experience in the Pacific and left us with the question, "Do you suppose...?"

We reached Guam on the 27th. This rugged volcanic island, southernmost of the Marianas, is roughly thirty miles long and from four to nine miles wide. Not far to the southwest in the Mariana Trench is located the deepest point in the earth — Challenger Deep, nearly 36,000 feet below sea level. Guam was liberated from the Japanese in July 1944 at the cost of more than a thousand American lives and was now a fortress controlled by the Navy. Rather remarkably, a Jap major and forty-one of his soldiers had held out in the jungle until a few weeks before our arrival, and a few others were believed to be still hiding in volcanic caves; furthermore, nearby Rota Island was still enemy-occupied simply because it was of no strategic value to the Allies.[3] Most of the native Chamorros had been relocated, so Guam was almost entirely occupied by Americans in uniform. In commodious Apra Harbor on the west coast of the island we joined five other minesweepers — *Sway* (AM-

120), *Swift* (AM-122), *Symbol* (AM-123), *Threat* (AM-124), and *Spear* (AM-322)—for three days of inactivity. We had traveled more than three thousand miles since leaving Hawaii.

Willard Green and I, who had been lazy during the rolling seas the past week or so, devoted our working hours to catching up on our typing and updating service records. I had the pleasure of adding this entry in mine, over the skipper's signature: "Eligible ... for the American Area and Asiatic-Pacific Campaign Medals. Hereby authorized to wear campaign ribbons for above areas." With little work, the crew was given several liberties, and my first stop was the Gab-Gab Club, run by the Red Cross, which provided a few refreshments, games, and reading materials. Two sheds on the coral reef encircling the harbor were more popular because of the availability of beer and Coca-Cola. Since I never liked the taste of beer, and the Cokes were about as hot as the tropical climate, I found the place of little interest. Jolicoeur, Watson, Leary, and I, on the other hand, were attracted to a jungle that extended beyond the harbor, but our safari started out badly and got worse. Not having seen off-limit signs, we examined an abandoned Jap pillbox before a sour-faced shore patrol raced up to us, lectured us on the danger of unexploded ammunition, and sent us in another direction. Our next mistake was to enter a thick jungle where we were met by a noisy, angry swarm of bees, whose dives reminded me of Stukas at Anzio. All of us sustained multiple stings, but mine were the most numerous and painful. Frog snapped a picture as I frantically sought escape down a rocky outcrop, and he jotted on the back of the photo, "Dans les jungles après s'être fait piques par les guêpes." I wrote home, with only a little exaggeration, "When I got to the ship, I had a hard time, with 3 witnesses, to convince the fellows that we hadn't been in a brawl. My [right] eye was closed, the left hand out of order, and my back looked like a mattress with inner springs."

Here I am with *Speed* shipmates Watson, center, and Leary, right, in the jungles of Guam. A few minutes later we were attacked by a swarm of bees, the stings from which closed one of my eyes.

On June 30, our captain was made escort commander of Task Unit 94.7.1, consisting of *Speed, Sway, Wateree* (ATF-117), and *Stallion* (ATA-193). Our destination: the dreaded kamikaze aerial circus of Okinawa, an assignment made more disagreeable because both tugs were towing other vessels, necessitating a painfully slow five-and-a-half-knot speed. On the second day out, without observing its source, our lookout sighted an object falling from the sky. *Speed* leapt at full throttle to investigate, fired upon the strange object, and cautiously approached what appeared to be a balloon with a tinfoil kite attached. Relieved, we assumed it was a runaway weather probe. We stopped at Garopan Anchorage on the northern Mariana island of Saipan long enough to add to our entourage USS *Wandank* (ATA-204) and its tows. Later that day off Anatukau Island we observed smoke bombs and were relieved when USS *Becuna* (SS-319) surfaced to assure us that she was both friendly and the source of the smoke bombs. The only other momentary scares during the voyage were a false sonar contact and a floating 500-pound chemical-horn mine; the latter we exploded by gunfire. The presence of the prickly explosive hundreds of miles out in the open ocean provided another reminder of the threat of fugitive mines to friend and foe. At the same time, we gave little thought to the possibility that the explosion of these mines could alert a Jap submarine of our presence with four other vessels. In addition, our crew got a little careless, with official approval, by celebrating Independence Day with a display of pyrotechnics. For his own reasons, the skipper ordered the shaving of beards that had sprouted after we left Pearl Harbor. Many cameras clicked.

The twelve days from Guam to Okinawa went excruciatingly slowly because the tugs, for which we and *Sway* provided antisubmarine protection, were severely tested by the weight of their tows in the rolling seas. As usual, musters, general quarters, and drills of imaginative types were regularly held, but there was much time for speculation about what lay before us. The battle for Okinawa had begun in March, and the island had finally fallen while we were at Guam. Thus our arrival at Buckner Bay on July 12 followed only by a few days the end of the last major Japanese resistance, and some enemy troops were known to still be holed up on the mountainous island.[4]

History will record Okinawa as one of the most horrifying battles in history, with an estimated 12,500 Allied and 66,000 Japanese soldiers killed or missing and 40,000 Allied and 17,000 Japanese wounded. These figures were dwarfed by the estimated 140,000 native Okinawans killed or missing, tens of thousands at their own or the hands of the Japanese, who encouraged mass suicide. The Navy lost about 75 ships sunk or scrapped, and more than 760 Allied planes were shot down, about one-tenth the number lost by the Japanese. Of those killed or missing, nearly 5,000 were seamen, many of them victims of more than 3,000 kamikaze attacks on our ships.[5]

Of course, the full horror of the battle for Okinawa was unknown to our crew — we knew only what we heard over the radio or saw from our deck. However, we realized that we were entering an entirely new kind of war — one in which the enemy held a different view of death and was prepared to accept it as a religious ritual in defense of the Motherland. Even though the worst of the kamikaze season was over by the time we arrived, our short exposure bore out Admiral Morison's description of those attacks: "For days and even nights on end, the crew had to stand general quarters while the ship was kept 'buttoned up.' Men had to keep in readiness for the instant reaction and split-second timing necessary to riddle a plane bent on sacrificial death. Sleep became the rarest commodity and choicest luxury, like water to a shipwrecked mariner."[6]

Long before the rugged hills of Okinawa came into view, we saw a tower of black smoke rising several thousand feet into the sky, and when the outline of the hills finally appeared,

"Welcome to Okinawa." This was the scene when in July *Speed* arrived in Nakagusuku Wan (renamed Buckner Bay). Hundreds of ships that gathered in this bay, in preparation for the invasion of Japan, dodged enemy aircraft and repeatedly put to sea to ride out horrific typhoons.

we could discern that there had been a huge fire or explosion in or near the bay. Even after directing our wards to their respective anchorages, we did not learn the source of the billowing smoke captured by the lens of my camera. It was, we assumed, just a regular occurrence in the huge bay filled with literally hundreds of vessels from battleships to small boats.

Except for "Flash Reds" (enemy airplanes approaching) and several changes of anchorages, our first four days at Okinawa passed fairly uneventfully, but on July 17, a new word entered my vocabulary: *typhoon*—a tropical cyclone somewhat analogous to an Atlantic hurricane. When winds became dangerous, we were ordered to get underway to execute Typhoon Plan X-Ray. Nearly every ship in Buckner Bay hurriedly battened down the hatches, hoisted anchor, and steamed seaward, lest she be capsized or blown onto the beach. *Speed* joined a column led by *Gladiator* (AM-319) and including *Toucan* (AM-387), *Surfbird* (AM-383), *Sustain* (AM-119), *Sway* (AM-120), and *Competent* (AM-316). It was a scene of utter feverishness as forty-two minesweepers and a dozen destroyers and destroyer escorts sought to keep in visual and radio communication. As we fled the anchorage, already the waves were breaking over the bow, but as we steamed seaward, the white-crested billows grew angrier and the helmsman had difficulty in holding the correct heading directly into the crest. Under no circumstance did we want the ship to get caught broadside against sixty-foot waves, a prescription for capsizing once the water penetrated the stacks and hatches. Consequently, we bucked the breakers, battled seasickness, and ate and slept little for three days before Typhoon Opal's eye passed and we were able to return to Yonabaru and begin restoring to their place equipment and supplies thrown helter-skelter during the rough ride. Sandwiches and coffee were about all we had to for sustenance during the roller coaster experience.

Safely back at Okinawa, *Speed* was reassigned to Lieutenant Commander E. B. Knowlton's Mine Division Seventeen, with *Strive* as flagship, with which she had operated in Africa and Italy. For veterans of the Mediterranean, however, four AM sisters were missing—*Portent*, sunk by a mine at Anzio; *Sentinel*, destroyed by bombs in the invasion of Sicily; *Skill*, torpedoed off Salerno; and *Swerve*, mined off Anzio-Nettuno.

I had been on *Speed* for seven months, but except for brief practice sweeps at Norfolk and off the coasts of California and Lanai, I was without experience as a minesweeping sailor. I was not a complete stranger to minesweepers, however. In the Mediterranean, I had become more familiar with YMSs than AMs because, like SCs, the yard minesweepers were made of wood, were only twenty-six feet longer than our SC, and often patrolled with us at sea and tied up to us in port. Besides, their small complement lived in cramped quarters without desalination equipment and thus shared the discomforts of subchaser sailors. Our hearts were with the crews of *YMS-30*[7] that went down at Anzio and *-24* and *-21* that were lost during the invasion of Southern France.[8] Having endured so many mutual discomforts and so many close shaves ourselves, we felt a comradery with the minesweeping sailors that proudly boasted "Where the fleet goes, we've already been"—or, as we joked, "Any ship can be a minesweeper—once."

Consequently, I did not share the air of superiority expressed by some of my *Speed* family who dismissed the smaller vessels as cannon fodder for shore batteries and who assumed that an exploding mine would do less damage to our metal Two-Twenties than to the little "wooden dreadnaughts." Only after the war were we able to count the heavy price paid by our plank-sided partners. In the broad expanse of the war in the Pacific and in the China Sea, they carried out their special minewarfare operations separately from the AMs, and we saw them usually only at a distance. However, our three Mediterranean losses and three off Normandy were surpassed by the toll in the Pacific—seven by mines and three by shore batteries. Add to that a dozen YMSs victimized by typhoons and storms in the Pacific and five British-crewed BYMSs lost in Europe, and the toll rose substantially among the 136-foot vessels.[9]

The steel-hulled AMs were *large* ships in the eyes of YMS and SC sailors. The Two-Twenties, like *Speed*, carried a complement four times that of a subchaser, and its armament put to shame my previous ship's peashooters. AMs also chased submarines—but with more sophisticated equipment. I felt quite at home in my sonar and yeoman specialties, but I had little notion of the use of all of the mysterious gear stashed, seemingly haphazardly, on deck behind the stacks. To me, our stern looked something like a junkyard. Nor did I know much about mines except for their lethal power. Through osmosis rather than formal study, however, I gradually learned a bit about mine warfare. Underwater mines, no matter what they were called, had been used against seagoing vessels since antiquity, but the sinking of the Russian battleship *Petropavlovsk* by a mine during the Russo-Japanese war changed sea warfare forever. During World War I, Allied mining of the edges of the North Sea helped turn the tide against German submarines.

Technology for both planting and destroying mines was improved between the wars; even so, the United States was ill-prepared for the massive manufacturing and sowing of enemy mines at the outbreak of World War II.[10] Faced with submarine-laid minefields blocking our Atlantic harbors, naval authorities quickly converted coastal vessels to mine defense, and specially designed sweepers were rushed into production. By the time I came aboard *Speed*, there were several classes of minesweepers in addition to steel-hulled AMs and wood-hulled

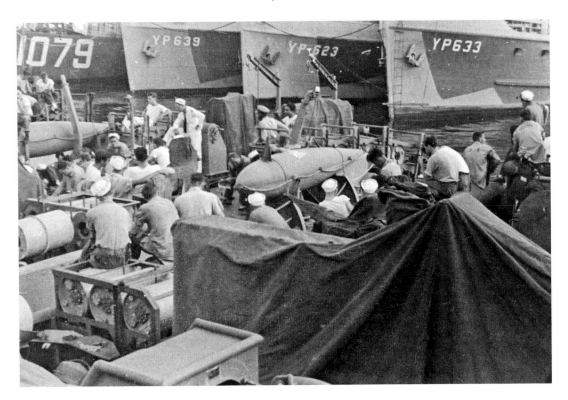

To a sonarman with no previous minesweeping experience, the stern of *Speed* looked like a seagoing junkyard. Fortunately, sonarmen and yeomen were not required to learn the function of every single piece of equipment.

YMSs, and some patrol and landing vessels such as PCs, SCs, LCMs, and LCVPs were jerryrigged and pressed into service for clearing mines nearer to shores before invasions.

Mines — typically containing from 250 to 1,600 pounds of trinitrotoluene — were either *controlled* or *independent* and could be anchored at specific depths or planted on the sea floor. The former, located close to land, could be remotely controlled by shore stations. Independent mines, our usual quarry, were fired by *contact* with a ship's hull or by the ship's *influence*— magnetic, acoustic, or pressure. As their classification indicates, *magnetic* mines were set off when a metal object such as a ship's hull tripped an electrical current; *acoustic* mines "listened" with microphones and fired when the noise level tripped an electrical circuit; and *pressure* mines were set off by movement of water, such as a ship's wake. To defend against magnetic mines, ships sought to minimize their attraction by means of energized electromagnets. Many were wrapped in a degaussing belt (a sort of chastity belt) that reversed the magnetic field and periodically were "degaussed" by passing through an energized field produced by underwater cables. Toward the end of the war, specially designed vessels — called Mobile Degaussing Unit (YDG)— were developed to make possible the "degoosing" of ships unable to reach the stationary degaussing fields.[11]

Mines were laid by air, submarine, or surface vessels, and regardless of the means that set them off, they did not discriminate between friend and foe.[12] Once laid, and until destroyed by man or neutralized by nature (age, silt, malfunctions), mines threatened any object that came within its means of activation. It was the objective of Allied minesweepers to outwit and destroy underwater weapons that threatened our war objectives.[13] Each type of mine required a different offense. The easiest to destroy was the moored mine, but even that was no simple task. A minesweeper towed long steel cables, directed to appropriate angles and depth by means of otters and paravanes, to which were attached a series of cutting blades that either exploded the mine on contact or cut its tether and allowed the horned weapon to rise to the surface, where it was exploded by gunfire. This type of sweeping used Oropesa gear (named after the British ship that perfected the gear); the procedure was spoken of as "making an O-sweep." The oropesa (or pig-float) was a streamlined steel float shaped like a fish, designed to keep the towed sweep at a predetermined depth, distance, and position from the minesweeper. This was the most commonly used sweeping procedure in Far Eastern waters. Great danger accompanied a mine caught in the cutters and not observed until the retracted gear approached the stern of the ship. In such cases the gear was usually restreamed, after which the vessel made erratic course changes in an effort to shake the culprit loose.

Electronically charged cables, sheathed in rubber and unwound from huge reels on the minesweeper, were towed behind the sweeper to set off magnetic mines; and loud noisemakers like a hammer box and parallel pipes sought to create enough water noise and disturbance to fire acoustic and pressure mines at a safe distance. Swept mines that rose to the surface were sunk or exploded by gunfire from a distance of at least two hundred feet, preferably more.

The first sweeper to enter a minefield was without protection. However, when an operation engaged several (or many) ships, various formations were devised to limit the danger to each following ship. A "protective echelon" allowed the second ship to sail in the wake of the lead ship's port (or starboard) paravane, with succeeding vessels fanning out similarly. In large

Tightening my life vest on the bridge of *Speed* during one of scores of general quarters off Okinawa. When on neither sonar gear nor typewriter, I often relieved buddies on bridge duty.

fields, both port and starboard echelons (called "wedge" formation) could be utilized, widening the swept field to several miles. The entire fleet could then — intricately, because of the danger of fouling gear — turn and double the width of the sweep. From the air, a wedge formation would appear as a huge inverted "V." Open echelon, in which each ship sailed in unswept waters, was of course the most dangerous; it was used only when no mines were suspected in the area.[14]

Not all of that did I know when we arrived at Okinawa, but I learned it fast, for on July 22, MinDiv-17 received orders to join Task Group 39.11 in a major minesweeping exercise in the East China Sea. Known as Operation Juneau under command of Rear Admiral Alexander Sharp and Captain Wayne R. Loud, the entire Task Force 39 involved more than a hundred minecraft — 7 DMs, 52 AMs, 6 DMSs, 49 YMSs, and 7 netlayers. Formidable protection was provided by Rear Admiral Jesse B. Oldendorf's Task Force 32 containing 3 battleships, 2 heavy cruisers, 1 light cruiser, 11 destroyers, and 4 destroyer escorts; the battleships in return were protected by Marines flying air cover. In fact, we were awed by this overwhelming sea power around the perimeters of the 9,000-square-mile rectangle of waters near Kobe Sho and Sekiki Sho northeast of Formosa (today, Taiwan). For our part in this operation, *Strive* (AM-117) became formation guide for the same ships that had together ridden out the typhoon, plus USS *Southard* (DMS-10).[15] The sweepers formed a row twelve miles long and moved across the sea in echelon formation, cutting a swath six miles wide.[16] For ten days *Speed's* log recorded entries such as this (July 24): "0625, Commenced streaming double 'O' type sweep gear using 345 fathoms scope of sweep wire, 45 fathoms of depressor wire, 110 ft. float pendants, two Mark II type 'T' cutters and two Mark XI cutters on each leg. 0645, Completed streaming sweep gear and commenced sweeping." Within three hours, *Speed* struck our first blow against the Japanese when our starboard leg cut a mine. The next morning, we cut another with the port leg. We were on a roll![17] Sweeping was usually limited to daylight hours when floaters could be spotted by eye; furthermore, the ships were strictly blacked out at night. We did, of course, maintain visual, radar, and sonar surveillance day and night. In the midst of this ten-day operation, surprised to see a "PC" approaching the fleet, we were elated to discover that the former *PC-1555* had been converted to a patrol gunboat, *PGM-24*, and that she was loaded with mail for our crews. An angel from heaven in the East China Sea.

Before returning to Okinawa on July 31, the ships of Operation Juneau cleared about 9,000 square miles of the vast East China Sea, and the result was impressive: In all, TF-39 had destroyed 404 mines.[18] We felt a little apologetic because *Speed* had accounted for only two of those, but there would be plenty of other opportunities to flex our minesweeping muscle. Three days before we returned to Buckner Bay, a kamikaze had sneaked in and sunk the *Callaghan* (DD-792), which was providing picket duty nearby. The destroyer was the last American ship sunk by a kamikaze, but *Lagrange*, an attack transport, was badly damaged by another the following month.

To our surprise and pleasure, *Speed* remained in Buckner Bay for the next eleven days, interrupted only by rushes to general quarters in response to "Flash Reds," frequent drills, routine movements of the ship for supplies and fuel, regular watches and other duties, and a visit from my old Key West Sound School buddy, W.B. Charles, who was also on an AM in the bay. The routine was broken when scuttlebutt spread around the fleet about a broad, sandy beach on Tsugen Shima, a formerly fortified island located at the northeastern edge of the bay. Inquisitive crew members learned that once the island had been scoured for mines, an LCT had been designated as "liberty bus" for the bay and would, with permission of respective captains, ferry sailors between ships and the island. I was among the first from *Speed*

Above and opposite: When crews discovered a good beach on the island of Tsugen Shima near Okinawa, *LST-1160* was pressed into service as a "liberty bus." Shipmates McGlynn and Geiger exhibited the most popular attire for the occasion; and after dressing more respectably, the sailors listened as the band of battleship *Nevada* performed on a makeshift stage. Several months earlier, *Nevada* had been hit by both a kamikaze and a shore battery that killed crew members and injured others, including some of the musicians.

to go down the gangplank and crowd into *LCT-1160*, which landed us on Tomai Hama (meaning beautiful beach), where modesty was thrown to the wind. It was a strange sight: Scores of naked or semi-nude men cavorting as teenagers and posing for my Kodak, which produced what in 1945 would have been classified as X-rated photographs. Some fellows were innovative; Radarman Vernon Paul Geiger of Pleasantville, New Jersey, posed in a jockstrap, but Radarman McGlynn of Watervliet, New York, simply used his sailor's dixie-cup to conceal his jewels. The more modest, like Ship's Cook Mavereaux and me, slipped on swim trunks. Of my favorite photographs, I regret most that I did not write down the names of twenty shipmates who posed (in our work clothes) with me on Tsugen Shima. Nearly two-thirds of a century later, I recognize the faces but remember only a few names. The years do indeed make us other men.

Several excursions to Tsugen Shima allowed us to swim, stretch our legs, and, on at least one occasion, enjoy warm beers and colas — rare luxuries in battle areas. The beach became so popular that the band of the battleship *Nevada* constructed a tarpaulin-roofed platform and on several occasions gave a rousing concert. It was an unlikely scene: hundreds of warships of all sizes anchored in the background, alert to air attacks, and here, lounging on a sandy beach, was a gaggle of sailors raptly listening to a military band concert. Not only that, but members of the band were survivors of a kamikaze crash into and a shelling of *Nevada* on the opposite side of Okinawa just a few months earlier.[19] We found an equally strange contrast a few hundred feet away — a Japanese cemetery filled with architecturally interesting above-ground concrete mausoleums in which human bones lay grotesquely. Gruesomely, these mausoleums had been used as caves by defending Japanese troops in the savage defense of the island against American forces. I am not proud of the photographs taken at what to the enemy, before the war, was a sacred place. Nearby stood a field of fourteen white wooden crosses marking graves of American Marines killed during the battle for the island; that sight reminded us that all men are human and that humans make war.

On one of those lazy days, several of our men narrowly averted disaster in an accident involving our boat crew. Let the ship's log of August 8 tell the story:

> 1248, Motor whaleboat returned to the ship in tow. Ensign Cole reported that while lying to 1000 yards on starboard beam of USS KA-13, engine off, coxswain, bow hook, engineer and assistant engineer in boat, whaleboat of this ship was struck slightly aft of midships section on starboard side by LCVP-9 of USS PA-76 [USS *Crenshaw* (APA-76)]. The LCVP rode over the whaleboat until it rested on port gunwale, then backed off. Boat crew of LCVP took our whaleboat in tow, brought it to AF-13, afloat but awash. No men injured. Damage: Engine inoperative, bulwark smashed to thwart.[20]

Nearly two dozen members of *Speed*'s crew posed near a Japanese bunker during one of the liberty parties at Tsugen Shima. I am standing bare-chested third from the right.

Not a word was entered in *Speed*'s log when on August 6 an atomic bomb was dropped from *Enola Gay* on Hiroshima by bombardier Thomas W. Ferebee of Mocksville, North Carolina.[21] Nor was there reference to the second bomb dropped three days later on Nagasaki, located only a few hundred miles from where we were anchored. We heard, of course, radio reports of the bombings and rumors that negotiations were underway toward a Japanese surrender. The word "nuclear" meant nothing to most of us, and the continued attacks from Japanese airplanes put us in a nasty mood toward concessions to the enemy. Nor was there an entry describing another extraordinary experience at Okinawa, but I recorded the exhilaration in a letter home:

> We got the news of Japan's offer [to surrender] at 9:02 P.M., the 10th. About a hundred of us were looking at a movie [*Frisco Sal*, starring Susanna Foster, Turhan Bey, Adam Curtis, and Andy Devine] in the mess hall when [Robert] Kelly, a SoM from Maine, announced over the public address system Japan's offer. To us, that meant the end of the war and a deafening roar went up from the fellows. Then outside the sky began to glow from gunfire, star shells, and pyrotechnics of all colors. The vast area covered with the fleet was completely lit up; the Navy really celebrated. The ships, from subchasers to battleships, made all the noise they could. Then the soldiers and marines on the beach joined in. It must have lasted an hour before the senior officer present got them (us) to quiet down.[22]

What we thought was a joyful celebration — shooting every gun toward the stars — was in fact a terrible mistake for which scores of impulsive gunners probably never forgave themselves. And I can never forget the radio plea of the "senior officer" referred to in my letter. I cannot be sure of his exact, anguished words, but in a shrill, pleading voice, it was something like "Cease fire! Cease fire! You're killing your own men!" We learned later that falling shrapnel from our wild, celebratory firing had killed American personnel on the beach.

Despite remorse for the accidental killing of our own men, most of us were euphoric over the prospect of peace. I wrote home, "By the time you receive this, I have every hope that the surrender will be signed. It is a very tense day — we're all just hoping." I added,

Yesterday and today have been filled with suspense — every one on board hoped that the Allies would accept — these fellows want to go home. It made our blood boil when the radio said 62 percent of the civilians in the States wanted to continue fighting. Every man who said "keep fighting" should be sent out here and made to do the fighting. There are going to be a lot of changes made when these far Pacific men get back.

I concluded, "If the war is over, get this straight: Don't expect us back anytime soon. We still have a big job, war or no war, and it will take time. It won't be near so hard on us (no more air raids, landings, etc.) if it's over, but we'll be here for quite a while."

On August 12 the glue was hardly dry on the envelope as I dropped it into the mail bag when, at 2102, another Flash Red sent every man in Buckner Bay to his battle station. The sky again lit up as hundreds of antiaircraft guns fired on targets flying right into the bay. A single plane penetrated the screen and launched a torpedo that missed *Speed* by several hundred yards but slammed into the battleship *Pennsylvania* (BB-38). The blinding flash, followed by an ear-splitting explosion, was soon accompanied by waves that rocked every ship in the enormous bay. Tugs rushed to the scene but, anchored, *Speed* could not move. The torpedo hit *Pennsylvania* aft, flooding many compartments and killing twenty men. Dawn revealed a sickening sight: The mighty warship had settled heavily at the stern, where tugs joined onboard pumps in keeping the massive and venerable vessel afloat.[23] The attack on *Pennsylvania* proved to us that the war was not over, further confirmation of which came the next day when a kamikaze crashed into attack transport *Lagrange* (APA-124), killing twenty-one and wounding eighty-nine. Another clipped the kingpost and splashed twenty feet away. *Lagrange* earned the distinction for being the target of the last kamikaze attack of the war.[24]

There was little sleep following the torpedoing of *Pennsylvania*, for at 0545, *Speed* weighed anchor and sailed out of Buckner Bay with Task Group 95.4 for Operation Skagway, a seventy-six-ship flotilla of minesweepers and protective vessels under command of Captain Henry J. Armstrong, Jr. Our column, led by *Prevail* (AM-107), included in order *Strive* (AM-117), *Speed* (AM-116), *Sustain* (AM-119), *Token* (AM-126), and *Tumult* (AM-127). Among the dozens of vessels in the operation, *Swift* (AM-122), *Spear* (AM-322), and *Success* (AM-322) later worked with us.

For eleven days, our tasks were repetitive. Each morning, dozens of ships would position themselves to form, collectively, an inverted fan, following the lead ship and covering a miles-wide triangle of the East China Sea between Tokarra Retto and Nagasaki. Daily, each ship streamed intricate gear, recorded mines exploded by the gear or by gunshot on the surface, retrieved the gear, and, after a productive day against mines, prepared for a quiet evening of coasting in the waters swept during the day, leery only of a Jap torpedo or a fugitive floating mine. Perhaps a typical log entry was made for *Speed* on August 18; it read:

0527, Formed m/s formation starboard echelon ... 0631, Streamed 'O' type m/s gear using 300 fathom scope sweep wire, 48 fathom depressor wire, 120 foot float pendant, 3 Mk II type 'T' cutters and 2 Mk XI mechanical cutters on each leg ... 0732, Cut two moored chemical horned mines with port and starboard gear in position 127°03'E longitude, 29°42'N latitude in about 65 fathoms of water.

The same afternoon, we destroyed three additional mines, and the following day, five more. Of the latter, one was found lodged in the port gear as it was being retrieved — a particularly dangerous predicament if not observed at a safe distance from the ship. Fortunately, the contact mine was spotted early enough, so the gear was streamed again and the mine was finally exploded.

When we returned to Okinawa on August 25, TG-95.4 had destroyed in Operation Skagway 896 of 3,700 known mines planted in 3,600 square miles of water.[25] *Speed* accounted for eleven. More memorable to me was the fact that the announcement of Japan's surrender actually was heard while we conducted Operation Skagway. Again, a momentous historic event passed unmentioned in the ship's log, but I recorded that at 0804 on August 15 we heard by radio the official announcement from President Truman that the Japanese had acceded to the Potsdam demands.[26] However, remembering the false report five nights before, my attitude — and that of many others — was, "Yeah, I've heard that before." We simply did not trust the Japanese, so we continued with our sweeping as if nothing had happened. At the moment of the president's announcement, we were a little more than a hundred miles from Nagasaki, and, unknown to us at the time, we were sweeping the channel for Allied invasion forces that were scheduled to land between Nagasaki and Kagoshima on November 1.[27]

Events happened fast following our return to Okinawa. *Mona Island* (ARG-9) became our mother ship, and on her I attended Sunday religious services conducted by Chaplain John Cummings, whose topic was "Working Together with God." We took on water from the battleship *California*; and the crew again found time to enjoy the beach at Tsugen Shima. On the 26th, Lieutenant John F. Maddox, Jr., succeeded Lieutenant Commander Raymond C. Dryer as captain of *Speed*, and two days later the first real consequence of the war's end on our crew was demonstrated when I typed transfer papers for F.W. Bostwick, E.E. Dillon, G.M. Gatlin, L.R. Goodman, A.B. Guidry, E.L. Herren, R.G. Lachance, and R.S. Ulmer. Their destination: "to Demobilization Center, Nearest Point of Entry of United States for discharge." I snapped pictures as the veterans — sad to leave their shipmates but gleeful about returning home — loaded into the ship's whaleboat. My days aboard *Speed* also were numbered, but more than six months would pass before I too would join "Operation Magic Carpet" and head back to the "Good Ole U. S. of A." In fact, I was about to take a surprising detour.

16

Finishing Off the Japanese

September–October 1945

On paper, the war was over in August 1945, and nearly every serviceman wanted to go home. The simple solution suggested that we sail our ship back to the West Coast, decommission her, accept individual discharges, and go home. Finis. Back in civvies. "Ain't gonna study war no more." On second thought, we realized the simple-mindedness of such a solution. The Japanese had surrendered their ships, not their mines — nor had we surrendered ours. Thousands of square miles of waters in the Far East were pregnant with mines planted by both the Japanese and the Allies, and those weapons would not discriminate between nationalities. For years to come, each one of them would endanger any ship sailing near it. All would need to be destroyed or neutralized. Our minesweepers faced many months of dangerous work before returning to the States. Most urgent was the clearing of channels through which Allied ships could deliver occupation troops and bring out thousands of American prisoners-of-war held in Japan and on the Asiatic mainland.

New recruits were on their way to the Pacific fleet, so the Navy designed a point system under which naval reserve enlistees could qualify for honorable discharge based on length of overseas service. By late August I had already typed transfer orders for six of my *Speed* shipmates, and others were scheduled to leave when replacements arrived. During the coming months, men with fewer than forty-one points chafed and cussed as they watched their long-serving shipmates heading home. We yeomen chafed and cussed because we were declared "essential" for handling the paperwork associated with the mass transfers; three additional points were required for us to qualify for release. Adding to our victimization, some shipmates, who had considered ours a privileged rating, seemed to get pleasure from our outrage.

I had earned only thirty-six points; my "time" was months off, so I joined the grumbling until good fortune intervened. My first discussion with Commander Dryer concerning this unexpected benefaction consisted of a sort of "What if?" scenario. Ed Murphy, flag yeoman serving Commander Elliott B. Knowlton, commander of both USS *Strive* (AM-117) and Mine Division Seventeen, had earned sufficient points to qualify for discharge, and he was anxious to return to civilian life. In other words, the position was opening for an experienced yeoman already serving on one of the ships in the division. Would I be interested? I was well satisfied on the *Speed* and was particularly happy with my captain, my ideal of a naval officer — firm and stern but fair and understanding. But when Commander Dryer revealed to me that *he* would be leaving the *Speed* soon, my interest in a possible transfer leaped.[1] Whether I stayed

While aboard *Speed* I apprenticed under Y1c Willard A. Green, right, and had my rating changed from sonarman to yeoman. On September 1, I was promoted to flag yeoman for the commander of Mine Division Seventeen and transferred to USS *Strive*.

or moved, I would need to adjust to a new captain. And, as the junior among the *Speed*'s two yeomen, I sort of liked the idea of becoming my own boss. I really didn't know what a flag yeoman was, but the title certainly sounded important.

Apparently my skipper's recommendation was sufficient to convince Commander Knowlton to order my transfer. Consequently, as September approached, I tried to complete all backlogged work, for I did not want to leave any unfinished tasks to Willard Green, who had been a congenial supervisor. I was ready on September 1, and I expected to be transferred by the ship's whaleboat. It was a shock, therefore, when the *Strive* drew within about a hundred feet of the *Speed* and the bosun hove across a hawser to which a breeches buoy was attached. Plopped down in the dangling canvas seat, I was unceremoniously whizzed above the raging waters of Nakagusuku Wan and plunked down on the deck of the *Strive* like a sack of potatoes. I was too petrified to look back and wave goodbye to my snickering (now former) shipmates. Consequently, at 1340 on September 1, 1945, my name appeared in *Strive*'s log as having "reported aboard for temporary duty in accordance with verbal orders of Commander Mine Division Seventeen"—no mention whatsoever of my unorthodox delivery. My service record accompanied me, but the log noted that my health and pay accounts would remain on the *Speed*. In other words, I was on probation, on trial. In a letter home on October 27, I wrote:

> You asked what a flag yeoman is. Well, it's a nickname in the Navy. My boss is the commander of a division of minesweepers. He is given a flag which is flown on the ship and makes the ship a "flagship." And the commander himself is referred to as the "flag." Therefore, the commander's yeoman is the "flag yeoman." My job is to take care of the division's records, reports, and run the office. My only superiors are the commander and a lieutenant, senior grade, who is his assistant.

In another letter, printed in *Jefferson Standard Life*,[2] I added, "My duties consist chiefly of handling administrative matters dealing with problems of personnel and distribution of men in the division."

There was no time to ponder my probationary status, for within a hour and a half of my boarding, *Strive* and MinDiv-17 sailed out of Buckner Bay on a perilous mission—to lead the first American occupation troops into Japan's southernmost island of Kyushu. Our assignment was to clear a channel into Kagoshima Wan so that transports could safely land American troops who would seize the Chiran and Kanoya air bases from where kamikaze pilots had struck many of our ships and killed hundreds of our fellow sailors and soldiers.

Thus, at the moment of glory when General MacArthur and a Japanese official were signing the formal treaty of Japan's surrender in Tokyo Bay on September 2, my new ship was facilitating the peaceful landing of troops of the 32nd Division, who had prepared to invade Kyushu two months later. The invasion plans — made unnecessary by Japan's surrender — were unknown to us at that time, but hundreds of ships and tens of thousands of American troops had been rendezvousing throughout the Pacific in preparation for a massive assault on the Japanese mainland. The overall plan, under code name Operation Downfall, called for the landing of fourteen combat divisions on the island of Kyushu (subnamed Operation Olympic) on November 1, 1945. As those troops fought their way northward, twenty-two more combat divisions would invade the main island of Honshu near Tokyo (subnamed Operation Coronet) on March 1, 1946. An amusing irony of Operation Olympic — in view of the flooding of the United States with Japanese-manufactured automobiles in the postwar era — lay in the designation of the invasion zones as Taxicab, Roadster, Limousine, Station Wagon, and Town Car, and the naming of the individual beaches for American-made automobiles — such as Zephyr, Packard, Chevrolet, and DeSoto. The estimate of potential casualties among American troops — had the invasion been necessary — varied widely, but, alarmingly, the War Department ordered the manufacture of 400,000 additional Purple Hearts. We will never know how many American lives were saved when the invasion became unnecessary after the bombing of Hiroshima and Nagasaki, but none of us in harm's way questioned the decision to use the atomic bombs.[3]

As we gingerly approached Kyushu, the commander of Task Unit 95.3.81 was in USS *Adams* (DM-27), with which *Strive* and the other AMs sailed past numerous islands of Ryukyu Retto (Nansei Islands) and Tokara Retto. In the predawn darkness of September 3, for the first time in the Pacific, *Strive* turned on her running and range lights. Condition III was set, and our crew wore sidearms as we cautiously approached a Japanese vessel in Osumi Kaikyo (Van Diemen Strait). By prearrangement, we took aboard three uniformed Japanese, later identified as M. Myoi, lieutenant commander and pilot; K. Tokahashin, sub-lieutenant first class, interpreter; and M. Tokashima, signalman. It was an apprehensive feeling — we were putting our lives in the hands of three of our erstwhile enemies who, just three weeks before, would have killed us on sight. We felt our vulnerability and wondered if these little brown-skinned men might deliberately pilot our ships into the minefield rather than steer us through a secret channel. Heartbeats accelerated when each AM streamed "O" type gear and began a sound and visual search for mines. All day, almost under the shadow of 3,000-foot conical Mt. Kaimon, the ships swept the approach to Kagoshima Kaiwan, and when our equipment was retrieved in the evening, we found Japanese gear fouled in *Strive*'s port gear — meaning that the Japs had previously made an effort to open a channel for their own vessels to emerge for suicide missions. We only relaxed a bit when at 1744 the three Japanese were returned to their pilot vessel.

Remarkably, confidence had been established on the bridge during the day, and Commander Knowlton and several of our officers accepted an invitation to pay a brief visit to a Japanese vessel, where pictures were taken as evidence of the rapport between former enemies. Still apprehensive, however, the unit commander again ordered darkened ships at night, lest we attract suicidal swimmers bearing limpets. Sweeping continued the following day, but we took time out to lead through the minefield six LSTs loaded with troops of General Walter Krueger's Sixth Army, who landed in 100-degree heat at Takusu about four miles southwest of Kenoya Airfield[4] from where death had so often taken wings in the form of kamikazes. In the mouth of Kagoshima Kaiwan, *Strive* found a mine fouled in our port gear, but we restreamed and eventually shook it loose and exploded it by gunfire.

On September 5, we had a banner day. With gear streamed, *Strive* entered the Kagoshima mined area as guide ship in a starboard echelon formation, completely exposed to unswept waters but providing some protection for the vessel that followed our starboard cutter, which in turn offered a bit of protection of the third ship, etc. Just after noon, we cut one mine, and within an hour, five more. The next day's toll was an astonishing record of twenty-five mines, two of which had to be shaken from the cutters.

From the anchorage off the village of Furue, we saw little of Kagoshima, the major city in a district with that name, nor did we get to the two nearby airbases, Chiran and Kanoya, from where more than a thousand pilots had taken off on suicide missions. The peaceful occupation of the peninsula, therefore, was a sweet victory for the soldiers and sailors who had witnessed kamikaze attacks that took heavy tolls upon the American Navy.[5] The dockyards around Kagoshima, and much of the city, had been heavily bombed by American planes, so our most lasting impression was of Sakurajimi, the stratovolcano towering 3,665 feet just east of the city. The volcano's last violent eruption occurred in 1914 and was powerful enough to turn the island into a peninsula, but it still acted up periodically and smoked almost continually.

Sweeping continued until the September 9; *Strive* alone destroyed thirty-two mines, and our sister ships accounted for 222 more.[6] Just one of those missiles could have sunk a transport loaded with thousands of men. But we had done our duty, and we happily witnessed the arrival of troops to take up positions around the military establishments. We were also glad to join Task Group 32 and head back to Okinawa, where two days later we tied up to USS *Wabash* (AOG-4) and took on 24,526 gallons of fuel oil and 1,300 gallons of lubricating oil.

After nearly a fortnight and my baptism of fire aboard my third ship, I was still a stranger because of my newness and because I was a member of the flag staff rather than the *Strive*'s regular crew. However, when on the 12th I returned to *Speed* and retrieved my seabag and hammock, there was no turning back. I had a new allegiance and new shipmates. In addition to Commander Knowlton and me, the flag staff consisted of Lieutenant D.R. Sellers, assistant to ComMinDiv-17; R.F. Lotz, radioman; A.C. Netzel, signalman; and J.L. Spells, steward's mate. The "flag" affiliation carried conflicting consequences, for although some may have viewed us as elitist, we had few perquisites beyond those enjoyed by the ship's crew. I consciously sought to fit in as a "regular joe," and I helped the ship's yeoman when my own work was done. This cooperation was especially important because my predecessor flag yeoman, Edward Thomas Murphy, was transferred on September 13, and the ship's new yeoman, Cody R. Rust, did not report aboard until October 4 to replace Otto Eric Benson, Y2c, who was transferred a couple of weeks later. Meanwhile, other new men were replacing veterans, and soon I was no longer a novice among the crew. Besides, *Strive*'s physical configuration generally paralleled that of *Speed*, so I could find my way around the ship. I gradually learned of her valorous service by listening carefully to plankholders as they described *Strive*'s role in the various Mediterranean operations, including her assistance to the bomb-damaged *Mayrant* (DD-402), whose executive officer was Lieutenant Franklin D. Roosevelt, Jr. I realized that I was among more heroes.[7]

A week of relative inactivity at Okinawa was interrupted on Sunday, September 16, when another typhoon bore down on the island, and ships were ordered to execute Typhoon Plan X-Ray, which meant sailing out of the bay into the rising sea. *Strive* took station astern of USS *Macomb* (DMS-23) as we headed northward around the island. Among our partners were, in addition to the vessels of MinDiv-17, *Ptarmigan* (AM-376) and *Tumult* (AM-127), with Captain W. R. Loud in *Ellyson* (DMS-19) as officer in tactical command. For two days

I had to brace myself to capture this picture of USS *Straus* (DE-408) with her bow out of the water during Typhoon Ida off Okinawa. A moment later, another towering wave covered her forward gun turret.

we alternated course to battle the huge waves, and during that time I photographed USS *Straus* (DE-408) with her bow first out of water and then under the water, an unidentified destroyer with its bow submerged back to the gun turret, and seas slanted at grotesque angles. *Strive* suffered no structural damage, but as in all typhoons, unsecured objects became weapons flying from beam to beam. Several other vessels were less fortunate; *YMS-98* and *—341* went down; Liberty ships *Richard V. Oulahan* and *John A. Rawlins* were lost; the hospital ship *Repose* (AH-16) recorded winds of 173 miles per hour and a barometer reading of twenty-six inches; and the supply ship *Beagle* (IX-112) claimed to have measured waves up to eighty feet high. Most tragic of all, *YMS-472* capsized with the loss of twenty-five, including one man devoured by sharks as his shipmates watched helplessly. The storm was called Ida by Americans but Makurasaki by the Japanese.[8]

Badly shaken up but safely back in Buckner Bay, we refueled from *Saugatuck* (AO-75) and were grateful for four days of relative quiet, during which time I nursed a nasty head cold contracted during the rough seas. I almost became homesick when *SC-1034*— looking so much like my old *SC-525*— came alongside and begged for fresh water, which our captain, an old sea dog from New England, freely granted.

Entries in a ship's deck logs often required clarification and interpretation. For example, the entry for 0700, Saturday, September 22, reads: "JONES, Houston Gwynne, 656 97 02, Y3c(T), V-6, USNR reported aboard for duty in Flag Allowance of Commander Mine Division SEVENTEEN. Authority: Verbal orders from Commander Minecraft, Pacific Fleet." Translation: I had survived my probationary period and Commander Knowlton was satisfied with me. I was now officially the flag yeoman, and my health and pay records were transferred from *Speed*. I belonged to *Strive*. The date coincided with my third anniversary in the Navy, for which I was awarded the Good Conduct Medal and a five-percent increase in salary. Simultaneously, nine crewmen were transferred to *LST-804* for eventual return to the States.

Later that morning, Mine Squadron Six was ordered back to Japan, this time to Bungo Suido, the broad neck that separates the home islands of Kyushu and Shikoku and provides the gateway from the Pacific to the Japan's Inland Sea. We sailed east of the northern Ryukyu Islands, then up the coast of Kyushu and over to the southern tip of Shikoku. Upon arrival at the entrance to the strait on the 24th, Commander Knowlton was placed in charge of Task Unit 52.9.22 with instructions to clear a channel for the transports bringing the 41st Infantry Division to occupy the Hiroshima-Kure area. Many of the 3,400 mines to be swept in Bungo Suido had been planted in these waters by American submarines as early as 1942, and we were welcomed by a genuine made-in-America floater, which was sunk by small arms fire. Another bobbed up the next day with the same result, and we got down to business on the 26th, exploding ten mines, one of which had to be dislodged from the sweep gear. Obviously, we were in the right place, whether we liked it or not. Each day's work for five weeks became repetitive but not always boring, for issues frequently arose with the sweeping gear. The log on several occasions recorded problems like "Lost starboard float while anchoring; float pendant fouled in starboard screw pulling float into screw. Examination by diver disclosed slight damage to port screw." We anchored many nights in Fukuru Wan, which, with nearby Sukumo Ko, provided some protection from rough waters off southern Shikoku, but by the 29th we had crossed the strait to Kyushu and tested the waters of Tsukumi Wan, then sailed up to Beppu Wan on the Inland Sea. Fearful of treachery on the part of suicidal Japanese, armed seamen circled the ships in the whaleboat to deter potential saboteurs. Sweeping back from Beppu to Fukuru, we cut five mines but in the process lost the port leg, recovered it, lost it again, and recovered it a second time. These were nerve-wracking hours, trying to recover gear in the middle of a minefield. On October 3, ships passed through carrying elements of the Sixth Army into Hiroshima Wan, and the next day, with the threat of another typhoon, our *Strive* put in at Tsukumi, after rescuing and taking ashore a crew of five Japanese from a small vessel flying the international distress signal. Only two months after accepting their surrender, we were playing good Samaritan for our erstwhile enemy. Near Yonozu Ko, still on the Kyushu side, we sank a mine with small arm fire. On October 7, the log recorded, "Maneuvering through many mines, mines detonating ahead." *Strive* got two of them before returning to Fukuru Wan, but the real "fun" came the following day south of Fukuru when, between the hours of 0900 and noon, *Strive* destroyed twenty-five mines, equaling the previous month's record at Kagoshima.

The Lord was with us on October 9, for we were in Bungo Suido when Typhoon Louise wreaked havoc on the fleet still in the vicinity of Okinawa. That storm, which unexpectedly changed course and caught three hundred ships in vulnerable Buckner Bay and other anchorages around Okinawa, only sideswiped us at Sukumo Ko. But at Okinawa, an estimated eighty percent of the military buildings around Buckner Bay were blown away or damaged, and many servicemen, in wet uniforms and without food for days, sought shelter in caves previously used by Japanese holdouts. The Navy Department reported the sinking of 12 ships, the grounding of 222 (most of which were eventually salvaged), and severe damage to 32 more. Among those numbers were 14 PCs, 20 SCs, 19 YMSs, and the *Mona Island*, on which I had attended church services the previous month.[9]

The back-and-forth sweeps between Shikoku and Kyushu continued for three additional weeks with consistent success for *Strive*— four mines on the 12th, eight the next day, and twenty on the 16th. We came up empty five days but the next week swept ten more. When we were relieved of duty in Bungo Suido, the ship's log recorded the destruction of 87 lethal mines that had threatened the troopships heading for Hiroshima. However, in the history that I prepared for the third anniversary celebration, I credited *Strive* with 107 mines in Bungo Suido.[10] The discrepancy probably is accounted for this way: The log may have recorded only mines actually exploded by *Strive*, whereas my anniversary figure probably included those that were cut loose by *Strive* but some of which were exploded and sunk by ships behind us. Cooperative destruction was essential because mines usually surfaced several hundred feet astern of the ship whose gear cut them.

There were a few pleasant experiences during our dangerous work in Bungo Suido. A squadron of several dozen ships required regular replenishment of fuel and provisions, and *LCI-423* was our most frequent visitor, bringing fresh foodstuffs and supplies. *LCI-917,* -*1088,* and -*1089* were also welcome. In turn, *Strive* shared provisions and fuel with the smaller YMSs, including -*93* and -*343*. The large oiler, *Saugatuck* (AO-75), kept the sweepers supplied with diesel fuel and lubricating oil. We all rankled at the infrequent delivery of letters to our remote location, but morale peaked when bags and bags of mail finally caught up with us at Fukuru.

Considerable excitement awaited in Fukuru Wan as we anchored after sweeping the record-tying twenty-five mines on October 8. The log simply reads, "1925, Lt. Comdr. Francis G. Moore, (D), USNR, 110923 reported aboard for duty as commanding officer Strive (AM-117) and additional duty as Commander Mine Division Seventeen." As the flag yeoman, I had typed Commander Knowlton's letters and records, so I knew about the impending change in command, but I was careful not to reveal more than the skipper wanted to be known. Keeping secrets was not easy, because the crew regularly pumped me for information. Besides, the change would most directly affect me and the other flag personnel, and I was disappointed to lose my boss, Commander Elliott Burris Knowlton, who at age thirty-one was wise beyond his years. A Harvard man and an avid sailor, "Buzz" Knowlton had participated in a 14,500-mile non-stop "grain race" between Australia and England in 1939, and he had served as captain or navigator in four transatlantic ocean races. He was, then, a seaman of the first order, and the crew looked upon him as an outstanding officer. He demonstrated his management style when I typed his first letter, a draft of which he had written out in longhand. Shorthand was not required of yeomen, and office copiers and correction fluids had not yet been invented, so letters with multiple copies were produced by interleaving onionskin paper with sheets of carbon paper—a painstaking exercise requiring almost flawless typing. That first letter required several carbon copies, and when I absent-mindedly typed a word that was similar to but not exactly what the commander had written in longhand, I took a chance that the minor substitution would go unnoticed. Not so. Instead of upbraiding or embarrassing me, however, Commander Knowlton calmly explained the subtle difference between the two words; afterward I followed his instructions to the letter.

I was, therefore, apprehensive as October 14 arrived and Lieutenant Commander Moore assumed the captaincy of the *Strive* with additional duty as commander of Mine Division Seventeen. Two days later Commander Knowlton was piped aboard USS *Bauer* (DM-26) for further transfer back to the States.[11] My concern was eased when Commander Moore, though an older seadog who had commanded several ships in civilian life around New Orleans, turned out to be a warm, almost folksy, officer. Commander Knowlton had been a rather formal New

Englander who dressed impeccably, but the new captain was not impressed by pomp and polish, so he made the crew feel comfortable around him. He would have been at home on our Caswell County tobacco farm, so I was at ease with him. My feelings were expressed in a letter home (October 27): "We have a new commander now and I like him better than the old one. He hasn't turned down a single suggestion or recommendation that I have made so far. He made me Yeoman Second Class less than a week after he took over." That promotion was accompanied by a salary increase: "Now I get a base pay of $96; 5% for longevity; and 20% for sea duty. Total, $120 per month (insurance, etc., out of that).... That extra money will come in handy. The longer I stay over here, the more I can save.... Incidentally, Y2c is the same grade as staff sergeant in the army." I wanted the folks in Caswell to know that I was no longer just a lowly swab.

The most memorable event of the Bungo Suido operation occurred while *Strive* was at anchor in Sukumo Ko, Shikoku, on October 27. The new captain declared a holiday, we watched the movie *Marriage is a Private Affair*, and Lieutenant (jg) R.B. Ferrell and I arranged a third anniversary commemoration of the commissioning of the *Strive* in Cleveland, Ohio. The lieutenant handled the logistics, the commissary department provided the food, and I prepared the crew roster, wrote a short history of the ship, and mimeographed the five-page anniversary program. We all regretted that Commander Knowlton and about two dozen of the veteran crew members had been transferred shortly before the celebration, but we proudly honored the remaining seven plankholders who sailed from Cleveland in 1942: J.A. Bata, Jr., H.A. Bell, and L. Besse, Jr., all boatswain's mates; C.W. Belzer, gunner's mate; W.A. Bernhard, carpenter's mate; B.A. Drexler, chief motor machinist; and G.D. High, sonarman. The menu was exceedingly sumptuous for a war zone: Mulligatawny soup, olives, carrot and raisin salad, roast stuffed Princess Anne turkey, spinach, minced eggs, potatoes, green peas, and for dessert, chocolate layer cake, vanilla ice cream, and chocolate sauce. I wrote home about the "biggest chow we've had in years ... really delicious." The dinner was followed by cigars and beer, which further boosted morale. Everyone felt that we had a "good joe" at the helm of the *Strive*.

For the occasion, a collaborative effort by members of the crew produced silly lyrics to be sung to the popular tune, "Blues in the Night." It went:

> From Bungo to Beppu
> From Beppu to Bungo
> Wherever the typhoons blow
> We're heaving the hook up
> And dropping the hook down
> Not in the same place you know
> A mine is a four horned
> A worrisome thing, that leaves us to sing
> The blues in the night.
>
> Now the sweeps are forming
> In the early morning
> Streaming, their gear they are streaming
> Now the orders come in
> We're to start the run in
> Leaving, the sweeps are all leaving
> But where are we going?
> We've heard it and then
> It's all changed again
> So we stream — through the night.

> The evening breeze is strong
> Our scope is long
> And we are anchored in a lee
> But of course you see
> We must go
> Orders from SOPA come
> And we start heaving in our chain
> And again we're steaming
> To and fro.
>
> We take on our fresh chow
> And load up on fuel oil
> But not in the same place, NO!
> We're ready for steaming
> The staff is all scheming
> Where do you think we will go
> We'll go 'cross the mine line
> From Bungo to Beppu and Beppu to Bungo
> We move in the night.

Except for typing transfer orders for men who attained their forty-one points, relatively little office work was required of me during the forty-day Operation Bungo Suido. I spent a lot of time around the bridge, away from the clutter and clatter of the minesweeping gear toward the stern, and I played checkers and chess with other bored crew members. Frustratingly, we were not permitted to go ashore — the Japanese in these remote areas may not have fully accepted their country's defeat — so we could not put a foot on land. From the deck, however, I sent home the following description of Fukuru (September 26):

> For the past two nights we have anchored in a little cove back under the cliffs in the Straits. There are a number of little villages in the cove and are interesting. The hills are very steep..., but the Japs have terraced off the hills and now they appear like giant steps. They plant their crops on these steps and make use of the steep hills that we would let go to waste in the States. Many of the homes are dug in caves and they don't bother with glass windows; they just leave a whole [*sic*] in the side of the houses and let it go at that. Some of the roofs are made of straw and weeds, but some of them are of terra-cotta clay.... We have two whale boats patrol all night with tommy guns just in case any Japs try to swim out with depth charges.

I added, "We still don't trust them too much." That distrust increased dramatically when we solved the mystery of hundreds of small dark spots visible along water's edge on the coast of Shikoku. We debated the purpose of the tiny holes in the cliffs. After anchoring in Fukura Wan on October 14, I joined a whaleboat crew for a closer look. The question became more perplexing when we drew closer and discerned two thin lines running from each cave to the water's edge. Closer still, we suddenly realized the awful truth: Each cave served as a midget submarine pen, and the dual lines were in fact flimsy rails on which the diabolical suicide weapons were to be launched into the water. Along the rugged coast of the Japanese islands, in case of an American invasion, hundreds of young Japanese had been prepared to give their lives to the emperor by guiding these small explosive-laden contraptions into American ships. Historians may debate the wisdom of atom-bombing Hiroshima and Nagasaki, but in 1961 at the Truman Library in Independence, Missouri, I had a chance to tell my wartime commander-in-chief, "Mr. President, I want to thank you for your decision to drop the atomic bombs, for otherwise I probably would not be here today." The exact moment when former President Truman put his left arm around my shoulder and said "You don't know how good that makes me feel" was captured in a photo made by my assistant state archivist, Rear

When in 1961 I thanked former President Truman for his decision to use the atomic bombs to end the war, he put his arm around my shoulder and said, "You don't know how good that makes me feel."

Admiral Alex M. Patterson. I did not know at the time, but the former president did, that some armchair academicians had begun to criticize his approval of the bombing of Hiroshima and Nagasaki. I was proud to have cheered a great statesman by my simple but heartfelt appreciation.

When we left Bungo Suido on November 1 ("*at last*," I wrote in my note book), our sweepers had destroyed 1,687 of the estimated 3,400 mines endangering shipping; in addition, Japanese vessels — impressed into the same service — accounted for 222 more. That meant that nearly 1,500 other underwater missiles remained to threaten every ship that sailed between Kyushu and Shikoku. Some of the weapons aged out to impotency, but others remain a threat two-thirds of a century later, particularly to strollers who find the encrusted curiosities washed up on Pacific coast beaches. We disarmed the Japanese, not their (or our) mines.[12]

As *Strive* again headed for the East China Sea, I typed in my service record, over the signature of Commander Moore, three new entries:

4 July–18 August 1945: Participated in operations Juneau and Skagway in East China Sea. Tentatively authorized to wear one bronze star in Asiatic-Pacific ribbon in accordance with AlPac 211–45.

1–11 September 1945: Participated in minesweeping operations preceding American occupation force landings in Kagoshima Kaiwan, Kyushu, Japan.

24 September–1 November 1945: Participated in Bungo Suido minesweeping operations preceding Sixth Army landings in Kure-Hiroshima area, Honshu, Japan. This vessel accounted for 107 Japanese mines.

17

Formosa, China, and Japan Again

November 1945–January 1946

After concluding Operation Bungo Suido on November 1 and sending seven men aboard *LCI-423* for further transfer back to civilian life, *Strive* and our squadron, augmented by USS *Spector* (AM-306), sailed out of Tsukumi Wan, tipped our hat as we passed Kagoshima, and headed for Sasebo on the southwest side of Kyushu. We looked forward to tying up to a dock for the first time since leaving Pearl Harbor five months earlier, but again we were relegated to the anchorage. The reason was evident when we were allowed liberty in the city, whose dock area and much of the built environment had been devastated by American bombing. The Fifth Marine Division had already occupied the city, only a fraction of whose prewar population of 300,000 had begun to return.[1]

A Christian church stood lonely but apparently undamaged, and a few shops had managed to reopen in the rubble, so I bought some trinkets — a porcelain saki jug and cup, a serving tray, a miniature kabuki figure, and a bowl that I used for my smoking tobacco. The most colorful purchase was a hand-painted original folder featuring Japanese symbols and the image of a ship, which I mailed to my parents after adding in ink, "Sasebo, Japan. November 1945. Merry Christmas. Love. Houston." This would be my fourth Navy Christmas away from home. I also mailed home three money orders, along with a fifty-sens note (half a yen) equal, in United States currency, to three cents. The registered air-mail letter required postage of forty-six cents because it went via "civilian" mail. The war really *was* over back in the States!

On my first Sunday in Sasebo Ko, I attended a religious and communion service on USS *Dauphin* (APA-97), conducted by Chaplain G. M. Warner. Two of the hymns were familiar — "Lead On, O King Eternal" and the Navy anthem, "Eternal Father, Strong to Save." On another Sunday I heard on USS *Yosemite* (AD-19) what I described as "the best sermon" I could recall. I added, "The Engineering Officer of the *Strive*, Lt. (jg) Jack Fleischli, of Missouri, is a strict Lutheran and has missed only one chance to go to church since being on board." My record was not nearly as perfect.

The next two weeks in Sasebo passed slowly and sluggishly, for I had almost no work to do except to help type transfer orders for departing crew members and endorse papers of new arrivals. In fact, the whole atmosphere of the ship rapidly changed as familiar faces were replaced by new ones, the latter mostly teenagers fresh from the States. Transfers became so wholesale that blocks of names were checked off alphabetized personnel lists and assigned en masse. For example, on November 5, we received aboard six seaman second class ratings:

Edward H. Schultz, Jacob Schwartz, Clifton J. Seliga, John H. Shantz, Abraham M. Shaponik, and Neil A. Sherman. Eleven days later we received five seamen first class: Charles D. Shaffer, John H. Sharp, Stephen Siebert, Henry F. Skropka, and Ernest L. Steward. I called them the "S-Eleven" (pronounced "Sleven"). Bodies appeared to have outweighed ratings in the rush to fill vacancies. To be sure, some petty officers came aboard also, but the ship's complement certainly underwent radical change as the need for particular skills, such as gunners, diminished with war's end. The complement of officers was also reduced; for example, Lieutenant Commander Hugh C. Wallis, the executive officer, left, along with Lieutenant D.R. Sellers, Ensign Charles E. Herin, and Chief Machinist George A. Fletcher.

More minefields awaited our clearance, however, and on November 17 *Strive* weighed anchor and steamed from Sasebo with MinDiv-16, -17, -32, and -33, the OTC in *Henry A. Wiley* (DM-29).[2] The destination was an area included in the huge Operation Sherlys, this portion of it northeast of Formosa in the vicinity of the Sakishimi Islands, and on the 23rd we rendezvoused with the remainder of Task Group 70.5 and began sweeping in violent waters, only to be embarrassed by the loss of both starboard and port gear. Additional gear was streamed just before a mine was spotted dead ahead. A change of course evaded that one, but almost immediately another was cut by the starboard gear. The following day *Implicit* (AM-246) hogged the show by cutting five mines while we only exploded one. The sight of *Implicit* brought back memories of *SC-525* and our game of hide-and-seek with German gunners firing from the mountains above Monte Carlo the previous year.[3]

Our arrival in Kiirun (Keelung, Chilung) at the northern tip of Formosa on November 25 provided a couple of days' respite from the rough waters of the East China Sea, but more importantly, for the first time since leaving Pearl Harbor on June 11, my ship tied up to a shore-bound dock. Actually, *Pinnacle* (AM-274) beat us to the dock, but *Strive* hugged her port side, with *Steady* (AM-118) snug against us to port. At least we could walk across a sister ship and reach terra firma without being ferried back and forth by boat. A few steps ashore, we discovered that we were in a whole new world. The harbor and much of the city had been wrecked by war, but the populace was smiling and bowing. I recorded, "Place littered with sunk ships & wrecked buildings. But better than Japan at that." After returning from a wobbly walk ashore, I repeated in a letter home:

> This is a very fine port, but it is littered with sunken Jap ships and wrecked buildings. The air force really did a swell job of knocking the Nips out of here. The people here in Formosa are the friendliest I have yet run up on and they have higher regards toward the Americans than any other country that I have visited. It isn't put-on; they really look up to us. Altho they are out of clothes, the people dress neatly and smile at everything. They love to hear fireworks and all day they stay around the docks shooting firecrackers. We have a fleet of our own in Kiirun and we feel like we own the place.

My chief complaint—a recurring one—was the tardiness of the mail; the last letter from the States had been mailed five weeks earlier.

We relaxed in Kiirun only two days before moving out with Mine Squadron Six, our captain serving as CTU-70.5.4. An overnight cruise through the Taiwan Strait took us to Takao (now Kao-hsiung) in southern Formosa near the upper limit of the South China Sea. Just north of that large city was the village of Saei with a protective harbor; we sometimes docked there, but in the coming weeks we more often anchored at Ryukyu Sho. This sweeping assignment, still a part of Operation Sherlys, began November 27 and continued until December 15. *Strive* destroyed seventeen mines, not an impressive number, but ten of them were swept in one day, and one was a mine camouflaged as a barrel. Other vessels were more productive, so the operation was effective in opening the sea lanes to Saei and Takao, important ports of the island-state of Formosa, the name of which was changed to Taiwan when the island declared its independence from the Communist-controlled mainland of China. One tragedy occurred on November 30 when *LCS-56* struck a mine that killed one man.

I described a day in Saei in a letter home (December 10):

> I went on liberty with a friend [Neil Sherman] and came back loaded down with Jap swords, a watch, an arm full of fruit, and other odds and ends. We found a couple of nice Jap sabers and traded a pair of dungarees and a carton of cigarettes for one and two pair of dungarees for the other. I found a pretty good, but cheap, wrist watch and got it for 15 packs of Camels. We can't spend American money here and can't exchange for Chinese money, so we have to trade clothes, cigarettes, and other items to get anything. My watch is keeping good time and it only cost me 90 cents (we pay 60¢ a carton for cigarettes). We traded for tangerines, grapefruit (as big as a bucket and red meat), and bananas.... The town, with a population about like Reidsville, has only one main street and that is filled with ox-drawn carts and wagons. Very few automobiles of any kind. They grow fresh vegetables but live largely on fish.[4]

I added that the Chinese soldiers and sailors all saluted us regardless of rank, and that we had examined suicide submarines and a kaiten abandoned in the harbor. I could also have described the dozens of chattering Formosan males whose bumboats gathered beside our ships at each anchoring. They arrived on rafts made of eight or ten lashed bamboo reeds, each end plugged for water-tightness. Most were in tattered shorts, many in discarded Japanese army caps or typical Chinese pointed straw hats. They had almost nothing except fruit to offer but clamored for anything that the crew might offer them. Among them were children who had never seen a Caucasian. These youngsters would grow up to build a strong Taiwan that defied the Communists who conquered mainland China.

At Saei, wobbly legged men from the squadron's vessels played amusing baseball games, and I found a willing chess victim in the new fireman striker, Neil Sherman.

Local residents paddled their bamboo skiffs out to welcome *Strive* to Takao (now Kaohsiung) in southern Formosa (now Taiwan). Some of the children had never seen a Caucasian.

During Sherlys, he defeated me only once. Joe Johnson would have been proud. By trading movie reels with sister ships, the crew often passed early evenings in the mess hall watching titles such as *Tonight and Every Night, Klondike Katie, Saratoga Trunk,* and *Rhapsody in Blue.* Not all was perfect on *Strive,* however, for at a captain's mast on November 20 a steward's mate was given fifty hours' extra duty for disobedience and impertinence, and several weeks later a signalman and quartermaster were restricted to the ship for "disorderly conduct prejudicial to good discipline." Other cases involved warnings for absences over leave and one AWOL. Somehow, AWOL in Formosa didn't sound like a good idea to me.

I, too, had a brush with the ship's rules. To break the boredom and keep the crew alert to naval discipline, the officers thought up ways to keep their men on their toes, so one day they called for a top-to-bottom inspection of the ship. That included every fourth man's berth and locker. Mine happened to be in the unlucky category, and when Lieutenant Ferrell's fumbling turned up my pint of Prince George — a souvenir from Waikiki — he followed the rules and confiscated the bottle. A bit mortified, I cursed my fellow Tar Heel Josephus Daniels who, as Secretary of the Navy in World War I, outlawed alcohol aboard ships. My loss had an up side, however, for my stature peaked in the eyes of recent arrivals who quickly judged me to be a *real* gob. To live up to my suddenly won reputation for obstreperousness, Sherman and I slipped ashore and brought aboard several bottles of Espiro — a mean Chinese rice wine with a lot of kick — from which we drank far too much in the engine room as our squadron sailed overnight back to Kiirun. The result was a diary entry the next day, "And what a hangover! Slept all morning."

In southern Formosa, Alberta, the monkey mascot of *Sheldrake* (AM-62), found four friends from *Strive* in, from left, Neil A. Sherman, fireman, of Massachusetts; Joe Hoskins, motor machinist's mate, of West Virginia; Ed Schulz, seaman, of New York; and Don Bradish, electrician's mate, of Pennsylvania.

Strive began to take on the appearance of a zoo. The crew brought aboard Mike, a monkey; Boats, a dog; an unnamed cat; and a cackling chicken. In Takao, the boys tried to bring aboard a goose and a goat, but the skipper said enough was enough. Boats was sold to the *Speed*, and the hen disappeared just before we had fried chicken for dinner. Nobody asked the whereabouts of the monkey and cat, though there were some complaints to the cook about tough beef.

On December 16, *Strive* and sister ships arrived back in Kiirun before sailing out again. Mine Squadron Six resumed Operation Sherlys north of Formosa on the 19th but, with no success, abandoned the hunt and two days later sailed for Shanghai, a belated reward for minesweeper crews who had experienced no real liberty since leaving Hawaii. A few hours out of Kiirun, however, both *Strive* and *Staff* were hounded by onboard fires which, though quickly brought under control, provided some anxious moments. The anxiety was exacerbated when we were hit by a violent storm, and we arrived at the mouth of the Yangtze River too late for entry on December 22. We would have been more uneasy if we had known that since August three American ships had been mined near where we anchored.

The next morning Captain Scellery, a pilot, conducted our column of ten ships up the Whangpoo Kiang to the city of Shanghai. There, at anchor in the middle of the river sat the majestic cruiser, USS *St. Paul* (CA-73), Task Force 73 flagship, and as our minesweepers came abeam, the cruiser's public address system sounded attention and an honor guard saluted each ship. At last, a little respect for the humble vessels that boasted "Where the fleet goes, we've already been." We continued past the imposing buildings familiar from travel literature and docked across the river about a mile upstream. Before tying up, *Seer* scraped an underwater obstruction, but it caused no observable damage, so it was not reported. We were delighted upon learning that Commander Moore had been recommended for the Legion of Merit for serving as CTU-70.5.4 during the Formosan sweep. We also added another star on our Asiatic-Pacific service ribbon.

Shanghai was ready for us. Even though some sections of the city remained off-limits to uniformed Americans, an organization called the "Shanghai Joint Service Committee for Allied Force," under auspices of the War Area Services Corps, distributed a handy printed guide and operated information centers, money exchanges, voluntary guide services, and even a bazaar. Its map guide contained useful directions and information on recommended facilities and services, along with a few reminders on subjects like left-hand driving and the modesty of Chinese women. Representatives of the Joint Service Committee wore "A.A." insignia, meaning aid to Allied forces, and all spoke English, usually with a Limey accent. The city, already looking to the future, rolled out hospitality to the extent that it was able so soon after expelling the Japanese occupation forces.

For eleven days, the crew almost forgot the minefields. Liberty was generous, and I described my first three days in a letter home (December 26):

> Shanghai is the closest thing to a city in the U.S. that I have seen in a long time. It is very modern and if it were a little cleaner, it could be mistaken for an American city. Nice hotels, shops, stores, theatres, and fairly good food can be had. After being in the China Sea and Japan ... it is Heaven to us. Yesterday, Christmas Day, the Engineering Officer [Lt. (jg) J. E. Fleischli], a Radioman [Karl] Moe, and I went to church on board the USS *Saint Paul*, a heavy cruiser, here in the Whangpoo River.... [I]n the afternoon, I went with two friends [Neil Sherman and Harry Morris] into the city. Liberty commenced at 1300 and ended at midnight. We had a very quiet evening and enjoyed it very much. Went down to the Red Cross Club for real chocolate pie and Coca-Cola. Seems strange to see American food in such a distant land. Most of the people here speak some English; in fact, there are many Americans and British here as well as Russians,

Chinese, French, and Japs. We planned to do some bowling, but the place was too crowded. From there we walked around the city a ways and went to a show at a modern theatre. We had a very nice chow at the "Black Widow." I had fillit [sic] mignon and the other boys had steaks. They were surprisingly good and tasted just like in the States.

I did not share with my parents a note scrawled in my abbreviated diary admitting that almost before all lines were secured against the dock a couple of days earlier, Neil Sherman, Ed Schultz, J. T. Locke, and I "went to town & got drunk. Had swell time. Put Neil to bed. I'm still drunk but am last to go to bed." The resulting hangover apparently moderated our behavior, for I later recorded, "Neil & I went into town. No drink except a brandy & Manhattan. Excellent chow at Coconut Grove. By YMCA & picked up quart of Scotch at EMC. Back at 12:30." This temperance was short-lived, however, for Shanghai lit up at midnight New Year's Eve. I, too, was lit up, though not blindly. Neil and I had the afternoon and evening in the city, and we had good food and several drinks, but I came back in better shape than my buddy. Neil remembered, in a letter written December 31, 1946, "It's New Year's Eve! Some different from last year. I can remember it very clearly—at least part of it. You went to bed early & were annoyed by the ship's whistles; I was standing on the dock with a bottle of Scotch & yelling 'Happy New Year.' Eddie [Schultz] was holding me up." Looking back, both of us can count our Shanghai behavior as one of the perils of juvenile misjudgment.

New Year's Day was spent aboard; I was content to slip over to *Speed* and watch *Big Sleep* with my old shipmates. As I looked back upon those Shanghai liberties, I was conscious of one experience above all. I yielded to the temptation to taste absinthe, the power and danger about which I had been warned even by the owner of the dark, off-limits establishment. One taste of the "Green Fairie" and no one needed tell me to stay away from the stuff, which had long been banned by the international community but was still hawked to down-and-out addicts in the Far East. Even sixty years later, in my imagination I can feel the touch of my tongue to the awful liquid.

In another letter, I reflected on "Chink dollars":

> This Chinese money keeps us all balled up. I paid $3,000.00 for a pair of gloves; Cokes cost $65.00 each; a ride in a rickshaw cost $200.00 [each for three people]; and a hair cut cost $550.00. That sounds like a lot of money, and it is. I have in my pocket now over $20,000.00. Now if that was in American money, it would be better. The exchange rate for the money is changed each day. The first day we were here, we got $1,200.00 in Chinese for one American dollar. Yesterday, it was $1,320.00 in Chinese for one American dollar.... It is very confusing to say the least, but it feels good to have our pockets stuffed with thousands of dollars.[5]

Based on the widespread availability of silk clothing and decorative items, the Chinese people must have been resourceful and secretive during the long Japanese occupation of Shanghai. I really splurged by buying several stunning, colorful, and intricately embroidered silk items of women's wear, often with dragon motif; most of them I mailed to my sister Pauline when we reached Sasebo. I retained and used for six decades a handsome blue silk smoking jacket and white scarf, and I shared one of the pair of fine silk exotic bird prints with my old friends Bill and Anna Sharpe. On my last trip ashore, I used up some of the paper currency bulging my pockets by purchasing from a peddler on the landing a peck of peanuts for a thousand Chink dollars (less than one American dollar). The supply lasted for two months, mostly consumed during our yeoman's shack chess games.

For Flag Yeoman Jones, however, it was not all fun and drinks in Shanghai. A day after we docked, a delegation of Chinese officials arrived aboard *Strive* with a complaint. They

My old and new ships, *Speed* (AM-116) and *Strive* (AM-117), were photographed side by side in the Whangpoo River near Shanghai during our Christmas "vacation" in 1945. My flag yeoman's shack occupied two portholes under *Strive*'s bridge. Other vessels of MinDiv-17 are nested nearby.

reported that the little bump felt by the *Seer* just before she docked on the 23rd was in fact a collision with the waterlogged bridge of a Chinese ship previously sunk by American bombs. And they brought along a list of damages to equipment, including a ship's compass that had been under water for five months, and a bill against Uncle Sam for several million dollars. To avoid a diplomatic incident, Commander Moore as ComMinDiv-17 felt obliged to hold a hearing, and as flag yeoman, I was obliged to be the recorder. For two days the following week I took down in longhand — and later typed up — the testimony of the heavily accented Chinese officials. The whole subject was ridiculous, but international relations being outside the realm of the military, the commander knew that he had to handle the matter without upsetting Chiang Kai-shek and the Kuomintang, America's friends battling the Communists for the soul of China. When we left Shanghai on January 3, I didn't know that I would be plagued by the *Seer* incident two more times.[6] The many hours that I spent deciphering and typing testimony and documents impinged upon my liberty opportunities in Shanghai, but I did get into the city five times in ten days — fifty percent was not bad!

During our ten-day "vacation" in Shanghai, an eager bunch of Chinese, male and female, young and old, visited each of our ships and, to show their gratitude to us Americans for freeing them from the Japanese, very obligingly scrubbed the decks, cleaned equipment, and washed our clothes and dishes. Not until our grateful visitors departed and all liberty parties returned aboard did we notice the diminished stock of dishes and silverware. Even if the Chinks took them off simply as souvenirs, we found it inconvenient to beg seconds on a spoon or cup until we obtained replacements when we reached Sasebo.

Two of the friends with whom I libertied in Shanghai were from among the "S-Eleven" seamen who came aboard during our stopover at Sasebo. I can't remember how I got to know them, but Neil Sherman of Baldwinsville, Massachusetts, showed an interest in chess. Ed Schultz of New York had gone through training with Sherman, so he happened along at some point. Both, quite young, exhibited an educational bent, and we found a common ground in a number of intellectual discussions. Neil and I had serious philosophical debates, which continued through correspondence after we were both again civilians. Our daytime chess contests eventually moved to evening games in the yeoman's shack, which in turn led to little

**Dissipation from liberty excesses in Shang-
hai showed in this photograph in which I am
wearing my yeoman second class chevrons
and the insignia of the minesweeping fleet.**

treats and finally to rewards to the winner. The
cost of defeat was sometimes as simple as making hot chocolate, but my favorite reward for
winning was a shave or a shampoo.

On January 3, 1946, Pilot C.A. Rousselt
guided the column of ten minesweepers down
the Whangpoo past Liberty Landing, and again,
as each ship came abeam of *St. Paul*, attention
was sounded and the cruiser's honor guard
saluted us. Our morale boosted by the Shanghai interlude, we sailed to the entrance of the
Yangtze, where our MinDiv-17 joined Div-18,
with USS *Adams* (DM-27) as OTC and guide.[7]
The East China Sea was still angry, and *Strive*
and several other ships suffered breakdowns as
we sailed for Japan. The first night *Strive* lost
power on one engine, got it back on line, then
lost it again. An hour later we lost power on the
starboard shaft, then all lights and steering
power. We pulled out of the formation and fell
astern before regaining power. The log recorded,
"Casualties due to water in fuel oil." USS *Robert
A. Smith* (DM-23) became OTC the next day,
but our luck did not improve.[8] Two generators
kicked out and for a time we again became a
crippled duck. It was a relief, therefore, to drop
anchor in Sasebo Ko on January 5. There we would swing on the chain for ten days except
for repositioning. On my twenty-second birthday, January 7, I helped Rusty transfer twenty
veteran sailors to faster transportation to the States for discharge. These were, as a whole, representative of the men who won the war, and their absence dramatically diminished the cohe-
siveness of *Strive*. Twenty new men came aboard a week later. Now we were becoming a ship
of strangers.

These rapid changes ended my fleeting plan to reenlist in the Navy provided I could
retain my job as flag yeoman to Commander Moore. I had become so indecisive toward the
future that I briefly considered pursuing a twenty-year Navy career, retiring at age thirty-
eight with a nice pension, getting a college degree, and starting an entirely new profession.
The commander appreciated my loyalty, but when I discussed it with him, he sensed my
ambivalence and said, "You can go when the first line hits the dock in San Pedro."

The pint of Prince George confiscated from my locker back in Formosa was returned to
me in time for a little birthday celebration in the yeoman's shack. After typing transfer orders
for twenty men, I wrote in my diary, "Spent afternoon in bed — cold bad. Opened up pt. of
Prince George. Stayed up very late talking with Neil & having cocoa and grape juice." Just
how well cocoa, grape juice, and Prince George mixed, I did not explain. Four nights later,
I wrote, "Snowed today. Received a number of letters from various people. Three new men
aboard. Neil gave me a sham[poo] & message tonight — first in 16 months. Up to 0120 talking. Woozy for a while over several drinks of Vodka."

The days in Sasebo Ko passed slowly, but I was fortunate to be only a gangplank's distance from *Speed*, still the home of a number of my former mates. On the other hand, old buddies Frog Jolicoeur, Alex Watson, Willard Green, and John Larson were already in civilian clothes. I did take several more trips into the devastated city, but each one was equally unpleasant because of a stench that permeated the desolation. The smell of death was all around, and I wondered how much worse Nagasaki, just over on the next peninsula, must be. Although we were close to both, I was disappointed not to have gotten into the harbor of either Hiroshima or Nagasaki. A visit to either might have made me an instant arm-chair authority on atomic bombs.

Had I been unlucky, I might never have lived to regain civilian status. On January 14 in Sasebo harbor, as *Strive* approached the ammunition ship *Sangay* (AE-10) to unload armament, I was working in the yeoman's cabin, with the porthole open, oblivious to the movement of the ship. What transpired on the bridge was explained to me later: As *Strive* coasted toward the ammo ship at the usual angle for perhaps a one-point docking, the captain softly ordered "one-third back." The "jg" at the controls responded "one-third ahead," and the engine conformed. Not recognizing the misinterpreted command, the captain called for "two-thirds back," and the junior officer moved the lever to "two-thirds ahead." Instantly, the skipper recognized the junior's error and yelled in a booming voice unmistakable to anyone on the bridge and perhaps even to the engine room gang, "*back full!*" It was too late. Just when I heard the reversal of the engines and felt the shuddering of the ship's response, I jumped up and stuck my head through the open port and saw nothing but a dark wall approaching. Almost simultaneously with my head's withdrawal, I felt a crash and heard the crunching of metal. Our forward port quarter had hit and bounced off—and then was thrown back against—*Sangay*. Fortunately, the damage was minimal, and I was only shaken up as the frame of my porthole bumped and scraped up and down the hull of the other ship. I could only imagine the chewing out that the captain gave the "jg," whose naval career might well have been shortened by his inattention to a command.

At 2210, January 15, 1946, I sat down in my yeoman's office and started what would become a typed thirteen-page, single-spaced, circular letter with multiple carbon copies. It began:

> This is a date that we will all remember for a long time to come, just like 7 December 1941 [Pearl Harbor] and 15 August 1945 [when we heard that the war was over]. This morning at 0800, the *Strive*, after 11 hectic months in the Pacific (plus 21 in the European-African theatre), and her sister ships got underway for their last trip—and one for which we have all looked forward. We are heading for the United States, our objective during the past months of continuous minesweeping operations in the Japan-China-Formosa areas.

I then described another experience that left few dry eyes among old salts in our ten-ship convoy. With *Strive* in the lead, the line of sweepers, with all hands at attention in dress blues, sailed up Sasebo Ko, our going-home flag fluttering in the breeze. We rendered honors as we passed each dressed capital ship — *Yosemite* (AD-19), *Oklahoma City* (CL-91), *Monadnock* (CM-19), hospital ship *Samaritan* (AH-10), and several others. When we came abeam of the flagship of Rear Admiral A.D. Struble, Commander of Minecraft, Pacific Fleet, the band of the *Paniment* (AGC-13) struck up "Hail, Hail, the Gang's All Here."[9] That, though, was not the highlight; as we reversed course and slowly cruised down the port side of the anchored ships, *Paniment*'s band about-faced, marched over to the port side, and struck up "Auld Lang Syne."

Grown men later spoke of hair standing on end and frogs in throats as ten lowly Two-Twenties, finally having been given a salute by ComMinPac for a job well done, slipped out into the East China Sea, passed a short distance from Nagasaki and Okinawa, and steamed toward the North American continent.

18

The Long Way Home

January–March 1946

As we waved good riddance to Japan — "Auld Lang Syne" still ringing in our ears — we savored the moment. In our euphoria, it hardly occurred to us that former members of the crew, who had returned to the States earlier, would never know of the honor paid to them in absentia by ComMinPac.[1] Nor did we think of those left behind who, without the forty-one points required for discharge, would continue dangerous minesweeping work for many months. We did leave, however, with the sad knowledge that one of our sister ships, *Minivet* (AM-371), had been sunk by a mine in Tsushima Straits on December 29 — more than four months after Japan's surrender — carrying down thirty-one of her crew, including the brother of one of our cooks. This tragedy reenforced the truism that mines respect neither friend nor foe, and that thousands of the nefarious weapons remained a threat in international waters around the world. We were still within sight of the harbor when a Type 93 Japanese mine bobbled up ahead, still another reminder of that threat. The commander sent the *Seer* off-course to destroy the prickly sphere.

With *Strive*'s captain as CTU-52.3.13, the ships accompanying us were *Pilot* (AM-104), *Pioneer* (AM-105), *Prevail* (AM-107), *Seer* (AM-112), *Staff* (AM-114), *Speed* (AM-116), *Steady* (AM-118), *Sustain* (AM-119), and *Dextrous* (AM-341). Lieutenant Commander John F. Maddox, Jr., of Beaufort, South Carolina, at the youthful age of twenty-four already the new skipper of my old *Speed*, and Commander Moore were close friends, so our two ships very often tied up side by side. This relationship provided me many occasions to visit my former shipmates, and I may have taken undue advantage of their friendship. I occasionally joined them for chow (my favorite was fried chicken and apple pie), which always seemed to taste better than *Strive*'s food. In my continuing letter home (January 25), I wrote,

> I find it beneficial to be a friend of the ship's service operator of the *Speed*, Don Wetmore of Oregon. My cigars were running low and the *Strive* was sold out, so our friendship was worth two boxes of Garcia Grandes. I have quite a name now for being a moocher — when the *Strive* runs out of cigars, candy, cream, or good chow, I just step over on the 116 and make myself at home. It's very nice to have two "homes."

As we proceeded into the vast Pacific, I added:

> the 20 new men make the ship manned by 20% strangers. Two new guys sleep near me and I don't even know their names. We have only about 30 men aboard now who were aboard last 1 September when I came over from the *Speed*. The *Strive* is a good ship, but I will always look at

the *Speed* as my home. I have never known a better group of men than the 116 had up until the end of the war. I go over for a visit and feel just as much at home as I do on the 117, even tho there are many new men who I don't know well.... Neil Sherman, of Baldwinsville, Mass., was one of those who have been out only a short time and I am glad that he did not have to stay over. He's a swell fellow and we made some good liberties in Shanghai. That's the trouble with the Navy ... we meet some of the best fellows on earth and all of a sudden, pop, a transfer, and never see them again.

The first night out we celebrated our departure from Japan by watching the appropriately titled movie, *Thank Your Lucky Stars*, featuring Humphrey Bogart, Bette Davis, and a dozen of Hollywood's leading stars. We did indeed thank our lucky stars. Most of us had seen the film before, but movies were a way to pass the time. I had confiscated from the storeroom some ice-cream mix, cocoa, and juice, so we had something to chase the fruitcake that my folks mailed in November but which caught up with us after Christmas in Sasebo. Neil was a fireman striker, so I often carried refreshments to the engine room, where we ate and imbibed among the noisy and oily machinery. I bruised a couple of ribs when I fell down the boat deck ladder; a seaman had carelessly left a paint brush on a rung, and I carelessly did not see it. That, with a lingering cold from the rough trip across the China Sea, gave me reason to complain.

Our bow lookout the next day spotted two more floating mines, and, as instructed, *Speed* sped off and dispatched them. Those were the last mines that I ever saw, but thousands of them were left in the Pacific, ready for their unsuspecting victims. That night for the first time, Neil beat me at chess and I also lost a game to Ed Schultz; I was reminded again why Texas Joe in the Naples hospital enjoyed winning better than losing. The consolation was that I then won three straight, and the prize was another free shave.

On the 17th we passed Iwo Jima, which meant less to us at the time than when the real story of the battle was revealed later in the nation's reverence for Joe Rosenthal's famous photograph of the raising of the American flag. The erratic steering by one of the new men — the water was turbulent — brought back memories of my scare at the Bay Bridge many months earlier. Somehow we had acquired a doctor aboard — perhaps one returning to the States for discharge — and he ordered the entire ship disinfected to eradicate mosquitoes.

The next couple of days were too rough for me to work productively, but on the 21st the sun came out and I lay under it for five hours. The result was predictable, and I lamented, "For some reason I never seem to know when I have had enough. I am now sitting behind the after stack on an engine room vent trying to keep in the shade. This would be a wonderful trip, should the sea calm. Even the thought of going to the States doesn't help much." I took some consolation in observing that Seliga, seaman second class, was even redder. I griped because *Dextrous* was having engine trouble and was slowing down the entire flotilla.

Although nearly three years at sea had enabled me to pretend that I was not susceptible to seasickness, I often fooled myself by simply hitting the sack during rough seas. I learned that lying flat on my back with my arms folded over my eyes was the best way to avoid mal de mer, and I was glad during the Pacific typhoons that I was not required to be in the yeoman's shack during the worst sea conditions. I empathized with a man from *Adams* to whom we were giving a ride to the States: "He passed completely out when going up a ladder and since then Doc has had to keep him topside on a cot. All he has had to eat for these three days have been a few glasses of juice."

January 22 put me in a mood to write a long memoir on the second anniversary of *SC-525*'s role in the invasion at Anzio.[2] We were by then hearing English-language radio broad-

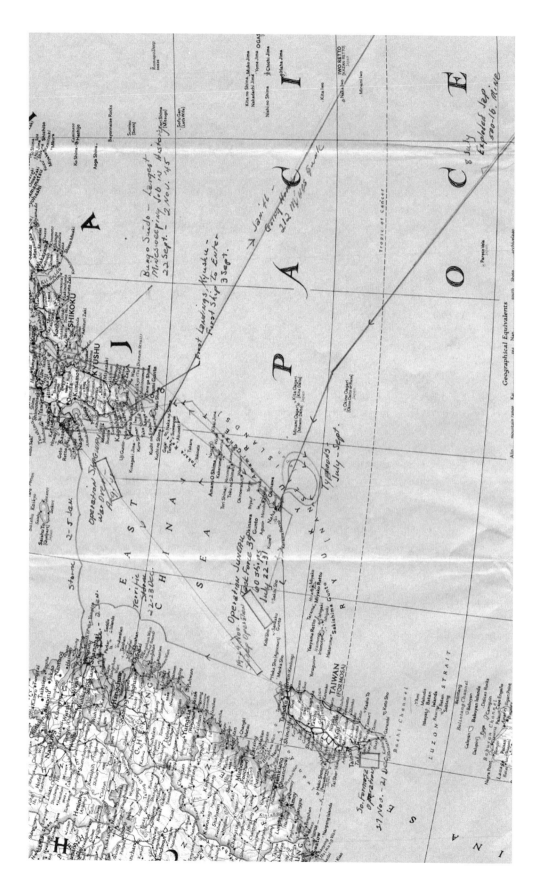

casts from Iwo Jima and Saipan, a welcome sound, for communication had been almost non-existent around Japan and Formosa. The next day, I continued to reveal much of myself when I added to my long letter:

> Last night, I was lying up here in the breeze in cogitation and began thinking of the things that I have enjoyed and things I have missed since being in the Navy.... A few of my "likes" about the Navy: traveling to places where I wanted to go; seeing and being in war in order that I might know the real meaning of it; testing myself to see how I could stand up under fire; finding out how men feel when danger is all around; examining men's actions and thoughts during a crisis; knowing what fear really is; learning what a decaying human body smells like; watching the attitude of our victorious "conquering" soldiers and sailors walking up a street in a devastated Japanese town.

Among my dislikes were "sameness of the chow; continuous life at sea — no recreation ashore; the continuously restless sea; no stiff collars and ties; not enough Milky Ways and Cokes; slow mail service; incompetent '90-day wonder' officers; and red tape." Sixty-five years later, I can name no more than a couple of officers whom I classified in the last intemperate judgment. We imagine stupid things when we are not held to account for our outbursts. I ended the paragraph with this reassurance: "I have never regretted being in the USNR and I know that these 3½ years have been more valuable than they could have been anywhere else."

Our convoy dropped anchor in Eniwetok on January 24, with *Strive* and *Speed* side by side. I remarked that nothing had changed since our stop seven months earlier: "The beached tanker still sits on the rocks and the anchorage is still filled with ships of all kinds." There was no village, only military buildings, so that night we provided our own diversion by setting up our movie screen on the fantail since *Speed* was showing her film on her bow. Our choice was *First Comes Courage* starring vivacious Merle Oberon ("better than the average run of war pictures"), and I made the mistake of sitting on the magnetic minesweeping reel for a better view of the screen. When I went into the head and looked into the mirror, I was as black as the ace of spades. I had failed to realize that I was sitting high up in the direct path of the soot from the stacks.

A couple of nights later, we showed *The Picture of Dorian Gray*, and I was deeply moved by the 1945 Oscar–winning (best black and white cinematography) film, based on a 1890s novel by Oscar Wilde. Featuring George Sanders, Hurd Hatfield, Donna Reed, and Angela Lansbury, *Dorian Gray* so impressed me that I wrote, "I think the one thing that is emphasized is that man's life on earth is what he makes it. Aside from the moral and immoral qualities of the picture, it turns out to be utterly gruesome in many ways."

One day at Eniwetok was enough to get one of our officers in trouble. Shockingly, it was the executive officer of *Strive*, Lieutenant G. J. Keating of Scranton, Pennsylvania, whom I admired for his loyal attendance at Catholic Mass whenever a priest was in the vicinity. His offense was excessive drinking at the base officer's club, which in turn led him to do "a few un-officer–like things." In other words, under the influence of alcohol, he tried to be a bigger man than he was, and an altercation occurred. Arriving back aboard in un-officer–like attire, he was promptly given a hearing by Commander Moore, who sentenced his second-in-command to ten days' confinement to the ship, beginning upon arrival in Pearl Harbor.

Opposite: On the way back to the States, I traced on this map a crude reminder of my Pacific war path aboard *Speed* (from the States to Okinawa) and *Strive* (to Japan, Formosa, China, and back to the west coast).

Boredom was difficult to hide and privacy was hard to find during the long cruise back to the States after the Japanese surrendered. Writing passed the time for this sailor with his feet propped on a 40-millimeter gun mount.

For a man who was returning to the United States after nearly a year in the Japanese-Chinese theater of war, this was not a light sentence; it meant no liberty at all in Hawaii.

Irritated by *Dextrous*'s engine troubles and determined not to be held back further, Commander Moore ordered the vessel to remain behind and to join a later — and slower — convoy of YMSs. So the nine other AMs sailed out of Eniwetok Atoll on the 25th. To remind us that we were still in the Navy, the crew regularly responded to "Bong. Bong. Bong. Now hear this" with rushes to general quarters for about every type of drill conceivable to officers with nothing better to think up. Log entries now appear quaint: "Mustered all hands at stations. No absences." Of course there were no absences; we were hundreds of miles from land, and we were heading home!

Still, the long, unexciting cruise that started ten days earlier provided me much time for reading, contemplation, and writing. There were few books on the ship, and magazines were often many weeks old. Unlike in the Mediterranean where we received *Stars and Stripes* fairly regularly, few copies of the Pacific edition of *S&S* reached the naval vessels at sea. I did take along or otherwise acquired several books, among them H.G. Wells's *Outline of History* and Elliott Arnold's novel, *Tomorrow Will Sing*. From Wells I copied the line, "In peace, sons bury their fathers; in war, fathers bury their sons" — hardly original with the author. I borrowed from Charlie Kane, a radioman from Buffalo, New York, H.B. Monjar's *Code of Ethics*, which I found informative, even profound. Among the passages that I quoted in a letter home were these: "A tree may be small or large, it may be a fruit or a shade tree, it may live long or die an early death, but if it fulfills the purpose for which it was created, it will have done its part, made the world a little better and brighter place to live in, and have brought some happiness to others"; "Moral courage is a weapon that can conquer every obstacle save death, and with its aid even death may be approached without fear or trembling, and accepted with nobility"; and "Those we love can never be entitled to more than justice and even our enemies are never entitled to less."

To help pass the time during the long return trip, one resourceful crewman cut the butts from expended three-inch brass shells, added lips, stamped them with "USS STRIVE AM 117," and traded the resulting ashtrays for whatever foresighted collectors were willing to exchange. Mine is a perpetual reminder of my old ship.

"Killer" Kane, I wrote home, was "one of the finest characters I've ever seen. I've never yet heard him utter a word of profanity or speak against another person. He has been in the Navy over two years, and it takes a lot of character and courage to go that long with a bunch of sailors and still have complete self-control." On another occasion, I described a naughty joke played on one of our shipmates: "John Hirt, radioman from Terre Haute, as fat and jolly as anyone on the ship, had Tom Sleap pretty worried for a while today when he made up a fake radiogram to Tom, informing him that his wife in Staten Island had given birth to a baby boy. However, Tom soon learned that it was all a joke.... He hasn't been home for over a year."

My back-country upbringing had deprived me of even the rudiments of music and I never *really* learned to dance, but I enjoyed listening to radio music and records played on the single phonograph aboard the ship. For example, on January 27, north of Rongalap, I wrote,

> This evening we gathered here on the main deck with the phonograph speaker and played records. Tom Sleap, the storekeeper of Staten Island, New York, bought some Japanese and Chinese recordings and they went along with everything from boogy-woogy to "Stardust." [B. L.] Hunt, the colored StM of Winston-Salem, did some fancy jitterbugging on the slippery deck to the juggle of those Japanese instruments.

Sixty years later, I am surprised that I did not commit to paper stories of other shipmates and our shenanigans. Nor did I characterize many of them — favorably or unfavorably — in my correspondence and notes. I did on many occasions express my admiration for Commander Dryer, my old skipper on *Speed*, and Commander Moore, to whom I reported as flag yeoman on *Strive*.

East of the Marshall Islands, we again crossed the International Date Line — this time happily heading east — and thus endured two January 29s and regained the day we lost the previous year. The sea was too rough for many hijinks; besides, nearly every mind was on reaching Hawaii, only three days away. But those days dragged all too slowly. I wrote on the 31st,

> Today, we picked up a Honolulu radio station, and believe me, it was good to hear real advertising and news broadcasts again. As much as I hate commercials, I did enjoy hearing them again. And it was novel to hear a news broadcast, especially with the dit-da-dit-da [clicking of Morse Code] at the beginning and end. The men actually sat down and listened to "Ma Perkins"—that's how glad we were to hear a real station again.

The sea remained rough, and we pitied Lieutenant Boyer, a passenger that we picked up at Eniwetok. Like the ship's laundryman, he suffered from chronic seasickness. The pharmacist's mate set up cots for them in shaded areas on deck, and they survived mostly on juices.

As we approached Pearl Harbor, I described my abhorrence of "Spam (at the head of the list), 3-year-old eggs, dehydrated eggs and potatoes, flapjacks, French toast, beans (for breakfast), navy coffee, string beans, asparagus, meat loaf, canned peaches, apricots, and other canned fruit, lumpy oatmeal, cold-cuts, and chlorinated water." I had no idea that decades later my taste buds would welcome some of those foods.

We celebrated our return to United States territory at 1300 on February 2, one day after seaman C.E. Smith sustained contusions and lacerations to his left foot when a metal bench fell from a mess table. Liberty was granted daily for just about everybody except Commander Moore, Lieutenant Keating, Seaman Smith, and me. The federal bureaucrats in Hawaii forced two days of hearings on the ridiculous Chinese claim for compensation of $9,000,000 (in Chinese National Currency, a little less than $1 million in United States dollars) for the sunken Chinese ship that the *Seer* scraped prior to docking in Shanghai. Again it was incredible that claims were made for electronic equipment that American bombs sent to the bottom of Whang-poo River the previous year. But the commander kept his cool and listened, asked questions, and made tentative rulings. That was the easy part; it was my task to record the hearing in longhand — again without benefit of shorthand — and then type up the findings in multiple carbon copies to be forwarded to Washington, where, very likely, the Chinks got what they asked for.

Rough waters since leaving Japan had given me an excuse to procrastinate in some work that I could have done on a smoother sea, so I was already behind in my assignments when we reached Hawaii. For example, the designation of our division was changed from Mine Division Seventeen to Mine Division Nineteen, and I had to transfer myself and our flag staff on paper, even though we went nowhere. The redesignation also meant alterations in many different documents; that was one of my early adventures in a bureaucracy that demands change whether it is needed or not. I also had begun training David M. Leet, a seaman second class from Louisville, Kentucky, as my "striker" — that is, yeoman-in-training — to succeed me as flag yogi. David was a fine young man, and I felt responsible for giving him good experience before the whole responsibility fell on his shoulders the following month. And, to interfere further with my liberty plans for Honolulu, the officers went ashore, leaving me to complain in a letter home (February 6) that I did "a half-way job of holding down the fort while the commander was away. In short, I was run to death. AdComMinPac's personnel officer tried to induce some of my men to come over to *Terror* [erstwhile flagship of Mine Force, First Fleet], but no one wanted to go. [Radioman G.E.] Nelson had only 16 points, so they took them anyway."

Of course, *Strive*'s executive officer, Lieutenant Keating, denied liberty because of his indiscretions at Eniwetok, and the injured seaman were there to share my hurt feelings, but they gave me little solace. Still, I was able to get ashore twice, both times with Neil Sherman, and I described (February 6) one excursion:

> And that *real milk* and those banana splits were good! The first day, Neil and I went to Waikiki and after swimming at the Royal Hawaiian, had that first banana split which I had been tasting for many months. We did a little exploring the place as Neil had not been here before, and had a good chow and movie and more milk and splits. Saw at the Waikiki *And There Were None*, very good and what a great feeling to sit down in a beautiful aircooled theatre and sink into those seats.

On the second liberty, with Sherman and Ed Schultz, we had a big dinner at The Tropics with more splits. Both of the liberties were very quiet; I recorded, "Not a drop of alcohol — and it was great to be back in civilization. I bought some good records which I will no doubt break before I get home...." The prediction was borne out, for Schubert on six sides never made it across the continent. It was just as well, therefore, that the store did not have my favorite, Debussy's "Clair de Lune." My other memorable purchase in Waikiki was a pair of fancy blue and white bathing trunks, which I thought enhanced my physique on the beach. The garment came to an ignoble end; it was among personal effects lost when my gold-colored Ford was stolen in Boston in 1952. The vehicle was eventually recovered by Boston's Finest, but the miserable thief kept my favorite souvenir trunks. At least he/she exhibited good taste.

In Pearl Harbor, Commander Moore, as CTU 70.5.4, was decorated with a Legion of Merit for the Formosan operation. He in turn recommended a Bronze Star Medal for all of the ships in the Takao-Saei sweeping. Crew members were authorized to wear stars on our Asiatic-Pacific service ribbon stars for the Juneau, Skagway, and Sherlys operations. These were not symbols of heroism but of survival. We had been there, done that, and lived to tell the story for those who died in unheralded missions to clear sea lanes for the evacuation of Allied prisoners of war and the landing of occupation troops.

February 6 was a happy day when Task Unit 18.2.20, with the OTC in *Strive*, cleared Pearl Harbor, sailed past Honolulu and Waikiki Beach, waved to the pink Royal Hawaiian Hotel, and hummed "Auld Lang Syne" as landmark Diamond Head faded behind us. We were again going to the "Good Ole U.S. of A."[3] Despite our euphoric anticipation, the trip was not an easy one, for I continued to transcribe testimony from the *Seer* investigation, finishing just as the California coastline showed up on radar. Furthermore, several of our ships, including *Pioneer*, *Seer*, and *Strive* herself, developed engine and other mechanical problems that slowed down our fourteen-knot programmed speed. Maintenance obviously had been neglected after the war's end because of the imminent return of the ships to the States and an uncertain fate for the fleet. In addition, a medical problem developed on *Incredible*, and *Pilot* and *Speed* were dispatched to provide assistance. From time to time I reflected that, in addition to "my" *Strive* and *Speed*, I was returning with two ships, *Pilot* and *Prevail*, that had been *SC-525*'s motherly companions on the voyage from Casablanca to Oran in August 1943. Gosh, could that have been two and a half years ago? So much had transpired in the interim. Join the Navy and see the world, indeed.

It was 0458 on St. Valentine's Day when a pilot boarded *Strive* and led us to the anchorage in San Pedro harbor. What followed in the afternoon was a mass exodus of twenty-two men, whose transfer papers I had helped Cody Rust — who was among the transferees — type during the cruise. The usual rats-deserting-a-sinking-ship joke was repeated ad nauseam, but there was generally good humor except among the newer enlistees with service still to be fulfilled. Additional transfers were made, and I was responsible for working up shore leave papers for many of the sailors who had not yet achieved the required points for discharge.

For me, the next eleven days were bittersweet. Although the commander had given me permission to leave immediately, I chose to remain to assist with the personnel goings and comings, take a few liberties in nearby Los Angeles, and help plan a big Ship's Party for men of the newly designated Mine Division Nineteen, then consisting of *Staff* (AM-114), *Speed* (AM-116), *Strive* (AM-117), *Steady* (AM-118), and *Sustain* (AM-119).[4] Despite transfers, scores of men remained aboard the five ships and, because all could not be spared for a single party, the affair was scheduled for two nights — February 20 and 21 — at the Diamond Room in Wilmington. An attractive printed folder, emblazoned with the Navy symbol, welcomed Mine Division Nineteen personnel to the Ships' Party, the schedule for which read, "1930 — All Doors, Hatches, Scuttles and Ports Opened Wide to Receive Guests. 2000 — All Hands Man Your Dancing Stations. 2015 — Strike Up the Band. 2030 — Pipedown Dinner. 2100 — Buffet Dinner. 2200–2400 — Dancing and Refreshments, Floor Show. 2400 — Abandon Ship." The

A blurry photograph suggests that we heeded the command to "eat, drink, and be merry" at Mine Division Nineteen's party in Wilmington, California, on February 21, 1946. Left to right: Neil Sherman, me, Edward Schulz, and Max Shaponik, together with two local ladies.

sumptuous buffet included turkey, ham, two kinds of beef, and a cake decorated with the words "Mine Division 19." To encourage the command, "Eat, Drink and Be Merry," local ladies, invited by the Terminal Island Recreation Office — combined with every imaginable drink, all free — assisted in making the two evenings lively. A faded photograph showing giddy Neil Sherman, Ed Schultz, Max Shaponik, and me, with arms around two unnamed hostesses, attested to a merry evening. Happily, the officers had arranged for busses to safely return us to the ship, and reveille was mercifully late the following morning. One shipmate, Quartermaster R.F. Leonard, apparently missed the bus, for, as recorded in the log, he arrived back "with a large cut on his head. Sent immediately to U.S. Naval Hospital, Long Beach, California."

Neil and I made two trips into Los Angeles, including, naturally, a longed-for visit to Hollywood. Even though the war had ended six months earlier, service men still were treated with great respect, and we were welcomed at stage shows and special events. On the 16th, we caught the train to LA, checked into the Ferguson Hotel, became "pleasantly stewed on gin and Southern Comfort," and went to Betty Rowland's burlesque show. The next day was spent on movies — *Lost Weekend, Getting Gertie's Garter,* and *Whistle Stop.* Two days later, after sending more friends on leave, we had a barbecue dinner in Long Beach and saw *The Dolly Pictures.* On successive days, I alternated between work aboard and liberty ashore, but on the 22nd, I recorded that I was "mad as hell all day" — I have no idea what about — and slipped off alone to Hollywood. Upon my arrival back at Long Beach that night, I couldn't find the boat to the ship because of fog, so I ended up in a fleabag hotel. The next morning there was still no boat, so I lucked up with Leet, Skropka, and Sharp at the Saratoga Cafe. I went back to the ship for a couple of hours of sleep in my dress blues, then returned to town for a dinner of buttermilk and rabbit, took a room at Yale Hotel, and slipped back to the Saratoga, where on the earlier visit I had taken a shine to Tini, a delightful hostess. The fun-filled evening culminated in a photograph of a pretty woman and a handsome sailor, which she signed, "Luck to you always. Too bad you get discharged so soon. Always a friend, Lorentine (Tini)." I returned aboard the next morning in time to leave again with Neil for Hollywood and a visit to the Roosevelt Hotel, Grumman's Chinese Theatre, and other places about which I had read. Best remembered was Ken Murray's *Blackouts of 1946* at the El Capitan Theatre. In addition to musical numbers, the variety program included skits, acrobatic and animal acts, "nautical moments" with a "whistling sailorette," and a performance by the "Elderlovelies." Murray, the host, and Marie Wilson provided the most laughs. Years later, Marilyn Monroe reminded me of Marie Wilson, an earlier "dumb blonde" who starred frequently on the Broadway stage and in Hollywood movies. She was a particular favorite of service men who visited the Hollywood Canteen during the war. As a political buff, I was impressed by the presence in the audience of flamboyant Governor Jimmy Davis of Louisiana. Back in Long Beach after midnight, we had fried oysters and spent the night at Yale Hotel, but after only a few hours of sleep, I rushed back to the ship for a very important "appointment."

The day had come for my goodbye to *Strive*. The log recorded at 1430 on Monday, February 25, the transfer, "with service records, pay accounts, and gear," of Chester A. Carter, Peter De Mattia, Samuel L. Logan, William D. Lowe, Henry F. Skropka, and Houston G. Jones. My service record carried a nice going-away present from Commander Moore; he had given me a final rating of 3.9 in proficiency in rank, 3.9 in leadership, and a perfect 4.0 in conduct. I left him sadly but with hope for the bright future that he predicted for me.

The six transferees took bunks for four nights in the Receiving Station at Terminal Island, San Pedro, to await travel orders. DeMattia and I spent the first evening in Long Beach for barbecue and the movie *The Harvey Girls*. The next day I met Neil at Mamie's, where I introduced him to fried rabbit, and we saw the movie *Stork Club*. On the last day of February, I met Neil, Leet, and Lowe for dinner and two movies, *Meet Me on Broadway* and *Pardon My Past*.[5] I had made plans to meet Neil for a last visit, but I did not merit liberty that day. Uncharacteristically, I committed a courtmartial-level offense by borrowing DeMattia's ID, with which I went into the city and met Neil for dinner and overnight at the Schuler Hotel. We were up at 0600

Tini in the Saratoga Café in Long Beach provided good company as my Navy days waned in California.

for our last breakfast together. In my notes, I wrote, "He's one great guy & I hope to see him again."[6]

On March 2 my on-the-way-home group was bussed into Los Angeles, where we boarded a Pullman train for a slow, sometimes torturous trip across America. Because of the shortage of berths, on alternate nights we slept two per bunk—not a pleasant experience for several score men, few of whom were known to each other. In fact, we mostly napped sitting up as we drowsily watched mountains and deserts from the train window. The rail trip was via the southern route, and about the only recompense came from my ability to boast that I had once "visited" cities like Phoenix, Tucson, El Paso, Houston, and New Orleans (Mardi Gras was being celebrated, described in my notes as "Very impressive"). Passing through Texas, I remembered the 1930s when Dr. John R. Brinkley, a Tar Heel native who transplanted goat glands in elderly men for sexual enhancement, operated the nation's most powerful radio station, XEAW, Del Rio, Texas, from across the Mexican border.

Thankfully, though, the long cross-country journey afforded me an opportunity to read two fascinating little books that Neil Sherman had recommended. One was *The Rubaiyat of Omar Khayyam of Naishapur*, and I found myself drawn to the poetry of the twelfth century Persian astronomer and mystic. Two verses contained such profound wisdom that I committed them to memory. One was quoted in the preface; the other reads:

> I sent my Soul through the Invisible,
> Some letter of that After-life to spell:
> And by and by my Soul return'd to me,
> And answer'd "I Myself am Heav'n and Hell."

The other was the work of an equally wise poet—*The Kasidah of Haji Abdu El-Yezdi*, one verse of which I quoted when describing my transfer from New York in December 1944. Additionally, whenever I become absolutely convinced that I am right, I still try to remember another of El-Yezdi's verses:

> All Faith is false, all Faith is true:
>   Truth is the shattered mirror strown
> In myriad bits; while each believes
>   his little bit the whole to own.[8]

A surviving souvenir of the transcontinental train ride—and a stopover in Atlanta—is a street cameraman's photograph of me striding confidently in my dress blues in front of the famous Winecroft Hotel on Peachtree Street. Interest in the twenty-five-cent photograph was heightened nine months later when 119 people—including the owner of the "fireproof" Winecroft building—died in what was to that date the worst hotel fire in American history.

The train arrived in Norfolk on March 7, and I was taken by bus to Shelton Separation Center. It required three days of physical and debriefing examinations for the Navy to assure itself that it owed me nothing more.[9] At 1355, March 10, 1946, I was handed my honorable discharge from the United States Naval Reserve. The accompanying NavPers-553, "Notice of Separation from U.S. Naval Reserve," added information: I had served three years, five months, and seventeen days, and I was owed $100 in initial mustering-out pay, $241.27 in salary, and $13.35 transportation fare to my home. I chose to retain my government service insurance policy that would require payment of $6.50 per month.[10] The document authorized me to wear the following medals: Good Conduct, Victory, American Theatre, European-African-Middle Eastern Theatre with four stars, and Asiatic Pacific Theatre with three stars.[11] Under the blank space for job preference, I optimistically furnished "College Washington &

Lee, Va." My thumb print and signature concluded my active duty in World War II. The handsome zippered leather folder bearing the naval eagle also contained a letter each from President Harry S Truman, Secretary of the Navy James Forrestal, and Veterans Administrator Omar N. Bradley; a referral sheet identifying sources of assistance to veterans; and, for a prospective employer, a small "Rating Description" booklet certifying the job skills of a yeoman second class. Separately, I was handed an honorable discharge lapel button, nicknamed "Ruptured Duck." My parents were sent a letter from Chaplain Joseph Howard Giunta reminding them, "Life in the military service, of necessity, is much different from life at home, and I am sure you will do all you can to assist him to readjust himself s a vital part of his family, his church, and his community."

March 10 was a Sunday, so I lugged my seabag into Norfolk, saw two movies—*This Love of Ours* and *Miss Susie Slagle's*—and, to give my thanks for a safe return from the war, attended evening service at Epworth Methodist Church, where I had first wor-

When I removed my dogtag on March 10, 1946, attached to its chain was the St. Christopher's medal given to me three years earlier by *Cinq-Deux-Cinq* shipmate George Franklin Klumpp. It had brought me home safely.

shiped during boot camp three and a half years earlier. I boarded the midnight bus, arrived at 0800 in Reidsville, bought some civilian clothes from my brother-in-law John Jones at Belk-Stevens Department Store, and slept until afternoon when he and Pauline drove me home to rejoin my parents, brother Buck and sister-in-law Vivian, and my faithful uncle and aunt, Bob and Nannie Willie Fowlkes. At age twenty-two, I removed the dogtag that had identified me for nearly four years as "656 97 02, USNR"; registered for the "52/20 Club"; made plans for college with the help of the "G.I. Bill of Rights"; and—the anxiety of my youth behind me—prepared for a new life.[12]

Uncle Sam and I had lived up to our bargain.

Chapter Notes

Preface

1. Samuel Eliot Morison, *The Two Ocean War: A Short History of the United States Navy in the Second World War* (Boston: Little, Brown, 1963), p. 585.

2. Edward Fitzgerald, trans., *The Rubaiyat [of Omar Khayyam]* (New York: Dodge, 1914), p. 79.

Chapter 2

1. The onerous tradition was repealed in 1945 by AlNav 278–45. See chapter 12, note 1.

2. The lyrics, written in 1860 by Englishman William Whiting, have long been in the public domain.

3. That information — along with other secrets — was revealed when after the war I obtained a copy of my service record from the National Personnel Records Center in St. Louis.

4. I did not know in 1942 that I would serve on both the smallest and largest of these classes of vessels.

5. Attack Teacher practice sessions were provided at additional bases as the war progressed. See "Sonar Gear and Sound Schools," *PCSA Newsletter* 64 (April–June 2004): 11–13.

Chapter 3

1. Built in the 1930s, Pier 92 extended a thousand feet into Hudson River. After the war, it and nearby piers became Manhattan's main passenger ship terminal. Immediately following the terrorists' attack on the World Trade Center on September 11, 2001, Pier 92 became the command center for emergency operations, and the hospital ship USNS *Comfort* tied up to the pier and provided medical attention, food, short-term lodging, and laundry service for firemen and disaster recovery personnel.

Chapter 4

1. During the war, *John Ericsson* made two trans–Pacific voyages and twenty-seven troop lifts from American shores to Europe and Africa. Afterward, she was damaged by fire in New York but, lavishly renovated and renamed *Italia*, resumed operation as a passenger ship. In 1964 she was converted into a floating hotel, *Imperial Bahama*, but the following year she was broken up at Bilbao, Spain.

2. Samuel Eliot Morison, *The Two-Ocean War: A Short History of the United States Navy in the Second World War* (Boston: Little, Brown, 1963), p. 242.

3. The rating of "soundman" was officially changed to "sonarman" before I reached Africa, but several months passed before the official shoulder patch became available to replace the left-arm quartermaster patch. The new one, bearing the image of a pair of earphones, was worn on the left sleeve with the eagle correctly facing inward. We could no longer be called "queer quartermasters." One of the best brief explanations of sonar gear and its use is found in "Sonar Defeated Subs," *Science News Letter* (April 13, 1946): 231.

4. Miller was soon promoted to chief petty officer as the ship's top-ranked enlisted man. Ensign King was relieved by Ensign Hugh P. McCormick.

5. *SC-515*, *-516*, and *-517* were among thirty submarine chasers built by the Elizabeth City Shipyard in my state of North Carolina.

6. Although I kept in touch with "Boats" for several years after the war, it was ironic that, unknown to me, he eventually retired back to Stanly County, North Carolina, and lived only a few miles from Reed Gold Mine, which was acquired and developed under my direction as a state historic site in the 1970s while I was director of the North Carolina Department of Archives and History. Only when I read his obituary on the Internet in 2000 did I realize the lost opportunity for a nostalgic reunion.

7. Mathis built twenty-six of the 438 SCs produced in World War II. More than 40,000 men served on subchasers during the war. www.splinterfleet.org.

8. For an example of my bodily transfer from one ship to another, see chapter 16.

9. Marynell Dyatt Reece, wife of Lieutenant Reece, in August 2005 gave me by email a version of the evaluation. Following the skipper's death in August 2008, she visited my home and gave me the longer evaluation, which was written on the back of a photograph show-

ing me in my white uniform. The captain took such an interest in his men that he requested from each a photograph, on the back of which he wrote his comments. I was flattered by his opinion, and I hope I became more "industrious" the longer I remained in the Navy.

10. Published by the Special Services Division of the United States Army (Washington: Government Printing Office, 1942).

11. The ARC Liberty Club on Rue Chavandier de Valdrome provided commissioned officers with similar but more elegant facilities. There was also an "Allies Club" on Boulevard de Paris and an American Merchant Seamen's Club at 32 Boulevard de la Liberte.

12. *Casablanca with Plan of the Town and Name of the Streets* (Casablanca, F.M.: Guides Moroc-Presse, 1943).

13. The article by Jane Hall appeared in the *News & Observer* (Raleigh, NC), August 17, 1958.

Chapter 5

1. Brave *PC-624* met an inglorious end. She ran aground off Palermo the following March but was salvaged and reclassified as *YW-120*, a self-propelled water barge; was lent to the French for a while; and ended up as *YWN-120*, a non-self-propelled water barge. Ah, the versatility of patrol craft!

2. Participation of a small number of United States Marines in the Mediterranean is often overlooked. Among the Americans on the ill-fated *Hartland* were six Marines; another small contingent landed at Arzeu and marched overland and captured the large fort overlooking the principal French port of Mers el-Kébir. Earl Burton, "The Invasion of Southern France," *Sea Classics* (September 2004).

3. We could not have imagined that within five months we would watch helplessly as *YMS-30* was blown to pieces at Anzio and that *YMS-24* would be sunk off Southern France the next August. See chapters 6 and 10, respectively.

4. *Siniai* had been a French ship that was seized by the Germans in 1942 and converted to a hospital ship. When the Allies invaded Southern France in August 1944, she was scuttled in Marseilles. *Aquileia* had been an Italian hospital ship seized by the Germans.

5. http://tdiumh.blogspot.com/2004/11/November-11.html.

6. Don Fortune, "Pioneer to the Rescue," *Silent Defenders* 22(2) (Summer 2005): 18–23.

7. *Vulcan* in 1978 became the first Navy ship on which women were deployed.

8. Years later I twice voted for one of the film's stars for president of the United States.

9. For that melancholic story, see chapter 10.

10. In June, Cain did spend five days in the brig in Bizerte.

11. "V — as in Victory Mail," *Smithsonian* 35 (May 2004): 28. Our communications were governed by Spencer S. Lewis [Chief of Staff], Northwest African Forces, Headquarters Administrative Order No. 1 (revised), 25 March 1944.

12. HE=high energy; AP=armor piercing; and AA= antiaircraft.

Chapter 6

1. For the sinking of *PC-558*, see chapter 9.

2. For the sinking of *LST-348*, see chapter 8.

3. Samuel Eliot Morison, *History of United States Naval Operations in World War II*. Vol. IX, *Sicily-Salerno-Anzio* (Edison, NJ: Castle, 2001), p. 332; F.J. Lowry, "The Naval Side of the Anzio Invasion," *United States Naval Institute Proceedings* 80(1) (January 1954): 23–30.

4. Peter Verney, *Anzio 1944: An Unexpected Fury* (London: B.T. Batsford, 1978), p. 27.

5. An LCVP (Landing Craft, Vehicle, Personnel), often called a "Higgins Boat" for its designer, Andrew Jackson Higgins of New Orleans, was approximately 36 feet long with a beam of nearly 11 feet, with a complement of three and capacity for 36 troops, a 6,000-pound vehicle, or 8,100 pounds of general cargo. With a speed of nine knots, the boat usually ferried troops (who had scrambled down a cargo net hung over the side of a transport) or supplies from a troopship. Its shallow draft of slightly over two feet forward allowed it to drop its ramp and disgorge its contents near the water's edge. General Eisenhower was said to have called Higgins "the man who won the war for us." *News & Observer* (Raleigh, NC), April 16, 2008.

6. An LST-1 class of tank landing ships was about 328 feet long and 50 feet wide with its wheelhouse and chartroom aft. It could carry a load of 2,100 tons at nine knots. Its short forward draft permitted the ship to push its bow close to the beach before dropping its ramp. Some were manned by American Navy and Coast Guard personnel, others by the British Navy. Crews jokingly referred to their LST as a "Long Slow Target." An LCI was 158 feet long with a 23-foot width and a landing draft of 5'4," allowing the vessel to approach the shore, lower two forward ramps, and discharge troops in shallow water. Troop capacity for an LCI was nearly 200.

7. There were several models of LCTs. The MK5 was about 117 feet long by 32 feet wide with a crew of 13 and capacity for four tanks or 150 tons of men or cargo. Its speed was only seven knots and its range 700 miles. These craft were adaptable to several special purposes, such as LCA (landing craft, assault), LCG (landing craft, gunship), LCM (landing craft, mechanized), and LCT(A) (landing craft tank, armored.) A DUKW (pronounced "Duck") was a 6.5-ton amphibious truck about 31 feet long by 8 feet wide with a crew of two or three and speed of 6 mph in water and up to 45 mph on the road. A "Duck" could carry a 2.5-ton payload (troops or goods) over land and water. Its acronym stood for D=production code for 1942; U=utility truck amphibious; K=front wheel drive; and W=two rear driving axles.

8. The number of small craft in a "wave" varied — up to six or seven LCTs or 30 LCVPs — each of which delivered its load to the beach and, like the escort, returned to the transport area for, if necessary, repeated missions. Many DUKWs might constitute a wave.

9. These buoyant pots, metal cans filled with smoke-producing hexachlorethane, were lit and dropped overboard in an effort to hinder the enemy's view of ships in the roadstead, which was within range of German

guns throughout the four-month struggle to sustain the Anzio beachhead. Electrically operated smoke generators were also used on deck.

10. Admiral Lowry doubled as commander of X-Ray Force while Rear Admiral Thomas H. Troubridge, RN, was in charge of landing Peter Force. The following summary is based largely on "Commander Task Group 81.3 [W.O. Floyd] to Commander-in-Chief, United States Fleet, 17 April 1944, Subject: Amphibious Operations, Anzio-Nettuno Area, Italy during January, 1944 — Report of." [The cover sheet reads "Secret Action Report Commander Task Force 81.3 Serial 046 17 April 1944"], National Archives, College Park, MD. Hereinafter cited as Floyd, "Secret Action Report." This report covers activities of January 22 to 31 for only the Red Beach Group of X-Ray Force. The document was later declassified and filed in the Office of Naval Records and Library but has subsequently been transferred to the National Archives. Also of value was Lowry, "The Naval Side." Secondary sources, such as Morison's and works by later scholars, are cited in other notes.

11. The total number of vessels participating in the invasion at Anzio-Nettuno depends upon the definition of "ship." The British Navy counted 154 American and 215 British and other Allied ships, making a total of 369. www.naval-history.net.WW2CampaignsItaly. htm. Martin Blumenson, in *Salerno to Cassino* (Washington: Center for Military History, 1993), p. 356, counted 354 vessels divided as follow: two command ships, five cruisers, 24 destroyers and destroyer escorts, 23 minesweepers, 32 submarine chasers, two antiaircraft ships, two gunboats, six repair ships, four Liberty ships, eight LSIs, 84 LSTs, 96 LCIs, 50 LCTs, and 16 landing craft carrying guns, rockets, or other weapons. He did not include PT boats. Flint Whitlock, in *The Rock of Anzio: From Sicily to Dachau: A History of the 45th Infantry Division* (Boulder, CO: Westwood, 1998), p. 137n, agrees with Blumenson. On the other hand, Carlo D'Este, in *Fatal Decision: Anzio and the Battle for Rome* (New York: HarperCollins, 1991), p. 443, counted 379 vessels but classified PCs and SCs as "scout craft." In addition to British and American vessels, two each flew Greek and Dutch flags, and there was one Polish craft.

12. In the account that follows, official reports and my memory are supplemented by voluminous manuscript notes that I made at the time (in defiance of censorship regulations) plus "Anzio: A Brief Memoir," written from my hospital bed in Naples on March 1, 1944. Of great value were the manuscript logs of USS *SC-525*, entries into which were made at least every four hours by the officer on duty; the logs are in the National Archives, and I have complete photocopies. Exact times of specific actions are recorded differently even in the official sources — sometimes because of inexact timepieces, sometimes because of delays in making entries — so I have used clock times as recorded in Floyd, "Secret Action Report."

13. Edward P. Stafford, *Subchaser* (Annapolis, MD: Naval Institute, 1988), p. 13.

14. The naval component of each group included both British and American vessels; only the nationality of troops was divided between the landing areas — the British in Peter Force and Americans in X-Ray Force.

15. The first and last naval losses at Anzio, *Portent* and *Swerve*, respectively, were minesweepers. I would remember that statistic the next year as my new ship approached Okinawa.

16. Morison, *Two-Ocean War*, p. 253.

17. The following chronology of the Red Beach landings is based largely on the log of *SC-525*; Floyd, "Secret Action Report"; and personal notes and memory.

18. This was Sweeping Unit One, consisting of *Dextrous*, *Pilot*, *Pioneer*, *Portent*, *Sway*, and *Symbol*, which had been sweeping a six-mile-long approach into Nettuno all night, with *Strive* and *Prevail* danning the sides of the swept channel with lighted buoys visible seaward. Thirty-four mines were swept at Anzio during the first week. Arnold S. Lott, *Most Dangerous Sea: A History of Mine Warfare, and an Account of U.S. Navy Mine Warfare Operations in World War II and Korea* (Annapolis, MD: U.S. Naval Institute, 1959), pp. 126, 129.

19. Morison, *Sicily-Salerno-Anzio*, p. 340.

20. These men, with their heavy backpacks and weapons, had been cramped aboard ship since sunset on January 20.

21. The craft were LCTs modified by the British as rocked launchers. We would pal again with *140* in Operation Dragoon in August. We called her our "security blanket."

22. The boats from *LST-197* and *-360* tied for the distinction of hitting the beach first.

23. Most of the DUKWs at Anzio were driven by black troops, working around the clock and winning compliments from a British general for "cheerfulness, cleanliness, and courage" and helping keep "the unending chain of 'ducks' running to and from the anchorage." Quoted in Morison, *Sicily-Salerno-Anzio*, p. 369.

24. Commander United States Naval Forces, Northwest African Waters [H.K. Hewitt] to Commander-in-Chief, United States Fleet, 23 June 1944, second endorsement to Floyd, "Secret Action Report."

25. Clayton D. Laurie, *Anzio 1944* (Washington: U.S. Army Center for Military History, CMH Publication 72–19, 2003), p. 8.

26. For more on Axis Sally, see chapters 8 and 11.

27. Barbara Brooks Tomblin, *With Utmost Spirit: Allied Naval Operations in the Mediterranean 1942–1945* (Lexington: University Press of Kentucky, 2004), p. 329; Rick Atkinson, *The Day of Battle: The War in Sicily and Italy, 1943–1944* (New York: Henry Holt, 2007), p. 368.

28. Atkinson, *Day of Battle*, p. 369.

29. Tomblin, *With Utmost Spirit*, pp. 330–332, 337.

30. As is lamented elsewhere, a Sicilian photo processor in Palermo ruined my film, and I salvaged only one grainy image — of the flotsam from an exploded Allied ship.

31. Lott, *Most Dangerous Sea*, p. 128.

32. For my relationship with this young sailor while we were patients in 118th Station Hospital, see chapter 7.

33. Ernie Pyle, *Brave Men* (New York: Henry Holt, 1944), p. 14.

34. Fred Sheehan, *Anzio: Epic of Bravery* (Norman: University of Oklahoma Press, 1994), p. 165n.

35. Atkinson, *Day of Battle*, p. 485; William Lusk

Allen, *Anzio, Edge of Disaster* (New York: Elsevier-Dutton, 1978), p. 71.

36. Tomblin, *With Utmost Spirit*, p. 334; Atkinson, *Day of Battle*, p. 370.

37. The heavy sea prevented my being transferred to a hospital ship, and *525* was fortunate to have been allowed to enter the harbor, where every minute was precious to ships delivering desperately needed personnel, ammunition, and provisions. LSTs, after unloading their cargo, often returned to Naples with about a hundred litter patients and a like number of ambulatory wounded. The one-way trip could be made in sixteen to twenty hours on a calm sea.

Chapter 7

1. Throughout six weeks of hospitalization, I repeatedly thought of the insignificance of my physical disability when compared with the agony of the soldiers in the beachhead. I am still reminded of that each time I read their accounts. For example, during the frightful two-day storm that led indirectly to my injury, PFC Paul Brown was put ashore at Anzio from an LST with the 45th Division's 179th Regiment. He penciled in his pocket notebook: "Had a rough ride last night. Many got sick. I had a bed on top of 2½ ton truck in lower deck.... They shot down three dive bombers. Had two raids.... Were unloaded in 1 hour 20 minutes. Good job. We are now bivouacked in open field just out of town. Enemy planes are regular." Then, as my pain was being eased by morphine aboard a warm ship a mile offshore, the soldier added, "Sleep [slept] in back of truck.... It rained and sleeted all night. My bed is on a stretcher. Had four air raids since yesterday.... They hit hospital ship [HMS *St. David*] 2 days ago. The rats!" http://members.aol.com/HizBeluved/WW2/Brown.htm. Thousands of other troops had the luxury of neither painkillers nor a stretcher for a bed.

2. *LST-327*, on the way from Cherbourg to Southampton the following August, was struck by what the crew assumed to be a mine. However, German naval records, opened after the war, proved that the explosion on the *327* came from a torpedo fired by Nazi submarine *U-92*. Despite the casualties, the ship remained afloat and returned to the States for repairs.

3. The only first-hand account of 118th Station Hospital that I have found is a newspaper interview with Lieutenant Mildred White Pusch of the Army Nurse Corps, who was stationed there. It was published in the October 10, 2004, issue of *Marco Magazine* of Fort Walton Beach, Florida, and appears in www.marconews.com/news/2004. Another document, http://history.amedd.army.mil/booksdocs/wwii/MedSvcs, gives an account of the several hospitals in Naples, and adds: "All hospitals in the Naples area faced problems of reconstruction and renovation. Even those sited in hospital buildings found a heritage of indescribable filth to be cleaned out before they could operate. Initial cleaning and minor remodeling were usually accomplished by hospital personnel; the Chemical Warfare Service was available for disinfecting the premises." The 118th had been operating only a little over three months when I was admitted, but I remember it as old but clean

and efficiently run. The 118th closed in Naples in May 1945, and its staff and equipment preceded me to Okinawa, where it retained its designation.

4. When a half century later I traced down Lowell Randall's papers and photographs at Bowling Green State University Library in Ohio, I was astounded to find a picture of him fitting a cast on a standing nude, a spitting image of me. It was negative number 33, labeled "Scene in cast room 118 S.H., APO 387 Italy, 1944." There was just one problem: Instead of covering "my" hands, Randall was applying a body cast. For a long time I was convinced that Randall had played a joke on me while I was under the influence of sodium pentothal — a sort of "Oops, wrong patient"— but physicians assured me that one so medicated could not stand, wide-awake, as "I" appeared to be in the photo. Eventually I was forced to conclude that the figure in the photo was simply a very handsome look-alike, the proof being a part of the fellow's anatomy that I could only envy.

5. Sheehan, *Anzio*, pp. 160–161. Of the 767 men in two battalions of Darby's Rangers who sought to capture Cisterna while I was in the hospital, only eight escaped death or capture. Atkinson, *Day of Battle*, p. 395.

6. Reading matter was always in short supply in combat areas. Cartoonist Bill Mauldin told of infantrymen at Anzio who were limited to reading and rereading the labels on K-rations. Mauldin, *Up Front* (New York: Henry Holt, 1944), p. 25.

7. For the sinking of *YMS-30* at Anzio on January 25, see chapter 6.

8. Coincidentally, *Hilary P. Jones* operated with us the following month at Anzio. After leaving *SC-525*, I again saw Eddie in January 1945 at the Mine Craft Training Center at Little Creek, Virginia, where he was anxiously awaiting his next assignment to sea. When I wished him good luck, he replied, "Don't worry about me pal. See that canteen over there? It's filled with beer. And it's not rationed. Don't worry about me pal."

9. For many men at war, mail call was their most important event. I have seen men weep from disappointment when the last letter was handed out, and I have seen tough men walk away with tears of thankfulness for a handful of mail. No doubt homefolks just as eagerly awaited mail, but Bill Mauldin explained why writing was not always easy for servicemen: "It's very hard to write interesting letters. About the only thing you ever talk about are what you are doing and where you are, and that's cut out by the censor." Mauldin, *Up Front*, p. 24.

10. Of course, we assumed, erroneously as it turned out, that the Germans had actually occupied the Abbey and were operating from within the sacred buildings.

11. Mark W. Clark, *Calculated Risk* (New York: Harper, 1950), pp. 292–294. The general's description of the episode is poorly written. A better account is found in Robert J. Buckley, Jr., *At Close Quarters: PT Boats in the United States Navy* (Washington: Naval History Division, 1962).

12. Unlike the 509th Parachute *Battalion*, the 504th was a parachute *regiment*, not a battalion — evidence of my ignorance of the Army's organizational pattern.

13. I had slept on the deck of a subchaser at Casablanca in March 1943. See chapter 4.

Chapter 8

1. Eddie Runof, our most interesting crew mate, was profiled in chapter 7.

2. Quoted in Tomblin, *With Utmost Spirit*, p. 348. Perhaps the best web address for the January 29 tragedies is http://artsweb.aut.ac.nz/hmsspartan/campaign, commemorating the activity associated with the sinking of HMS *Spartan*. Included is a photograph and log extract for *SC-1029*, which rescued many survivors of *Spartan*, then went to the assistance of *Alexander Martin*. *SC-1029*, like my *525*, was later damaged in the invasion of Southern France, and we were escorted together back to safety in August. See chapter 10. The role of *LCI-219* is also told in *Spartan*'s website. Gunner's mate Joseph W. Logan was commended for helping rescue ninety men from the oily waters.

3. "Window," in military parlance, was also called "chaff"; from a ship it looked like strings of tinfoil dropped from friendly planes. For more on the Hs-293, see Richard P. Hallion, "Bombs That Were Smart Before Their Time," *World War II* 22(5) (September 2007): 52–57.

4. Tomblin, *With Utmost Spirit*, p. 435.

5. At the end of the first week, seven Liberty ships and 20 LSTs had landed 68,886 Allied troops, 508 large guns, 237 tanks, and 27,250 tons of stores on the beaches and in the port of Anzio. The average trip between Naples and Anzio took sixteen to twenty hours. Morison, *Sicily-Salerno-Anzio*, p. 356; Jurgen Rohwer, *Chronology of the War at Sea 1939–1945* (Annapolis, MD: Naval Institute, 1972, 3rd rev. ed., 2005).

6. *LCI-219* compiled an illustrious record in the Mediterranean, including landing troops in four invasions and retrieving hundreds of survivors of various ships. Less than five months later during the Normandy invasion, on June 11, a German bomb broke her into two pieces, killing several members of the crew who had been generous to my shipmates after our vessels collided at Anzio.

7. USS *Frederick C. Davis* joined us again in August and provided similar service in the invasion of Southern France. After returning to New York for repairs, she was assigned to antisubmarine duty in the western Atlantic. On April 24, 1945, just two weeks before the Nazis surrendered, she was torpedoed in an encounter with German submarine *U-546*; she sank with the loss of more than a hundred men.

8. *LST-348*, with which we had worked in the Salerno simulations, was a "stores ship" sent to Anzio as a "mother hen for the covey of thirsty, hungry chicks that averaged twenty a day." *SC-525* was one of those hungry chicks. On January 25 in rough seas a tug had collided and punched a hole in the landing craft, and on January 27 she was the target of near-miss bombs. She was patched up, but on February 20, during another run from Nisida to Anzio, she was hit by two torpedoes from German submarine *U-410*. Most of the crew was saved by *LCI-219*, *LCI-195*, and *PC-627*, but nine men died and fifteen more were missing. Tomblin, *With Utmost Spirit*, pp. 353–354. That same day, February 20, back off Anzio, HMS *LST-305* was sunk by German *U-230*. A graphic description of the death throes of *LST-*

348 is found in D'Este, *Fatal Decision*, pp. 314–315. *LCI-219*'s engineering officer, William F. Becker, provided another graphic account of the tragedy at http://www.ibiblio.org/hyperwar/USN/ships/logs/LCIL/lcil219-Becker.html.

9. Like *Alexander Martin*, *Samuel Ashe* was a Liberty ship named for a North Carolina revolutionary leader.

10. *Penelope* was the second ship to be sunk in connection with the Anzio invasion by the skipper of *U-410*, 25-year-old Horst-Arno Fenski; the other was *LST-348*. For more of Fenski's exploits, see chapter 9.

11. For more on Axis Sally, see chapters 6 and 11.

12. Robert H. Adleman and George Walton, *Rome Fell Today* (Boston: Little, Brown, 1968), p. 168.

13. Pyle, *Brave Men*, p. 159.

14. Rick Atkinson, *An Army at Dawn* (New York: Henry Holt, 2002), pp. 428–429.

15. For the full text, see photograph of the flier in this chapter.

16. John S.D. Eisenhower, *They Fought at Anzio* (Columbia: University of Missouri Press, 2007), p. 204; D'Este, *Fatal Decision*, p. 328; Morison, *Sicily-Salerno-Anzio*, p. 367.

Chapter 9

1. "Swinging ship" refers to the necessity of compensating for compass deviations. The ship itself contains ferrous materials affecting the magnetic compass, so to compensate for the resulting variation, the ship is taken to sea, lined up with markers indicating north, south, east, and west, and "swung" (that is, it is pivoted so the bow points to each of the markers to ascertain the deviation).

2. Our tow sometimes reminded me of the CSS *Shenandoah*, under the command of North Carolinian James Iredell Waddell, which at the end of the Civil War in the Bering Sea captured dozens of Yankee whalers and strung them out for a mile off its stern.

3. www.warwingsart.com/12thairforce/vesuvius/htm.

4. That eerie experience is described in chapter 11.

5. One soldier described the sound as like an "outhouse going end-over-end with the door open and paper flapping." Quoted in Atkinson, *Day of Battle*, p. 414.

6. "Anzio Annie" and "Anzio Express" actually played minor roles at Anzio. The Germans used other railroad guns, including a 210-millimeter weapon, hidden in a tunnel near the Pope's summer palace at Castel Gandolfo, that inflicted much more damage. The best summary on the giant guns is found in D'Este, *Fatal Decision*, pp. 454–457.

7. An example of "making a mountain out of a molehill" is found in the climb of Lieutenant (junior grade) Joseph Walker Barr in Democratic Party ranks after the war. The commanding officer of *PC-651*, which shared in the sinking of a little *Neger*, later served as a congressman from Indiana and in several appointive positions, including a single month (December 21, 1968, to January 20, 1969) as Secretary of the Treasury at the end of President Lyndon Johnson's administration. By

then Barr's official biography credited him with "sinking submarine off Anzio Beach." Readers no doubt assumed that the "submarine" was one of the dreaded U-boats of the German Navy.

8. An intact Neger is pictured in Steven J. Zaloga, *Anzio 1944* (Oxford, UK: Osprey, 2005), p. 76.

9. Later in the war the new Liberty ships were strengthened, modified, and reclassified as Victory ships. In all, 243 Liberty and Liberty-class ships were built in Wilmington, North Carolina, between 1942 and 1946. Ralph Scott, *The Wilmington Shipyard: Welding a Fleet for Victory in World War II* (Charleston, SC: History, 2007).

10. E.V. Walls, "PC 1235 in Action," *PCSA Newsletter* 58 (October–December 2002): 9–10.

11. For more on the sinking of the famed cruiser nicknamed "Pepperpot," see chapter 8.

12. *Richard Henderson* was named for a North Carolinian. *LST-348* had been like a mother hen to *Cinq-Deux-Cinq* at Anzio. See chapter 8, note 8.

13. *Menges* was patched up and upon reaching New York had its mangled stern cut off and replaced by the stern of USS *Holder* (DE-401), which in another encounter had been hit midship, leaving its aft portion in good shape.

14. That excursion is discussed in chapter 11.

15. War correspondent Ernie Pyle, embedded with the troops, wrote, "On the beachhead every inch of our territory was under German artillery fire. There was no rear area that was secure.... They could reach us with their 88s, and they used everything from that on up." Pyle, *Brave Men*, p. 159.

16. Audie Murphy, *To Hell and Back* (New York: Henry Holt, 1949), p. 125.

17. William B. Breuer, *Agony at Anzio* (London: R. Hale, 1989), p. 239.

18. See Darrell L. Jackson, "Sinking of the USS Swerve (AM-121)," *Silent Defenders* 25(1) (Spring 2008): 14–17.

19. Morison, *Sicily-Salerno-Anzio*, p. 380; Tomblin, *With Utmost Spirit*, p. 483.

20. Floyd, "Secret Action Report," p. 18.

21. Perhaps that disappointment explains why in a later career I took such delight in boasting that I was the only yeoman second class to lord it over a retired naval officer. Rear Admiral Alex M. Patterson, USN Retired, was for twelve years my assistant before he succeeded me as state archivist of North Carolina.

22. Winston Churchill, *Closing the Ring* (Boston: Houghton Mifflin, 1951), p. 488.

23. Quoted in Lowry, "The Naval Side," p. 31.

24. Quoted in Tomblin, *With Utmost Spirit*, p. 378.

25. See chapter 10 for the sinking of *YMS-21* at Southern France on September 1.

26. This sad experience is discussed in chapter 11.

Chapter 10

1. The harrowing story of the destruction of *YMS-24* is given later in this chapter.

2. Limpets are explosives that could be attached to the hull of a ship by enemy swimmers.

3. Mondello, our favorite swimming spot in the Mediterranean, is discussed in chapter 11.

4. AA=anti-aircraft; HEI=high explosive incendiary; HET=high explosive detonating.

5. Long after the war, the name of the little town became known worldwide for the distinctive earthenware produced in Vietri, and the American distribution center was established at Hillsborough, North Carolina, near my home. Small world.

6. Despite his attitude, Churchill watched the invasion from HMS *Kimberly*, waving his ever-present cigar and holding his V-for-Victory sign. The play on names was revealing, for Operation Overlord (the Normandy invasion) had originally been called Operation Hammer, linking the northern and southern front as "Hammer" and "Anvil." The code name "Neptune" was also used occasionally in connection with the Normandy action

7. As at Anzio, the number of vessels participating in the D-Day landings in Southern France varies with the definition of "ship," but the Royal Navy counted 612 American and 285 British, French, and other Allied vessels, making a total of 897, that number exclusive of "smaller" craft. www.naval-history.net/WW2Campaigns/Amphibious2.htm. Alan F. Wilt, in *The French Riviera Campaign of August 1944* (Carbondale: Southern Illinois University Press, 1981), p. 70, counted 880 ships and "some 1,370 smaller vessels (mostly landing craft)." General Jacob L. Devers wrote that during Operation Dragoon 151,019 men and 19,371 vehicles, guns, and tanks were brought to Southern France aboard 479 cargo ships the size of an LCI and larger, and that at least 1,370 landing and assault craft were launched. Jacob L. Devers, "Operation Dragoon: The Invasion of Southern France," *Military Affairs* 10 (Summer 1946): 27. The beaches on which the landings were scheduled were usually called collectively "Cote d'Azur"; the area from Cannes eastward was more generally called "Riviera."

8. Ten days before the landings, Admiral Lewis assumed command after the previously designated commander, Rear Admiral Don R. Moon, committed suicide. Morrison, *Sicily-Salerno-Anzio*, pp. 237, 242.

9. "Action Report," Serial 0123, letter from Commander Task Force Eighty-Five (Delta Force) [B.J. Rodgers] to Commander-in-Chief, United States Fleet, 25 August 1944, in National Archives, Washington, D.C. (Herinafter cited as Rodgers, "Action Report.") Supporting Delta Force were the American battleships *Texas* and *Nevada*; cruiser *Philadelphia*; destroyers *Ellyson*, *Rodman*, *Emmons*, *Forrest*, *Fitch*, *Hambleton*, *Macomb*, and *Hobson*; and French cruisers *La Fantasque*, *Le Terrible*, *Le Malin*, *Georges Leygues*, and *Montcalm*. Utility and firefighting ships were fleet tugs *Narragansett*, *Pinto*, HMS *Aspirant*, HMS *Athlete*, HMS *Charon*, and an ATA and YTL. A squadron of ten American and British minesweepers and dan layers swept close to the shore prior to the actual landings.

10. Morison, *Sicily-Salerno-Anzio*, p. 340.

11. Near Red Beach was located the "Plage des Elephants," named for Babar, an elephant created in the works of Belgian illustrator, Jean de Brunhoff, who once lived nearby.

12. One of these diversionary forces, nicknamed "Rosie," was later highly publicized because of the name

of its leader, Lieutenant Commander Douglas E. Fairbanks, Jr., USNR. The commandos landed between Cap Roux and Cannes at 0140 and sought to cut the main road to prevent German reinforcements from attacking American troops scheduled to land at 0800. The men encountered a minefield, the explosions tipped off the Germans, and, when the Americans sought to retreat to their vessels, they were accidentally machine-gunned by two friendly planes. Forced to swim back to shore, the Americans were taken prisoner by the surprised Germans. Fortunately, the commandos were liberated the next day by the advancing Free French forces attached to the 36th Division. Morison, *Sicily-Salerno-Anzio*, p. 250.

13. Among the parachute infantry battalions dropped was the 509th, some of whose members assisted the French underground in taking control of the resort city of St. Tropez. I suspected that some of my old hospital buddies were among them.

14. Several of those zombies went awry, and one of them turned and blew up near *SC-1029*, killing two men and damaging the vessel.

15. Afterward we learned that Allied intelligence had erred in reporting that the Bay of Bougnon was mined; in fact, the mines were located just to the east in the Gulf of Frejus, where they claimed several victims during the Camel Force landings. Lott, *Most Dangerous Sea*, p. 198. At least six subchasers were engaged in minesweeping in Operation Dragoon, including *SC-770* of Anzio fame.

16. Admiral Rodgers's "Action Report" gave the landing time of the third wave as 0816. Even if he was correct, our wave arrived four minutes before its due time under the master plan. The troops that landed at La Nartelle encountered a ten-foot anti-tank wall six feet thick, and a hole had to be blasted through it before the first tanks of the 157th Regiment could advance from the shore. Jacques Robichon, *The Second D-Day* (New York: Walker, 1969), p. 179.

17. *Hambleton* (DD-455), like many ships with which we served in the Mediterranean, had an interesting history. During Operation Torch off Fedhala, she was torpedoed, but Seabees in Casablanca cut out a 40-foot midship section, pieced her bow and stern together, and sent her to Boston for a more permanent repair in time for participation in the Normandy invasion. She was converted to a high-speed minesweeper (DM-20) and sent to the Pacific, participating in the invasion of Okinawa, where she was damaged by a kamikaze but survived to operate in the East China Sea. She then helped sweep Tokyo Bay for the ceremonies associated with the surrender of Japan.

18. American soldiers discovered a number of "Quaker Guns" — wood logs made to appear from the air as gun barrels.

19. My incredibly bad photographic luck continued. Under censorship, I was not permitted to mail back to the States the film exposed during the invasion, so I unwisely took another chance on having my film developed in Palermo. Again, the Sicilian camera shop scratched the emulsion badly.

20. Apparently, that was one of the three unsuccessful glide-bomb attacks directed toward the destroyer *Charles F. Hughes*. Lott, *Most Dangerous Sea*, p. 487.

21. Rodgers, "Action Report," p. 7. During the first ten days, Delta Force only lost one man (member of the 1040th Construction Battalion, killed in a bombing on D+1). Ibid., p. 14. In the first nine days of Dragoon, Allied convoys unloaded 172,569 men and 98,328 tons of supplies. Tomblin, *With Utmost Spirit*, p. 484.

22. Tomblin, *With Utmost Spirit*, p. 410, concluded that the Delta Force landings constituted "one of the most beautifully executed amphibious landings of the war."

23. John R. Cox, Jr., was born April 14, 1913 in Cleveland, Ohio. He was a Phi Beta Kappa graduate of what now is Case Western Reserve University, where he took up acting. In Hollywood he adopted the name John Howard. His first memorable role was in *Lost Horizon* (1937). During the next two years he starred in several of the popular Bulldog Drummond series. He starred with Katharine Hepburn in *The Philadelphia Story* (1940). Following his decorated Naval Reserve service, Cox played minor roles but never regained his prewar prestige in Hollywood. He appeared occasionally on Broadway and television but ended his career a teacher of English in a private high school. He died in 1995 of heart trouble. A star on the Hollywood Walk of Fame and his decorations for bravery are his legacy.

24. Lott, *Most Dangerous Sea*, p. 202.

25. Among other ships damaged in a variety of mishaps during the Dragoon operation were *LCI-588*, *LCI-590*, *LST-391*, *LST-659*, *PT-555*, *SC-535*, *ML-559*, *ML-562*, *Livermore* (DD-429), *Forrest* (DD-461), *MacKenzie* (DD-614), *Seer* (AM-112), *Steady* (AM-118), and the freighter *Allen A. Michelson*.

26. This was not the only time *Catoctin*, flagship of the Eighth Fleet during Operation Dragoon, welcomed aboard special guests. A month before, she had been visited in Naples by King George VI of Great Britain, and a month later she hosted General Charles DeGaulle as he greeted the return of the French fleet to Toulon. In February 1945, escorted by *Incredible* and *Implicit*, she served as headquarters ship for the Yalta Conference in Russia and provided President Franklin D. Roosevelt and Fleet Admiral W. D. Leahy with beds for one night. Finally, in November 1945 in Tako, North China, she served as headquarters for negotiations between the Chinese Nationalists and the Communists. *Catoctin* was decommissioned the next year and later was transferred to the Maritime Authority.

27. That excursion is described in chapter 11.

28. *SC-1029* had distinguished herself at Anzio when on January 29 she rescued many men from the sinking HMS *Spartan*, then picked up more survivors from the merchant ship *Alexander Martin*. http://artsweb.aut.ac.nz/hmsspartan/campaign. See also "School Will Give Diploma to Man Killed in WWII," *Rutland Herald* [Vermont], March 21, 2008. *YMS-43* likewise performed valiantly at Anzio when on January 26 she rescued survivors from *LST-422* and *LCI-32*. The ship's log reported, "Heavy seas and high winds made it very difficult maneuvering ship along side the unfortunates. Most men were either too cold or too nearly drowned to help themselves.... Using the boat hook was the best method except many of the life belts tore under the strain. Survivors were drowning all around us while we

were picking up some of their shipmates." http://www.dvrbscom/history-mil/LST-422.htm.

29. The origin of the name "Jeep" is disputed. One theory is that it came from the abbreviation "GP" (general purpose vehicle) Another is that the name was suggested by the Popeye "Thimble Theater" comic strip's little animated character, Eugene the Jeep, who could scoot around with impunity. A good history of the versatile Jeep is Ronald H. Bailey, "The Incredible Jeep," *World War II* 24(3) (September 2009): 26–35.

30. Tomblin, *With Utmost Spirit,* pp. 448–449. The AMs fought back with their three-inch cannon, which must have sounded like pea shooters to the gunners on the destroyers.

31. Lott, *Most Dangerous Sea,* pp. 205–206. Commander Lott overlooked the fact that one of the vessels, my *SC-525,* was a veteran of previous experiences at Anzio. Still, we appreciated the rare published mention in print of *Cinq-Deux-Cinq.*

32. We had not returned to the front by August 26, but at the end of D+10, Delta Force alone had landed more than 92,000 personnel, 15,000 vehicles, and 49,000 tons of stores. In addition, 3,473 Allied casualties and 3,620 enemy prisoners had been evacuated. For the entire Operation Dragoon through September 18 (when the beaches were closed) 380,000 troops, 69,312 vehicles, 306,000 tons of cargo and 17,848 tons of gasoline had passed over the beaches. Morison, *Two-Ocean War,* p. 420.

33. See earlier in this chapter.

34. Tomblin, *With Utmost Spirit,* p. 463.

Chapter 11

1. My most memorable religious experience overseas occurred on the lawns of Palermo's Villa Igeia at Easter. The imposing palace with terraced gardens of palms and jasmines faced the harbor, almost in the shadow of Mt. Pellegrino with its hair-pin roads and the sanctuary to Saint Rosalie, the patron of Palermo. After the war the villa was converted into the luxurious Grand Hotel Igeia.

2. See chapter 14.

3. "U.S. Pays Up," *Time* (October 23, 1944). Note: "lira" is singular; "lire" is plural.

4. The letter, along with a photograph of Lieutenant Waldron and me at Mondello, was republished in Mary Best, *North Carolina's Shining Hour: Images and Voices from World War II* (Greensboro, NC: Our State, 2005), p. 75.

5. For example, the top five songs for the week of June 10, 1944, were "Long Ago and Far Away," "I'll Be Seeing You," "I'll Get By," "San Fernando Valley," and "Goodnight, Wherever You Are."

6. See also chapters 6 and 8. After the war, Zucca was convicted by an Italian court on collaboration charges and served nearly a year in prison. Whitlock, *The Rock of Anzio,* pp. 264–265. Gillers, born Mildred Elizabeth Sisk in Portland, Maine, gave up her teaching job in Germany at the outbreak of the war and became an effective propagandist for the Nazis, parroting the line, "a Jewish war but a Gentile's fight." With a sultry voice and calling herself "Midge at the Mike," she interspersed boasts of German victories with romantic music, including tunes by "Bruno and the Swinging Tigers," later revealed to be American and British musicians duped in POW camps. After the war, Gillers was brought to the United States and convicted of treason, for which she served twelve years in prison. See also Richard Lucas, "With a Sweet Kiss from Sally," *World War II* 24(3) (January–February 2010): 48–53.

7. *Stars and Stripes* (Mediterranean edition) 1(80) (February 17, 1944): 2.

8. War Department Publication T M 30–303 (Washington: Government Printing Office, June 2, 1943).

9. Two-sided mimeographed sheet titled "Cathedral at Monreale Sicily" prepared for American Red Cross Sightseeing Tours for Sicily, 1943–44.

10. John Lloyd Stephens, *Incidents of Travel in Egypt, Arabia Petrea, and the Holy Land* (Victor Wolfgang Von Hagen, ed.) (Norman: University of Oklahoma Press, 1970), p. 204.

11. John Ross Browne, *Yusef: Or the Journey of the Frangi: A Crusade in the East* (New York: Harper and Brothers, 1853), p. 25.

12. See Bob Drier, "The Well-Dressed Dead," *Archaeology* 56(3) (May/June 2003): 32–35; and mimeographed two-sided sheet titled "The Catacombe of the Cappuccini Friars," handed out to American Red Cross Sightseeing Tours Sicily, 1943–44. For recent X-ray tests on the body of Rosalia Lombardo and a new essay on the catacombs, see A.A. Gill, "Where the Dead Don't Sleep," *National Geographic* 215(2) (February 2009).

13. Best, *North Carolina's Shining Hour,* cover.

14. Norman Lewis, *Naples '44* (New York: Pantheon, 1978), pp. 200–204.

15. Atkinson, *Day of Battle,* p. 446.

16. My persistent praise for the war front services of the Red Cross was expressed again in a letter dated February 26, 1945, to Erwin D. Stephens, editor of the *Caswell Messenger:* "Look at Bizerte after the bloody battles of Tunisian campaign; or better still, Civitavecchia, whose capture came after days of pounding from the captors of Rome. In both of these towns, hardly a building stood after the battles, not a live person remaining in the rubble. Yet, within a matter of days, a small red and white sign went up on the front of four walls reading 'American Red Cross Servicemen's Club.' To the thousands upon thousands of soldiers and sailors who had come up to make what use they could of the newly captured cities, this was the only place that showed life; not only life, but a couple of real, genuine American girls, a hot doughnut, a cup of coffee, a few battered tables that held checkerboards, chess sets, and cards. And as soon as practicable, a movie screen is tacked up and the show is on. To a weary fellow who hasn't seen anything to remind him of home in many months, this means more than anyone can put into words."

17. *Time,* April 3, 1944. At the time, the 1944 eruption was said to have been the most damaging since 1872, but later studies indicated that an early twentieth-century eruption may have caused more damage.

18. Amedeo Maiuri, *A Companion to the Visit of Pompeii* (Naples: Tipi Artigianelli, 1944).

19. In the six decades since the war, archaeologists have conducted extensive investigations and partial excavations at the site, which promise to yield significant information on Roman history.

20. More recently, Fort Sangallo has been renovated, and a portion of it is used for an art museum.

21. A fire in 1978 caused heavy damage to the chateau, but more recently the building was registered as a historic site and in 2002 plans were laid for its restoration.

22. See chapter 10.

23. For the transfer of *SC-525* to the French Navy, see chapter 12.

Chapter 12

1. Inexplicably, however, when I submitted the form to the supply officer at Lido Beach upon my return to the States, a charge of $16.50 was placed against my pay account, a fact unknown to me until December, by which time I was aboard my new ship, USS *Speed*. I took this renege as a personal affront, and my blood boiled as I challenged the government in a mission that was successfully accomplished only three years later. Since this was the first of my many encounters with governmental bureaucracy during the next half century, the victorious effort merits recounting here. Still a sonarman third class, I went straight to my new captain, Lieutenant Commander Raymond C. Dryer, who readily saw the injustice being imposed upon me (and, presumably, upon all of my former shipmates). I prepared and typed, and the skipper endorsed, a letter dated February 10, 1945, to the Bureau of Naval Personnel under the subject "Claim for Reimbursement for Personal Property Turned Over to the French Enlisted Personnel." Careful to follow strict protocol, I referenced four documents, each bearing upon the case, particularly one from ABATU, Lido Beach, which stated that Public Law 176 of the 78th Congress could not be construed to cover payment for personal property except in "extreme emergency" and that "this case" could not be considered such an emergency. In polite language, I responded that the gear was turned over to the French by direct orders of Commander Escort Sweeper Group and that, inasmuch as my Navy oath forbade me to defy an order from a superior, "I should not be held personally responsible for the cost of this gear." All I asked for was credit in the amount of $16.50 to cover the loss which had been charged against my pay account. A response from the claims officer in the Bureau of Naval Personnel, dated February 23, asked that I submit my claim to the Bureau of Supplies and Accounts for payment from the Naval Emergency Fund. On March 2, I forwarded a copy of my original letter, along with that of the claims officer and my captain's endorsement recommending approval, to the BSA. I waited and waited for a response. Finally, on May 25, I wrote again, asking that I be informed as to the action taken on the previous request. Two months later the bureau chief finally replied, instructing me to submit S&A Form 378, "Claim for Reimbursement in Kind for Loss of Items of Clothing and Small Stores." By then *Speed* was at Okinawa dodging Japanese planes, riding out typhoons, and preparing for the invasion of Japan; consequently, it was not until August 27 that I was able to itemize the blanket at $7.50 and the mattress at $9, the exact charge made against my account, and submit the form through Commander Dryer. Nothing more was heard until August 8, 1948 — nearly *three years later*, when I received, with not a word of explanation, a check for $16.50. I felt vindicated. I simply was not going to take lying down such a miscarriage of justice. I carefully preserved the correspondence to prove to myself that indeed "no prius vincor quam desistam" (I am never defeated until I quit). Meanwhile, Alnav 278–45 decreed that henceforth the Navy would provide mattresses and that sailors would no longer be required to tote their bedding. See "No More Lugging of Mattresses and Hammocks," *PCSA Newsletter* 59 (January–March 2003): 8. Was the timing of the new policy —1945 — purely coincidental? I wondered, perhaps egotistically, if the persistence of an affronted sonarman third class might have come to the attention of the chief of the Bureau of Naval Personnel and influenced this radical repeal of a century-old tradition.

2. Keys was a professor at the University of Minnesota; he died at age 100 in 2004. *News & Observer* (Raleigh, NC.), November 24, 2004. See also Stephen Budiansky, "The Man Behind the Incredible, Nearly Inedible K Ration," *World War II* 24(1) (May 2009): 21.

3. The K-Ration was just one of several special-purpose rations (or supplements to other rations) introduced to the armed forces before and during the war. The D-Ration was essentially a 600-calorie, 4-ounce dark bar, made with chocolate, sugar, dry milk, cacao fat, oat flour, and flavoring. Sometimes the bar was halved and used as a supplement to other rations. Perhaps most familiar to — and least-favorite of— front-line soldiers was the three-meal (breakfast, lunch, dinner) C-Ration which, like the K-Ration, varied in contents but often contained biscuits, dried meat, compressed cereal, candy-coated peanuts or raisins, cocoa or coffee powder, sugar, flavored juice powder, hard candies, jam, and caramel. Cigarettes, book matches, water-purification tablets, chewing gum, granulated salt, salt tablets, toilet paper, can opener, and wood spoons were often included either with the ration or in supplemental packets. The rations were designed to provide nutrition to military personnel only in circumstances when normal meal service was unavailable. See Franz A. Koehler, *Army Operational Rations: Historical Background* (Washington: Office of Quartermaster General, 1958).

4. The Quonset hut, named for its initial place of manufacture (Quonset Point, Rhode Island), was a successor to the Nissen hut, a World War I British innovation. Made of lightweight corrugated steel, the half-oval building, with semicircular cross section, was prefabricated for shipment and later bolted together on site. The interior was open, allowing various configurations and uses. Several sizes of huts were manufactured; ours at Arzeu were about 40 by 100 feet. See Julie Decker and Chris Chei, *Quonset Huts: Metal Living for a Modern Age* (New York: Princeton Architectural, 2005).

5. Theodore R. Treadwell, *Splinter Fleet: The*

Wooden Subchasers of World War II (Annapolis, MD: Naval Institute, 2000), p. 233. The disposition of scores of other submarine chasers is documented by Commander Treadwell on pp. 233–235.

6. Theodore R. Treadwell, Danbury, CT, to H.G. Jones, June 5, 2004. Author's personal file.

7. The ship's namesake, General Montgomery Cunningham Meigs, the Union Army's quartermaster general, was largely responsible for the federal government's seizure of Arlington, the estate of the wife of Confederate General Robert E. Lee, and its conversion into Arlington National Cemetery. At the end of the war, the big ship was decommissioned and transferred to the American President Lines as a spruced-up passenger ship in the Pacific. However, during the Korean War, she was pressed back into military service until placed in the reserve fleet. On September 1, 1972, while *Meigs* was being towed from Olympia to San Francisco, wind and high seas caused the towline to break, and the liner went adrift; she struck a rocky ledge and broke apart near Cape Flattery, Washington. See Roland W. Charles, *Troopships of World War II* (Washington: Army Transportation Association, 1947), p. 106; Robert M. Poole, "The Battle of Arlington," *Smithsonian* 40(8) (November 2009): 50–57; *History: The History Channel Magazine* 1(3) (May–June 2008): 8; and www.nwc.navy.mil/usnhdb/ShipLookup.asp?Ship.

8. Uncle Kester was young enough for his nephews and cousins to call him by his first name.

9. The "front room" was built of mud-chinked logs covered by unpainted planks. My unheated room was directly above, reached by a narrow stairway under which Mamma stored her canned vegetables and fruits.

10. Having been overseas so long, I was surprised by the stringency and complexity of the government's domestic rationing regulations, which were altered by the Office of Price Administration with each of the four consecutive ration books issued during the war. War Ration Book Four was in use during my furlough. Originally, it contained 384 tiny coupons of different colors, letters, numbers, and icons, each keyed to strict instructions concerning use for commodities such as meat, sugar, coffee, butter, fats, oil, canned goods, alcohol, shoes, and clothing. Coupons were even required for restaurant meals. Most closely regulated was the use of rubber; to qualify for the normal allowance of three gallons of gasoline per week (one gallon requiring one stamp bearing the vehicle's license number), the driver certified that the automobile tires had been inspected for proper inflation every forty-five days. Ironically, the rationing of rubber rings and metal tops for glass jars contravened the government's encouragement of canning from "victory gardens." Despite the law, some ration coupons found their way onto the "black market," but more often they were traded between holders, an illegal (but seldom prosecuted) practice called the "gray market." To guard against fraud, only the merchant was authorized to remove the appropriate stamps from a ration book. No wonder, then, that my father's book number 316063EK was in virtual tatters.

11. That libel in my diary was quoted in chapter 1.

12. I did not live near Pelham. The farm on which I lived was located nearer the county seat, Yanceyville,

whose rural route ran within a mile of my house, even though our mail was received on Pelham's rural route. In fact, the carrier, Hester Fowlkes (not a close relative) turned his car around in our front yard, so our mailbox was affixed to an oak tree in the driveway.

13. I took some delight in repeating accusations made during the 1928 presidential campaign — that if Al Smith had been elected to the White House, the Lincoln Bedroom would have been permanently reserved for the Pope.

14. Sir Richard Francis Burton, trans., *The Kasidah [of Haji Abdu El-Yezdi]* (Girard, KS: Haldeman-Julius Company, 1880), p. 21.

15. "Four Die in Two Weekend Boating Accidents," www.rodnreel.com.news, January 7, 2002.

Chapter 13

1. For a profile of Runof, both my shipmate and hospital-mate, see chapter 7.

2. The inveterate packrat that I was, I preserved many programs, church bulletins, and even ticket stubs of events that I attended.

3. Oropesa gear is discussed in chapter 15.

4. The booklet was written by Evelyn Moore and Dorothy Jurney and was published by United Women's Service Organizations in cooperation with United Service Organizations in the Panama Canal Department, 1943. The Pacific exit from the canal was east of the starting point only if a line were drawn directly south from the Caribbean entrance. Other "facts" in the pamphlet have since become outdated with the modernization of the canal. In 1945 we could not have imagined that ownership of the canal would be ceded to the corrupt government of the Republic of Panama during Jimmy Carter's presidency.

Chapter 14

1. A pitometer is a pitot tube extending beneath the keel to measure speed and distance.

2. The San Francisco–Oakland Bay Bridge, opened for traffic only nine years previously, was officially named but seldom called the "James 'Sunny Jim' Ralph Bridge." Consisting of west and east spans, the bridge, including the island crossing, was 8.4 miles long. The clearance below the west span was 220 feet.

3. During my first six months on *Speed*, in addition to Kelly, Perry, and me, we had at least seven other sonarmen — Alfred R. Bishop Lawrence F. Fournier, Owen Winston Lile, Clarence M. Lickfield, William M. Reid, Clinton S. Roberts, and Myles E. Spainhower. Bishop, Fournier, Lickfield, and Reid were transferred to other stations during that time.

4. The wish came true the next January on our return from Japan; see chapter 18. However, on another visit sixty years later to speak at an international congress on the humanities, I was dismayed to find the Royal Hawaiian hidden behind a new high-rise Sheraton Hotel that looked like any of scores of Sheratons in the world. The image of 1945 was gone.

Chapter 15

1. Although our Auk-class AMs were actually 221 feet 3 inches long, we called them "Two-Twenties" to emphasize our size superiority over the Admirable-class AMs (like *Implicit*) that measured only 184 feet 6 inches and were called "One-Eighties."

2. Eniwetok became the site of more than forty nuclear tests from 1948 to 1958, including the first hydrogen bomb test, code-named Ivy Mike, in 1952.

3. As late as the following December, three Marines were ambushed and killed by Japanese hold-outs. One Jap sergeant survived in a remote cave for twenty-seven years before surrendering.

4. Shortly before we arrived on July 12, Nakagusuku Wan (which included the smaller Yanabaru Wan) had been renamed by the Americans in memory of Lieutenant General Simon B. Buckner, who was killed only a few days before the island fell. Our official orders used the new designation, but the charts still carried Japanese place names.

5. Samuel Eliot Morison, *History of United States Naval Operations in World War II*, vol. 14, *Victory in the Pacific* (Edison, NJ: Castle, 2001), p. 282 and passim; and Morison, *Two-Ocean War*, p. 556 and passim. Later works give differing figures of casualties. See, for example, Bill Sloan, *The Ultimate Battle: Okinawa 1945 — The Last Epic Struggle of World War II* (New York: Simon and Schuster, 2007); and "The Last Big One," *U.S. News & World Report* 118(13) (April 3, 1995): 12.

6. Morrison, *Two-Ocean War*, p. 556.

7. The loss of this friend was described in chapter 6.

8. The sinking of these two vessels was described in chapter 10.

9. In all, 481 YMSs were constructed by thirty-three shipyards in the United States. Eighty more were made for Britain, ten percent of them by the Barbour Boat Works in New Bern, North Carolina. Interestingly, *YMS-21*, sunk by a mine off Southern France, was salvaged, repaired, and transferred to Thailand in 1956 as *Ta Dindeng*. John Dixon Davis, *Wooden Dreadnaughts: The Biography of YMS 183* (Bloomington, IN: Authorhouse, 2004), pp. 358–361; William N. Still, Jr., "Wooden Ship Construction in North Carolina in World War II," *North Carolina Historical Review* 77 (January 2000): 43–44.

10. There are almost as many types of underwater mines as there are diabolical minds devising them, and each type varies in its firing and defusing mechanism. See, as examples, Appendix I in Maurice Griffiths, *The Hidden Menace* (Greenwich, UK: Conway Maritime, 1981), pp. 149–153; also Peter Elliott, *Allied Minesweeping in World War 2* (Annapolis, MD: Naval Institute, 1979), passim. "A mine can neither be seen nor heard; leaves no wake, makes no noise, and is made with self-defense mechanisms which make them difficult to detect and even more difficult to destroy." "The YMS," *Silent Defenders* 25(1) (Spring 2008): 30. Illustrations of various mines may be found in Max Gadney, "An Undersea Killer Evolves," *World War II* 23(6) (February–March 2009): 64–65; and "Sweeping Up Sudden Death," *Popular Mechanics* (January 1946): 28–34.

11. Old salts warned new recruits that "degoosing" could turn a virile man into a eunuch.

12. Another type of mine, the limpet, could be attached to the hull of a ship by a swimmer. The minesweeper had no natural defense against these hand-carried explosives, so in Japanese ports a "limpet watch" was often posted at night.

13. We also were charged with removing, when appropriate, mines sown by our own military forces. At the end of World War II, for example, American ships spent months sweeping from Japan's Bungo Suido mines that had been laid by our own submarines and airplanes. See chapter 16.

14. The intricacies of minesweeping explained why it was the Navy's second-most hazardous occupation (after submarine duty) in World War II. Of the forty-nine minecraft lost during the war twenty-four struck mines, ten were sunk by enemy aircraft, four by enemy gunfire, and one by submarine. Forty-three other U.S. Navy ships, mostly landing craft, were sunk by mines; so were six Army or Coast Guard vessels. More than a hundred American merchant ships were sunk or damaged by mines; twenty-seven Allied ships were sunk or damaged in United States defensive minefields; and eleven Allied ships were sunk or damaged by enemy mines laid in American waters. Lott, *Most Dangerous Sea*, pp. 288–295. Fifteen percent of naval casualties during Operation Iceberg (Okinawa) alone were associated with minesweeping. Morison, *Two-Ocean War*, p. 117.

15. *Southard*, which had already survived two kamikaze attacks, was grounded during a typhoon the following month.

16. Lott, *Most Dangerous Sea*, p. 246.

17. Actually, these were meager pickings; see the story of Bungo Suido below, chapter 16.

18. Lott, *Most Dangerous Sea*, p. 246.

19. *Nevada* had been hit by a kamikaze in March and by a shell in April; men were killed and wounded in both attacks; yet her band played on, providing inspiration for the remainder of the fleet. Morison, *Victory in the Pacific*, p. 180. The previous year during the invasion of Southern France, I was aboard *SC-525* sailing within the shadow of the ancient battleship.

20. The log's identity for two ships may have been in error, for neither *Titania* (AKA-13) nor *Tarazed* (AF-13) appears to have been at Okinawa at that time.

21. Ferebee had preceded me as a student at Lees-McRae College.

22. I smoked cigars when they were available in the Navy, and I was smoking one in the blacked-out, stuffy mess hall when Perry's announcement came over the PA system. I preserved the stub of that cigar for many years as a souvenir of one of the most dramatic moments of my life. Alas, the stub eventually disintegrated. The Soviet Union had entered the war against Japan on August 8, between the time of the two atom bomb drops. See Mark Grimsley, "What If the Japanese High Command Had Refused to Surrender," *World War II* 23(3) (August–September 2008): 83, 85.

23. *Pennsylvania* remained afloat and on August 18 was towed by tugs to Apra Harbor, Guam, where the torpedo's damage was repaired. On the way from Guam

the following October, one of the shafts was lost; and the ship limped into Puget Sound Navy Yard. Although repaired and put back in service, *Pennsylvania*, which had compiled a valorous record, was given an inglorious assignment after the war as a target ship in the Bikini atomic bomb tests. In 1948, after being used in further tests, she was sunk off Kwajalein.

24. *Lagrange* remained afloat, was repaired, and returned to the States.

25. Lott, *Most Dangerous Sea*, p. 258.

26. Nagasaki time was thirteen hours ahead of Washington time, so people back home had heard the news the evening of August 14.

27. For more on the aborted invasion of Japan, see chapter 16.

Chapter 16

1. Commander Dryer was relieved as skipper of *Speed* on August 26 by Lieutenant John F. Maddox, Jr.

2. *Jefferson Standard Life* (January 1945): 19.

3. Among useful books on the planned Operation Olympic are John Ray Skates, *The Invasion of Japan: Alternative to the Bomb* (Columbia: University of South Carolina Pres, 1994); Thomas B. Allen, *Code-Name Downfall: The Secret Plan to Invade Japan and Why Truman Dropped the Bomb* (New York: Simon and Schuster, 1995); and Richard B. Frank, *Downfall: The End of the Imperial Japanese Empire* (New York: Random House, 1999). See also Adam Goodheart, "The Invasion That Never Was," *Civilization* (January/February 1995): 40–43.

4. *Durham Morning Herald* (Durham, NC), September 7, 1945.

5. Although Japan had lost about 2,550 kamikaze planes, they still had 5,350 left, and 5,000 suicide pilots were in training at war's end — in addition to a million men in arms in the home islands. Morison, *Two-Ocean War*, p. 572. Decades later, the Japanese still commemorate their suicidal heroes with the Chiran Peace Museum of Kamikaze Pilots and the Kanoya Naval Air Base Museum, each exhibiting the last words and photographs of the pilots as they left on their fatal missions.

6. Lott says that Kagoshima was blocked with 320 mines, of which 166 American and 88 Japanese mines were destroyed. Lott, *Most Dangerous Sea*, p. 254. The Army Air Force dropped more than 12,000 mines around Japan in "Operation Starvation" between March and August 15. Richard P. Hallion, "Operation Starvation," *World War II* 23(1) (April–May 2008): 48–55.

7. Stafford, *Subchaser*, p. 164, describes *Strive*'s furnishing electrical power to *Mayrant*.

8. The experience aboard *Beagle* is described in Robert Esson Rew, Jr., "Typhoon Off Okinawa," *Reader's Digest* 48(285) (January 1946): 67–72. The gruesome story of *YMS-472* is told in Elmer Renner and Kenneth Birks, *Sea of Sharks: A Sailor's World War II Survival Story* (Annapolis, MD: Naval Institute, 2004).

9. For a list of minecraft lost during this typhoon, see "U.S. Navy Minecraft Losses from All Causes,"

Silent Defenders 23(4) (Fall 2006): 23–26. One of the most graphic descriptions of the battering of ships by typhoons at Okinawa is found in the chapter titled "Buckner Bay" in Treadwell, *Splinter Fleet*, pp. 221–230. See also Jim Myers, "Typhoon Louise and *SC-1012*," *PCSA Newsletter* 84 (April–June 2009): 11.

10. "History of the USS *Strive*" in H.G. Jones, *USS Strive Anniversary, October 27, 1945* (mimeographed, 5 pages), in the North Carolina Collection, University of North Carolina Library, Chapel Hill, NC).

11. After being discharged, Knowlton entered the public relations field and served as vice president of Barre Publishers and as development officer for the American Antiquarian Society in Worcester, Massachusetts. I probably saw him when, as State Archivist of North Carolina, I conducted research in the AAS, but out of uniform, neither would have recognized the other. He died in 2000.

12. It is estimated that a half-million mines were laid by the combined Allied and Axis powers before and during the war, and only about 12,000 had been destroyed in the Pacific by February 1946. Lott, *Most Dangerous Sea*, pp. 256, 263. A story in the *New York Times*, August 25, 1946, reported, "Pacific mariners were warned today that some 30,000 mines had broken loose from Japanese minefields and were floating in trade currents. The mines explode by magnetic or pressure influence and remain dangerous to shipping for five years." Some have already had deadly effect upon postwar travel; some have washed up on beaches around the world; and more will undoubtedly be encountered in the twenty-first century.

Chapter 17

1. Sasebo served as a major staging port during the United Nations' war with North Korea a few years later.

2. The destroyer minelayer *Henry A. Wiley* was a veteran of the battles for Iwo Jima and Okinawa, having shot down four kamikazes and earned a Presidential Unit Citation.

3. See chapter 10 for *SC-525*'s service with *Implicit* at Southern France.

4. The swords and fruit were bargains, but the wrist watch turned out to be worth about what I paid for it — 90 cents — because it soon stopped keeping correct time. I still have the handsome Japanese sword.

5. About thirty years later, the burglar who broke into my home in Chapel Hill and took off a huge wad of Chinese money must have been sadly disappointed when he or she discovered the virtual worthlessness of the Chinese yuan of World War II. Interestingly, many of the notes were printed by the E.A. Wright Bank Note Company in Philadelphia.

6. See chapter 18.

7. The destroyer minelayer *Adams* had compiled an illustrious record against Japanese air attacks, suffering twice from enemy planes that splashed near the ship. Her guns shot down seven Japs, including a kamikaze.

8. The destroyer minelayer *Robert A. Smith* likewise compiled a heroic record, surviving many air attacks and destroying at least five enemy planes.

9. *Paniment* was built in 1944 by the North Car-

olina Shipbuilding Company in Wilmington, originally as a Liberty ship named *Northern Lights*. She was scrapped in 1961.

Chapter 18

1. The naval historian of the war, Rear Admiral Samuel Eliot Morison, observed, "The most consistently unsung naval heroes of World War II, however, were the minecraft." *Two-Ocean War*, p. 364.

2. Portions of the memoir were quoted in chapter 6.

3. Although Hawaii was a United States possession, it was not admitted as the fiftieth state until 1959.

4. The numerical sequence of the "S" group of fleet minesweepers had been broken on July 10, 1943, when *Sentinel* was destroyed by German bombs during the invasion of Sicily; on September 25, 1943, when *Skill* was blown in half by a torpedo following the invasion at Salerno; and on July 9, 1944, when *Swerve* succumbed to a mine off Anzio. *Seer* and *Sway* apparently had been placed in another mine division at the time of the party. *Speed* and *Strive*, both with seven battle stars, were decommissioned shortly after returning to the States. However, both eventually were called back for further service. In 1955, *Speed* was reclassified as MSF-116; then on November 17, 1967, she was transferred to the Republic of Korea and given the name *Sunchon* (PCE-1002). *Strive* was put back into commission in 1952 and operated in the Atlantic and Mediterranean. In 1955 she was redesignated MSF-117 and berthed at Green Cove Springs, Florida. Subsequently given the designation MMC-1, she was transferred to the Kingdom of Norway on October 1, 1959, and operated as KNM *Gor* (N-48) until 1975 when she was decommissioned and sold for 25,000 kroner to a company that scrapped her in Stavanger. *Sic transit gloria.*

5. Readers living in the twenty-first century with a profusion of televisions, videos, and myriad other digital means of audio and visual communication cannot possibly understand the importance of motion pictures to service personnel in World War II. Except for an exceedingly rare stage show, movies were the chief means of escaping the drudgery of duty.

6. In fact, we have remained good friends over the years, corresponded, and visited together as his and Phyllis's family grew in Vermont, where they live next to the Round Church in Richmond. Neil revealed in one letter that, when we said goodbye that morning in Long Beach, he really was worried that I might become an alcoholic. Funny, I had the same worry about him at that time! Both of us can be proud that neither had anything to worry about; we had simply occasionally used poor judgment characteristic of boys on their way to becoming men. Po-

litically, I was then a radical Democrat, but the only Democrats that Neil knew in Massachusetts, he claimed, were "gangsters." After nearly two-thirds of a century, our political views have changed. So now I can blame the sorry state of the nation on his political backsliding.

7. Edward Fitzgerald, trans., *The Rubaiyat [of Omar Khayyam]* (New York: Dodge, 1914), pp. 74, 79.

8. Sir Richard Francis Burton, trans., *The Kasidah [of Haji Abdu El-Yezdi]* (Girard, KS: Haldeman-Julius Company, 1880), p. 38.

9. The physical examination revealed that I was still 68 inches tall, but I had added 13 pounds in nearly four years (up to 145). My "circumference of abdomen at umbilicus" was 29 inches. Except for both hands broken at Anzio, the examiner could find no abnormality. An examination by the Veterans Administration later adjudged my handicap to be less than 10 percent, and, consequently, I was ineligible for disability benefits. The St. Christopher medal given me by George Klumpp in Casablanca had brought me safely home.

10. Unwisely, I dropped the insurance after I entered college.

11. Actually, on the EAME bar I personally qualified for only two stars (Anzio and Southern France); I was not aboard *Speed* or *Strive* when their crews earned stars for the invasions of Sicily and Salerno.

12. Veterans who registered for work but could not find a job were eligible for a weekly unemployment check of $20 for up to 52 weeks; I "joined the club" for a few weeks before entering college. By 1956, I was among 7.8 million veterans who had participated in educational programs under the G.I. Bill, and 2.4 million had taken out home loans backed by the Veterans Administration under provisions of the Servicemembers Readjustment Act of 1944. I used every day of my sixty-month educational entitlement for college expenses; it ran out only a few weeks before I qualified for my Ph.D. at Duke. The low-interest loan for my first home in Raleigh was guaranteed by the Veterans Administration.

My appreciation for governmental assistance in my education was inferred when, more than half a century later, President Barack Obama in a public address on the passage of a new "G.I. Bill" said, "H.G. Jones, a Navy man from North Carolina, said, 'What happened in my rural Caswell County happened all over the country — going to college was no longer a novelty.' Indeed, one of the men who went to college on the G.I. Bill was my grandfather, and I would not be standing here today if the opportunity had not led him West in search of opportunity." White House press release, "Remarks by the President on the Post/9/11 GI Bill," August 3, 2009.

Bibliography

Personal Manuscripts

Diaries, notes, and letters by, to, and from Houston G. Jones, 1937–2009. (Originals in possession of author.)

Official Government Records

Deck Log of USS *SC-525*, October 1-December 31, 1943; August 1–October 8, 1944, National Archives, College Park, MD. (Copy in possession of author.)

Deck Log of USS *Speed* (AM-116), January 1, 1945–August 31, 1945, National Archives, College Park, MD. (Copy in possession of author.)

Deck Log of USS *Strive* (AM-117), September 1, 1945–March 31, 1946, National Archives, College Park, MD. (Copy in possession of author.)

Floyd, W.O. "Action Report, Commander Task Group 81.3, Serial 046, 17 April 1944, Amphibious Operations, Anzio-Nettuno Area, Italy, during January 1944 — Report of." This report from Commander W. O. Floyd with endorsement dated 23 June 1944 by Vice-Admiral H.K. Hewitt was initially classified "Secret" but was later marked "declassified" on March 21, 1963. The original is in the National Archives in College Park, MD. Commander Floyd was in charge of LST Group Three (Red Beach Group). Herein referred to as Floyd, "Secret Action Report." (Copy in possession of author.)

Medical Records of Houston G. Jones (656–97–02), 1942–1946, in Veterans Administration, Winston-Salem, N.C. (Copy in possession of author.)

Military Service Records of Houston G. Jones (656–97–02), 1942–1946, in National Personnel Records Center, St. Louis, MO. (Copy in possession of author.)

[Rodgers, Bertram J.] Commander Task Force Eighty-Five (Delta Force) to Commander-in-Chief United States Fleet, 25 August 1944. The cover page of the document reads "Confidential Action Report Commander Task Force 85, Serial 0123, 25 August 1944, Action Report, Southern France Landings. Report of Rear Admiral B.J. Rodgers Concerning Delta Attack Force Which Landed US 45th Infantry Division on Beaches in Baie de Bougnon, 15 August 1944." Originally classified as confidential, the report was declassified on 19 March 1963, and is preserved in the National Archives at College Park, MD. Herein referred to as Rodgers, "Action Report." (Copy in possession of author.)

Books

Adleman, Robert H., and George Walton. *Rome Fell Today*. Boston: Little, Brown, 1968.

Allen, Thomas B. *Code-Name Downfall: The Secret Plan to Invade Japan and Why Truman Dropped the Bomb*. New York: Simon and Schuster, 1995.

Allen, William Lusk. *Anzio, Edge of Disaster*. New York: Elsevier-Dutton, 1978.

Anzio Beachhead, 22 January–25 May 1944. Washington: Center of Military History, U.S. Army, 1990.

Atkinson, Rick. *An Army at Dawn: The War in North Africa, 1942–1943*. New York: Henry Holt, 2002.

_____. *The Day of Battle: The War in Sicily and Italy, 1943–1944*. New York: Henry Holt, 2007.

Best, Mary. *North Carolina's Shining Hour: Images and Voices from World War II*. Greensboro, NC: Our State, 2005.

Blackwell, Ian. *Anzio*. Barnsley, UK: Pen and Sword, 2006.

Blumenson, Martin. *Anzio: The Gamble that Failed*. New York: Cooper Square, 2001.

_____. *General Lucas at Anzio*. Washington: Center for Military History, U.S. Army, 1990.

_____. *Salerno to Cassino*. Washington: Center for Military History, 1993.

Bovbjerg, Richard V. *Steaming as Before*. Lanham, MD: Hamilton, 2004.

Breuer, William B. *Agony at Anzio*. London: R. Hale, 1987.

_____. *Operation Dragoon: The Allied Invasion of the South of France.* Novato, CA: Presidio, 1987.

Bruce, Colin John. *Invaders: British and American Experiences of Seaborne Landings, 1938–1945.* Annapolis, MD: Naval Institute, 1999.

Buckley, Robert J., Jr. *At Close Quarters: PT Boats in the United States Navy.* Washington: Naval History Division, 1962.

Burns, James, Jr. *Friends at Anzio: Alva (Al) Bacon and James (Bud) Burns: Their Stories in the 180th Infantry Regiment, 45th Division during World War II.* Fayetteville, NC: Old Mountain, 2006.

Burton, Sir Richard Francis, trans. *The Kasidah [of Haji Abdu El-Yezdi].* Girard, KS: Haldeman-Julius, 1880.

Charles, Roland W. *Troopships of World War II.* Washington: Army Transportation Association, 1947.

Churchill, Winston. *Closing the Ring.* Boston: Houghton Mifflin, 1951.

Clark, Lloyd. *Anzio: Italy and the Battle for Rome, 1944.* New York: Atlantic Monthly, 2006.

Clark, Mark W. *Calculated Risk.* New York: Harper and Brothers, 1950.

Clarke, Jeffrey J. *Southern France 15 August–14 September 1944.* U.S. Army Center of Military History, [CMH Publication 72–31], [1944].

Cressman, Robert. *The Official Chronology of the U.S. Navy in World War II.* Washington: Naval History Center, 2000.

Critchell, Brad. *Minewarfare.* Washington: Navy and Marine Corps WWII Commemorative Committee, Navy Office of Information, 1994.

Daly, Bob. *Steaming As Before: World War Two 173 Foot Steel Hulled PC Subchaser Histories and Stories.* N.p.: "pc daly press," 2004.

Davis, John Dixon. *Wooden Dreadnaught: The Biography of the YMS 183.* Bloomington, IN: Authorhouse, 2004.

Decker, Julie, and Chris Chei. *Quonset Huts: Metal Living for a Modern Age.* New York: Princeton Architectural, 2005).

D'Este, Carlo. *Fatal Decision: Anzio and the Battle for Rome.* New York: HarperCollins, 1991.

Dictionary of American Naval Fighting Ships. Ed. James L. Mooney. 13 vols. Washington: Naval History Center, 1957–1981. Vol. 5 includes minecraft; vol. 6 includes subchasers.

Dodge, Robert E. *Memories of the Anzio Beachhead and the War in Europe.* New York: Vantage, 2004.

Eisenhower, John S.D. *They Fought at Anzio.* Columbia: University of Missouri Press, 2007.

Elliott, Peter. *Allied Minesweepers in World War 2.* Annapolis, MD: Naval Institute, 1979.

Fehrenbach, T.R. *The Battle of Anzio: The Bloody Beachhead that Turned the Tide of World War II.* N.p.: E-reads Publications, 1999 [c. 1962].

Fitzgerald, Edward, trans. *The Rubaiyat [of Omar Khayyam].* New York: Dodge, 1914.

Frank, Richard B. *Downfall: The End of the Imperial Japanese Empire.* New York: Random House, 1999.

Frankie, D.M. *Damn Cold Water and the Navy.* North Charleston, SC: BookSurge, 1999.

Franklin, Robert J. *Medic! How I Fought World War II with Morphine, Sulfa, and Iodine Swabs.* Lincoln: University of Nebraska Press, 2006.

Friedman, Norman. *U.S. Small Combatants, Including PT-Boats, Subchasers, and the Brown-Water Navy: An Illustrated Design History.* Annapolis, MD: Naval Institute, 1987.

Griffiths, Maurice. *The Hidden Menace.* Greenwich, UK: Conway Maritime, 1981.

Hackman, Willem. *Seek and Strike: Sonar, Anti-Submarine Warfare and the Royal Navy, 1914–1984.* London: Her Majesty's Stationery Office, 1984.

Hartmann, Gregory Kemenyi. *Weapons That Wait: Mine Warfare in the U.S. Navy.* Annapolis, MD: Naval Institute, 1991.

Haycock, D. J. *Eisenhower and the Art of Warfare: A Critical Appraisal.* Jefferson, NC: McFarland, 2004.

Henry, Chris. *Depth Charge! Mines, Depth Charges and Underwater Weapons, 1914–1945.* Barnsley: Pen and Sword Military, 2005.

Hewitt, H. Kent. *The Memoirs of Admiral H. Kent Hewitt.* Ed. by Evelyn M. Cherpak. Newport, RI: Naval War College, 2004.

Hibbert, Christopher. *Anzio: Bid for Rome.* New York: Ballantine, 1970.

Hoyt, Edwin Palmer. *Backwater War: The Allied Campaign in Italy, 1943–1945.* Westport, CT: Praeger, 2002.

Juergensen, Hans. *Beachheads and Mountains: Campaigning from Sicily to Anzio: A Journal.* Tampa, FL: American Studies, 1984.

Katz, Robert. *The Battle for Rome: The Germans, the Allies, the Partisans and the Pope.* New York: Simon and Schuster, 2003.

Koehler, Franz A. *Army Operational Rations: Historical Background.* Washington: Office of Quartermaster General, 1958.

Lambert, John, and Al Ross. *Allied Coastal Forces of World War II.* Vol. 1. London: Conway Maritime, 1990.

Laurie, Clayton D. *Anzio 1944.* Washington: U.S. Army Center of Military History, 1994.

Lewis, Norman. *Naples '44.* New York: Pantheon, 1978.

Lott, Arnold S. *Most Dangerous Sea: A History of Mine Warfare, and an Account of U.S. Navy Mine Warfare Operations in World War II and Korea.* Annapolis, MD: U.S. Naval Institute, 1959.

Lund, Paul, and Harry Ludlam. *Out Sweeps: The Story of the Minesweepers in World War II.* London: W. Foulsham, 1978.

Marshall, Charles F. *A Ramble through My War: Anzio and Other Joys.* Baton Rouge: LSU Press, 1998.

Mauldin, Bill. *Up Front.* New York: Henry Holt, 1945.

McKay, James C. *Bill Creelman's Conflicts: A Story of a Boy's Coming of Age.* N.p.: No publisher, 2000.

Melia, Tamara Moser. *Damn the Torpedoes.* Washington: Naval History Center, 1991.

Mitchell, Brad. *Mine Warfare.* Washington: Navy and Marine Corps World War II Commemorative Committee, Office of Information, 1994?

Morison, Samuel Eliot. *History of United States Naval Operations in World War II.* Vol. IX: *Sicily-Salerno-Anzio;* Vol. XI: *The Invasion of France and Germany*; Vol. XIV, *Victory in the Pacific.* Edison, NJ: Castle, 2001.

_____. *The Two-Ocean War: A Short History of the United States Navy in the Second World War.* Boston: Little, Brown, 1963.

Murphy, Audie. *To Hell and Back.* New York: Henry Holt, 1949.

Powell, William S., ed. *Encyclopedia of North Carolina.* Chapel Hill: University of North Carolina Press, 2006.

Pyle, Ernie. *Brave Men.* New York: Grosset and Dunlap, 1944.

Renner, Elmer, and Kenneth Birks. *Sea of Sharks: A Sailor's World War II Survival Story.* Annapolis, MD: Naval Institute, 2004.

Robichon, Jacques. *The Second D-Day.* New York: Walker, 1969; c.1962.

Rohwer, Jürgen. *Chronology of the War at Sea 1939–1945.* Annapolis, MD: Naval Institute, 1972; 3rd rev. ed., 2005.

Roland, Charles W. *Troopships of World War II.* Washington: Army Transportation Association, 1947.

Schorer, Avis D. *A Half Acre of Hell: A Combat Nurse in WW II.* Lakeville, MN: Galde, 2000.

Scott, Ralph. *The Wilmington Shipyard: Welding a Fleet for Victory in World War II.* Charleston, SC: History, 2007.

Sheehan, Fred. *Anzio: Epic of Bravery.* Norman: University of Oklahoma Press, 1994.

Skates, John Ray. *The Invasion of Japan: Alternative to the Bomb.* Columbia: University of South Carolina Press, 1994.

Sloan, Bill. *The Ultimate Battle: Okinawa 1945— The Last Struggle of World War II.* New York: Simon and Schuster, 2007.

Stafford, Edward P. *Subchaser.* Annapolis, MD: Naval Institute, 1988.

This Is Our War, Selected Stories of Six War Correspondents Who Were Sent Overseas by the Afro-American Newspapers. Baltimore: Afro-American, 1945.

Tomblin, Barbara Brooks. *With Utmost Spirit: Allied Naval Operations in the Mediterranean 1942–1945.* Lexington: University Press of Kentucky, 2004.

Treadwell, Theodore R. *Splinter Fleet: The Wooden Subchasers of World War II.* Annapolis, MD: Naval Institute, 2000.

_____. *Taste of Salt: A WWII Skipper Looks Back.* New York: iUniverse, 2007.

Trevelyan, Raleigh. *The Fortress: A Diary of Anzio and After.* London: Collins, 1956.

Vaughan-Thomas, Wynford. *Anzio.* New York: Holt, Rinehart and Winston, 1961.

Veigele, Wm. J. *Seabag of Memories: Images, Poems, Thoughts & Crafts of the Small Ship Sailors of World War II.* Santa Barbara, CA: Astral, 2003.

Verney, Peter. *Anzio 1944: An Unexpected Fury*: London: B.T. Batsford, 1978.

Wells, Lloyd M. *From Anzio to the Alps: an American Soldier's Story.* Columbia: University of Missouri Press, 2004.

Whitlock, Flint. *The Rock of Anzio: From Sicily to Dachau: A History of the 45th Infantry Division.* Boulder, CO: Westview, 1998.

Wilt, Alan F. *The French Riviera Campaign of August 1944.* Carbondale: Southern Illinois University Press, 1981.

Wings of War Series, No. 1–6: An Interim Report. Washington: Center for Air Force History, 1992.

Youngblood, Norman. *The Development of Mine Warfare: A Most Murderous and Barbarous Conduct.* Westport, CT: Praeger Security, 2006.

Zaloga, Steven J. *Anzio 1944: The Beleaguered Beachhead.* Oxford, UK: Osprey, 2005.

Booklets, Leaflets, and Maps

Casablanca with Plan of the Town and Name of the Streets. Casablanca, F.M.: Guides Moroc-Presse, 1943.

Cathedral at Monreale Sicily. [Palermo]: American Red Cross Sightseeing Tours, 1943–44.

Italian: A Guide to the Spoken Language [Introductory Series]. War Department Publication T M 30–303. Washington, DC: Government Printing Office, June 2, 1943.

Jones, H.G. *History of the USS Strive.* Mimeographed, 1945. Copy in University of North Carolina Library, Chapel Hill, NC.

Maiuri, Amedeo. *A Companion to the Visit of Pompeii.* Naples: Tipi Artigianelli, 1944.

Moore, Evelyn, and Dorothy Jurney. *Panama in Your Pocket.* Panama Canal Zone: United Women's Service Organizations, 1943.

Napoli. Naples, Italy: American Red Cross, [1943].

Pocket Guide to North Africa. U.S. Army Special Services Division, Washington, DC, 1942.

Shanghai Guide. Shanghai, China: Shanghai Joint Service Committee for Allied Forces, 1945.

Soldiers Guide to Naples. Naples, Italy: Special Service, Metropolitan Area, Peninsula Base Section, 1944.

Journal and Newspaper Articles

Atkinson, Rick. "What is Lost?" *World War II* 24(4) (November 2009): 32–35.

Bailey, Ronald H. "The Incredible Jeep." *World War II* 24(3) (September 2009): 26–35.

Budiansky, Stephen. "The Man Behind the Incredible, Nearly Inedible K Ration." *World War II* 24(1) (May 2009): 21.

Burton, Earl. "The Invasion of Southern France." *Sea Classics* (September 2004).

Devers, General Jacob L. "Operation Dragoon: The Invasion of Southern France." *Military Affairs* 10(2) (Summer 1946): 2–41.

Drier, Bob. "The Well-Dressed Dead." *Archaeology* 56(3) (May/June 2003): 32–35.

Evans, James E. "A Letter to My Sons [service on *SC-697*]." *PCSA Newsletter* 80 (April–June 2008): 1, 7, 9; 81 (July–September 2008): 7, 9.

Fortune, Don. "Pioneer to the Rescue." *Silent Defender* 22(3) (Summer 2005): 18–24.

"Four Die in Two Weekend Boating Accidents." *Rodnreel.com.news* (January 7, 2002).

Friedman, Norman. "World War II Patrol Craft (PC) History." *PCSA Newsletter* 66 (October–December 2004): 12–14.

Gadney, Max. "An Undersea Killer Evolves." *World War II* 23(6) (February–March 2009): 64–65.

Gerson, Irving B. "Small Boat Minesweeping, Invasion of Southern France, Operation Dragoon." *Silent Defenders* 21(3) (Summer 2004): 14–20.

Gill, A.A. "Where the Dead Don't Sleep." *National Geographic* 215(2) (February 2009).

Goodheart, Adam. "The Invasion That Never Was." *Civilization* (January/February 1995): 40–43.

Grimsley, Mark. "What If the Japanese High Command Had Refused to Surrender?" *World War II* 23(3) (August–September 2008): 83–85.

Hall, Jane. "Long Journey Ends: After 15 Years, Ring Back With Owner." *News & Observer* (Raleigh, NC) (August 17, 1958).

Hallas, Stanley. "Another Look at SC 525." *PCSA Newsletter* 83 (January–March 2009): 6–7.

Hallion, Richard P. "Bombs That Were Smart Before Their Time." *World War II* 22(5) (September 2007): 52–57.

"History of the YMS." *Silent Defenders* 23(2) (Spring 2006): 8–11.

Jackson, Darrell L. "Sinking of the USS Swerve (AM-121)." *Silent Defenders* 25(1) (Spring 2008): 14–17.

Jones, H.G. "60 Years Ago: Chasing Submarines, Sweeping Mines, Dodging Kamikazes, and Sayonara to World War II." *Silent Defenders* 23(3) (Summer 2006): 8–10.

_____. "Skeletal History of USS SC 525." *PCSA Newsletter* 83 (January–March 2009): 1, 5.

"The Last Big One." *U.S. News & World Report* 118(13) (April 3, 1995): 12.

"Last Fighting Ship Sunk in WW II: The Story of the USS Minivet AM 371." *Silent Defenders* 23(1) (Winter 2006): 12–26.

Lowry, Vice Admiral F.J. "The Naval Side of the Anzio Invasion." *United States Naval Institute Proceedings* 80(1) (January–February 1954): 23–30.

Lucas, Richard. "With a Sweet Kiss from Sally." *World War II* 24(3) (January–February 2010): 48–53.

"The Man Who Won the War [Andrew Jackson Higgins]." *PCSA Newsletter* 76 (April–June 2007): 7, 910.

Myers, Jim. "Typhoon Louise and SC-1012." *PCSA Newsletter* 84 (April–June 2009): 10–11.

"No More Lugging of Mattresses and Hammocks." *PCSA Newsletter* 59 (January–March 2003): 8.

Poole, Robert M. "The Battle of Arlington." *Smithsonian* 40(8) (November 2009): 50–57.

Rawlings, Charles. "Oh, the Jolly Old Ash Cans!" *PCSA Newsletter* 59 (January–March 2003): 1, 3, 9.

Rew, Robert Esson, Jr. "Typhoon Off Okinawa." *Reader's Digest* 48(285) (January–February 1946): 67- 72.

"School Will Give Diploma to Man Killed in WWII." *Rutland Herald*, March 21, 2008.

"Sonar Defeated Subs." *Science Newsletter* (April 13, 1946): 231.

"Sonar Gear and Sound Schools." *PCSA Newsletter* 64 (April–June 2004): 11–13.

Stafford, Edward. "August Moon [Story of *SC-694* and *-696*]." *PCSA Newsletter* 62 (October–December 2003): 1, 4.

Stars and Stripes. Various editions in Africa and Italy; various dates 1943–1944.

Still, William N., Jr. "Wooden Ship Construction in North Carolina in World War II." *North Carolina Historical Review* 77 (January 2000): 43–44.

"Sweeping Up Sudden Death." *Popular Mechanics* (January 1946): 28–34.

"U.S. Navy Minecraft Losses from All Causes." *Silent Defenders* 23(4) (Fall 2006): 23–26.

"U.S. Pays Up." *Time* (October 23, 1944).

"V — as in Victory Mail." *Smithsonian* 35 (May 2004): 28.

Waldby, Ronald W. "USS Steady, AM-118." *Silent Defenders* 25(2) (Spring 2008): 12–15; 25(3) (Fall 2008): 7–10; 26(4) (Winter 2008): 8–13; 27(1) (Spring 2009): 22–28.

Walls, E.V. "PC 1235 in Action." *PCSA Newsletter* 58 (October–December 2002): 9–10.

"World War II Subchaser (SC) History." *PCSA Newsletter* 64 (April–June 2004): 6, 8.

"The YMS." *Silent Defenders* 25(1) (Spring 2008): 30.

Web Sites

http://artsweb.aut.ac.nz/hmsspartan/campaign

http://history.amedd.army.mil/booksdocs/wwii/MedSvcs

http://members.aol.com/HizBeluved/WW2/Brown.htm

http://tdiumh.blogspot.com/2004/11/November-11.html

www.dvrbscom/history-mil/LST-422.htm

www.ibiblio.org/hyperwar/USN/ships/logs/LCIL/lcil219-Becker.html

www.marconews.com/news/2004

www.naval-history.net.WW2CampaignsItaly.htm

www.naval-history.net/WW2Campaigns/Amphibious2.htm

www.nwc.navy.mil/usnhdb/ShipLookup.asp?Ship

www.splinterfleet.org

www.warwingsart.com/12thairforce/vesuvius/htm

Index

Numbers in **bold italics** indicate pages with illustrations.

ABATU, Lido Beach, New York 155, 159
Abdiel 143
Aberdeen Proving Ground, Maryland 100
absinthe 208
Achelous (ARL-1) 108, 119, 147
Adams (DM-27) 195, 210, 213, 236
Admirable Class (184-foot AM) 235
Aeneid (book) 137
Agadir (French Morocco) 27, 39, 40
Aheron, Ray 158
Ain el Turck (Algeria) 50
Ajaccio (Corsica) 114, 119–120, 147–148
Alameda, California 169–173
Alberta (monkey) *206*
Alcatraz 169
L'Alcyon (French) 103
Alexander Graham Bell 102
Alexander Martin 87, 102
Algeria 42–58
Algiers (Algeria) 23, 43
Allen, Fred 20
Allen A. Michelson 231
Alpha Force (TF-84) 112
Altman, Thelma 20
American Red Cross 20, 38, 43, 49, 79–80, 120, 128, 133, 135, 137, 141, 148, 159, 181, 207, 226, 232
American Shipbuilding Company 161
Anatukau Island 182
"Anchors Aweigh" 12
Les Andalouses (Algeria) 13
Anderson, Eddie ("Rochester") 10
Anderson, Wilbur Kenneth 157
Anika, Virgil 46, *97*
Anne Arundel (AP-76) 46
"Annie Express" (German gun) 100, 104, 229
antisubmarine weapons *180*, *185*
Anzio *see* Operation Shingle
"Anzio Anxiety" 104
Anzio-Nettuno: ashore at 145–146

"Anzio Stoop" 100
Apex boats 113, 120
Aphis 119
Apra Harbor (Guam) 180
Aquileia 48
Arab Bowl (Oran) 56
Armstrong, Henry J., Jr. 191
Arnold, Elliott 216
artillery (German) 119, 123–124, *125*–126
artworks *see* souvenirs and artworks
Arzeu (Algeria) 43, 46–47, 152–154
Atherstone 49
Atkinson, Rick 1–2
Atlanta, Georgia 222
Atlantic Fleet Sound School 15
Atlas Bar (Casablanca) 39
atomic bomb 190, 202
ATR-1 17
Attack Teacher 15, 33–34, 50, 88, 225
Augustine Le Bourgne 47
Augustus 145
Auk (class of minesweepers) 235
Avery, A.M. 172
Axis Sally 70, 92–94, 131, 232

Bagnoli (Italy) 59–60
Baker, George 131
Balog, Michael 27, 31, 36, 55, *97*, 107
Baltimore, Maryland 166
Barbour Boat Works 235
Bardot, Brigitte 122
Barefoot, J.C. 7
Barnegat (AVP-10) 164
Baron, Luzette 39
Barr, Joseph Walker 229
barrage balloons 70
Barricade (ACM-3) 108, 148
Barrier, Smith 8
Barton, John Underwood 48, 56, 97, 128, 150–*151*
Bason, Sam 156
Bata, J.A., Jr. 200
Bauer (DM-26) 199
Bay Bridge (San Francisco) 169, 173, 234
Bayfield (APA-33) 112

Bayonne, New Jersey 18
"Beach-Head Death's Head" *90*–*91*
Beagle (IX-112) 197, 236
Beasley, J.R., Jr. 173
Becker, William F. 229
Becuna (SS-319) 182
Behm, Robert D. 99
Belknap, R. 154
Bell, H.A. 200
Bell, Ivan B. 136
Belzer, C.W. 200
Beni Saf (Algeria) 44, *45*–47
Bennett, C. E. 6
Bennett, James E., Jr. 27
Benny, Jack 20
Benson, Otto Eric 196
Benson, Paul B. 14–85
Beppu Wan (Kyushu) 198
Bernadou (DD-153) 48, 50
Bernhard, W.A. 200
Besse, L., Jr. 100
Bessler Fog Generator 108, 110
Best, Mary 136
Binzart *see* Bizerte
birthday: 1942 (New York) 19; 1943 (Bizerte) 58; 1944 (Norfolk) 163; 1945 (Sasebo) 210
Biscayne (AVP-11) 62, 88, 112, 119, 122
Bishop, Alfred Raymond 163, 234
Bizerte (Tunisia) 42–44, 56–58, 88, 98, 107, 129
Black, Bruce 158
Blackwelder, Keith 158
Blankney 103
Block, Ray 20
Bluejacket's Manual (book) 11, 14
"Blues in the Night" (song) 200
Boats (dog) 206
bodies: recovery of 50
Boise (CL-47) 43
Bolton, Charlie 179
Bonaparte, Napoléon 120, 147–148
Bonnans (French crewman) 151
Boot Camp 11–*13*
Borgo, Count 120
Bostwick, F.W. 192
Bougie (Algeria) 49
Bourgeaius, B.H.J. 154

Bousbir (Casablanca) 39
bow watch 114
Bradish, Don *206*
Bradley, Omar N. 123
"Brad's Drink" 51, 159
Brave Men (book) 176
breeches buoy 194
brig 18, 107
Briggs, Hulon 157
Bringman, John B. 17
Brinkley, John R. 122
Bristol (DD-453) 143
British Broadcasting Company (BBC) 130
Brooklyn (CL-40) 11, 89, 92, 99, 104, 123, 153
Brooklyn, New York 156, 159
Brooks, Douglas 7
Brown, Harold 124–125
Brown, Paul 228
Browne, John Ross 135
Bruce, Carol 20
Brunhoff, Jean de 230
Brutus, Marcus 137
Buchanan, Billy 158
Buck (DD-420) 143
Buck, Pearl 8
Buckner, Simon B. 135
Buckner Bay (Okinawa) *183*
Buffalo 44
Bungo Suido: operation in 198–202

C-Ration 32, 233
Caesar, Julius 137
Cafe-Brasserie de la Vallette (Casablanca) 19
Cain, Edward 27, 51, *97*, 107, 128, 150, 226
Calculated Risk (book) 14
California 168–175
California (BB-44) 192
Caligula 145
Callaghan (DD-792) 187
Camden (AS-6, IX-42) 18
Camel Force (TF-87) 112
camel riding 50
Campi Flegrei (Italy) 137
Cape Blanc (Algeria) 16
Capp, Al 131
Capri (Italy) 13, 98, 103, 144
Capuchin Monastery (Palermo) 134
Caravaglia, Nuzio J. 11
Carter, Chester A. 121
Carter, Lewis 179
Carter, Myrtle 127–128, 130, 144, 158–159, 171, 179
Casablanca (French Morocco) 12–42, 82, 133, 219
Casbah 38, 39
casualties 69, 105, 117, 182, 195, 198, 229–232
Caswell (AKA-72) 157
Caswell Messenger (newspaper) 1, 55, 128, 130, 132, 156, 157, 232
catacombs (Palermo) 19, 134–135
Catoctin (AGC-5) 112, 119, 231
Causey, Jack 7
censorship of mail 52, 128–129
Cercle Civil Café (Nemours) 14

CH-102 (French) 154
Challenger Deep 180
Chambers, Felix 8
Chamorros (Guam) 180
Chance, Edna 6
Charles, W.B. 187
Charle's [*sic*] Bar (Casablanca) 16
Charles F. Hughes (DD-428) 119, 126
Charles Piez 102
Chateau de la Punta (Corsica) 148
chess (game) 18, 129, 201, 205, 209, 213
Chiang Kai-shek 209
Chilung see Kiirun
Chinese claims against *Seer* 208–209, 218
Chiran air base (Kyushu) 194, 196
Chocron, Joseph 39
Christmas: (1942) 17, (1943) 57, (1944) 162; (1945) 203–207
Churchill, Winston 22, 34, 39, 62, 105, 111, 230
CIC Training School 163
Cicero 137
Cieslak, Boleslaus L. 17, 44, 46, *97*, 118, 124, 150
Cinq-Deux-Cinq see *SC-525*
Civil Defense Control Center (Greensboro) 1
Civitavecchia (Italy) *106*–108, *107*, 146–147
Clabaugh, Horace Albert 163, 175–176
Clark, Mark 46, 84
Clark Mills 102
Clarkson, Robert J. 16–*97*, 150
cleanliness 27, 95, *96*, 136
Cobb Memorial School 6, 8, 13, 38, 127–128, 158
Coco-Solo 166
Code of Ethics (book) 116
Cohen, S.L. 164
Cohn, David L. 176
Cokalis, James 158
Cole, Bernard 178, 189
Cole (DD-155) 18
Colon (Panama) 166
Combustion on Wheels (book) 176
Comfort 225
commendations/medals/decorations 33, 74, *76*, *93*, 119, 169, 181, 197–198, 202, 207, 219, 221, 223, 237
ComMinPac 211–212
Companion to the Visit of Pompeii (booklet) 142
Competent (AM-316) 183
Connally, Senator Tom 171
Convoy KMF-26 19
Convoy NAM-1 13
Convoy NAS-1 13
Convoy SS-1A 113
Cooke, Fred 6
Cormick (DD-223) 119, 126
Corrao, John 135
Corsica 113, 119–120, 147–148
Costa Rica 168
Cox, John R., Jr. 11, 119, 231
Crenshaw (APA-76) 189
Cristobal (Panama) 166

Cummings, John 192
currency: Allied military 130; Chinese 205, 208; yellow seal 130

Dahlgren (DD-187) 16
Dale's Dance Studios 159
Dallas (DD-199) 10, 49
dance lessons 159
Daniel Chester French 102
Daniels, Josephus 15, 206
Dar-al-Baida (Casablanca) 17
Darby, William O. 14
Darby's Rangers 228
Dauman, Stanley 82, *97*, 103, 105, 129, 150, 152–*153*
Dauphenais, William E. 16, *97*
Dauphin (APA-97) 103
David L. Swain 108
Davis, Jimmy 221
degaussing ship 57, 185
Delta (AR-9) 17
Delta Force (TF-85) 112, 117
DeMarquo, Wally 41
DeMattia, Peter 221
Dempster, William J. 169
depth charge explosion *89*
Deweese, C.S. 11
Dewey, Thomas E. 157
Dextrous (AM-341) 112–213, 216
Dido 104
Dillon, E.E. 192
"Dirty Gertie from Bizerte" (poem) 132
discharge from Navy 223
discipline 56, 107, 163, 165–166, 171, 174, 206
dogtag *223*
"Donald Duck Navy" 19, 115
donkey riding 51
Doppler effect 15, 100
Dormer, George H. 17
Dorsey, Jimmy 29
Dour (AM-223) 166, 168
Drexler, B.A. 100
drone boats 113, 120
drydock: Alameda 169–173; Bizerte 88; Oran 55; Palermo 94, *120–121*
Dryer, Raymond C. 163, 169, 172–173, 192–193, 217, 233, 236
Duane, USCG 112
Duke-Army football game 156
DUKW: described 61, 226
Duncan, Gregor 131
Dutton, C.S.S. 171

E-boats 71, 101–102, 123
Eagle (PE-56) 16, 21
Early, Joyce V. 165
Ebro (Spanish) 12
Edison (DD-439) 12
Edward Bates 102
EFM telegrams 121, 140, 156
Egret 49
83rd Chemical Mortar Battalion 62, 74
Eisenhower, Dwight 46–47
El Hank (Casablanca lighthouse) 13, 39
El Paso, TX 122

El Salvador 168
El-Yezdi, Haji Abdu (author) 160, 222
Elihu Yale 89
Elizabeth City Shipbuilding Company 225
Ellis, Norman 24
Ellyson (DMS-19) 196
Empire Gawain 118
Endicott (DD-495) 119
Eniwetok 179, 215–216, 235
Enola Gay (bomber) 190
Ericsson (DD-440) 18–99
Ericsson, John 22
Escaburt (German) 117
Escort Sweeper Dispatch 191127A 151
Euphrat, Jack 179
Exercise Oboe (British) 10
Exercise Webfoot 60

F-lighters 71, 101
F. Marion Crawford 102
F.A.C. Muhlenberg 72
Fairbanks, Douglas E., Jr. 131
farm work 6, 54
Fedhala (French Morocco) 17, 40
Fenski, Horst-Arno 103, 229
Ferebee, Thomas W. 190, 235
Feree, Marjorie 7–9, 158
Feree, Worth 7
Ferrell, Bob 21
Ferrell, R.B. 100, 206
Fifth Marine Division 203
"52/10 Club" 123, 237
First Division (British) 10, 62
Fitch, Lois 55, 127–128
509th Parachute Infantry Battalion 62, 79, 228, 231
Flag Yeoman 194
flares 70
Fleet Sound School (Key West) 13–16
fleet post offices 52
Fleischli, John E. 103, 207
Fletcher, George A. 104
Floyd, William O. 13, 65, 68
food and meals 32, 152, 200, 215–218
Ford, Henry 15
Forester, C.S. 14
Formosa (Taiwan) 187, 202–**205**, 207
Fornier, Lawrence F. 134
Forrest (DD-461) 131
Forrestal, James 119, 223
Fort (French) 19
Fort Santa Cruz 50
Forty-fifth Division *110*, 112, **115–116**
Forty-first Division 198
Foster, Clark 7
Foster, John 6
Fouasson (French crewman) 151
Fournier, Lawrence J. 174
Fowler, Ned 7, 9
Fowlkes, Charles, Jr. 157
Fowlkes, Doris 7
Fowlkes, Frances Jane 156
Fowlkes, Hester 55

Fowlkes, Jackie 156
Fowlkes, John Wesley 6, 157
Fowlkes, Kester L. 1, 7, 130, 156, 158
Fowlkes, Laura Ieropol 156
Fowlkes, Nancy 156, 158
Fowlkes, Nannie Willie 54, 156, 223
Fowlkes, Robert Jennings 54, 156, 223
Frankford (DD-497) 119
Frederick C. Davis (DE-136) 17, 89, 229
Frejus (France) 124
French Morocco 22–42
Friegleit Lines 48
Frisky 100
Fritz X 17
"From Bungo to Beppu" (song) 100–201
Fukuru Wan (Shikoku) 198–199, 201
Furue (Kyushu) 195
Future Farmers of America 8

"G.I Bill of Rights" 12, 223, 237
"G.I. House" (Beni Saf) 16
Gardiner's Bay (AVP-39) 168
Garner, Thomas E. 12
Garvin, Lewis James 36, **97**–98, 197
gas mask instruction 13, 56, 99
Gatlin, G.M. 192
Geiger, Vernon Paul 174, 176, 178, **189**
General Engineering & Drydock Company 169
General M.C. Meigs (AP-116) 154, 169, *155*, 234
Geoffroy (French crewman) 151
George (Axis Sally's partner) 12, 131
George Cleeve 102
Germany: surrender of 171
Ghazaouet *see* Nemours
Gibajo (French crewman) 151
Gibraltar 33–34, 43, 48–49, 82
Gillars, Mildred 131, 232; *see also* Axis Sally
Gillis 47
Giovanni, Tallo 139, 143
Gipp 47
Giunta, Joseph Howard 223
Gladiator (AM-319) 183
Glasse, John A. 170
Gnecco, Louis J. 163
Goddard, Paulette 20
Golden Gate Bridge (San Francisco) 169, 173
Good Conduct Medal 198
The Good Earth (book) 1
Goodman, Benny 20
Goodman, L.R. 192
Gor (N-48) (Norwegian) 137
Gorry (French crewman) 151
Goureous (French crewman) 151
Graham, Margaret 7
Grand Café Mers-Sultan (Casablanca) 19
"Grasshopper" (L-4 airplane) 104
Graves, Richard L. 175

Green, Willard A. 164, 166, 170, 172, 175, 181, **194**, 211
"Green Fairie" 108
Greensboro, North Carolina 1–10, 158
Greensboro Daily News (newspaper) 1–9, 158
Greenwich Meridian 46
Greenwood Presbyterian Church 158
Gregory (cook on *Speed*) 178
Grosz, Wilhelm 145
Guam 180
Guatemala 168
Guidry, A.B. 192
Gunn, Johnny 156
Gustav Line 62
Guyomaid (French crewman) 151
Gwynn, Houston Lafayette 156

Hall, H.L. 161
Hall, Jane 226
Hall, Roy 5, 8
Hallas, John Stanley 34, 36, 39, 80–82, 88, **96**–**97**, 136, 150, 152
Hambleton (DD-455, DM-20) 115–116, 231
Hamilton, Allen Knowles 107
"handlessness" 18
"Hands Gone Jones" 18, 85
"Happy Hour" (Anzio) 10
Harding (DD-625) 119, 126
Harmon, Coward 163
Harpolyeus 44, 46
Harrelson, Jimmy 157
Harriet (stage play) 170
Harris, Martha 13
Harris, O.D. 12
Harris, Wade A. 12
Hartland 43
Harton, Fred B. 1
Hasty, Joseph 159
Hauser, Jimmy 1
Hawaii 176–178, 218–219
Hayes, Helen 170
Hebe II 17
hedgehogs (bow rockets) 16
Hendrickson, Paul **97**, 99
Henry A. Wiley (DM-29) 104, 236
Henschel Hs-293 (flying bombs) 19, 87, 92
Herbert C. Jones (DE-137) 17, 89
Herculaneum (Italy) 141
Here Is Your War (book) 176
Herin, Charles E. 104
Heroic (AMC-84) 166
Herren, E.L. 192
Hewitt, H. Kent 68, 112, 119, 161
Higgins, Andrew Jackson 226
"Higgins boat" *see* LCVP
High, G.D. 100
Hilary A. Herbert (DD-160) 14
Hilary P. Jones (DD-427) 11, 119, 126
Hillsborough, North Carolina 130
Hippo Diarrhytus *see* Bizerte
Hiroshima 190, 198, 201–202, 210
Hirt, John 217
Hodges, Jimmy 6
Hodges, Nellie Jones 6

Hodges, Tom 54
Holden, William 20
Holder (DE-401) 130
Holloway, Sterling 50
Hollywood, California 120–221
Hollywood Canteen 221
home: description of 10, 163, 165, 234
homeward bound: Oran 154; Sasebo 211
Honduras 168
Honolulu 176–177, 218–219
"Honorary Thunderbirds" 114
Horace (poet) 145
Horace H. Lurton 102
Horne, Lena 38
Horner, Jack 8
Hornpipe 87
Hoskins, Joe **206**
hospitals: 23rd General 59; 70th Station 139; 103rd Station 139; 106th Station 139; 118th Station 75–76, **77**–85, 88, 98, 129, 133, 137, 139, 228
Houston, TX 122
Howard, John (pseud.) 11, 119, 231
Huangpui *see* Whangpoo
Huffines, Thomas 7
Huger 47
Hull, Cordell 171
Hunt, B.L. 117
"Hunter Killer Mission" 179

I-75 12
"I and I trucks" 140
Illinois (BB-7) see *Prairie State (IX-15)*
illness and injury 9, 21–22, 73–85, 99, 213
Implicit (AM-246) 123, 125, 204, 231
Improve (AM-247) 125
Incessant (AM-248) 125
Incredible (AM-249) 123, 125, 219, 231
Indiana 47
Inglefield 17, 92
International Date Line 178, 217
Intrigue (AM-253) 166
Iris 174
Isaac, William C. 17–58, **96–97**
Isle Habibas 48
"Isle of Capri" 145
Italian: A Guide to the Spoken Language (booklet) 133
Italy: surrender of 47, 52
Iwo Jima 213

Jackson, Willie Frank, Jr. 163
Jalbert, H.H. 16
James, E.W. 1
James Guthrie 102
James Iredell 102
Jamison, Chaplain 129
Janus 71, 92
Japan: Iwo Jima 213; leading troops into 194–196; plans for invasion 195; surrender 190, 192
Jared Ingersoll 102
Jean Bart (French) 14

Jeep 232
Jefferson Standard Life (magazine) 15, 128, 194
Jefferson Standard Life Insurance Company 6, 7, 9, 14, 15, 128, 130, 158
Jernigan, R.H. 12
Jervis 71, 87
Jessell, George 20
John A. Rawlins 197
John Armstrong 102
John Banvard 74
John Bell 103
John Ericsson 12–24, 154, 224
John M. Harlan 98
John Paul Jones 13
John Rodgers (DD-574) 11
Johnson, Joe H. 18, 80, 94, 129, 179, 206, 213
Jolicoeur, Luke Joseph 163, **170**–171, 174–176, 181, 211
Jolson, Al 20, 38
Jonathan Worth 47
Jones, Billy Webster 6, 157
Jones, Cecil 157
Jones, Edward 82
Jones, Fred Reid 158
Jones, John Malloy 55, 158, 223
Jones, Joseph Hodges 158
Jones, Judith 158
Jones, Lemma Sue Fowlkes 54, 156, 223
Jones, Marie 158
Jones, Paul Hosier 10, 54–55, 156–157, 223
Jones, Pauline Jones 54, 130, 156, 158, 208, 223
Jones, Ronald 158
Jones, Vivian Hodges 54, 158, 223
Jones, William Henry 129
Jones, William Joseph (Buck) 14, 156, 158, 223
Joseph E. Campbell (DE-70) 103
Joseph Hewes (AP-50) 10
Junker-87 102

K-Guns 16, **180**
K-Ration 32, 152, 228, 133
Kagoshima (Kyushu) 182, 192–196, 236
Kamikazes 182, 187, 191, 236
Kane, Charlie "Killer" 116–217
Kanoya air base (Kyushu) 194, 196
Kaohsiung (Takao, Formosa) 24–206, **205**
Karouba (Tunisia) 16, 88
The Kasidah (book) 160, 222
Kassan Bay (CVE-69) 117
Kate (cow) 1
Kaye, Danny 20
Kaye, Sammy 20
Kearney (DD-432) 18
Keating, G.J. 115, 218
Keelung *see* Kiirun
Kei see *Camden* (IX-42)
Kelly, Robert 190
Kelly, W.R. 174
Kendall, H.A. 12
Kennedy, Jimmy 145
Kesselring, Albert 105

Key West, FL 13–16
Keys, Ancel 152, 233
Khayyam, Omar (author) 1, 22
Kiirun (Formosa, Taiwan) 102, 207
Kill Quick, North Carolina 10
Killman, John R. 177
Kimberly 230
King, J.G. 16
Kingston, Addison F. 165, 175–176
Kinitra (Port Lyautey, French Morocco) 10
Kitty (cat) 163
Klumpp, George Franklin 25–26, 31, 35–39, 41–44, 46, 50, 56–57, 73–74, 79, 81–82, 88, 96, **97**, **99**, 100, 103, 110, 119, 122, 129, 135–138, 140–144, 147–148, 150, 152, 155, 158–160, 223
Klumpp, Mary 37
Knowles, Hamilton A. 150
Knowlton, Elliott Burris 184, 193, 195–200, 236
Kobe Sho 187
Krueger, Walter 195
Kungsholm see *John Ericsson*
Kuomintang 209
Kyushu: landing troops on 194–196, 198

Lachance, R.G. 192
Lafayette see *Normandie*
Laforey 98
Lagrange (APA-124) 187, 191, 236
Lamonnier, Contre-Amiral 119
Lamour, Dorothy 20
Lanai (Hawaii) 176
Landing Craft Flak (*LCF*): *LCF-4* 70
Landing Craft Infantry (*LCI*) description of 61, 226; *LCI-12* 12; *LCI-20* 19–70; *LCI-32* 14, 231; *LCI-34* 101; *LCI-41* 105; *LCI-42* 151–152; *LCI-219* 16–87, 229; *LCI-233* 13; *LCI-273* 12; *LCI-277* 101; *LCI-423* 199, 203; *LCI-588* 117, 231; *LCI-590* 131; *LCI-592* 117; *LCI-917* 199; *LCI-948* 108; *LCI-951* 119; *LCI-1088* 199; *LCI-1089* 199
Landing Craft Support (*LCS*): *LCS-56* 105
Landing Craft Tank (*LCT*): description of 61, 226; *LCT-26* 19; *LCT-32* 17, 70; *LCT-33* 18, 70; *LCT-34* 10; *LCT-35* 10, 89; *LCT-36* 19; *LCT-152* 120; *LCT-203* 10; *LCT-204* 18, 70; *LCT-217* 17; *LCT-220* 19; *LCT-277* 17; *LCT-333* 10; *LCT-1160* 188; *LCT(R)-140* 17, **113**, 117
Landing Craft, Vehicle, Personnel (LCVP): description of 226
Landing Ship Infantry (*LSI*): *LSI-590* 117
Landing Ship Medium (*LSM*): *LSM-386* 176
Landing Ship Tank (*LST*): description of 11, 226; at Nisida **111**; LST-4 191; *LST-76* 109; *LST-141* 108; *LST-174* 100, 103; *LST-197*

17, 89, 97, 227; *LST-210* 109; *LST-211* 105; *LST-263* 103; *LST-282* 117, 126; *LST-305* 12, 229; *LST-321* 16; *LST-322* 10; *LST-327* 18, 70, 74–**76**, 96, 145–146, 228; *LST-348* 19, 72, 86–87, 89, 103, 229; *LST-349* 19; *LST-359* 19; *LST-360* 127; *LST-365* 109; *LST-366* 14; *LST-384* 18; *LST-386* 18; *LST-387* 16; *LST-391* 131; *LST-394* 18, 103–104, 109; *LST-418* 12; *LST-422* 14, 231; *LST-602* 109; *LST-659* 131; *LST-691* 152; *LST-804* 198; *LST-1012* 153

Larson, John C. 165, 175–176, 211

latrine problems 78

Latta, Don R. 165

Laub (DD-613) 104

laundry/washing 95–96, 136

Laurentine (Tini) *121*

Leahy, W.D. 131

Leary, Earl *181*

leave, official 13, 155–159, 163, 165

LeBorgne (French crewman) 151

Ledger-Dispatch (newspaper, Norfolk) 163

Lee, Harry 176

Lees-McRae College 5–7, 10–12, 128, 130, 158, 160

Leet, David M. 118, 221

Legion of Merit 207, 219

Leinster 71

Leonard, R.F. 120

"Leopold" (Nazi gun) 100

Le Riche, Alphonse Albert 27, 57

Levy (DE-162) 180

Lewis, Norman 139

Lewis, Spencer S. 12, 112

"Liberty Bus" *188*

Liberty ship: description of 102, 230

Lickfield, Clarence Michael 163, 234

Lido Beach, New York 153, 155

Lile, Owen Winston 234

"Lili Marlene" 131

limpets 230, 235

Liri Valley (Italy) 12

Little Creek, Virginia 163

Livermore (DD-429) 131

Locke, J.T. 108

Locust Hill Methodist Church 8, 10, 130, 156–158

Lofberg (DD-759) 174

Logan, Joseph W. 129

Logan, Samuel L. 121

Lombard, Carole 6

Lombardo, Guy 20

Lombardo, Rosalie 135

Long, Bernard N. 100, 150

Long, Johnny 20

Long Beach, California 120–221

Longtin, Gustave 20

Lonsdale (DD-426) 162

Lornaston 17

Lorraine (French) 10

Los Angeles, California 120–222

Lott, Arnold S. 1, 72, 125

Lotz, R.F. 196

Loud, Wayne R. 187, 196

Louis II, Prince 123

Lovell, Larry 157

Lowe, William D. 121

Lowry, Frank J. 10, 62, 84, 112, 114

Ludlow (DD-438) 19, 123, 162

Lyautey, Louis Hubert Gonzalve 40

M-691 (French) 154

"Ma Perkins" (soap opera) 117

MacKenzie (DD-175, DD-614) 19, 104, 231

MacLennan, J.M. 132

Macomb (DMS-23) 196

Maddox, John F., Jr. 192, 212

Madison Square Garden (New York) 19, 159

mail 52–55, 81–82, 88, 127–128, 204, 213, 228

Mainstay (AM-261) 123, 125

Maiuri, Amedeo 142

Le Malin (French) 123, 126

Malone, Millard 40, *97*, 100

Manzanillo (Mexico) 168

Marabout Mountain (Algeria) 10

Marder midget "submarines" 101–103, 123, 125–126

Mardi Gras (New Orleans) 122

Mariana Islands 180

Mariana Trench 180

Marie, Rose 20

Marines: at Oran 126

Marlow, Earl 12

Marsa 47

Marshall Islands 179, 217

Martin, W.M. 16

Marzean, Walter Leo 16–27, 36, 40, *97*, 99

MAS torpedo boats 71, 101–102

Massachusetts (BB-59) 14, 33

Mathis Yacht Building Company 27–28, 225

Mattia (French crewman) 151

Mattole (AO-17) 17

mattress and bedding 11, 151, 233

Mauldin, Bill 121, 228

Maumee (AO-2) 16

Mavereaux (ship's cook) 188

Mayo (DD-422) 11

Mayrant (DD-402) 196

McAdoo, Mrs. 1

McArthur, Douglas 194

McBride, Stuart J. 18, *121*

McCabe, E. Jack 41

McCormick, Hugh P. 16, 31, 42, 44, 48–51, 63, 69, 79, 82, 88, 96–97, 122, *124*, 128–129, 150–*151*, 225

McDowell, Roddy 20

McGlynn (radioman) 188–*189*

McIlvain, W.E. 15

McLanahan (DD-615) 126

McLaughlin, John Frederick 27, 36, *97*

medals *see* commendations

medical report 77–78

Medina (Casablanca) 18–39

Meeks, Haywood 160

Meier, Helen 79

Meigs, Montgomery Cunningham 154, 234

Melusine (French) 19–40

Menges (DE-320) 103, 230

Menton (France) 123, 125

Merchant Mariners 102

Merckling, Charles E. 15, *97*, 120, 150

Mers el-Kébir (Algeria) 13, 43, 48, 50, 52

Mersa Bou Zedjar (Algeria): landings at 43

Messmer, W.L. 151, 154

Metropolitan Opera 20

Mexico 168

Meyer London 102

midget submarines 101, 103, 123, 125–126, 201

Mike (monkey) 107

"Milk Run" 132

Milland, Ray 20

Millelli, Les 148

Miller, Edward Lewis 26–27, 36, 50–51, 82, 88, 96–*97*, 99, 107, 110, 122, 129, 225

Miller, Glenn 7

Mine Division: Eighteen 210; Nineteen 118–**220**; Seventeen 161, 184, 193, 204, 210; Sixteen 204; Thirty-three 204; Thirty-two 204

Mine Squadron: Eleven 125; Six 161, 198, 204, 207

Minecraft: lost in Typhoon Louise 236

mines destroyed 236; in Operation Bungo Suido 199–202; in Operation Juneau 187; in Operation Kagoshima 196; in Operation Sherlys 204; in Operation Skagway 192

mines, types of 185, 235

minesweeping formations 186–187

minewarfare: description of 184–187, **185**, 236

Minivet (AM-371) 112

Minster, John J. 17

Miriam (New York) 155, 159–160

Mitscher, Marc A. 178

ML-559 131

ML-562 131

ML-563 119

ML-566 19

Moal, F. (French crewman) 151

Moal, G. (French crewman) 151

Mobile Degaussing Unit (YDG) 185

Moe, Karl 207

Mona Island (ARG-9) 192, 198

Mona Loa, HI 176

Monadnock (CM-9) 111

Mondello (Sicily) 110, **135**–136

money *see* currency

Monitor 22

Monjar, H.G. 116

Monreale (Sicily) 134

Montcalm (French) 115

Monte Carlo (Monaco) 121, 123–126, **125**, 162

Montecassino (Italy) 13, 228

Montgomery, Bernard L. 121

Moon, Don R 130

The Moon Is Down (book) 1
Moore, Francis G. 199, 202, 207, 209–210, 212–215, 217–219, 221
Moore, Herman 157
Morison, Samuel Eliot 2, 60, 65, 105, 126, 182
Moroccan Sea Frontier 22–42
Morris, Harry 207
Most Dangerous Sea (book) 1, 125
Mostaganem (Algeria) 16–48, 153
motion pictures: importance of 237
motorcycle 96, 110
Mount Vesuvius 58–59, 85, 97–98, 100, 139–143
MTB-710 126
Mull 92
Murphy (DD-603) 117
Murphy, Audie 104
Murphy, Edward Thomas 193, 196
Murray, Ken 221
Museo dello Sbarco di Anzio 1
music 217–218
Myoi, M. (Japanese pilot) 195
mysterious visitors 136

Nagasaki 190–192, 201–202, 210–211
Nakagusuku Wan (Okinawa) *183*, 235
Naples (Italy) 18, 59, 61, 75–85, 97–98, 103, 120, 127; liberty in 136–144
Naples '44 (book) 139
Napoli Compliments of the ARC (booklet) 138
Narragansett (ATF-88) 18, 118
National Geographic (magazine) 130
Naval Operating Base: Bizerte 56–58; Casablanca 24; Coco Solo 166
Naval Training Center, Lido Beach 155
Naval Training Station: New York (Pier 92) 17–21; Norfolk 11–13, 161, 222–224
Navy V-12 Program 37
Navy YMCA (Brooklyn) 156, 159
Nazi propaganda 70, *90*–94, *91*, 131, 232
NBC Symphony Orchestra 20
Neal, Billy 159
Neal, David 7
Nebelwerfer 100
Neger (midget submarine) 101, 103, 123, 126
Nelson, G.E. 118
Nemours (Algeria) 14, 47–48
Nero 145
Nettuno *see* Anzio
Netzel, A.C. 196
Nevada (BB-36) 188–*189*, 235
New Bern, North Carolina 11, 159, 235
New Orleans, Louisiana 122
New York, New York 17–21, 154–155, 159–160
Newfoundland 143
News & Observer (newspaper) 11
Nicaragua 168
Nice (France) 123–124, 148

Niles (hospital mate) 12, 80
Nimitz, Chester W. 16
99th Fighter Squadron 82
Nisida (Italy) 19–60, 63, 137, *111*
Nixon, Jim 79
Noble, Ray 145
Norfolk, Naval Training Station 11–13, 161, 222–224
Norfolk Navy Yard, Portsmouth 161–166
Normandie 18
Norment, William 9
North Carolina Collection 108
North Carolina Shipbuilding Company 102, 157
North Carolina's Finest Hour (book) 136
Norton, J.J. 168

Oak Ridge Military Institute 9
Obama, Barack 237
Okinawa 182–*183*, 186, 190–194, 196, 198, 211
Oklahoma City (CL-91) 111
Oldendorf, Jesse B. 187
"One-Eighties" (184-foot AMs) 1, 235
157th Regiment, 45th Division *110*, 112, *115*–*116*
"One-Tens" (SCs) 1, 25
"Opera Bar Gang" 15–37, 39
Operation Anvil 112
Operation Avalanche 59
Operation Blackstone 40
Operation Brushwood 40
Operation Buffalo 104
Operation Bungo Suido 198–202
Operation Coronet 195
Operation Diadem 104
Operation Downfall 195
Operation Dragoon (Southern France) 109–126; casualties of 119–120, 126; German artillery off Monte Carlo 123–*125*, *124*; invasion of 109–126, 230; plans for 111–113; practice landings for 109–111; *SC-525* leads Thunderbirds into 114–*116*, *115*; *SC-525* rammed and leaves battlefront 117–119, *118*; *SC-525* returns to battlefront 122; *SC-525* transferred to French Navy 150–151, 153–154; sister ships sunk 118–119, 126
Operation Goalpost 40
Operation Hammer 230
Operation Husky 42
Operation Juneau 186–188, 202
Operation Kagoshima 194–196, 202
Operation Magic Carpet 192
Operation Neptune 230
Operation Olympic 195
Operation Overlord 111
Operation Reservist 43
Operation Sherlys 204, 206
Operation Shingle (Anzio) 62–107; author with battle star from *93*; author's certificate from *76*; author's injury at 73–74; author's

return to sixty years later 1; black troops at 82, 227; depth charge exploding at *89*; farewell to 108; history of Anzio-Netunno 145–146; invasion of 62–107; map of landings *64*, *66*; Nazi propaganda at *90*–*91*; practice landings for 59–60; *SC-525* at 67–74, 86–89, 93, 100–107, 145; scene from *72*
Operation Skagway 191–192, 202
Operation Torch 23, 33, 42, 55
Opponent (AM-269) 166
Oran (Algeria) 13, 42–58, 152–154
Oropesa gear 166, 186
Orr, M.S. 11–*13*
Ostergren, D.L. 19–80, 85, 129
Ostrowski, Joe 8
Ostrum, Lieutenant 122
Osumi Kaikyo (Van Diemen Strait) 195
Ouahran *see* Oran
Outline of History (book) 116
Owen (French crewman) 151

P-691 (French) 154
Pagano, Liana 139
Page, L.G. 156
Paige, Raymond 159
Palermo (Sicily) 14–100, 109, *120*–*121*, 127, 133–137, 153
Palo Alto 44
Palomares 70
Panama Canal Zone 166–167
Panama in Your Pocket (booklet) 166, 234
Paniment (AGC-13) 111, 236
Park, A.I. 1
Parker, R.E. 112
Parks (DE-165) 179
Party (Mine Division Nineteen) 119–*220*
Pashley, W.H. 17
"Passion Wagons" 140
Patch, Alexander M. 112, 119
Patterson, Alexander M. 102, 230
Patterson, George E. 14–85
Paul (Apostle) 137
Paul Hamilton 102, 162
Payne, Buster 159
Peale, Norman Vincent 20
Pearl Harbor 176–178, 218–219
peccadillo 36, 39, 167
Pelham, North Carolina 158, 234
Pelletier, Wilfred 20
Penelope 92, 103
Peninsula Base Section, Naples 131, 138
Pennant 178
Pennsylvania (BB-38) 191, 235
Pennsylvania Sun 16
Pensacola (CA-24) 173
"Pepperpot" 12
Pepsi-Cola 51; canteen, New York 155, 159; center, San Francisco 169
Perry, Robert E. 174
"Peter Charlies" (PCs) 1, 24–25; *PC-472* 14; *PC-474* 12; *PC-475* 14; *PC-480* 14; *PC-482* 14; *PC-*

496 15, 42; *PC-545* 102, 117; *PC-546* 18; *PC-551* 13, 67; *PC-556* 18, 102; *PC-558* 18, 101–102; *PC-559* 109; *PC-591* 101; *PC-621* 18, 101; *PC-624* 12, 226; *PC-625* 109, 150; *PC-626* 18, 50, 56, 63, 101–102, 104; *PC-627* 19, 101–102; *PC-676* 12; *PC-811* 174; *PC-826* 14; *PC-1226* 13, 67; *PC-1227* 13; *PC-1235* 102; *PC-1555* 187; *PC-1596* 117–118; *PCS-1442* 174
Peter Force (British) 12
Peter Skene Ogden 102
Petit, F. (French crewman) 154
Petropavlovsk (Russian) 184
Pettigrew, Edna 54
Pfau, Bernard 48, 74, 81–82, 88, **97**
PGM-24 187
Philadelphia (CL-41) 13, 89, 99, 104, 113, 125, 153
Philadelphia Navy Yard 26
Phlaegrean Fields (Italy) 137
Phoenix, Arizona 122
physical examinations 11, 78, 237
Pier 92, New York, New York 17–21, 159, 225
Pilot (AM-104) 12–43, 65, 74, 89, 212, 219
Pinnacle (AM-274) 125, 204
Pioneer (AM-105) 19, 212, 119
pitometer 173, 234
"Place of the Farmer" 1
Plage des Elephants 230
Plage Mehdiya (French Morocco) 11
plankholders 27
Planter (ACM-2) 109, 126, 150
Platoon 526, Norfolk 11–*13*
Pleasant, Janie Ruth 158
Pleasant Grove Primitive Baptist Church 8
Pliny the Elder 141–142
Pliny the Younger 141–142
Plummer, Howard C. 19
Plunkett (DD-431) 11
Pocket Guide to North Africa (booklet) 14
poetry, camp 132
point system (for discharge) 193, 201
politics 5, 157, 171
Polo Grounds 156
Pompeii (Italy) 19, 103, 139, 141–*143*
Pontchartrain see *Hartland*
Port Lyautey (Kinitra, French Morocco) 17, 40
Port Slave 44, 46
Portent (AM-106) 19–70, 105, 184
Poteat, Paul 6
Pozzuoli (Italy) 19, 61, 63, 75, 111, 113, 137
Prairie State (IX-15) 19, 159
Prevail (AM-107) 12, 71, 191, 212, 219
Preyer, Father 129
Price, Albert 27, **97**–98
Price, Julian 7
Pride (DE-323) 103
Prime Meridian 46

Pritchett, Leo K. 1
"Pro Stations" 140
Proctor, Jim 15
Promp, Otto H., Jr. 17, 40, **97**. **106**, 108, 147
propaganda, Nazi **90**–94, **91**, 131, 232
prophylactic kit 39
Prosperous 68
prostitution 36, 39, 46, 167
Pruett, Samuel R. 119
PT-201 14
PT-202 119
PT-207 101
PT-216 14
PT-218 119
PT-555 131
Ptarmigan (AM-376) 176, 196
Punta di Pozzo di Borgo (Corsica) 148, 233
Purple Heart 105, 195
Pusch, Mildred 228
Pyle, Ernie 73, 92, 131, 176, 230

Q-499 (French) 154
"Quaker Guns" 131
Queen (mule) 1
Quonset hut 152, 233

R-boats 71
radar training 176
radio 52, 130–131, 190, 192, 217
Radio Belgrade 131
Raft, George 20
Rains, Claude 20
Raleigh, North Carolina 10
Ralph, James "Sunny Jim" 134
Randall, A. Lowell 78, 85, 228
Ranger (CV-4) 14
rangers 44, 62
rationing, wartime 8, 55, 157–158, 164, 234
rats and rodents 55–56
Reece, Harry William 25–27, 31, 33, 37, **47**–48, 128
Reece, Marynell Dyatt 225
Reed, Jesse Francis 168, 225
Reed Gold Mine 225
Refresh (AM-287) 174
Reid, William Mason 163, 174, 234
religious services: Alameda 170; Bizerte 57, 107, 129; *Mona Island* 192, 198; Naples 140; Norfolk and Portsmouth 162, 165, 223; 118th Station Hospital 85; Oran 51; Palermo 99, 136, 232; Pearl Harbor 177; Ste. Maxime 122; San Francisco 171; Sasebo 203
Repose (AH-16) 197
Rhona 49
Richard Henderson 103, 230
Richard V. Oulahan 197
Richards, Alfred H. 15
Richmond P. Hobson 102
Rickenback, Rick 24, 39
Rigoletto (opera) 140
Ritchie, Commander 68
roaches 50, 55–56
Robb, Fred E. 177

"Robert" (Nazi gun) 100
Robert A. Smith (DM-23) 110, 236
Roberts, Clinton S. 134
Roberts, Francis R 117
Rocco, Carlo 147
Rochester (Eddie Anderson) 10
Rocky Mount, North Carolina 17
Rodgers, Bertram J. 112, 116–117
Rogan, Virginia 155, 159, 160
Rongalap 217
Roosevelt, Franklin D. 1, 8, 22, 34, 39, 52, 62, 92, 130, 157, 171, 231
Roosevelt, Franklin D., Jr. 196
Rose, Anna 9
Rosenthal, Joe 213
Rota Island 180
rough seas 29–31, **30**, 88, 183, 196–**197**, 207, 210, 218
Rousselt, C.A. 110
Routh, Guy 7
Routh, Kathryn 7
Rowan (DD-405) 143
Rowland, Betty 220
The Rubaiyat of Omar Khayyam (book) 1, 222
Runof, Edmund Emil 17, 36, 40, 50, 55–56, 80–82, 86, 88, 93, **96**, 98, 100, 103, 105, 122, 150, 163, 228
Russo-Japanese War 184
Rust, Cody R. 196, 210, 219
Ryukyu Retto 195
Ryukyu Sho 204

S-boats 71
"Sad Sack" (cartoon) 131–132
Saei (Formosa, Taiwan) 104–205
Safi (French Morocco) 17, 38, 40
St. Andrew 71
St. Christopher medal 37, 160, **223**
St. David 11, 131
St. Helena Barrack 163–164
St. Paul (CA-73) 107, 210
St. Raphael (France) 148
St. Tropez (France) 122, 124, 126, 148
Ste. Maxime (France) 122
Saipan 182
Sakishimi Islands 204
Salafia, Alfredo 135
salary and savings 130, 176, 194, 198, 200, 223
Salerno (Italy): landings at 47, 59–60, 103, 109–114, **110**; liberty in 143–144, 162
Salinger, J.D. 12
Samaritan (AH-10) 111
Sampson, C.O. 11
Sam's Cigar Store 19
Samuel, Noah E. 11, 128
Samuel Ashe 89
Samuel Huntington 87
Samuel Johnston 102
San Carlo Opera House, Naples 140
San Diego, California 168, 174
San Francisco area, California 168–173
San Francisco Examiner (newspaper) 171

San Pedro, California 119, 221
San Salvador Island 166
San Sebastiano (Italy) 141
Sangay (AE-10) 111
Santa Barbara, California 174
Santa Cruz Cathedral (Algeria) 10
Sardenia 114
Sasebo (Japan) 103–204, 210–211
Satterlee (DD-626) 126
Saugatuck (AO-75) 197, 199
Savannah (CL-42) 13, 87
savings *see* salary
Scarab 119
Scellery, Captain 207
Schaefer, Gerald M. 103
Schira, John S. 17, 40, *97*, 150
Schnellboots 101
Schroeder (DD-501) 11
Schultz, Edward H. 104, *206*, 208–210, 213, 218, 220, *220*
Schwartz, Jacob 204
Scipio 50
"Screamin' Meemies" 100
scrugnizzi 138
Sebago, USGS see *Walney*
Sebou, Wadi 40
Sechler, David 24
Seer (AM-112) 176, 212, 219, 231, 237
Seer Incident 208–209, 218
Sekiki Sho 187
Seliga 213
Seliga, Clifton J. 104
Sellers, D.R. 196, 204
Sénégalais (French) 103
Sentinel (AM-113) 184, 237
Seventh Army 112
Seventh Regiment, Third Infantry Division 63–64, 66–67
Shaffer, Charles D. 104
Shanghai (China) 107–210
Shantz, John H. 104
Shaponik, Abraham Max 204, *220*
sharks (*YMS-472*) 197
Sharp (crew member) 121
Sharp, Alexander 187
Sharp, John H. 104
Sharpe, Anna Rose 9, 208
Sharpe, Carolyn 9
Sharpe, Sandy 9
Sharpe, William J. 1, 9–10, *14*, 208
Sheldrake (AM-62) 106
Shelton Separation Center 222–223
Shenandoah 229
Sherman, Neil A. 204–*206*, 207–210, 213, 218, *220*–222, 237
Shikoku 198, 201
Shiloh 47
The Ship (book) 12
shore patrol duty 19
Siebert, Stephen 204
Sigma Chi ring 41
Silseth, M.J. 17
Simpson, Barbara 7, 8, 127–128
Sinatra, Frank 159
Siniai 48
Sisk, Mildred Elizabeth 232
Sixth Army 195, 198
Sixth Corps 62, 112

Skelton, Red 20
Skill (AM-115) 143, 161, 184, 237
Skropka, Henry F. 104, 221
Slade, Dorothy 127–128
Sleap, Tom 217
Smith, C.E. 118
Smith, George Robert, Jr. 1
Smith, George Robert, Sr. 1, 10, 54
Smith, Steve 158
Smith, Thomas 54, 129, 157
smoke (smudge) pots 61, 73, 101, *124*, 226
Sockman, Ralph W. 159
Soldiers Guide to Naples (booklet) 138
Somers (DD-381) 117
sonar (acronym) 14
sonarman (rating) 15–16, 225
Soto, Edward A. 107
soundman *see* sonarman
Southard (DMS-10) 187, 235
Southern France *see* Operation Dragoon
souvenirs and artworks 136, 139, 147, 203, 205, 208; Capri scene 144; Civitavecchia documents 147; Japanese sword 208; *Strive* shell 217; Tallo Giovanni painting 143; Tearotini painting 134; Toulon pen set 149; Vittorio caricature *139*
Spainhower, Myles E. 134
Spartan 87, 92, 229
Spear (AM-322) 181, 191
Speckin, Bill 47
Spector (AM-306) 103
Speed (AM-116) 1, 159; author serves aboard as sonarman and yeoman 161–194; crew liberty at Tsugen Shima *188–190*; crew pictured *190*; damaged by fire 163–165; early history of 161–162; at Eniwetok 179; at Guam 180–181; passes International Date Line 178; in Hawaii 176–177; in Operation Juneau 187; in Operation Skagway 191–192; operates out of Okinawa 182–192; overhaul in Norfolk Navy Yard, Portsmouth 161–167; pictured *162*, *179*, *180–186*, *209*; postwar history of 237; in San Francisco area 169–173; in Southern California 174–175; transits Panama Canal 167; in Typhoon Opal 183–184; warpath of *214*
Spells, J.L. 196
"Spitkit Convoy" 16
Splinter Fleet (book) 1, 154
SS-34 174
Staff (AM-114) 112, 219, 207
Stafford, Edward P. 1, 65
Stage Door Canteen 20
Stallion (ATA-193) 182
Stancil, Mokie 7
Stars and Stripes (newspaper) 12, 82, *83*, 94, 121, 131–132, 216
The State (magazine) 55, 130
Staten Island, New York 12
Statue of Liberty 154

Steady (AM-118) 19, 204, 212, 219, 231
Steinbeck, John 7
"Stella the Bella of Fedela" (poem) 132
Stephen F. Austin 102
Stephens, Erwin D. 15, 156–157
Stephens, John Lloyd 135
Steubenville, Ohio 156
Steward, Ernest L. 104
Stirling, Alison B. 1, 128
Stockton 47
Strait of Bonifacio 114
Straus (DE-408) *197*
Strive (AM-117) 1, 60, 70, 74, 184, 187; adopts song 200–201; author serves aboard as flag yeoman 193–222; avoids Typhoon Louise 198–199; crew liberty 220–221; departure salute in Sasebo 211; at Eniwetok 215–216; in Hawaii 217–219; leads troops into Kagoshima 194–196; Mine Division Nineteen party 219–220; observes suicide caves 201–202; operates out of Okinawa 193–198; in Operation Bungo Suido 198–202; in Operation Sherlys off Formosa 204–207; passes International Date Line 217; pictured *209*; plankholders 200; postwar history of 237; returns to States 219; in Sasebo 203–204; in Shanghai 207–211; third anniversary of 200; in Typhoon Ida 196–197; warpath of *214*
Struble, A.D. 111
Stuka 102–103, 181
Sturzkampfflugzeug 102–103
Subchaser (book) 1, 226
Subchaser Training Center (Miami) 15, 26
submarines, midget *see* Marder; Neger; suicide submarines
Success (AM-310) 191
"Sugar Charlies" (SCs) 15; *SC-497* 15, *28*, 48, 59, 63, 69, 88; *SC-503* 108, 118, 122; *SC-506* 13; *SC-507* 17; *SC-515* 17, 48, 50, 59; *SC-516* 17; *SC-517* 17; *SC-519* 17, 39; *SC-524* 17, 39, 48, 56, 59, 108; *SC-525*: author serves aboard as sonarman 25–151, crew pictured *97*, damaged 87–88, 118, in drydock 55, 88, 94, *120–121*, early history of 25–27, insignia of *54*, in invasion of Anzio 58–108, 145, in invasion of Southern France 109–*116*, *113*, *115*, mysterious visitors aboard 136, operates out of Casablanca 25–41 27, operates out of Oran 42–56, physical description 27–30, pictured *30*, *45*, plankholders, practice landings at Salerno 59–60, 103, 109–114, practice landings at Volturno 59, second anniversary 100, subsequent history of 154, transferred to France 150–154, under German fire off Monte

Carlo 123–*125*, *124*; *SC-526* 18, 98; *SC-529* 17; *SC-530* 111; *SC-532* 18, 98; *SC-534* 19, 63, 67, 86; *SC-535* 108–109, 231; *SC-561* 18; *SC-619* 15; *SC-638* 19; *SC-639* 18, 63, 67; *SC-649* 19; *SC-651* 19, 101, 123, 229; *SC-655* 18, 108; *SC-666* 18, 107; *SC-691* 103, 107; *SC-692* 19, 63, 67, 69, 72; *SC-693* 19, 99; *SC-694* 12, 109; *SC-695* 18; *SC-696* 12, 109; *SC-697* 18; *SC-770* 10; *SC-771* 13; *SC-978* 19, 108; *SC-1029* 108, 120, 231; *SC-1030* 108; *SC-1034* 197; *SC-1044* 108–109
suicide submarines 201
Sukumo Ko (Shikoku) 198, 200
Sulfatara 137
Suncheon (Korean) 137
Surfbird (AM-383) 183
Sustain (AM-119) 18, 103, 164, 183, 191, 212, 219
Suzie (dog) 16, 136
Sway (AM-120) 14, 176, 180, 182–183, 237
Sweeping Unit One, Anzio 227
Swerve (AM-121) 105, 184, 237
Swift (AM-122) 176, 181, 191
swimming party 41, 108, 136, 176, 187–*190*, *188*, *189*
swinging ship 95, 229
Symbol (AM-123) 105, 176, 181

Tacitus 141
Takao (Kaohsiung), Formosa 204–*205*, 207
Tarazed (AF-13) 135
Tarleton Brown 117
Task Force: 32 (Oldendorf) 187, 196; 39 (Juneau) 16, 187–188; 73 (Shanghai) 107; 81 (Anzio) 12; 84 (Southern France) 112; 85 (Southern France) 112; 87 (Southern France) 112
Task Group: 39.11 (Juneau) 187; 70.5 (Sherlys) 104; 81.2 (Anzio) 12; 81.3 (Anzio) 12; 81.4 (Anzio) 12; 95.4 (Skagway) 191
Task Unit: 18.2.20 (homeward) 119; 52.9.22 (Bungo Suido) 198; 70.5.4 (Formosa) 107, 219; 94.7.1 (Guam-Okinawa) 182; 95.3.81 (Kagoshima) 195
Taylor, Ed 5, 7, 9
Tearotini (artist) 134
Teel, Almon 24, 39
Terminal Island (San Pedro, California) 174
Terror (CM-5) 118
Thaddeus Koscuiszko 47
Third Battalion, 157th Regiment *110*, 112, *115–116*, 146
Third Division 60, 62–63, 66–67, 112
Thirty-second Division: enters Kagoshima 195
Thomas, F.P. 15
Thomas G. Masaryk 102
Thompson, Ralph L. 171
Thompson, W.M. 12

Threat (AM-124) 176, 181
340th Bombardment Group 98
Thruster 68
"Thunderbirds" (45th Division) *110*, 112, *115–116*
Ticonderoga (CV-14) 17
Time (magazine, Pony Edition) 132, 141
Tini (Laurentine) *121*
Titania (AKA-13) 135
"Toeless Joe" 168
Tokahashin, K. (Japanese interpreter) 195
Tokara Retto 191, 195
Tokarz, Stanley 85, *97*, *106*, 108, 147
Tokashima, M. (Japanese signalman) 195
Token (AM-126) 191
Tomblin, Barbara Brooks 2, 105
Tomorrow Will Sing (book) 116
Toscanini, Arturo 20
Toucan (AM-387) 183
Toulon (France) 126, 132, 148, 150–153
Treadwell, Theodore R. 1, 154, 233
Trippe (DD-403) 19
Truman, Harry S 171, 192, 201, 223
Truscott, Lucian K., Jr. 112
Tsugen Shima (Okinawa) 187, *188*–*190*, 192
Tsukumi Wan (Kyushu) 198, 203
Tucson, Arizona 122
Tufts, Anna Lois 8
Tufts, Edgar H. 1
Tulagi (CVE-72) 117
Tumlin (drillmaster) 12
Tumult (AM-127) 191, 196
Turner, Arthur 127–128
Turner, B.F. 12
Tuscaloosa (CA-37) 119
Tuskegee Airmen 82
"Two-Twenties" (220-foot AMs) 1, 161, 184, 235
Typhoon Ida 196–*197*
Typhoon Louise 198
Typhoon Makurasaki *see* Typhoon Ida
Typhoon Opal 183

U-223 18
U-230 102, 229
U-343 12
U-371 103
U-375 42
U-410 12, 103, 229
U-450 12
U-546 129
"Ugly Ducklings" (Liberty ships) 102
Ulisse, Millefiorini 147
Ulmer, R.S. 192
Ulster Queen 17
Union Jack (British Army newspaper) 131
Unitarian Church of the Larger Fellowship 171
United Nations 171–*172*
United Service Organizations

(USO) 18, 51, 128, 135, 159
University of North Carolina 108
"Up Front" (cartoons) 121

V-E Day, San Francisco 171, 173
V-Mail 52–*53*, 79; *see also* mail
Vaccinations 12, 21, 24, 96
Vergil 137
Vestal, J.R. 17
Vesuvius *see* Mount Vesuvius
Viera, Joe 178
Vietri earthenware 144, 230
Vietri sul Mare 110, 144
Virginia Dare 102
Vittorio (caricaturist) *139*
Volle (French crewman) 151
Volturno River 59
Vulcan (AR-5) 10, 226

Wabash (AOG-4) 196
Waddell, James I. 129
Wahran *see* Oran
Waldron, John Charles 26, 31, 40, 48, 50, 61, 65, 68, 73, 82, 88, 93, *97*, 105, *118*, 122, 128, *135*, 136, 150, *151*, 153–154
Walker, B. 154
Walker, Lillie Jones 158
Waller 44
Wallis, Hugh C. 104
Walney 43
Wandank (ATA-204) 182
war bonds 157
Waring, Fred 20
Warner, G.M. 103
warpath of *Speed* and *Strive* *214*
washing machine 51
water conservation 27, 95–*96*, 136
Wateree (ATF-117) 182
Watlington, Peg 159
Watson, Alexander, Jr. 163, *170*–171, 174–176, 179, *181*, 211
Webster, V.W. 157
Wells, H.G. 116
Wertz, Captain 166
West Coast Sound School, San Diego 15, 174
Western Task Force 112
Wetmore, Charles 158
Wetmore, Don 212
Whangpoo River 207, 210
Wharton, Lenox B., Jr. 10–21, 24, 39
Whiting, William 225
Whitlow, R.N. 157
Whitworth, Fuller B. 17
Wichita (CA-45) 13
Wilkins, Lane 83
William A. Richardson 47
William B. Woods 102
William Patterson 51
Williamson, Mrs. Walter 157
Willkie, Wendell 5, 171
Wilmington, California 119
Wilmington, North Carolina 102
Wilson, Marie 221
Wilson, Robert T. 10
"window" 17, 229
Winecroft Hotel (Atlanta) 122
Winkler, Ernest 118

Wintle (DE-25) 180
With Utmost Spirit (book) 1
Wolfe, Thomas 131
Womack, Susan Anne 127
Woman's Army Corps 50
Wood, Bill 12
"Wooden Dreadnaughts" (YMSs) 184
World War II (magazine) 1
Wrenn, Frances 158
Wrenn, Mary 158
Wrenn, Susan 158
Wright, Julia 127–128, 158–159
Wynn, L.E. 16

X-Ray Force (Anzio) 12, **64**–65
XEAW (radio station, Del Rio, Texas) 122

Yanabaru Wan 135
Yangtze River 207, 210
Yank (magazine) 132

Yarbrough, Webb 38
yeoman (rating change) 17, 129, 161, 172, 174, 200
yeoman (flag) 194
Yew (YN-32) 19
YMS (yard minesweeper), description of 126, 184, 235; *YMS-17* 125; *YMS-21* 107–108, 126, 184; *YMS-24* 14, 48, 51, 109, 118–119, 126, 184; *YMS-26* 12; *YMS-27* 12, 42; *YMS-28* 12; *YMS-29* 14, 48; *YMS-30* 14, 48, 72, 80, 184; *YMS-34* 13; *YMS-36* 14, 127; *YMS-37* 107; *YMS-43* 107, 119–120, 231; *YMS-62* 12; *YMS-63* 119; *YMS-69* 12; *YMS-77* 12; *YMS-78* 15; *YMS-93* 199; *YMS-98* 197; *YMS-146* 174; *YMS-164* 125; *YMS-179* 125; *YMS-226* 13; *YMS-250* 123, 125; *YMS-301* 174; *YMS-341* 197; *YMS-343* 199; *YMS-359* 123–125; *YMS-373*

123–125; *YMS-472* 197, shark attack 236; *YMS-2022* 119
Yonozu Ko (Kyushu) 198
Yosemite (AD-19) 103, 211
Young, Robert 20
YP-645 174
YT-196 114
YT-198 19
YT-207 101
YT-633 177
Yukon (AF-9) 166
YW-120 126
YWN-120 126

Zanino, Frank J. 17, 19, 21, 35
Zarrytus *see* Bizerte
Zimmerli, R.M. 16
Zimmerman, Evelyn 127–128
Zouaves 37
Zucca, Rita Luisa 131, 232; *see also* Axis Sally